THE REAL ECONOMY

THE REAL ECONOMY
ESSAYS IN ETHNOGRAPHIC THEORY

Edited by Federico Neiburg and Jane I. Guyer

Hau Books
Chicago

The Real Economy by Federico Neiburg & Jane I. Guyer, with support from the
Instituto de Economia Real, is licensed under CC BY-NC-ND 4.0
https://creativecommons.org/licenses/by-nc-nd/4.0/legalcode

Cover and layout design: Daniele Meucci

Typesetting: Prepress Plus (www.prepressplus.in)

ISBN: 9781912808267
LCCN: 2019956202

Hau Books
Chicago Distribution Center
11030 S. Langley
Chicago, IL 60628
www.haubooks.com

Hau Books is printed, marketed, and distributed by The University of Chicago Press.
www.press.uchicago.edu

Printed in the United States of America on acid-free paper.

Table of Contents

Contributors

Maxim Bolt is a Reader in Anthropology and African Studies at the University of Birmingham, UK, and a Research Associate at the University of the Witwatersrand, South Africa. His first book, *Zimbabwe's migrants and South Africa's border farms: The roots of impermanence* (2015), explores wage labor in a place of transience and informal livelihoods.

Jane I. Guyer is Professor Emerita at Johns Hopkins University. A graduate of the London School of Economics (1965) and the University of Rochester (1972), she undertook field research projects on economic life in Nigeria and Cameroon. She has held faculty appointments at Harvard, Boston, and Northwestern Universities. At Northwestern, she was Director of the Program of African Studies (1994–2001). Book publications include *Family and farm in Southern Cameroon* (1984), *An African niche economy* (1997), *Marginal gains: Monetary transactions in Atlantic Africa* (2004), *Legacies, logics, logistics* (2016), and a new translation of Marcel Mauss, *The gift* (Expanded Edition, 2016).

Deborah James is Professor of Anthropology at London School of Economics. She is the author of *Money from nothing: Indebtedness and aspiration in South Africa* (2015), which documents the precarious nature of both the aspirations of upward mobility and the economic relations of debt that sustain the newly upwardly mobile in that country. Other books include *Gaining ground? "Rights"* *and "property" in South African land reform* (2006) and *Songs of the women migrants: Performance and identity in South Africa* (1999).

Mariana Luzzi is Associate Professor of Sociology at the University of General Sarmiento (Argentina) and a researcher at Consejo Nacional de Investigaciones Científicas y Tecnológicas (CONICET). She holds a PhD in Sociology from the École des Hautes Études en Sciences Sociales (EHESS-Paris). She has conducted research on Argentina's economic crisis of 2001–2, on community currencies experiments, and on the conflicts over economic reparations to the victims of State Terrorism in Argentina. She is currently doing research on the uses and meanings of the US dollar in Argentina's economy.

Bill Maurer is Professor of Anthropology and Law and Dean of Social Sciences at the University of California—Irvine. He is also the Director of the Institute for Money, Technology, and Financial Inclusion (www.imtfi.uci.edu). He conducts research on law, property, money, and finance, focusing on the technological infrastructures and social relations of exchange and payment. He has particular expertise in emerging, alternative, and experimental forms of money and finance, and their legal implications.

Eugênia Motta has a Postdoctoral Fellowship (PNPD/Capes) and is Assistant Professor in the Sociology Graduate Program of the Institute of Social and Political Studies (IESP) of the State University of Rio de Janeiro (UERJ).

Fabian Muniesa is a researcher at the Centre de Sociologie de l'Innovation, École des Mines de Paris (Mines ParisTech, PSL Research University, CNRS UMR 9217). He studies the culture of business performance and the politics of economic expertise. He is the author of *The provoked economy: Economic reality and the performative turn* (2014) and the coauthor of *Capitalization: A cultural guide* (2017).

Federico Neiburg is Professor in Social Anthropology at the Museu Nacional, Universidad Federal do Rio de Janeiro. He is also lead researcher for the Brazilian National Research Council (CNPq) and the coordinator of the Center for Research in Culture and Economy (NuCEC, www.nucec.net). Neiburg has held many fellowships and awards for his work including the Wenner Gren Foundation for Anthropological Research, the John Simon Guggenheim Foundation, and the Institute for Advanced Study (Princeton). He has done fieldwork in México, Argentina, Brazil, and the Republic of Haiti. His most recent publications are *Conversas Etnográficas Haitianas* (2019) and *The cultural history of money in the age of Empire* (edited with Nigel Dodd, 2019).

Gustavo Onto is a Postdoctoral Fellow at the Graduate Program in Sociology and Anthropology of the Federal University of Rio de Janeiro. He is also an associate researcher of the Center for Research on Culture and Economy (NuCEC), where he coordinates the Anthropology of Finance Study Group (GEAF) in partnership with the Brazilian Securities and Exchange Commission (BSEC). He was a visiting researcher at the École Normale Supérieure (ENS) in Paris and at Copenhagen Business School. He is also a member of the Behavioural Studies Group of the Brazilian SEC and a collaborator on the website Estudios de la Economia (http://estudiosdelaeconomia.wordpress.com).

Horacio Ortiz is associate professor of the Research Institute of Anthropology, East China Normal University, and researcher at Université Paris-Dauphine, PSL Research University, CNRS, IRISSO. He graduated from Sciences Po, Paris, obtained an MA in philosophy from the New School for Social Research, New York, and a PhD in social anthropology from the Ecole de hautes études en sciences sociales, Paris. His research focuses on the global financial industry from a perspective of political anthropology. He is the author of *Valeur financière et vérité: Enquête d'anthropologie politique sur l'évaluation des entreprises cotées en bourse* (2014).

Juan Pablo Pardo-Guerra is Assistant Professor in Sociology at University of California—San Diego and Research Fellow at the University of Edinburgh. Trained in physics (Universidad Nacional Autónoma de Mexico) and Science and Technology Studies (University of Edinburgh), he is author of *Automating finance: Infrastructures, engineers, and the making of electronic markets* (2019).

Fernando Rabossi is Professor of Cultural Anthropology at the Federal University of Rio de Janeiro. He coordinates the graduate program in Sociology and Anthropology (PPGSA) at the same university. He is author of *En las calles de Ciudad del Este: Una etnografía del comercio de frontera* (2008). His research is focused on the relation between rules and economic practices, dealing with informal economies, informal politics, markets, borders, mobility, and circulation.

Ariel Wilkis is Researcher at Consejo Nacional de Investigaciones Científicas y Tecnológicas (CONICET) and Dean of the Instituto de Altos Estudios Sociales, Universidad de San Martín (IDAES-UNSAM). His most recent books are *The moral power of money: Morality and economy in the life of urban poor* (2017) and *Las sospechas del dinero: Moral y economía en la vida popular* (2013). He has edited *El poder de (e)valuar* (2018) and *El Laberinto de las finanzas. Nuevos estudios sociales de la economía* (with Alexandre Roig, 2015). His book *The moral power of money* received "honorable mention" for the Best Book Award 2016–17 by the American Sociological Association Section on Economic Sociology (Zelizer Award). A French version will be published by École de Hautes Études en Sciences Sociales in 2020.

Caitlin Zaloom is a cultural anthropologist and Associate Professor of Social and Cultural Analysis at NYU. Her book *Indebted: How families make college work at any cost* (2019) examines how the struggle to pay for college transforms family relationships and defines middle-class life in America today. Zaloom has held many fellowships and awards for her work, including from the Center for Advanced Study in the Behavioral Sciences at Stanford, the Russell Sage Foundation, and the National Science Foundation. She is also the author of *Out of the pits: Traders and technology from Chicago to London* (2006) and is Editor in Chief of *Public Books*.

The real in the real economy

FEDERICO NEIBURG and JANE I. GUYER

THE SHIFTING MEANINGS OF REAL

"Economic reality ignores political expectations," writes one of the Brazil's main newspapers on the ongoing national crisis.[1] "All will depend on the behavior of the real economy," claimed an expert on CNN, talking about the future of the United States after Donald Trump's election.[2] "Evidence is mounting that the real economy is suffering from Brexit," writes the *Economist*.[3] Over the last few decades, and especially after the 2008 financial crisis and the following period of turbulence and uncertainty that affected the biggest democracies and strongest national economies, "the real economy" has been transformed into one of the most important concepts shaping public debates about the present and future of our collective existence.

1. "Realidade econômica ignora a retórica política," *Folha de São Paulo*, July 17, 2016. http://www1.folha.uol.com.br/colunas/laura-carvalho/2016/11/1832883-realidade-economica-ignora-a-retorica-politica.shtml.
2. "Money," *CNN*, May 14, 2016.
3. "Straws in the wind," *Economist*, July 16, 2016. https://www.economist.com/britain/2016/07/16/straws-in-the-wind.

In this introduction, we wish to trace the shifting referents of *the real* from its first use as a term in economics in the sixteenth century to its formalization in the early twentieth century. We will also trace the concept, via its more recent historical connotations, to the present, when "real life" for global populations as well as for sectors of the "formal economy" has become sufficiently turbulent to make daily practice a frontier for anthropological understanding. As we emphasize later, it is here that anthropologists can simultaneously mediate official terms through the details involved in their implementation, and attempt to comprehend people's own concepts and practices, their "realities", desires, and expectations, as they come to terms with them.

In the chapters that comprise this volume, we also draw attention to the fact that—in addition to its technical referent—the word *real* has moved beyond the technical economic domain into many new vernacular modes within public arenas. "Really!" and "Get real!" are exhortations made in everyday exchanges. In most places, it is people who see themselves as the custodians of the referent of "the really real" and engage in public discussion with this conviction. Only close ethnography can capture this range of referents in different contexts and languages, while paying close attention to its formal existence as a device of knowledge and government. This reflects the elasticity of the concept of "the public" itself, from the population in general through their legal representatives in governance and experts.

The *real economy*, as an official concept of economic governance, was initially created to track the relationship between money and commodities over time. It is still a key concept in the organization of the contemporary world, circulating among experts and ordinary people, through scientific and vernacular spaces, in multiple contexts, with shifting meanings. It is something that "real persons" can feel in their pockets, like the value of money, economic growth, or recession. People's sense of the real economy is linked to its realization in experiential life. In technical terms, we can measure and visualize it, as in the case of index numbers for prices, GDPs, interest, or risk rates, organized in the form of tables and graphics. In the terms used by Fabian Muniesa, "reality is really real when it is provoked, and hence realized" (2014: 17).

The reality of the real economy evokes something that endures, as indicated by its Latin etymology *res* (a thing), and thus also evokes a set of opposites: virtual, fictitious, black, or false economies. As we discuss later, in some contexts "real" is employed to analyze monetary valuations that may fluctuate for several different reasons. Discussions of slogans such as "Wall Street versus Main Street," widely deployed in the popular press, also enact these oppositions. Some social movements denounce the dominance of a spurious financial economy, arguing that people are losing the real value of their wages and their currencies.

These assemblages of vernacular and scientific realizations and enactments of the real economy are linked to ideas of truth and moral values: the realization of the real economy is also a moral judgment—like the index numbers themselves, those devices designed to know and govern turbulent realities, such as hyperinflations and recessions. As Jane I. Guyer argues in an article that served as the cornerstone of our project, "the concept of the 'real economy' is in itself real, in the sense that it has endured, as a large umbrella concept for centuries, adaptable in many contexts, a source of precise devices as well as vague allusions, but always indexing, in some direct or indirect way, as a counterpoint to, or mode of dealing with, turbulence and its mitigation" (2016a: 252).

By examining the formal concepts and actions *in* action, the essays included in this book apply a classic ethnographic methodology toward understanding how people grapple with the indeterminacies of time and meaning within the formal sector and at its interfaces. Our main aim in this collection is to launch a new program of research on the anthropology of economy/economics that combines intensive ethnographic reserach with contributions from economic history, taking a long-term and broad view of both national and international dynamics of change. Our focus is on the pragmatics of the *real*: we wish to scrutinize the real as a technical meaning in the international standardization of terms, yet at the same time, having varied philosophical and vernacular usages and meanings, link it to the "common sense-ism" of pragmatism—as proposed by Charles S. Peirce (1905) or even Thomas Reid ([1785] 1997), as suggested by Guyer (2016a: 259ff.)—with the kind of ethnographic theory proposed by Bronisław Malinowski (1935: 5ff.), where language and concepts are taken to be tools, documents, and "cultural realities."

QUESTIONING THE REAL

What are the shifting meanings of the "real"? In which situations and processes is it enacted and realized? How do these meanings form part of assemblages of vernacular and expert experiences, enactments, and realizations of the real economy? What processes are responsible for generating the "self-evidence" of the real? What practices, materialities, ideas, and devices are used to experience, live in, and live with real economies in diverse ethnographic settings? What kinds of persons and relations does the real economy enact and realize? Do we find both translational nuancing in local languages and cultures and also active policy interventions designed to redefine old meanings and modify their application as the global economy moves through different phases and changes? Do the philosophical interrogations of "the real" add yet another voice to our attempts to grapple with the dilemmas of contemporary life? How do we realize these experiences and realizations ethnographically?

Here we wish to distinguish our approach from the subdisciplinary field of "economic anthropology," born in the mid-twentieth century through classic ethnographies such as Paul Bohannan's work on the Tiv of Central Nigeria, including his analyses of production in *Tiv farm and settlement* (1954), distribution within spheres of exchange (1955), and eventually linked to the ambivalent and ambiguous (like all moral domains) realities of "development." Economic anthropology, we argue, has always dealt laterally with the real economy, never explicitly focusing on it as either its main subject of inquiry or analytic concept. The debate between formalists and substantivists was just the most developed instance of a more general problem raised by economic theory: What do we describe as the "economic" and how do we describe it in any given "real" situation? What is this reality composed of? Is it constituted by behaviors or by institutions? Is it an aspect of individuals or of collectives? Is it a term that people use descriptively or performatively? And in what contexts do they use it? That is, do they use it in their own languages, drawing on their own cultural archive of concepts, proverbs, sayings, inherited poetics, or (perhaps) religious invocations?

In a number of recent anthropological studies (see, for example, Neiburg et al. 2014; Narotzky and Besnier 2014), these questions have begun to be posed from a fresh angle that finally problematizes an earlier issue: Why and how does the "economy" or the "economic" appear as something taken for granted, by both actors and analysts, a given and objectified reality that limits and allows for different possibilities for human life? In this sense, Keith Hart was a pioneer in exploring radically different viewpoints on monetized economies in his trailblazing article "Heads or tails? Two sides of the coin" (1986), the two sides being the state (top-down) and the markets and social life (bottom-up). How, then, are these realities realized and recognized as such?

FOCUSING ON THE CONCEPT OF THE REAL

To be "real," the economy (it appears) needs to be adjectivized: micro, macro, national, global, popular, grassroots, financial, informal economy(ies). But the use of the adjective *real* implies some singular inflections, a very particular political epistemology linked to the two Latin roots of the term *real*: *realis*, *res*, "something that exists, truly and effectively," and *regalis*, "something that belonged or is related to the king or to royalty." As a development of this latter sense, "real" also turned into a substantive thing, associated with the king, and became the name for a small Spanish silver coin. Over time, it also came to denote various coins in different countries under Spanish and Portuguese colonization. *Real* has likewise been the denomination used for the Brazilian currency since 1994 (Neiburg 2006). In countries like Venezuela, Nicaragua, and El Salvador, the word *real* is used as a synonym for money.

The use of the adjective real to depict the economy is also linked to the sociogenesis of the term *economy* itself, associated with the world of the house and the family, as in the well-known ancient Greek definition elaborated by Aristotle: the *oikos* as the natural space of real persons to govern and administrate the house, as opposed to the *chrematistic*, the multiplication of money or the accumulation of wealth in the form of money. As Guyer has also shown (2016a: 246), it is time to examine the contemporary inflexions of the real economy, where the house is linked to the housing market (as "real estate") and debts, with an aim to develop a much deeper understanding of contemporary forms of relating the real to life: not only in the baskets of goods that serve to measure the value of money and inflation but also in the body itself, or parts of it, in the DNA or the global climate, all of them, among many other commercialized "goods," distant from a world in which the real referred, paradoxically perhaps, to the Polanyian "fictitious commodities": land, labor, and money.

The concept of the *real* in economic thought is centuries old, dating back to early European thinking on the quantity theory of money. Tracing its historical, social, and geographical mutations can provide to us a creative inroad, therefore, to understanding the present postcrisis, turbulent, economic world. Luigi Einaudi ([1936] 1953) showed how the wide use of imaginary monies in medieval Europe (that is, pure units of account, without any physical existence as coins or notes) gave traders a fixed point from which to think of "real values," generating confidence between traders in a world full of monies and material media. Fictional monies were, in this sense, more real for the traders than physical coins, since their value endured over time. This idea was developed to some extent by Marc Bloch (1954), who contributed to our comprehension of the multiplicity and articulation of units of account and means of payment in premodern Europe, which underpinned the calculative dimension of money as a device for the commensuration of "reality." Akinobu Kuroda (2008a, 2008b) developed these ideas in the context of Chinese history, providing valuable elements for other inquiries into the reality and realization of contemporary imaginary monies in Africa (Guyer 2012, 2016a) and the Caribbean (Neiburg 2016b).

Real tends to imply stability, something to be relied upon. As an analytic term, the concept of *the real* was first put forward by Copernicus in 1517 as part of his argument for vigilance over the quality and quantity of currency issued by the governing powers, so that the currency would always operate in a sufficiently stable way, and so that prices would reflect the real values for the people. Copernicus saw the relative stability of prices and confidence in the money issued by the government as vital components of the nationhoods developing in Europe during his era. In this sense, *real* reflected the shared values of a people.

The concept of the real exchange economy, based on a theory of the value of a measurable, stable component of the economy such as the classical labor theory of value of the nineteenth century, declined in the twentieth century with the rise of marginalist thought and the rise of capital as the key component of the triad: land, labor, and capital. The concept of the real became specifically applied to the purchasing power of money with respect to the same goods over time (producing "real prices") and the corresponding purchasing power of money wages ("real wages"), with the implementation of the Consumer Price Index (CPI) and the Gross Domestic Product (GDP) as indices for tracking economic life in the twentieth century, after World War II. Inflation, the decline in the purchasing power of money, would depress real wages and raise the cost of living. Under an updated quantity theory of money, and in the expanding colonial economies, the concept of *the real* thereby became the formal measure of inflation.

These numbers form part of the modern economic cosmology: they became central concepts in the making of a "cosmoeconomics" of different conceptions of *prosperity* and the radical uncertainty of their sources (da Col 2012), linked to new modulations of the real. They form an object of belief; they have won public trust; they seem to have always existed, like a natural fact with immanent force, but they nonetheless have a singular history. According to some authors (for example, Kendall 1969; Kula 1986: chap. 8; Poovey 1998: chap. 2; Mirowski 1991;

Crosby 1996), the first registers of price variation date back to fifteenth-century Europe. They were linked to the attempt to calculate and control fluctuations in the monetary value of certain products (like bread) and money in the context of rises in prices and monetary plurality (Einaudi [1936] 1953; Bloch 1954; Bompaire 2006; Bompaire and Dumas 2000; Fisher 1922: chap. 1; Kendall 1969; Diewert and Nakamura 1993; Balk 2008: chap. 1; Allen [1975] 2008).

From the eighteenth century on, more abstract numbers began to be calculated, whose content was no longer directly linked to specific products but to nondirectly observable agglomerates of goods and services making up "baskets," which serve to realize the reality of the people's economies. The index numbers were directly associated with the idea of the cost of living. In 1822, Joseph Lowe wrote on the troubles caused by the Napoleonic Wars, in which he argues: "What would be the practical application of this knowledge? The correction of a long list of anomalies in the real economy, in regards to rent, salaries, wages, etc., arising out of the unfortunate fluctuation of our currency" (Lowe 1822, quoted in Kendall 1969: 6). However, it would be necessary to wait until the end of the nineteenth century when, in the context of the marginalist revolution, the concept of index numbers was formulated. The first Consumer Price Index was created in Britain in 1913, and "a formalized monitoring of the correspondence, from year to year, between money prices and standardized 'basket of goods' to measure the cost of living within national economies, was installed as a technique of governance at the time of the Great War" (Guyer 2016a: 5). Irving Fisher produced the first national price index in the United States some years later (Fisher 1921; see also Neiburg 2010).

So, between the First World War and the end of the Second World War—during the Great Depression and the European hyperinflations of the 1920s—the price index became widespread as a standardized instrument of knowledge and action with respect to the real economy (in this sense, something measurable and dependable; "The Economy," in the terms set by Tim Mitchell [2002]). Index numbers, like the Consumer Price Index, are produced through abstractions of aggregates of price variations for "real" goods, expressed in a singular form of numbers: percentages.[4] These are used "to measure the change in some quantity which we cannot observe directly, which we know to have a definite influence on many other quantities which we can so observe, tending to increase

---

4. See Guyer (2014) on percentages—those particular figures linked to a sense of totality (and reality).

all, or diminish all, while this influence is concealed by the action of many causes affecting the separate quantities in various ways" (Bowley 1926: 196, quoted in Allen [1975] 2008: 2). According to Irving Fisher (1922: 3–4), "they express proportions represented by percentages and changes of magnitude between two points in time."

Later in the century, after World War II and the foundation of the International Financial Institutions, the GDP and CPI became key variables in international monitoring and mediation, commercial contracts, national social payment policies, and eligibility for international investment. All of these have an implicit or explicit temporal horizon, meaning that they project value into the future based on configurations of "the real" from the past. At the same time, index numbers became a privileged field of battle and controversy about the real: technically, there are different ways to measure the value of money, and such divergences could transform into conflicts between agents and agencies (governments, number laboratories, trade unions), each trying to impose their own figures to govern the real economy (Neiburg 2011). Since the mid-twentieth century, the Bretton Woods institutions (the IMF and the World Bank) have overseen and examined how countries make these calculations, submitting them for assessment in the broad policy contexts where these institutions play an important role.

In recent economic writing, *the real* appears to refer largely to these macroeconomic measurements (Cochrane 2005), at precisely the same time that popular and critical economics is seeking terms to analyze the experience of populations living in soft currency economies, where many factors affect the stability of the purchasing power of their money, given that financial capital is increasingly—and worldwide—held in hard currencies and real estate assets (see Piketty 2014 on the rising proportion of total capital held in housing). Both the concept and the analysis of *the real* is thus becoming complex and even contradictory. Economic historians Massimo Amato and Luca Fantacci (2014) have made the critical point that the increasing identification of capitalism with *financial* capitalism, and the real with purchasing power means that local-regional markets are very largely neglected as sources of livelihood—in this sense echoing some of the critics of contemporary mainstream economics for its supposed lack of attention to the real, instead privileging financial or fictitious economies. During the 2008 crisis and after, the press searched for terms to apply to people's values and experiences and came up with expressions such as "Wall Street versus Main Street" (as mentioned earlier). Internationally, there was also a powerful sense that the world's financial elite were strengthening a huge rift between the investment economy and the economy of those dispossessed by it (Hammar 2014).

The money economy and the real economy, the latter in the mundane sense of "making" a stable and predictable living (to "make a living"), have apparently been parting ways. The privatization and financialization of land and urban real estate, along with the expansion of extractive industries, have led to a migration of a sense of the *real* both in and out of the popular economic world. In official circles such as the International Monetary Fund, *the real*, in the sense of the purchasing power of money and the value of incomes, is still central to the calculation of the Consumer Price Index. Indeed, the CPI and risk rates have become two of the most important indices, informing a broad spectrum of policies.

A particular challenge arises from the increased sense that the conditions of the present economic and political world produce high levels of indeterminacy and turbulence in the "real lives" of ordinary people. The *real* and the *turbulent* are converging. But how is this being experienced and managed vis-à-vis people's individual search for some kind of temporal reach into their own futures, while at the same time an overarching technical and political locus is devoted to what is conceived as a "world order"? How do these realities and temporalities entangle with people's search for better lives, linking the real and the real economy to the stabilization and destabilization of collectives and persons?

It is here that anthropologists can both mediate the official terms—through the details of governmental policy implementation—and attempt to comprehend people's own concepts and practices, desires, and expectations as they come to terms with them. The recent works of Jane I. Guyer and Federico Neiburg on the "emergent" and "economic emergencies" provide ideal fields to further develop our theoretical framework.[5] Both concepts have the same etymology, the Latin *emergere*, which simultaneously means a process of coming forth (or becoming) and an unforeseen occurrence requiring immediate attention. The first sense (emergent) underlies the process of coming into being or becoming prominent; the second sense (emergency) accentuates the need to act. We will address emergency first.

---

5. Here we incorporate some of the ideas from the papers presented by the two authors at the Rio de Janeiro workshop: Jane I. Guyer, "The real economy: Past, present, and emergent" (2016b) and Federico Neiburg, "Economic emergencies and the real economy: Some ethnographic threads of thought" (2016a).

TURBULENT TIMES: ECONOMIC EMERGENCIES

The real economy seems to be traversed by the actuality of crisis and the need for its prevention. The concept of crisis is closely linked to the concept of emergency. Whether seeking to avoid or cure it, economic reality must be diagnosed and fixed. Idioms of medicine and warfare are prevalent in the realization of the real economy—going back to the connections established by Nicolas Oresme in his *De moneta* (c. 1360) between the rapid fall in the real value of money and the Black Plague (Kaye 1988). Crisis is also linked to truth and lies, to the accuracy or falsity of numbers, as we have recently seen in countries like Greece or Portugal, because of the lack of reliable "real" risk rates and "real" national deficit figures.

Some authors have shown how the crisis today is a kind of narrative, a structuring idiom and an existential device (Mbembe and Roitman 1995), a language of exceptionalism (Riles 2011), an omnipresent sign in almost all forms of narrative, which is mobilized as a defining category of historical situations, past and present, a term that seems to be self-explanatory, relating to a "moment of truth" (Roitman 2014).[6] Like the Latin *emergere*, the ancient Greek *krisis* denotes a mixture of revelation and truth, a power to distinguish, a capacity or a demand to choose and to diagnose. Both involve moral judgments and imperatives to act, providing a remedy without delay, urgently.

In the contemporary world, this entanglement of moral judgment and imperatives to act is performed in the concept of a "state of economic emergency," an exceptional yet nonetheless extremely frequently used way to suspend constitutional rights and the rule of law during times of crisis. It also alerts citizens to change their supposed normal behavior and orders government agencies to implement emergency plans. States of economic emergency are linked to states of exception, as studied by Giorgio Agamben (2005). Elaborations in the juridical field concerning "states of economic emergency" (see, for example, Scheuerman 2000a, 2000b) base themselves on Agamben's reading of Carl Schmitt, underlining the role of economic crisis (as well as war) in the construction of states of exception.

The theory and practice of the states of economic emergency were linked to World War I and its effects: European hyperinflations and the Great

---

6.   Claudio Lomnitz (2003) has explored the concept of "times of crisis," referring to wars, natural catastrophes, or major economic breakdowns, in order to stress the temporal character of crisis in two senses: a duration and a perception linked to the notion of a "saturation of the present" (as proposed by Reinhardt Koselleck [1972] 2006).

Depression. In his classic study of German inflation, Gerald Feldman describes the establishment of states of emergency (*Notstand*) to ensure the food supply and, especially, to issue "emergency currencies" (named as such by law) to meet the demands of the real economy for paper money, first to finance the war, later to deal with inflation. All sorts of emergency money were issued in Germany by firms, municipalities, the states, and other public and private agencies (Feldman 1997: 785). The relations between monetary instability, emergency money, and the war economy were, as we know, the topic of intense debates (see, for instance, Mendershausen 1943; Meyler 2007; Keynes 1940; and the responses to the latter by Hayek [1982] 1998: 124–26).[7]

In Britain, the British Emergency Powers Act of 1920 is especially illuminating. With the memory of wartime emergency provisions still fresh in people's minds, Lloyd George's postwar cabinet succeeded in pushing through regulations granting it substantial exceptional powers to limit strike activity that might interfere with the supply and distribution of food, water, fuel, or light, or with the means of locomotion (Scheuerman 2000b: 1877). In the United States, President Franklin D. Roosevelt demanded and acquired unprecedented wide-ranging executive powers to wage an economic war against the emergency. Taken as a whole, the dozen or so important statutes enacted at the time constitute the single largest instance of delegated power in US history. Although the Supreme Court soon declared parts of this original New Deal legislation unconstitutional, some of the laws survived the New Deal itself (Scheuerman 2000b: 1875n5). Despite legal and institutional variations (for example, Anglo-American models of martial law versus French-inspired conceptions of a state of siege), virtually all twentieth-century liberal democratic polities have been willing to declare economic emergencies before delegating generous (and often poorly defined) discretionary authority to the executive for the sake of tackling problems in the real economy.[8] The core of the argument is located in the two

---

7. Discussing German hyperinflation, André Orléan (2007: 205) asks, "what is real about currencies in war time" when the element of trust is radically thrown into question due to the absence of guarantees of victory or defeat? In response, he proposes the concept of a "self-referential currency" for those currencies imbued with uncertainties about the very future existence of the community within which they circulate.

8. Friedrich Hayek's responses to Carl Schmitt are well known: although the Austrian author was quick to recognize the need for states of emergency during wartime, he was always a staunch defender of the rule of law as a defense against despotism (e.g. Hayek [1945] 2001: 63–96).

world wars, in the interwar period (pervaded by hyperinflation and by economic depression), and in the postwar period, with its series of food supply crises (Guyer 2016a: chap. 2), monetary rearrangements (the end of the gold standard and the order that emerged from Bretton Woods), and injunctions for reconstruction—notably, through the launch of the Marshall Plan.[9]

Over recent years, various countries have decreed economic emergency devices. In the United States, the most relevant was perhaps the Emergency Economic Stabilization Act signed by President George W. Bush in October 2008—a law enacted in response to the subprime mortgage crisis, authorizing the United States Secretary of the Treasury to spend up to US$700 billion to purchase distressed assets, especially mortgage-backed securities, and supply cash directly to banks. One year later, the Icelandic legislature passed an emergency law that enabled the Financial Supervisory Authority to assume control of financial institutions and made domestic bank deposits priority claims. In the following days, Iceland's Prime Minister Geir Haarde announced: "The crisis in the real economy struck so violently that it turned into a concept of international law applied to countries at war or experiencing systematic crises. It is precisely what happened here [in Iceland]."[10] Similar examples in recent history can be mentioned apropos of Greece, Portugal, Spain, France, and Venezuela, among others. A curious case comes from Argentina: in December 2015, the new President Mauricio Macri declared a "state of national statistical emergency," the intervention of the National Institute of Statistics and Censuses (INDEC), and the freezing of any publication of the "main index numbers of the real economy." The president claimed, "up to now the state has lied systematically, blurring the boundary between reality and fantasy," and his economic minister added, "we want to stop lying and start telling the truth, to give back transparency and credibility, to know the real numbers of the Argentinean economy."[11] In

---

9. On the relationship between inflation and economic emergencies, see also McCormack (2015).

10. "Financial crisis: Full statement by Iceland's prime minister Geir Haarde," *The Telegraph*, October 6, 2008. http://www.telegraph.co.uk/news/worldnews/europe/iceland/3147806/Financial-crisis-Full-statement-by-Icelands-prime-minister-Geir-Haarde.html.

11. "Discurso completo de Mauricio Macri ante la Asamblea Legislativa," *La Nación*, March 1, 2016.
    http://www.lanacion.com.ar/1875715-discurso-completo-de-mauricio-macri-ante-la-asamblea-legislativa.

economic emergencies, the real economy becomes a public concern and a field of government, an issue for experts and for ordinary people, too, who need to "make a living" in extremely uncertain conditions.

CHANGING REALITIES: ECONOMIC EMERGENCES

The concept of emergence has itself "emerged" in recent years as a means to capture the relative imprecision surrounding prediction in a world where definitive historical developments are no longer anticipated in precise step-by-step fashion, projected from now into the future, or according to clearly defined plans. We see this implicit—although perhaps exemplary—indeterminacy in such popular publications as Alec Ross's *Industries of the future* (2016), where he observes several of these future industries, such as digital money, developing fastest in Africa. Jean Comaroff and John Comaroff (2011) suggest that new forms of labor organization are being tested out in the Global South for subsequent application elsewhere. The concept of emergence itself comes from the science of complex systems, which are composed through the ongoing dynamic interactions between smaller and simpler entities.

The two macroeconomic indices in which "emergence" is a concept, and where the CPI figures in some of its "real economy" referents, are the Emerging Markets Index (which ranks the "65 most influential cities") and EAGLEs (Emergent and Growth Leading Economies), which now includes thirteen countries whose GDP growth rates (also dependent on normalization through the inflation rate and the CPI) are comparable with the G6 (wealthiest) countries. Strangely, membership of this category overlaps with the BRICS group, but then this latter acronym is formed from the names of the countries themselves (Brazil, Russia, India, China, South Africa, which were the first to "emerge" into the global economy, post-1989), probably selected due to their size and industrial dynamism rather than being defined by a comprehensive inventory of all their qualities. Brazil, Russia, India, and China are still EAGLEs. Results of the national CPIs are applied to define inflation, largely for investment purposes. For comparison, we can note that inflation for the so-called hard currencies was, until the British vote on Brexit, recently less than 1 percent. Hence, emergence can be treated as a methodological concept through which an ethnographic approach can explore surprise and indeterminacy as temporal processes in economic life rather than as a completely formalized concept to slot cases into international indices.

Here we could also briefly evoke an earlier engagement with the concept of emergence in anthropology, where Bill Maurer writes of "ethnographic emergences" precisely as a way to enable "a rethinking of ethnography as a method and a retooling of the theoretical apparatus of the discipline" (2005: 1). He advocates new interfaces with other disciplines. In a world where interconnectedness is pervasive, the grasping of "the enmeshment of the observer and the observed, together with their mutually reinforcing, yet oftentimes incongruent, knowledge formations," which infuses anthropology's method, should "go along for the ride, in mutual, open-ended, and yet limited entanglements" (Maurer 2005: 4). "Entanglement" is an old concept in Western history, as Stanley Edgar Hyman (1962) pointed out in his book *The tangled bank* (a phrase taken from Charles Darwin) on great thinkers, including the early anthropologist James Frazer. We even learn from the press coverage of unexpected happenings, such as—to cite a recent case from Nigeria that adds further detail to the situation described by Guyer for the Nigerian CPI (Guyer 2016b)—the discovery that some shipments of rice imported from China were adulterated with plastic, a symptom of the price lurches in the local markets and the profits to be gained by importers. A 50 kg bag now sells for around 20,000 naira (US$63), more than double the price fetched in December 2016. Nigeria's inflation rate stood at 18.5 percent at the end of that year its thirteenth consecutive monthly rise, driven by higher food prices.[12]

Such surprising and indeterminate dynamics, involving many participants, relate to the real in several ways: What exactly is "real" rice? What can the rapidly inflating Nigerian currency actually buy, especially for those consumers who earn their incomes in unpredictable ways? We can ask, then, how the force of the concept of the real economy is created and combines in multiples realities, mobilizing concepts in ways that only in-depth ethnographically based research and mutual engagement can illuminate—as many of the essays in this book seek to demonstrate.

Emergence is not a state but a flow, something that springs into being, entangled in global assemblages and personal, experiential, and subjective lives. But there is nothing teleological in emergence: real economies can both emerge and submerge. Crisis is always a possibility, as shown by the current decline in some of the largest national "emergent economies" (such as the Brazilian economy,

---

12. "Fake plastic rice seized in Nigeria amid rocketing food prices," *Guardian*, December 22, 2016. https://www.theguardian.com/world/2016/dec/22/fake-plastic-rice-seized-in-nigeria-amid-rocketing-food-prices.

for example). Personal and collective lives need to come to terms with these variations, seen by specialists as cycles of economic expansion and contraction. As the chapters in this volume show, this is an extremely fertile field of research when it comes to formulating an ethnographic theory of the real economy: the experiential and the subjective, struggling to come to terms with the emergent and its opposite, allow us to ethnographically reframe the aspirations created by the massive absorption of populations into the contemporary market economy, through the expansion of indebtedness and financial devices, and their contrary: stagflation, the impossibility of paying, the dramatic change in personal and collective expectations, the transformation of uncertainty into some kind of normalcy that must be navigated through, lived with, and used to fashion lives.

TOWARD AN ETHNOGRAPHIC THEORY OF THE REAL ECONOMY

The study of the mutation of words and terms over time, space, and social context is itself an inspiration in ethnographically based theory. During Guyer's reading on the "emergent," she found the concept in the title of poet-cleric John Donne's meditations on life in general, written during his own illness and his sense of impending death: *Devotions upon emergent occasions* ([1624] 2014). The 27th Meditation contains terms that became part of the literary and conceptual life of the twentieth century: "No man is an island," and "Ask not for whom the bell tolls. It tolls for thee." All of us live in both the certainty and uncertainty of life, in Donne's poetic and religious register. In the twenty-first century, we stand poised to think deeply about emergence in a secular and pragmatic register, and to be attentive, through use of the classic ethnographic method, to people's own words, sayings, proverbs, and invocation of sources from their shared religious, philosophical, and performative archives, in their own languages. For example, what did Confucius write about reality and economy, or the dynamics of indeterminate emergence? Is it still quoted in China, and if so, in what contexts, by whom, and with what consequences? Ethnographic theory's great strength resides in its inquisitive receptivity to people's own lives and thoughts, expressed in their own terms, which in this case includes domains of formal expertise and everyday life, in their own discursive modes, social contexts, and temporal frames.

The question of *realism* is pervasive in Western philosophy: the idea that there is some kind of real world independent of our thoughts is intrinsically linked to the idea of truth and to moral values. As we know, Émile Durkheim's "social realism" was a singular instantiation of this concept: society (simultaneously immanent and transcendent to the individual) is truly real and its realization by the sociologist is, at the same time, an imperative to act upon it (see Durkheim [1895] 2013; Jones 1999). In a different register, much more recently, John Searle (1995) proposed that there are two kinds of realities: the raw and the institutional. The latter, as in the case of money mentioned by Searle himself, depends on people's trust and on institutional assemblages. Both kinds are "speech acts"—concepts that allow us to realize the reality of the real. This explains why reality is also a key issue for Actor Network Theory, especially for its critique of constructivism, which tries to build what is seen to be a realistic account of reality, proposing instead an inquiry into the effects and the "effectuation" made by human and nonhuman actants (see, for example, Muniesa 2014). Luc Boltanski has argued that the very concept of the real is linked to a sense of totality also expressed in the imagination of some kind of stable "world." In his words, the "reality of the reality," despite its viscosity and seriality ever present in the devices of realization deployed to tame uncertainty, suffers from "a sort of weakness which must incessantly be reinforced in order to endure" (Boltanski 2011: 36–37).[13]

Here, though, we have moved far away from research into the ontology of the real (or more modestly, the real economy). As João de Pina-Cabral (2017: 11) proposes apropos the similarly self-evident concept of *world*, we argue the need to abandon "the established dichotomy between rather crude forms of realism and equally crude forms of semiotic idealism," proposing an ethnographic rather than philosophical question about the real. At the same time, following Tom Boellstorff's (2016) recent work on the "ontological turn" and the "digital real," we propose to problematize the diverse ontologies of the real, showing, at the same time, similarities and differences, the multiple realities of the virtual, and the multiple virtualities of the real.

THE POLITICS OF THE REAL ECONOMY

In the first volume of his well-known series *Spheres*, German philosopher Peter Sloterdijk (2011) links the modern concept of the *real* to the spherical form of the material coin and its opposite, the aerial concept of the bubble. Since

---

13. See also Boltanski's (2011: chap. 2) differentiation between world, real, and reality.

Ancient Rome, the sphere has contained the reality of money, its real value, minted to avoid the deleterious and unrealistic economy of lies associated with airiness and fictitiousness (see also Marsh 2019). The concepts of *reality* and the *real economy* are linked, then, to the utopias of collective well-being—blended by circular coins of real monies and good economies—and with the dystopias of bubbles and balloons in which people's lives "crash" with the reality of their economies, from the famous Dutch Tulip bubble of 1636 to the 2008 mortgage credit crisis, and today. As we proposed at the outset of this Introduction, when the real economy is provoked—that is, realized mostly in monies, numbers, and graphics, or even in the "Reality Test" made by macroeconomic forecasters (see Pilmis 2018)—it reveals its constitutive links with concepts of force and weakness (hard and soft monies, strong and fragile economies), with moral values and with the value of truth. To adopt Michael Jackson's terminology (2009: xiv), provoking the real leads us to navigate the turbulent and challenging waters of "juxtapositions, analogies, poetic images, epiphanies and anecdotes" that allow us to experience at close range and realize reality; that is, to quote William James (quoted in Jackson 2009: 4), the place "where things happen," or as we have suggested, where something exists and must be governed.

These themes are found at the core of the chapters of this volume. They explore our proposal for an ethnographic theory of the real economy, offering insightful perspectives on singular assemblages of vernacular and scientific realizations and enactments of the real economy, along with their links to ideas of truth and to moralities. They show how these multiple and shifting realities become present and entangled with historically situated lives, the different ways through which the experiential lives of ordinary people engage with the formal realizations of the real in the governance of the economy (or economies).

Fabian Muniesa and Horacio Ortiz focus on business in education and practice. Muniesa shows how people teach and learn about the real economy in a leading business school, where a culture of realization of the economy is lived and cultivated, linked to a type of anxiety to deal with reality through the subjective and experiential lives of the business students themselves. Muniesa offers an ethnography in which the vernaculars of the business world are entangled, revealing the different perceptions of business reality and the reality of the economy nurtured by the subjective excitement of its realization. Ortiz analyzes different concepts of economic reality put into play by cross-border financial consultants, located between Shanghai and Europe. Based on long-term fieldwork in a Shanghai consultancy company, his article shows that the analytic claim of a "real economy," against which financial practices are to be gauged, misses the multiple meanings through which these practices make sense for those who carry them out.

Deborah James and Maxim Bolt explore the relations between reality and formalization and how the formal sector is made real. Bolt focuses on Zimbabwean labor on South African border farms in order to explore the relations between reality and formalization and the process of making workers real through real documents. His ethnography reveals how "spotlights" and "stepping-stones" are found at the points where formal regulation and livelihood plans mutually constitute each another, establishing the shared ground for negotiating the "reality" of a wage economy in the process. James focuses on dealing with debts and indebtedness from the official viewpoint and from the viewpoint of the debtor, showing their multiple articulations and disjunctures. Proposing a deep ethnography of the links between the formal "deductions" and "counter-deductions" of debts and the current explosion in South African "unsecure lending" by profitable big retailers and new microlenders, she reveals how financialization, in its multiple dimensions, has become a privileged field for an ethnographical appraisal of the real economy.

Caitlin Zaloom goes to the heart of the concept of the real economy, discussing the temporality of the *oikos*, household planning and the operation of calculative devices to project family futures. Under financial capitalism, Zaloom argues, the future, even the distant future, becomes a "central category for citizens' household operations." To plan a child's future education is "a hallmark of middle-class and aspiring US parenthood." Ordinary people thus craft and live regimes of foresight and projective fictions as a means to deal with financial policies and make financial plans in changing and uncertain times. At stake are moral ideals and concepts of (good) parenthood and family life—simultaneously rejecting finance, as opposed to the real and genuine family life, and incorporating finance and dealing with debts to make good lives.

Mariana Luzzi and Ariel Wilkis explore the contingent properties of money, its temporality, and its relationality. Contemporary Argentina offers the authors an extraordinary field in which to examine the changing meanings of the real economy and real monies through the dynamics of monetary pluralism. Entangled in the long cultural history of the use of US dollars in Argentinean daily life, Luzzi and Wilkis examine new units of account and stores of value (soybeans and bricks) that provide insights into the changing reality of money and economic lives. As the authors show, the creation and use of new currencies relies on, and reveals, changing concepts of the real.

Eugênia Motta scrutinizes the relations between Brazilian favelas and numbers. How is this unquantifiable and unstable reality measured and stabilized? How do numbers circulate and how are they reinterpreted by the favela inhabitants themselves? How do alternative figures emerge and compete with state statistics? Motta focuses on the statistical concept of the "subnormal agglomerate" used by state experts to realize the favela's reality, stabilizing and spatializing urban poverty, while also exploring resistance to this concept from favela residents (through self-counting) and local organizations (through alternative censuses). She then shows us how reality is also disputed and resisted.

Inquiring ethnographically into the concept of legal personhood in antitrust policy (which aims to regulate mergers, acquisitions, and joint ventures), Gustavo Onto discusses what a real economic agent is. Companies, individuals, and networks reveal and mask three key economic concepts: economic agency, markets, and competition. How do regulators realize economic agency and individualize real economic actants, identify "relevant markets" and distinguish between good and bad competition? How do they cultivate the knowledge (and sensibility) needed to regulate real markets and true competition and to realize economic realities?

What is a real or fictitious transaction? This is the main question scrutinized by Juan Pablo Pardo-Guerra in his chapter. In a deep ethnography of high-frequency financial trading and infrastructure, he focuses on the "realism" of electronic, automated stock markets, looking specifically at those transactions conceptualized as "spoofing"—"performances of reality" that constitute true trades and markets. Through this field, Pardo-Guerra addresses a key question for this project that articulates regimes of truth and the morality of exchanges regarding the real economy.

Fernando Rabossi's chapter sheds light on the dark sides of the real economy, on the difficulties of realizing "hidden" economic realities, black economies, smuggling, and piracy. Taking as his starting point fieldwork carried out on the border between Brazil and Paraguay, he asks who defines what it is legal and visible or illegal and invisible, how these boundaries are made and how the controversies over the real make the (un)real and the (un)realizable. (Un)quantifiable realities, Rabossi shows, are political.

The volume ends with Bill Maurer's Afterword. Inspired by Constantin Stanislavski, Maurer explores the affinity and disjuncture between playing theater and doing ethnography: it is necessary to put oneself in other people's shoes in order to experience and realize others' realities. It has nothing to do with a metaphysics of the real but rather with the concrete lives of persons and the very nature of the ethnographic project. It is also about enabling bridges, pluralities, and what Maurer calls the intentional ethnography that links the real economy to the ethnographic reality, being "radically empirical without being irreducibly empiricist." And it is also, as always . . . about politics.

Political struggles are found at the core of the pragmatics of the real and the real economy we propose in this project. As the Argentinean filmmaker Lucrecia Martel pointed out in speaking about fiction, to discuss and question the legitimacy of the real is itself a political act and a political fight.[14] This is true even more so in contemporary times, when the political battles over the real (and the real economy) are gaining new forms in public space through the concepts of "fake" and "fake news."

In a passage of the *Philosophical investigations*, Ludwig Wittgenstein stated that the question "Is a sum [or a calculation] in the head less real than a sum [or a calculation] on paper?" is less philosophical than practical (Wittgenstein [1953] 1986: §366ff.). This is also valid for the debate between those who denounce the supposed incapacity of mainstream economics to provide an account of reality (as proposed by Keynesians and the so-called critical economists, such as Lawson 1997) and those preoccupied with the ways through which economics perform social reality (Callon 1998). The theoretical, political, and moral dimensions at stake in these debates are part of the research program on the real economy that we propose in this volume. As the articles show, the real is a shifting and pluri-scalar concept, which involves multiple agencies, agents, engagements, and enactments, claims of truth and claims of justice, collective and personal lives, emergent and submergent personhoods, experiences, and feelings. The singular power of contemporary ethnography and ethnographers to navigate between worlds, realms of experience, scientific and vernacular scenarios, global assemblages, and the "imponderables of everyday lives" (to cite Malinowski on focal points of method) of ordinary people, reinforced by the collective nature of this project (which enhances the heuristic power of ethnography), can serve as an invitation to further develop the ethnographic (pragmatic, comparative, historical) theory of the real economy that we propose in this book.

---

14. http://revistacinetica.com.br/home/entrevista-com-lucrecia-martel/.

ACKNOWLEDGEMENTS

We would like to thank Giovanni da Col, Michael Lambek, Hylton White, and Anne-Catherine Taylor for their encouragement and patience, and the generosity of their insightful ideas during the long and intense process of making this book. We especially thank the battalion of reviewers who helped us improve each essay and the project as a whole, contributing to its collective nature. This project was born in multiple meetings and conversations that materialized in a workshop in Rio de Janeiro in June 2016, supported by the Wenner-Gren Foundation for Anthropological Research (Gr. CONF-700) and the Brazilian Science Research Council (CNPq, Gr. 442254/2015-6). We would also like to thank all the participants and organizers of this meeting: in addition to those who feature as authors of this volume, we thank Caetano Berenguer, Benoit de l'Estoile, Viviane Fernandes, Andrés Góngora, Keith Hart, Jeanne Lazarus, Taylor Nelms, and Jorge Pantaleón.

REFERENCES

Agamben, Giorgio. 2005. *State of exception*. Chicago: University of Chicago Press.

Allen, Roy G. D. (1975) 2008. *Index numbers in economic theory and practice*. Piscataway, NJ: Aldine Transaction.

Amato, Massimo, and Luca Fantacci. 2014. *Saving the market from capitalism*. Cambridge: Polity Press.

Balk, Bert M. 2008. *Price and quantity index numbers: Models for measuring aggregate change and difference*. Cambridge: Cambridge University Press.

Bloch, Marc. 1954. "Esquisse d'une histoire monétaire de l'Europe." *Cahiers des Annales*, no. 9: 40–70.

Boellstorff, Tom. 2016. "For whom the ontology turns: Theorizing the digital real." *Current Anthropologist* 57 (4): 387–407.

Bohannan, Paul. 1954. *Tiv farm and settlement*. London: British Colonial Office, Colonial Research Studies 15.

———. 1955. "Some principles of exchange and investment among the Tiv." *American Anthropologist* 57 (1): 59–70.

Boltanski, Luc. 2011. *On critique: A sociology of emancipation*. Malden, MA: Polity Press.

Bompaire, Marc. 2006. "Compétences et pratiques de calcul dans les livres de changeurs français (XIVe-XIVe siècles)." In Écrire, compter, mesurer: Vers une histoire des rationalités pratiques, edited by Natacha Coquery, François Menant, and Florence Weber, 143–62. Paris: Éditions rue d'Ulm.

Bompaire, Marc, and Françoise Dumas. 2000. Numismatique médiévale: Monnaies et documents d'origine française. Turnhout, Belgium: Brepols (L'atelier du médiéviste).

Callon, Michel. 1998. "Introduction: The embeddedness of economic markets in economics." In The laws of the market, edited by Michel Callon, 1–58. Oxford: Blackwell Publishers.

Cochrane, John H. 2005. "Financial markets and the real economy: Working paper 11193." Cambridge, MA: National Bureau of Economic Research.

Comaroff, Jean, and John Comaroff. 2011. Theory from the south; or, How Euro-America is evolving toward Africa. London: Routledge.

Crosby, Alfred W. 1996. The measure of reality: Quantification and Western society, 1250–1600. Cambridge: Cambridge University Press.

da Col, Giovanni. 2012. "Introduction: Natural philosophies of fortune—Luck, vitality, and uncontrolled relatedness." Social Analysis 56 (1): 1–23.

Diewert, Walter Erwin, and Alice O. Nakamura, eds. 1993. Essays in index number theory, vol. 1. Amsterdam: Contributions to Economic Analysis.

Durkheim, Émile. (1895) 2013. The rules of sociological method: And selected texts on sociology and its method. London: Palgrave.

Donne, John. (1624). 2014. Donne's devotions. Cambridge: Cambridge University Press.

Einaudi, Luigi. (1936) 1953. "The theory of imaginary money from Charlemagne to the French Revolution." In Enterprise and secular change: Readings in economic history, edited by Frederic C. Lane and Jelle C. Riemersma, 153–81. London: George Allen and Unwin.

Feldman, Gerald D. 1997. The great disorder: Politics, economics, and society in the German inflation, 1914–1924. Oxford: Oxford University Press.

Fisher, Irving. 1921. "The best form of index number." Quarterly Publications of the American Statistical Association 17 (133): 533–37.

———. 1922. The making of index numbers: A study of their varieties, tests, and reliability. Boston: Houghton Mifflin Company.

Guyer, Jane I. 2012. "Soft currencies, cash economies, new monies: Past and present." Proceedings of the National Academy of Sciences 109: 2214–21.

———. 2014. "Percentages and perchance: Archaic forms in the 21st century." *Distinktion: Scandinavian Journal of Social Theory* 5 (2): 155–73.

———. 2016a. *Legacies, logics, logistics: Essays in the anthropology of the platform economy.* Chicago: University of Chicago Press.

———. 2016b. "The real economy: Past, present and emergent." Paper presented at the Real Economy: Ethnographic Inquiries into the Reality and the Realization of Economic Life workshop, Rio de Janeiro.

Hammar, Amanda, ed. 2014. *Displacement economies in Africa: Paradoxes of crisis and creativity.* London: Zed Books.

Hart, Keith. 1986. "Heads or tails? Two sides of the coin." *Man* 21 (4): 637–65.

Hayek, Friedrich A. (1945) 2001. *The road to serfdom.* London: Institute of Economic Affairs.

———. (1982) 1998. *Law, legislation and liberty: A new statement of the liberal principles of justice and political economy.* Vol. 3, *The political order of free people.* London: Routledge.

Hyman, Stanley Edgar. 1962. *The tangled bank: Darwin, Marx, Frazer and Freud as imaginative writers.* New York: Ahtenaum.

Jackson, Michael. 2009. *The palm at the end of the mind: Relatedness, religiosity, and the real.* Durham, NC: Duke University Press.

Jones, Robert A. 1999. *The development of Durkheim's social realism.* Cambridge: Cambridge University Press.

Kaye, J. 1988. "The impact of money on the development of fourteenth-century scientific thought." *Journal of Medieval Studies* 14: 251–70.

Kendall, Maurice G. 1969. "The early history of index numbers." *International Statistical Review*, no. 37: 1–12.

Keynes, John Maynard. 1940. *How to pay for the war: A radical plan for the Chancellor of the Exchequer.* London: Macmillan.

Koselleck, Reinhart. (1972) 2006. "Crisis." *Journal of the History of Ideas* 67 (2): 357–400.

Kula, Witold. 1986. *Measures and men.* Princeton, NJ: Princeton University Press.

Kuroda, Akinobu. 2008a. "What is the complementary among monies? An introductory note." *Financial Historical Review* 15 (1): 7–15.

———. 2008b. "Concurrent but non-integrable currency circuits: Complementary relationships among monies in modern China and other regions." *Financial Historical Review* 15 (1): 17–36.

Lawson, Tony. 1997. *Economics and reality.* London: Routledge.

Lomnitz, Claudio. 2003. "Times of crisis: Historicity, sacrifice, and the spectacle of debacle in Mexico City." *Public Culture* 15 (1): 127–48.

Marsh, Nicky. 2019. "'t'was only a balloon': Seeing and satire in the cultural history of money." In *The cultural history of money: The age of empire*, edited by Nigel Dodd and Federico Neiburg, chapter 5. London: Bloomsbury.

Maurer, Bill. 2005. "Introduction to 'Ethnographic emergences.'" *American Anthropologist* 107 (1): 1–4.

Malinowski, Bronisław. 1935. *Coral gardens and their magic: A study of the methods of tilling the soil and of agricultural rites in the Trobriand Islands*. London: Routledge.

McCormack, Derek. 2015. "Governing inflation: Price and atmospheres of emergency." *Theory, Culture & Society* 32 (2): 131–54.

Mbembe, Achille, and Janet Roitman. 1995. "Figures of the subject in times of crisis." *Public Culture* 7: 323–52.

Mendershausen, Horst. 1943. *The economics of war*. New York: Prentice Hill.

Meyler, Bernadette. 2007. "Economic emergency and the rule of law." *DePaul Law Review* 56 (2): 539–68.

Mirowski, Philip. 1991. "The when, the how and the why of mathematical expression in the history of economic analysis." *Journal of Economic Perspectives* 5 (1): 145–57.

Mitchell, Timothy. 2002. *Rule of experts: Egypt, techno-politics, modernity*. Berkeley: University of California Press.

Muniesa, Fabian. 2014. *The provoked economy, economic reality and the performative turn*. Oxford: Taylor and Francis.

Narotzky, Susana, and Niko Besnier. 2014. "Crisis, value, and hope: Rethinking the economy." Introduction to Supplement 9, *Current Anthropology* 55 (S9): S4–S16.

Neiburg, Federico. 2006. "Inflation: Economists and economic cultures in Brazil and Argentina." *Comparative Studies in Society and History* 46 (3): 604–33.

———. 2010. "Sick currencies and public numbers." *Anthropological Theory* 10 (1–2): 96–102.

———. 2011. "La guerre des indices: L'inflation au Brésil." *Genèses: Sciences Sociales et Histoire* 3 (84): 25–46.

———. 2016a. "Economic emergencies and the real economy: Some ethnographic threads of thought." Paper presented at the Real Economy: Ethnographic Inquiries into the Reality and the Realization of Economic Life workshop, Rio de Janeiro.

———. 2016b. "A true coin of their dreams: Imaginary monies in Haiti." 2010 Sidney Mintz Lecture. *HAU: Journal of Ethnographic Theory* (6) 1: 75–93.

Neiburg, Federico, Fernando Rabossi, Eugênia Motta, and Lucia Müller. 2014. "Ethnographies of economy/ics: Making and reading." *Vibrant* 11 (1): 50–55. http://www.vibrant.org.br/downloads/v11n1_foreword.pdf.

Piketty, Thomas. 2014. *Capitalism in the twenty-first century*. Cambridge, MA: Harvard University Press.

Orléan, André. 2007. "Crise de souveraineté et crise monétaire: L'hyperinflation allemande des annés 1920." In *La monnaie dévoilée par ses crises, vol. II: Crises monétaires en Russie et en Allemagne au xxe siècle*, edited by Bruno Théret, 187–219. Paris: Éditions EHESS.

Peirce, Charles Sanders. 1905. "Issues of pragmatism." *Monist* 15 (4): 481–99.

Pilmis, Olivier. 2018. "Escaping the reality test: How macroeconomic forecasters deal with 'errors.'" In *Uncertain futures: Imaginaries, narratives, and calculation in the economy*, edited by Jens Beckert and Richrd Bronk, 124–43. Oxford: Oxford University Press.

Pina-Cabral, João de. 2017. *World: An anthropological examination*. Chicago: University of Chicago Press/HAU Books.

Poovey, Mary. 1998. *A history of the modern fact: Problems of knowledge in the sciences of wealth and society*. Chicago: University of Chicago Press.

Riles, Annelise. 2011. "Too big to fail." In *Recasting anthropological knowledge inspiration and social science*, edited by Jeanette Edwards and Maja Petrović-Šteger, 31–48. Cambridge: Cambridge University Press.

Reid, Thomas. (1785) 1997. *An enquiry into the human mind: On the principles of common sense*. Edinburgh: Edinburgh University Press.

Roitman, Janet. 2014. *Anti-crisis*. Durham, NC: Duke University Press.

Ross, Alec. 2016. *Industries of the future*. New York: Simon & Schuster.

Scheuerman, William W. 2000a. *Carl Schmitt: The end of law*. Oxford: Rowman & Littlefield.

———. 2000b. "The economic state of emergency." *Cardozo Law Review* 21 (5–6): 1869–93.

Searle, John. 1995. *The construction of social reality*. New York: Free Press.

Sloterdijk, Peter. 2011. *Bubbles: Spheres*. Vol. 1, *Microspherology*. Translated by Wieland Hoban. Los Angeles: MIT Press / Semiotext(e).

Wittgenstein, Ludwig. (1953) 1986. *Philosophical investigations*. Oxford: Basil Blackwell.

CHAPTER ONE

The live act of business and the culture of realization

Fabian Muniesa

Notions of reality significantly permeate the contemporary business curriculum. A prominent requirement of business schools today is to provide students with a realistic sense of managerial, entrepreneurial, and financial operations, a requirement that is often expressed as a critical response to purely abstract, theoretical, or academic approaches to the conduct of economic business. Experiential educational techniques, such as the case method of instruction in business administration, are now pervasive in business schools worldwide. They typically rely on participatory deliberation, focusing on the discussion of pedagogical materials consisting in the presentation of real or realistic practical cases, often involving several forms of staging and role-playing. Mainstream theories of business leadership tend to indicate that the felicitous attainment of a directorial disposition involves a transformation of the self, which requires the empirical exercising of the reality of the act of business decision. Promotional materials abound in which the semantic field of the real is put to work in a way that is not without relation to the exigency of adventurousness and courage in the face of reality that characterized the early ideological programs of institutions such as the Harvard Business School (Fraser 1931; McNair 1954; Copeland 1958;

Christensen, Garvin, and Sweet 1981; Cruikshank 1987; Barnes, Christensen, and Hansen 1994; Snook, Nohria, and Khurana 2012).

Specifying the meaning and function of the cluster of notions and intuitions that converge into this culture of the business real is a complicated venture. One can ask how this repertoire of the real relates to other common ideas widespread in economic critique, such as that of monetary gain as the ultimate reality test, or that of a materially tangible, genuine underlying ground that shall distinguish from spurious, artificial, fictitious, or unreal representations (cf. Guyer 2016). The difficulty augments with the evidence of ethnographic appraisal, since the examination of the actual practices that correspond to the discourse of the real in business education provides evidence of an ostensible level of contrivance and artifice, which may suggest the presence of a problematic concept of reality.

In the present study, I develop a characterization of the problem of the business real while drawing from ethnographic investigation. The first section provides a description of three situations observed in three different fieldwork sites in which the vernaculars of the business real are articulated. The first one is a course on the use of the case method, attended by business instructors at a business school established in Europe (2008–9, Winter Term). The second one is a case teaching session in the MBA program offered by a prominent business school established in North America (2011–12, Spring Term). The third one is an international case-solving competition for business school students in a business school established in Europe (2009–10, Winter Term).[1] I selected these situations from fieldwork records both because they are representative of the ordinary process of case-based business pedagogy and because they express most saliently the ordinary tensions produced by the problem of the business real. I do not venture here into a comparative analysis of specific cultural contexts but rather into a broad interpretation of these tensions. How can they be made sense of, then?

In the second section, I proceed to an examination of the concept of reality implied in these materials. For that task, I draw partly on Hans Blumenberg

---

1.   I spent three days in the instructional workshop, one month in the North American business school, and one week at the case competition, having had in all cases the opportunity to talk to organizers, instructors, and students. These ethnographic experiences were part of a wider, multisited research project carried out from 2008 to 2015 that involved multiple qualitative methodologies (archival research, qualitative interviews, and ethnographic observations) in various business education establishments in Europe, North America, and Asia.

(1979). Known primarily for his philosophical contribution to the intellectual history of the categories of modern thought, for his discussion of secularization, and for his study of metaphors, Blumenberg offers in his essay on the concept of reality a helpful resource for the examination of the tensions these materials offer. Four concepts of reality are discussed in that essay. The reality of instantaneous evidence found in ancient philosophy, Blumenberg writes, can be contrasted with the request for a guarantee of objective truth present in medieval and modern thought and, further, with a more contemporary idea of reality as intersubjective, experiential realization, that in turn may finally evolve into an idea of reality as what resists such realization. I locate in the notion of realization, as articulated in these two last concepts of reality, the crux of an anthropological understanding of the business real, as manifest in the ethnographic materials. I then observe the paradox that the culture of realization constitutes, with the ideal of the business real being caught between the excitements of an intersubjective provocation of reality, on the one hand, and on the other hand, the contained, almost fetishistic quality of the vehicle of realization.

THE CASE METHOD IN BUSINESS EDUCATION

Instruction workshop[2]

The three-day course offers two workshops, one on successful case teaching and one on how to write effective cases. We are in a small room located on the premises of a business school that hosts this event offered by an organization that specializes in the commercialization of cases. There are six participants in the course, all instructors working in different business schools. I am among them, having enrolled in the course as a regular participant (I introduce myself as a social science instructor in an engineering school). The first workshop is led by a professor of strategy and international management. She opens the workshop with a general introduction to the case method. She refers to the method's origins and development at the Harvard Business School. She insists on business education being "practical," centered on participants being confronted with "complex situations" that require a "project-solving" methodology.[3] She refers to

---

2. Description from fieldwork notes: workshop for case instructors.

3. I use quotation marks henceforth for verbatim expressions (my translation to English when required).

instructors as "facilitators" and to students as "participants." She situates the case method in a scale of increasing interactivity and pedagogical accommodation, from one-way action from facilitator to participant at the bottom, to higher interaction among participants at the top. "The more the case is lived by the participant," she indicates, "the more it is understood," adding: "You've got to get it just like that," snapping her fingers expressively, pointing to her head and raising her eyebrows. The case, she says, might be real or fictional: a real case might be more effective, but what ought to be real in any case is the "setting of the situation." The workshop involves practical work with actual examples of case teaching.

The facilitator, the workshop tutor demonstrates, needs to "manage" carefully a learning process: constructing it, but without obstructing its participatory and experiential dynamics. The "scenario" is the central ingredient: the situation is to be presented as realistically as possible, "as a real decision-maker confronts it in real life"—that is, most distinctively, "without all necessary information." The method, she explains, is "cooperative" (as opposed to individualistic), "dynamic" (as opposed to passive), and "democratic" (as opposed to magisterial). Students need first to read the case individually. Then they typically have to meet in small groups in order to confront interpretations and prepare for discussion. They finally attend a plenary session in which viewpoints are debated collectively. The workshop tutor insists on "decision": "Participants have to position themselves; the situation demands resolution." She insists on the fact that there is no "one best solution" to the "problem" featured in a case.

The bulk of the workshop revolves around the idea of the "scenario." This refers to the narratives that ought to be employed in order to convey to participants a clear comprehension of the particular state of affairs they need to maneuver in and of the particular agencies at play: where are "we," what happens, what is the problem, and who ought to make a decision. The "discussion" is also central in case teaching know-how. Practical aspects such as how and when to start and close a discussion need to be dealt with, also how to "make disagreement salient" or, conversely, how to "make consensus emerge," how to gratify participants, how to pick up claims as they come and write them down on the blackboard, how to avoid a professorial attitude, and how to value positively the production of "well-argued decisions." In order to further illustrate these points, a short video is screened that presents the views of experienced case instructors on the method's philosophy ("maieutics," "dialectics") and a few staged examples— some openly parodic—that illustrate common errors. The workshop concludes with a discussion on the crucial importance of using suggestive—"sexy"—cases and of entertaining a recreational—"game"—atmosphere.

The second workshop is led by a marketing professor. He embarks on a critical commentary on the historical import of the case method from the Harvard Business School, emphasizing a few paradoxes that other business schools encounter in the emulation of the model, such as "the lack of means." He is adamant in signaling that the method ought to focus on the communication of "concepts" and "fundamentals" in order not to become a spurious "salon conversation." The workshop tackles specifically the case-writing process. The tutor develops the topic of case "sources." The most usual one would be "students"—that is, a student's report on a company or an essay following a visit or an internship. The student's name ought to be mentioned in the acknowledgements. "Friends" in the corporate world do also serve well the purpose of acquiring "sources." The key justification of authorship does not rely on a sense of case investigation but on the writing process proper—that is, on the composition of the case narrative and also, most specifically, on the writing of the "teaching note." The teaching note is the document that the facilitator, having purchased the case, will use as a source of inspiration for the setting of the teaching. The content (and even existence) of that note, we are told, should be concealed from participants. A point is explicitly made about the confidential character of the teaching note. Anonymization of case company may be necessary in some cases but most companies, the tutor says, are "very happy" with being featured in cases: "Of course, not when the case is critical, but cases shouldn't be critical."

The workshop is almost entirely devoted to the "opening pages" of the case: that is, to the introductory narrative that sets the scene and introduces the problem. The writing of the actual documentation of the case (i.e., the presentation of empirical elements) is not considered as a central topic. The importance of the introductory narrative is illustrated with a case that includes some video material—that is, a short documentary film that presents the case company facing a competitive situation. Participants are asked to write down a list of keywords and suggest topics for development that could be made explicit in an accompanying teaching note. We also take part in a most amusing exercise, which consists in writing down a short dialogue that could serve as an introductory narrative for a human resources case, and then performing it theatrically. The workshop concludes with a complaint by the tutor about people not always paying the fees for the purchase and use of cases. The method's commercial system requires that an instructor purchase from the case repository as many copies as students in a case-teaching session, and complies with the rules concerning the confidentiality of the teaching note. A conversation arises about how case authoring and teaching connect to faculty evaluation and, more generally, to business school rankings. A few participants comment on how they felt pressure from their employers to enroll in this kind of instructional course.

Amphitheater discussion[4]

The case session lasts eighty minutes. The classroom—a large amphitheater—is fully packed with about a hundred students from the MBA program. Members of the staff carefully clean the several chalkboard panels from the previous session. The instructor arrives and introduces a few guest visitors, including me (I am presented as a sociologist from France researching teaching practices in business schools). The case featured this day is a finance case. The topic is the use of stock options as employee incentives. Students have already had the opportunity to read the case and discuss it in small groups, which they did the previous day. Specific sections from a corporate finance textbook were also given as required reading. The case recounts the story of a company facing the challenge of repricing its employee stock options (i.e., an "option exchange program") as a response to a dramatic decrease of the stock's price in the midst of the stock market crisis of 2008. The case is documented extensively. Students are asked to decide what to do, and explain their reasons, first putting themselves in the position of a shareholder ("Would you vote for or against the proposed option exchange program?") and then of an employee owning company options ("Would you participate in the option exchange program?"). The case refers with an actual name—"Nancy"—to the imagined employee featured in the situation.

The instructor introduces the case, setting up the scene and writing down the two questions on the blackboard. He mentions that at least two students had the experience of participating in comparable exchange programs, and points at them. "What is going on?" is the question he uses in order to initiate the participatory dynamics. Hands are in the air; he picks one, then another. As students comment on the main characteristics of the situation and of the corresponding challenges, the instructor writes down condensed versions of the claims on the blackboard, in an organized manner. He seeks to sharpen the terms in which the

4.   Description from fieldwork notes: case teaching session at a business school.

problems are expressed: "How is the stock doing? . . . Is it a disaster? . . . Yes, it is!
. . . How is the company doing? . . . Is it a disaster? . . . No! . . . See why we are
doing the exchange program?" Hence dramatized, the rationale for the option
exchange program is then complemented by a characterization of the situation
employees holding options are put in: constraints, risks, but also a "culture of
stock options" in which "you want employees acting as shareholders." He asks
how many students had stock options in previous jobs, and about twenty students raise their hands. The atmosphere is quite cheerful, and gently amusing
comments are made about the culture of risk-taking and the recurrence of the
experience of failure in business life.

The instructor calls for a vote. He roughly estimates the number of hands
raised and writes the following in the blackboard: "Shareholders approve plan:
Yes 90%, No 10%." And then: "Employees participate: Yes 50%, No 50%." He
emphasizes excitement about the scale of the disagreement: "Fifty-fifty! That's
what we like in case teaching!" He then orients the discussion toward how the
price of these options is calculated—that is, the use of the Black-Scholes model.[5]
Another student asks the two students that had participated in that company's
option exchange program how they proceeded with the calculation, to which
they respond that they really did not calculate anything. The instructor makes
a point about how these decisions are usually taken without expert knowledge.
He also tells the classroom: "Next year you'll get stock options, so now you will
know how to make decisions." He draws a valuation table on the blackboard,
comparing the old price with the new price. He raises concerns, such as the
number of options in the plan or the conditions of execution. When he mentions that one should consider the value of the option but also how many options one gets, he always refers to a student who actually raised the issue ("That
was your point, right?"). He then opens from the classroom computer desktop,
projected onto a screen, a spreadsheet that contains a Black-Scholes options
valuation calculator. One student makes a point about the psychological, behavioral aspect of financial decisions: people in the actual case did not make these
calculations. The instructor acknowledges, pointing at the guest "economic sociologist" (me), explaining that for psychologists these phenomena are individual

---

5.   The Black-Scholes model is a standard mathematical model widely used in the
     financial industry for the theoretical estimation of the price of financial derivative
     contracts such as options, which confer to their holder the right to buy or sell an
     underlying asset (e.g., a stock) at a predefined price and at a predefined date.

and for sociologists they are collective. "But let's focus on Nancy," he says referring to the imagined employee actually featured in the case. He plays with the stock price value in the spreadsheet calculator to see how both the old and the new option price evolve.

A student asks a question to which the instructor responds: "Who are you talking about when you say 'you'? Nancy? Or the shareholders?" He then indicates that the student had spotted a major issue: these are two possibly conflicting views. Another student intervenes, further developing the behavioral aspects of the problem. The instructor acts as if the student had actually revealed the nitty-gritty of the case. "If you got what she just said, then you got the thing entirely," he says, rubbing fingers in a gesture that connotes an idea of fine-grained intellectual perception.

The case session does not constitute a rebuttal of a purely formal, calculative approach to decision-making. "We couldn't have had this discussion before last week," says the instructor, in reference to an introduction to option pricing that was given previously in lecture form and that had introduced a shift in the students' capacity to "discuss hot topics." That said, the bulk of the session is oriented to a sense of pragmatic realism, with emphasis put on the behavioral, psychological dimension and on the fact that "it all depends on expectations on the evolution of the stock price." A final vote on the decision to participate in the option exchange program gives a result more favorable to participation. The instructor closes the session with a nicely spectacular video animation of the evolution of the stock price as it actually happened in reality, with the price going below the two option limits (old and new) then up one and then up the second one, too.

At the end of the class, a couple of students take pictures of the blackboard with their smartphones. The instructor himself takes a picture. In a private debrief with me after class, he says he had also recorded the session, as this was the first time he was teaching that case. He also explains the depth of the preparatory work, which includes rehearsing and, most prominently, studying and memorizing the profile of students: their experience, the companies they have worked for, and so forth. A preselection of the students that can offer better performances for the felicitous conduct of the session is necessary. He tells me straight-out (without me asking) and with visible relief that he wanted to use the student who asked the final question, because "she has a medical background," which seems to imply something about her capacity to think differently.

Real competition[6]

The case competition takes a full week, with a program packed with a number of events. Presented in communicational materials as a "real life case," the competition is announced copiously on the campus of the business school. A dozen teams representing business schools from around the world and each composed of four students are to compete in their capacity to provide strategic guidance to a real company. They are expected to give their views on "what are the most important challenges" of the company and on "how they should be solved" to a jury panel, which includes executives from the company. The nature and identity of the "case company" is not revealed until day four. Until then, participants mostly engage in social activities, visits, conferences, and "team-building" events. They also have some time to interact with the coach assigned to their team by their home business school. Once the identity of the case company is "revealed" and the case documentation distributed, teams engage in "case solving," a task they have thirty-two continuous hours to perform, which potentially involves overnight work. Each team has a room provided with computer connectivity; organizers provide snacks and assistance. The coaches are removed from the premises and prevented from interacting with their teams. At the end of that period, each team hands in an "executive summary" and a "presentation." The next day, a preliminary round of presentations takes place in small rooms. Four finalist teams are selected, which then perform again in the main amphitheater on campus in front of a vast audience. Following these "finals," the winner is announced at an "award banquet."

I attend the competition as an academic guest of the institution hosting the event. The organizing team has been instructed to take me around and allow me to mingle with staff, participants, and coaches for the full week (I introduce myself to informants as a social scientist studying the practice of the case method). During the days preceding the actual "case solving," my informants insist on the importance of "creating a friendly, social atmosphere," "preventing the formation of a too competitive atmosphere and a situation in which groups won't talk to each other." For example, each team is asked to present itself in a jovial manner, with each team engaging in cheerful stereotypes or "fun facts" about their national cultures. The organizing team is actually composed of students from the host business school. They resolutely value the task

---

6. Description from fieldwork notes: international case competition hosted by a business school.

of organizing the case competition: this is for them "an actual business experience," which involves taking responsibilities, being creative, and interacting in
a professional fashion with executives of the case company. It also satisfies a
"need for concrete reality."

A series of team-building exercises take place in the form of several kinds
of "games." Game teams do not correspond to actual case competition teams,
thus making participants mingle together. One exercise involves blindfolded
participants, going around in a room while making the sound of an animal that
has been assigned to their team, with the task of recognizing team members
through this noise, then crowding together, and then removing the blindfolds
to discover who is on their team. Again blindfolded, they have to play at "war"
in the following manner: each group forms a "train," with the last member, not
blindfolded, having to give the instruction "move forward" by tapping into the
next person's shoulder. Each "train" is in fact a "torpedo" that has to break up the
other "torpedoes." Each "torpedo" holds a banner with the image of their animal
and sings its motto occasionally ("Go, Tigers!"). A number of several comparable exercises follow. An organizer later indicates to me that these exercises
follow the methodologies developed by a consultancy firm that specializes in
the design and facilitation of team-building games. When I ask about the fact
that these games are about competition, he insists that the games are "all about
having fun" and "building great networks."

In a dinner conversation with organizers and team coaches, the issue of
how to select team participants is discussed. One coach talks about a group
that "was very good at analysis, very deep," but that "failed" because "they were
not capable of making a clear-cut decision and defend it." This is about "business reality," he claims, adding: "You won't find the best solution, but you need
to find one." More importantly, he indicates, "you need to defend it, you need
to be convincing, showing that you are yourself convinced; you need to show
that you love your solution" (with emphasis on "love"). He explains that when
he examines potential team members from his business school, he very much
cares about how they perform "on stage" and that he also favors students "that
do well in sports." An organizer who contributed to the writing of the competition case recalls the performance of a winning team in a past edition of the
case competition, and criticizes it because, although "the pitch was excellent,
very convincing," their proposal did not look "real enough," in the sense of not
likely to be effectively implemented by the case company. She adds that, in
order to test the realism of the case in the present edition, the text was shown

to consultants from a top management-consulting firm "who provided very valuable feedback."

On the morning of day four, the identity of the case company is revealed in a plenary presentation. The name appears on the screen after a moment of suspense, followed by a video projection and a talk by the company's CEO. A copy of the case is handed to participants, coaches, and visitors. Participants are taken to a separate room in order to read it, and then taken on a "surprise" visit to the headquarters of the company, which is located in the same city. The "case solving" thirty-two-hour period has started. Coaches are kept busy with social activities and visits during that time. An organizer tells me that they have to be kept under surveillance and prevented from "cheating"—for example, passing along some tips to the students by email or text message. I observe the anxiety of coaches: failure of their team means a serious burden on the reputation of their employers, and even possibly a threat to their own career.

The fact that the case ought to be "solved" in thirty-two hours is meant to simulate the pace and constraints of "real" business life. I am told the next morning that most teams opted for a shuttle ride back to the hotel for a short sleep, but some teams decided to spend the entire night working in the room that had been assigned to them. One coach tells me with some sense of pride that she is sure that her team did not go to sleep: "They have taken blankets to the room." The interior of the rooms is partially visible through transparent doors. I observe that some participants have obstructed the view—for example, with a flag of their business school. Some can be seen in casual wear, gesticulating, eating snacks, taking naps, working on their laptops. They have access to coffee and energy drinks. I talk to one organizing staff member about her views on all this: she is a student at the host business school, and she volunteered because she was "pissed off" with the "abstract" aspect of more professorial approaches to business learning. "You have to think in terms of reality," she says with a rebellious, transgressive tone. She is concerned that missing study time will affect her grading. She says, with emotion, that she has "learned much more" with the case competition. Late afternoon on day five, teams hand in a USB drive containing two files: an "executive summary" in the form of a PDF file and the "presentation," the PowerPoint slideshow document that they will use the next day in front of the jury. There is an atmosphere of excitement; it's almost party-like.

On day six, each team delivers a presentation in front of a jury. Participants dress smartly—that is, in compliance with conventional business dress code. Many teams play the game of impersonating a team from a consulting firm (some have even designed a mock company logo), sometimes an executive team within the case company ("We as a company"). Slideshows generally comply with the semiotic requirements of management consulting, with synthetic formulations and formalistic concepts augmented with acronyms and embedded in schematic shapes. One "key message" would, for example, read "Augment Core Business" (dubbed "ACE"); another would be "Optimize Existing Portfolio." Assessment of the company's situation is recurrently provided in the form of "SWOT analysis"—that is, a matrix in which "Strengths," "Weaknesses," "Opportunities," and "Threats" are listed. Pictures are used abundantly in order to illustrate marketing ideas (e.g., brand partnering, expansion of consumer base, new facility). Numeric information for "financials" (e.g., "DCF" for "Discounted Cash Flows") is usually provided in the last part of the presentation, eventually backed with the visualization of an Excel spreadsheet. "Q&A" follows each presentation. The guest executives from the case company take the lead. The emphasis on realism is palpable. At some point, a jury member addresses the question of the "communication" of the project just presented, a comment that team members misinterpret as being about the "marketing" dimension: the jury member then reframes the question in terms of "acceptance by stakeholders." The reaction of the team proves disappointing. The four teams that have made it to the "finals" perform again the same presentation in front of a larger audience, in the main amphitheater.

BUSINESS EDUCATION AND THE CONCEPT OF REALITY

Symbolic realization

In his 1949 essay on the therapeutic efficacy of shamanistic incantation for the management of childbirth, "*L'efficacité symbolique,*" Claude Lévi-Strauss expressed emphatically the fine impression he had of the results obtained by Marguerite Sechehaye with the psychoanalytic psychotherapeutic method she had developed for the treatment of schizophrenia (Lévi-Strauss 1963: 186–205). In her attempt at going beyond the barriers of narrative operation, Lévi-Strauss wrote, Sechehaye had discovered the effectiveness of engaging the patient through acts that symbolize a fundamental element of the problematic situation. In order to confront a weaning complex, for example, the psychoanalyst would enact a maternal setting by actually drawing the patient's cheek to her own breast. Lévi-Strauss did even conjecture that the parallel between

shamanism and psychoanalysis could be further confirmed by advances in phys-
iology and biochemistry, suggesting that an organic transformation could be
indeed induced through the manipulation of symbols. The only relevant difference between shamanism and psychoanalysis would reside in the location of the
scenario—or myth—that ought to be enacted: in one case, the healer provides
the myth and the patient performs the operations and, in the other, it is the
medic who performs the operations whereas the patient produces her myth
(Lévi-Strauss 1963: 200–204).

The name that Sechehaye had given to her method in the psychotherapy
case monograph published in 1947—"symbolic realization" ("*réalisation symbolique*")—seemed quite appropriate and became an important reference in the
field of the psychoanalytic psychotherapy of psychoses (Sechehaye 1951). The
name suited well a method in which the patient ought to acquire the conscience
of things through her involvement in the actual manipulation of symbols. But
the name was also perhaps quite meaningful from the standpoint of the general conceptual culture the psychoanalytic movement was part of. The notion of
realization obviously communicates with the German vernaculars of psychoanalysis, and most distinctively with the vocabulary of fulfillment (*Erfüllung*,
with *Wunscherfüllung* for the Freudian notion of wish fulfillment). Psychoanalysis aside, the notion of realization (*Realisierung*, also *Verwirklichung*) has been
aptly signaled by Blumenberg as a salient marker of the concept of reality that
characterizes the epoch (Blumenberg 1979). An attempt at demarcating different historical concepts of reality, Blumenberg writes in his 1964 essay, necessarily stumbles upon a contrast between the reality of instantaneous evidence
prevalent in ancient philosophy and the request for a godly guarantee of reality
elaborated in medieval and modern thought (cf. Blumenberg 1983, 1987). But
it also has to identify another contrast between the latter and a contemporary
concept of reality understood as the outcome of realization: that is, of reality as
the establishment of a context that is confirmed in intersubjective experience.

Blumenberg's instructive diagnosis, originally located in a critical examination of the problem of fiction, is clearly of use for situating a concept of reality
that has come to characterize heavily the social sciences and the humanities, and
which is perhaps best exemplified by the vast influence of *The social construction
of reality* (Berger and Luckmann 1966; cf. Muralt 1974). It may be even possible to argue that the idea that what is real to someone may not be to someone
else—and that reality depends on how it is realized—is now a defining part of
popular culture. Presented in many guises, it is also a feature of the concept of

reality that is articulated in the experiential movement in business education. Quite strikingly, the concept of the real that is explicitly advocated for in the philosophical meditations of early inceptors of the case method of instruction in business administration at the Harvard Business School, quite influenced by vitalism and pragmatism (such as Arthur Stone Dewing), is fundamentally about realization in that sense (Dewing 1910, cf. 1931).

There are numerous ways in which the culture of the business real exemplified in the preceding ethnographic accounts connects to this concept of reality. The realization of the business insight is formulated as a psychological event that is characterized by its dramaturgical unfolding and by an experience of intersubjective excitement. A therapeutic element is sometimes openly present, with realization understood as the elicitation of the will to decide. Rather than being concealed, the scenic contraptions that facilitate this event (and that constitute the bulk of the pedagogical apparatus) are celebrated in their capacity to produce a felicitous simulacrum. The demonstration of the love of decision, and hence the transmission of an ideal of reality as provoked reality, appears to be quite more salient than any notion of scientific inquiry. The disregard for empirical adequacy and the emphasis on the vagaries of human expectations in the real world is consistent with a constructivist, existential conception of reality. The prevalence of an individual self that affirms a context in an orchestrated social interaction stands as the prime vehicle for the acquisition of a business disposition, best understood as a process of symbolic realization.

True, the web of economic activities and power relations business schools are part of is not controlled by this concept of reality only. A vast portion of the notions of truth and order that characterize dominant approaches to economic value in contemporary business life draw, for example, from a tradition of liberal political philosophy and economic science that is by far closer to the scholastic, modern concept of reality (Dumont 1977; Ingrao and Israel 1990). And the notions of financial valuation present in the mainstream pedagogical narrative (e.g., DCF, Black-Scholes) certainly require the establishment of a deeply naturalized sense of value creation that revolves around the idea of considering things (including oneself, as a successful businessperson) in their capacity to maximize a return on investment (Ortiz 2013, 2014; Muniesa 2016; Muniesa et al. 2017). But the breadth of the experiential movement in business education and of the distinctive concept of the business real that it conveys should not be disregarded. As the preceding ethnographic accounts show, the medium of business education exemplifies a concept of reality as an ideal—even epic—conquest based on the confirmation of the experience of a context (Blumenberg 1979: 32–33).

The lack of reality

In his essay, Blumenberg discerns yet another distinctive concept of reality—a fourth one—that would be based, rather, on the experience of resistance: that is, a concept of reality as what the self does not—or cannot—hold, master, manipulate, or even make available for consideration (Blumenberg 1979: 34). This concept is expressed, most typically, in the form of a paradox. Often articulated in relation to the threat of the unreal that marks the projection of desire, and surely recognizable in psychoanalytic theory too, this concept does also permeate the constructivist enigmas of particle physics and the epistemology of surrealism. Stretching the idea further, one could even claim that the real stands now for what cannot be realized, if not in a delirious or hallucinatory manner (Lacan 1993).

It is possible to claim that the ideal of the business real that emerged in early justifications of the experiential curriculum partially wears the traits of this concept of reality too. Frequent reference to adventure, disorder, uncertainty, and courage suggests, indeed, that the existential flow business reality arguably consists of cannot be made explicit in full and can be approached only as a fantasized limit (Dewing 1931). The ethnographic accounts offered in this study do also, in part, support this view. The emphasis that is put on deliberation and cooperation is presented as an attempt at reproducing faithfully the reality of an actual business setting but constitutes also, paradoxically, a normative approach that may conflict heavily with the mundane experience of arbitrary power in the conduct of business. The business student attempts to experience a fulfilling encounter with an ideal medium of executive deliberation but is also exposed, simultaneously, to the fact that actual reality might be systematically located elsewhere. Strong insistence on promptness and nerve in decision-making places the business student in a position that possesses the qualities of the acting out, with all that this implies in terms of a materialization of anxiety. The acts of moral exercising conducted in small groups that often accompany these pedagogical vehicles can be infantile, if not openly surreal (Lezaun and Muniesa 2017). The therapeutic component can shift indeed, implicitly, from an emancipatory ideal of self-realization to a recreational happening in which the phantasm of the business real can be safely played with.

Within this perspective, the experiential apparatus in business education can in part be considered in the light of the psychoanalytic notion of the fetish—a shield against the painful awareness of reality—albeit augmented with the elements of suspense, contract, and disavowal that have been identified in the problem of masochism (Deleuze 1971). One conclusion that can be fairly drawn from the ethnographic materials presented above is that the creation of the experience of the business real inside the business school consists indeed most essentially in the elaboration of a shield (Lezaun and Muniesa 2017). It is certainly a paradox that the exacerbation of a taste for reality in contemporary experiential business education does not translate, simply, in the affirmation of the superiority of apprenticeship programs or internship jobs—that is, of the access to the business real from outside the business school, directly. Instead, an immense educational apparatus is required in order to provide a medium propitious for the simulation of the business act or, more exactly, for the maintenance of the simulation as the only approachable notion of the business real.

CONCLUSION

The vast network of meanings that characterize the global industry of business education in the present time is certainly marked by multiple concepts of reality, often poorly connected to each other, connected in contradictory manners, or not connected at all. The philosophical history of the concept of reality sketched out by Blumenberg (1979) proves nonetheless useful for an attempt at characterizing the parts of that industry in which the praise for the real is advertised the most: namely, in the experiential tradition in business pedagogy and, more particularly, in the widely institutionalized practice of the case method of instruction in business education, famously developed at the Harvard Business School. An examination of the philosophical sources that may have informed or accompanied the origins of the method—for example, through the pivotal contribution of Arthur Stone Dewing, philosopher, investor, finance professor, and notable case method instructor and advocate (Dewing 1903, 1910, 1920, 1931)—can unquestionably provide evidence of the importance of a vitalist, existential, constructivist, almost epic ideal of business reality as the outcome of a courageous process of realization. This ideal is vividly present, in variable forms, in the ways in which the case method is presented, practiced, and made sense of in the global business curriculum today. An ethnographic investigation in a number of paradigmatic sites indeed demonstrates the extent to which the notions of the business real that are articulated there correspond to what Blumenberg characterized, under the rubric of realization, as the intersubjective confirmation of the performance of a context.

But ethnographic inquiry also reveals a critical tension between this concept of reality and an interpretation of the business real as what cannot be realized. The conceptual repertoire of the real in psychoanalysis provides an appropriate analytical correlate to this conception, as the latter typically precipitates the possibility of anxiety. In the three fieldwork sites I referred to above, I observed instantiations of anxiety in relation to the articulation of the problem of reality, in both instructors and students (cf. Anteby 2013). These were found, for example, in expressions of excitement about the radical, revelatory effect of the case method, expressions that would nonetheless refer to the ineffable character of the reality hence revealed. The case method was also often conceived of by students as a technique for coming to terms with a sense of personal insecurity in the task of acquiring a leadership disposition, but sometimes with the impression that this could mean coming to terms with one's own self, which can be thought of as an illusory (or dangerous) task. The crucial notion of decision—of the need to emit a decision and display assurance in doing so—was also operational in creating this troubling sense of the real. In an interview after class with a student enrolled in the MBA program described in the second situation above (the amphitheater discussion), the topic of anxiety was brought up spontaneously. After a fervent vindication of the sense of realism the case method brings to business education, the student characterized as a necessary form of psychotherapeutic counseling the career coaching services the MBA program offered. These were helpful in coping with the tensions prompted by a climate of permanent decision, which prevented students such as her from taking the necessary time to think. She illustrated emotionally the idea of decision with reference to Stanley Milgram's obedience experiments—a reference that had been introduced to her in a program course as a way to illustrate the human challenges of decision-making, and that is known for its deeply traumatic form and content (Lezaun, Muniesa, and Vikkelsø 2013).

What conclusions can be drawn from these analyses for an anthropological appraisal of the cluster of meanings of reality that control the conduct of mainstream economic business? Limited as these results may be, they suggest that the subject matter cannot be dealt with satisfactorily only through a critical examination of the empiricist epistemology the notion of economic datum depends on. It cannot simply revert to a moral denunciation of the lack of realism that would be implied in economic policies or financial conduct. What this task requires, once the location of different notions of reality in contrasting conceptual assemblages has been acknowledged, is an exploration of the paradoxes these notions entail for an anthropological critique of the business real. At the center of such paradoxes lies the fact that an openly constructivist, performative, therapeutic—and perhaps even properly anthropological—ideal of symbolic realization becomes a cultural engine of business reality as we know it. Add to this the fact that such an ideal comes accompanied by the trouble of its own negation, in the form of a recurring reference to realization's exhausting impossibility. The possibility of an anthropological critique of the business real (that is, a critique of the business real as a condition of being human) remains nonetheless available, but only insofar we consider the part these paradoxes play in anthropology's own problems (Rabinow 2002).

ACKNOWLEDGMENTS

This study has benefited from funding by the European Research Council (ERC Starting Grant no. 263529). I thank Javier Lezaun, Horacio Ortiz, Signe Vikkelsø, and Damian O'Doherty for collaborations and conversations that have led to this analysis.

REFERENCES

Anteby, Michel. 2013. *Manufacturing morals: The values of silence in business education*. Chicago: University of Chicago Press.

Barnes, Louis B., C. Roland Christensen, and Abby J. Hansen. 1994. *Teaching and the case method: Text, cases, and readings*. Boston: Harvard Business School Press.

Berger, Peter L., and Thomas Luckmann. 1966. *The social construction of reality: A treatise in the sociology of knowledge*. Garden City, NY: Anchor Books.

Blumenberg, Hans. 1979. "The concept of reality and the possibility of the novel." In *New perspectives in German literary criticism: A collection of essays*, edited by Richard E. Amacher and Victor Lange, 29–48. Princeton, NJ: Princeton University Press.

———. 1983. *The legitimacy of the modern age*. Cambridge, MA: The MIT Press.

———. 1987. *The genesis of the Copernican world*. Cambridge, MA: The MIT Press.

Christensen, C. Roland, David A. Garvin, and Ann Sweet, eds. 1981. *Education for judgment: The artistry of discussion leadership*. Boston: Harvard Business School Press.

Copeland, Melvin T. 1958. *And mark an era: The story of the Harvard Business School*. Boston: Little, Brown & Co.

Cruikshank, Jeffrey L. 1987. *A delicate experiment: The Harvard Business School, 1908–1945*. Boston: Harvard Business School Press.

Deleuze, Gilles. 1971. *Sacher-Masoch: An interpretation*. London: Faber and Faber.

Dewing, Arthur Stone. 1903. *Introduction to the history of modern philosophy*. Philadelphia: J. B. Lippincott Company.

———. 1910. *Life as reality: A philosophical essay*. New York: Longmans, Green & Co.

———. 1920. *The financial policy of corporations*. New York: The Ronald Press.

———. 1931. "An introduction to the use of cases." In *The case method of instruction: A related series of articles*, edited by Cecil E. Fraser, 1–10. New York: McGraw-Hill.

Dumont, Louis. 1977. *From Mandeville to Marx: The genesis and triumph of economic ideology*. Chicago: University of Chicago Press.

Fraser, Cecil E., ed. 1931. *The case method of instruction: A related series of articles*. New York: McGraw-Hill.

Guyer, Jane I. 2016. *Legacies, logics, logistics: Essays in the anthropology of the platform economy*. Chicago: University of Chicago Press.

Ingrao, Bruna, and Giorgio Israel. 1990. *The invisible hand: Economic equilibrium in the history of science*. Cambridge, MA: The MIT Press.

Lacan, Jacques. 1993. *The seminar of Jacques Lacan, book III: The psychoses, 1955–1956*. New York: W. W. Norton & Co.

Lévi-Strauss, Claude. 1963. *Structural anthropology*. New York: Basic Books.

Lezaun, Javier, and Fabian Muniesa. 2017. "Twilight in the leadership playground: *Subrealism* and the training of the business self." *Journal of Cultural Economy* 10 (3): 265–79.

Lezaun, Javier, Fabian Muniesa, and Signe Vikkelsø. 2013. "Provocative containment and the drift of social-scientific realism." *Journal of Cultural Economy* 6 (3): 278–93.

McNair, Malcolm P., ed. 1954. *The case method at the Harvard Business School: Papers by present and past members of the faculty and staff.* New York: McGraw-Hill.

Muniesa, Fabian. 2016. "Setting the habit of capitalization: The pedagogy of earning power at the Harvard Business School, 1920–1940." *Historical Social Research* 41 (2): 196–217.

Muniesa, Fabian, Liliana Doganova, Horacio Ortiz, Álvaro Pina-Stranger, Florence Paterson, Alaric Bourgoin, Véra Ehrenstein, Pierre-André Juven, David Pontille, Başak Saraç-Lesavre, and Guillaume Yon. 2017. *Capitalization: A cultural guide.* Paris: Presses des Mines.

Muralt, André de. 1974. *The idea of phenomenology: Husserlian exemplarism.* Evanston, IL: Northwestern University Press.

Ortiz, Horacio. 2013. "Financial value: Economic, moral, political, global." *HAU: Journal of Ethnographic Theory* 3 (1): 64–79.

———. 2014. "The limits of financial imagination: Free investors, efficient markets, and crisis." *American Anthropologist* 116 (1): 38–50.

Rabinow, Paul. 2002. "Midst anthropology's problems." *Cultural Anthropology* 17 (2): 135–49.

Sechehaye, Marguerite A. 1951. *Symbolic realization: A new method of psychotherapy applied to a case of schizophrenia.* Oxford: International Universities Press.

Snook, Scott, Nitin Nohria, and Rakesh Khurana, eds. 2012. *The handbook for teaching leadership: Knowing, doing, and being.* Thousand Oaks, CA: Sage.

CHAPTER TWO

Deductions and counter-deductions in South Africa

DEBORAH JAMES

In 2015 and 2016, reports in the South African press gave the newest episodes in a long-running saga. There was the story of a washing machine sold to a gardener on installment plan (known locally as "hire purchase") that cost three times the normal price; the company in question was accused of "reckless lending" by the gardener's employer; the company threatened, in turn, to seek legal advice to protect its reputation from that employer's "defamatory allegations." There was a report on a groundbreaking decision by the High Court, which placed restrictions on the way in which creditors (including the sellers of over-priced washing machines, various microlenders, and second-tier collectors who had bought debt from other creditors) would in future be able to recoup the unpaid installments owed to them. There was an account of debt collectors who were taken to court by a corporate employer to prevent their making deductions from mine workers' salaries to repay outstanding debts for appliances, motor vehicles, and other goods. And there were stories anticipating legal action against a moneylending and insurance company that had been deducting repayments from social grants before they were given to recipients.

The *real economy* as a concept has taken root not only in stable or highly developed economies (or both) but also in those characterized by "the rapid growth of aspiration accompanied by massive incorporation of people into the current market economy, through the expansion of indebtedness and financial devices . . . [and] the impossibility of paying" (Neiburg and Guyer 2017: 272). As Federico Neiburg and Jane Guyer note, the real is a "shifting and pluri-scalar concept, which involves multiples agencies, agents . . . engagements and enactments, claims of true and claims of justice, collective and personal lives, emergent and submergent personhoods, experiences and feelings." Here, as in other similar settings, one finds "a progressive fractioning of products; multiplication of mediations; the amplified reproduction of small gains; and interplay between different units of measure and scales" (to use a description coined by Federico Neiburg [2016: 82] about economic life in Haiti). This plurality, in the South African case, exists in a setting in which forces of state, market, and reciprocity intertwine: where "neoliberal means interweave with and facilitate redistributive ends" (Hull and James 2012: 16).

In South Africa, debates about the real economy have been muddied, in particular, by the imperfect data on indebtedness. The stories outlined above tell us about an economic system in which debt, repayment (or nonrepayment), and deduction (and counter-deduction) have come to play a major role, yet are not always fully acknowledged. They point to a new context in which financial markets and services have overtaken labor-intensive industrial growth, making for a growth that has been termed "jobless" (Hull and James 2012; Marais 2011: 130–32).[1] By drawing attention to the phenomenon of payments (Maurer 2012), here in the form of deductions directly from employees' or grant-recipients' bank accounts, the stories also seem to indicate a highly routinized set of arrangements in an economic system that is predominantly formal. The extent of that formality has been said to leave less space for the emergence of what scholars dub a "second" or "informal" economy than in southern—and African—contexts beyond South Africa itself (Cichello, Fields, and Leibbrandt 2005; Neves and du Toit 2012). Yet tactics and techniques used by these debt collectors, companies, and microlenders often turn out, when challenged, to be illegal—or at least to contravene the spirit of the constitution. They also, in many cases, belong within the zone of transactions that are "unrecorded" (MacGaffey 1991) and are hence unavailable to statisticians. Nevertheless, the prominence

---

1. The process, echoing global trends, is marked by an increasing dominance of financial markets and services as a proportion of national economies, and a corresponding decline in labor-intensive industrial growth (Hull and James 2012).

of court judgments and legal action in the stories above speaks of a world in which formal regulations and legality *do* prevail. They also indicate the importance placed, in South African life, on establishing the rights of those once disenfranchised by using the law (Chanock 2001). Fierce battles are fought out in the courts to rule in favor of—or against—practices that seem intrinsic to the country's economy, despite existing in an ambiguous space on the boundaries of the law. Do uncollected debts, debts collected through deductions, and debts whose collection is actively resisted or countered (often with the help of legal actors), form an intrinsic part of a "real" economy conceptualized as seamlessly integrated?

The challenges posed by the editors of this volume invite us to unsettle the sets of binaries often used to analyze the basis of communities' and nations' livelihoods. They also call for some comparisons: How is indebtedness calibrated elsewhere in relation to aspiration, precarity in economic life, and the role of the state? Both points are attended to in the work of economic anthropologists. Keith Hart coined the term "informal sector" (1973) at the moment when "the post-war era of developmental states was drawing to a close" (2015). After the enthusiastic adoption of this term by development professionals, Hart pointed out that he had always intended to show the inseparability of the formal and the informal, conceptually and empirically (2015). The work of Jane Guyer bears this out, with her now well-accepted insights into the way that the formalization and financialization of economic arrangements are often accompanied by their opposite, all held within the same frame but not necessarily subject to some dominant hegemonic force originating in the capitalist West. She speaks of the need to think in multiplicities rather than binaries and shows how a West African logic of economic activity dovetailed with—while also countermanding—a capitalist one (2004: 11–12). Showing similar plurality and likewise repudiating polarities is the work of Parker Shipton. He maintains that the Luo of Kenya "are at times profit-seeking marketeers and at times reciprocators and redistributors" (2007: 28). Janet MacGaffey's book *The real economy of Zaire* [now the Democratic Republic of Congo] (1991) is an earlier account that shows how these varied aspects must not be separated along binary lines but must all be reckoned as belonging within the entirety of economic activity. To understand the "real economy," she insists, we need to recognize the "second economy," which does not appear in official reports and statistics or in "national accounts of the official economy." That arena of activity must be acknowledged, and not simply because of its size. It is also, she claims, intrinsically intertwined with the state-linked economy (rather than being distinct from it). In intervening decades, state power everywhere has both weakened and simultaneously intensified to favor the interests of market players, giving new valence to informal economic activity. Hart claims that "the informal economy seems to have taken over the world, while cloaking itself in the rhetoric of free markets. . . . Money and markets have escaped from public control and cannot be put back in that straitjacket" (2015: 2).

These debates take on a particular character if we look at South Africa. The country industrialized far earlier and to a much greater extent than its African counterparts and levels of wage labor were far higher (Cooper 2002: 194), although these were combined with a continued dependence on cultivation and herding, which has inspired Marxist-inspired theorists to debate whether and how to conceptualize diverse aspects of production, profit, and subsidy in one single frame (Wolpe 1972).[2] Later, as unemployment soared following the peak years of growth in the 1960s and 1970s, and even more so after the country's democratic transition in 1994, scholars explored the interrelation of what looked like diverse sectors of the economy. Economists and policy-makers, adopting Hart's concept, were puzzled about the failure of the "informal sector" to expand and to make up for the dwindling of its formal counterpart. Given the strength of the state and the capitalist sector in what was otherwise a developing country, informal economic activity, some thought, had been crowded out (Lund and Skinner 2003). Others, however, showed that the two were entwined. According to David Neves and Andries Du Toit (2012: 143), although informal economic activity seemed to present only few economic opportunities, the "varied, variegated and non-linear . . . trajectories of economic development" it afforded seemed to go against the assumption "that the economy becomes progressively disconnected from society as it becomes more formal." Its practitioners were able to negotiate "practices of economic governance— both formal (state-led) and informal—which provide the conditions of possibility for economic activities." Such practitioners positioned

---

2. The "cheap labor thesis" (Wolpe 1972) held that capitalist growth was premised upon, articulated with, and only profitable because of, household labor performed in rural settings, which thus subsidized the capitalist sector. Challenging this account, economic historian Charles Feinstein showed that apartheid's work force, largely unskilled and migratory, cost too much in relation to its productivity, rather than too little, achieving less for higher wages than their equivalents in other countries (2005: 245–51; see also Beinart 2012: 13).

themselves "to harness the benefits of formalization, while evading its considerable constraints" (Neves and du Toit 2012: 143). Such insights into the intertwining of state-regulated and off-the-record activities parallel the points made by Hart, MacGaffey, and Guyer. MacGaffey's claims about the complex and often contradictory role of the state are particularly relevant to the present study, especially the part played by state employment. In South Africa, civil service salaries—and in this case, welfare payments—are not (as in MacGaffey's discussion of Congo) just a point of access to opportunities. They are also a reliable source of steady income that acts, in effect, as collateral for debt—and thus as a source for deductions.

In some respects, the economic activities of those formerly seen as excluded from the single economy are indeed governed—if not wholly subsumed—by the banks, furniture companies, clothing stores, and "micro-lenders" to whom they are in hock. Financial formality, in other words, *is* more prevalent here than in many other African settings and other parts of the Global South. It is also the case, however, that multiple registers coexist, enabling formalizations and informalizations to interpenetrate (Guyer 2004). Alongside the spread of sophisticated financial technologies, and partly interwoven with these, the dynamics of a second economy of lending and repayment *are* in evidence: to argue that these interconnected sectors have come entirely under the sway of one single financialized arena would be to underestimate the plurality and multiplicity of arrangements.

While "credit apartheid" had previously restricted black people from borrowing in a single market (DTI 2002, 2004), loans of all kinds, in the 1990s, became readily available. It seemed as though the part played by those (primarily black) people, who for years had been partially excluded—if not from the wage economy then certainly from the formal financial sector—had been inverted. Instead of laboring for capitalist corporations while securing part of their sustenance from rural cultivation or informal economic activities, their chief contribution, and a new site of exploitation, was now that of making repayments on consumer credit agreements via highly routinized and technologized means: deductions. Many social actors, however, are intent on evading these technologies in various ways. Activists and human rights lawyers make efforts to shore up consumer rights. They devise systems of registration or regulation, or try to render illegal the proliferating technologies of debt collection by seeking redress and appeal through the courts. In a kind of arms race, lenders then invent new systems of payment or repurpose old ones. The struggle between those activating deductions and those striving to enable counter-deductions is ongoing.

As economic life in this newly liberalized, newly democratized country turns toward financialization (Neves 2018), new questions must then be asked about its *real economy*. This financialization is taking shape in a space where borders of legality/illegality and ethical/unethical practices overlap, which allows for contests about and shifts of the limits or reach of the state. It is not only the case that we need to note the unrecorded alongside the recorded—and nonmonetized alongside monetized—aspects of the economy, as MacGaffey suggests (1991). We also need to pay attention to how the state both facilitates the intensification of the repayment regime through providing civil service salaries and grants and also—by outsourcing grant payments to private companies—enables the emergence of a kind of parallel state, with its own database and payment system. At the same time, the financially incorporated have agency themselves, and are not reduced to mere conduits for flows of money.

DEDUCING INDEBTEDNESS

The extent of indebtedness—or over-indebtedness—has been difficult to ascertain. Although much of the money owed was being taken off—often through practices of borderline legality—in automated repayments or deductions, these do not necessarily show up in the official census or in reports by the newly established National Credit Register, surveys conducted by commercial companies keen to estimate their likely market share, or reports by agencies such as the Bureau of Market Research, which sell their results to such companies.[3] The figures offered by such sources reflecting the extraordinary growth in "unsecured" indicated debts that remained unpaid, rather than those that were being collected. By 2014, the World Bank reported that 80 percent of the South African population was borrowing money (against a global average of 40 percent).[4] Leading up to this high figure, sources showed that the sharpest rise had been in the early 1990s (Ardington et al. 2004). By 2008, nearly half the credit market's 17.56 million

---

3.   This Bureau is attached to a university, UNISA, but its results are available only to those who pay for them.

4.   Tanya Farber and Bobby Jordan, "Maxed out: SA's debt headache," *Times Live*, January 3, 2016. https://www.enca.com/money/maxed-out-sas-debt-headache.

consumers had "impaired records."[5] By 2011, household debt as a percentage of disposable income was at 76 percent, ratcheting up from 50 percent in 2002; consumer debt stood at R1.2 trillion, up from R300 billion in 2002. By 2013, around half of consumers were at least three months behind on debt payments.[6]

Central to policy debates over this epidemic of borrowing (and nonrepayment) were disagreements over whether it resulted from consumers' over- or underexposure to financial formality, and over the socioeconomic profile of these consumers. During the 1990s, one study argued, it had been among the urban black working class that the growth rate in credit consumption had exceeded the growth in incomes. They were taking out unsecured loans from small lenders and retailers rather than the big banks, and more from informal lenders or *mashonisas*—estimated at about 30,000 in number at the end of the twentieth century— than from formal institutions, and many were borrowing at high interest rates to repay their other debts. People from this sector were getting into debt to buy consumables at high interest rates rather than solid assets at affordable ones, so borrowing increased their vulnerability. The authors of this study, writing in a high modernist paradigm, claimed that the answer was to enable greater financial "deepening" and thus to facilitate more borrowing from banks. This would help such people move away from their reliance on less formal and more exploitative loans and toward cheaper ones from financial institutions (Ardington et al. 2004: 607, 619). Other analyses—reflecting similar patterns elsewhere (see Anders 2009 for Malawi; Parry 2012 for India)—emphasized that those with greatest levels of debt after 1994 were not those at the bottom of the pile but regular earners in the middle of the scale who were well placed to take advantage of the banking and retail sectors. Since their salaries served as collateral (Roth 2004: 78), they qualified for credit, but their "social obligations"—in other words, their embeddedness in networks of reciprocal exchange and care—placed "pressure on them to borrow" at "unsustainable" levels (Daniels 2004: 842).[7]

---

5.   Noted in the National Credit Regulator's maiden report; Sikonathi Mantshantsha, "7.3m in SA behind on bills," *Fin24.com*, May 24, 2009. https://www.fin24.com/ Money/Money-Clinic/73m-in-SA-behind-on-bills-20090324.

6.   Patrick McGroarty, "In South Africa, a consumer debt bubble forms," *Wall Street Journal*, December 26, 2012. https://www.wsj.com/articles/SB1000142412788732 4296604578177884108022670.

7.   But being in debt, for such people, was not necessarily seen as all bad. One report claimed that whereas buying consumables at high interest rates was ultimately detrimental, buying solid assets at affordable ones constituted the basis of a solid

While these debates evinced great concern over the prevalence of unregistered lenders offering unsecured loans and plying their trade in the borderlands of financial formality, the deduction stories with which this article is concerned tell of practices more central to that realm. These are practices that use devices within the terrain of legality, which benefit from the sheltering embrace of the law, and which have only recently begun to be challenged in the courts. These legal/illegal, formal/informal zones have interpenetrated: they have resulted from, generated, and also sought to control, the exploitative processes of "credit apartheid" over more than a century. To understand this, we need to look in more detail at two distinct historical moments. The first, dating back to the end of the nineteenth century, involved an uneven combination of unbridled market freedom and paternalistic state control. The second, at the end of the twentieth century, again saw market forces given free rein and again saw the authorities attempting to curb these excesses.

BETWEEN STATE AND MARKET

Although the rises of financialization, indebtedness, and "debtfare" have been documented worldwide (Anders 2009; Han 2012; Guerin 2014; Kear 2013; Martin 2002; Soederberg 2015; Wilkis 2015), the South African debt story has some noteworthy particularities. The historical underpinnings of credit apartheid lie in the colonial roots of South African capitalism. In the later years of the nineteenth century, mercantile capital was pervasive. While antiapartheid campaigners have complained about white ownership of the land, at that time it was large companies that appropriated vast swathes of the countryside, and the role of big finance houses was crucial: an "oligopoly" of British-owned banks rooted in the English-speaking capitalist sector established, from early on, a fully-fledged system of property, mortgages, and frequent repossessions (Trapido 1978; Verhoef 2009: 157, 181). The scene was set for a swift and uncompromising form of capitalist penetration. This was linked to the country's thoroughgoing proletarianization, and in turn to the phenomenon of indebtedness. Whereas, in most of Africa, "wage-labor capitalism . . . takes place on islands in a sea of other sorts of socio-economic relations; in South Africa, wage-labor capitalism

---

middle-class lifestyle. Kevin Davie, "Drowning in debt or rolling in riches," *Mail and Guardian*, July 22, 2011. https://mg.co.za/article/2011-07-22-drowning-in-debt-or-rolling-riches.

pervades the economy," noted Fred Cooper (2002: 194).[8] The means through which that labor force was recruited was intrinsically tied to the extension of credit. And accumulation continues to operate, even after the heyday of capitalist growth had passed and despite high levels of unemployment, which stood at 43 percent in 2012, through new incarnations of the creditor/debtor relationship.

Provided that cultivators could be persuaded to become wageworkers, the regular payment of wages was what opened up a stream of income for small-scale traders, imbued with a pioneering spirit of enterprise in the late nineteenth/early twentieth century. These traders doubled up as labor recruiters who sold to locals on credit and later obliged them to "work it off." Rural cultivators in the Eastern Cape, for example, were induced into work contracts, or tempted to leave employment in one sector in favor of another, by traders who gave "cattle advances" against these migrants' future earnings (Beinart 1979). The relationship between wage advances and labor procurement was even more direct in Bechuanaland (now Botswana), a British protectorate at the time. Agents recruiting for the South African mines "induced" locals to enter into contracts by paying them wages in advance, thus automatically indebting them (Schapera 1947: 108). These arrangements were open to abuse by those on both sides, with agents often extending such large advances that the borrower "remained in debt even after having worked for several months," but with borrowers often accepting advances from several agents at the same time, with no intention of honoring their debts to any of them (Schapera 1947: 109; Beinart 1979: 209). These cowboy-capitalist excesses were later regulated by the colonial authorities, who saw them as exploitative and unsustainable. Such regulatory measures did not, however, result in migrants' getting free access to their earnings. Instead, fearing that cash received immediately would be too readily spent or diverted from "legitimate" uses (primarily the payment of various colonial government taxes and levies), or might encourage migrants to neglect or desert their families, the authorities devised a system of deferring part or all of miners' pay rather than giving it to them at the work site (Schapera 1947: 106–7; First 1983). The reliance on such measures, in which earnings were subject to various forms of external or social control rather than being individually "owned" by workers themselves, proved to be long-lived.

---

8.   The (former) ubiquity of, and reliance on, paid work, has left in place an assumption that the main route to both a livelihood and citizenship is through a paid job (Barchiesi 2011).

Overall, a combination of freewheeling enterprise on the one hand, and its regulation by paternalistic authorities on the other, laid the basis for a mixed system. On the one hand, "external judicial control" (Haupt et al. 2008: 51) has meant that workers' finances and salaries/wages, and even—eventually—the bank accounts used to transfer these, have tended to be viewed, unquestioningly, as controlled or regulated (or both) from the outside. On the other hand, earners have become accustomed to dodging, negotiating, and evading the forms of entrapment represented by such systems of finance and loan/advance. In their most recent form, these evasions—including confrontations in the courts— have become the counter-deductions of this essay's title.

We skip forward—over a century during much of which a particularly stringent form of "national capitalism" was in operation (Hart 2009, 2015)—to examine the moment of democratic transition in 1994. In a muffled echo of earlier arrangements, the economy began to liberalize. It also became extensively financialized. The move away from—and the concerted attempt to abolish—credit apartheid, combined with a rise in expectations for personal material wealth, laid the grounds for a huge demand. This was met by a burgeoning supply, as short-term loans became available at high rates of interest. These were provided both by a rapid growth in informal lending—including the loan sharks or *mashonisas*—about whose proliferation economists and policy-makers had despaired (Ardington et al. 2004) (see fig. 1, sector 3)—and through an expanded willingness by the formal (formerly white-dominated) retail and banking sector (see fig. 1, sector 1) to open its doors to black people. Alongside this, a new microlending sector was emerging: it was initially borderline illegal but it gradually became formalized and regulated.

The resulting credit landscape, perhaps unsurprisingly, mapped itself along racial lines. Sector 2 (see fig. 1) largely comprised white, Afrikaans-speaking civil servants. Fearing an abrupt end to state patronage, they had taken redundancy packages with the onset of the new democracy. Seeking a place in which to invest their payouts, and emboldened by the repeal of legislation that for many decades had capped the interest rate but had now been abolished in the interests of extending credit to all, many of these ousted civil servants established microlending businesses to lend money to black people at high interest rates. In this setting of newly ballooning aspiration, the new (black) civil servants and grant recipients in turn, despite receiving regular payments, needed more than what those could buy, so they turned to borrowing. Replacing the fixed assets that lenders traditionally require by way of security (Roth 2004: 62),

Sector	Lender	Type of loan
1	Mainstream/formal financial sector (mainly English-speaking capitalists)	Loans from the "big four" banks, recently joined by African Bank and Capitec; housing loans; vehicle finance; store cards for clothing and food; furniture and appliances on installments.
2	New microlending sector (mainly Afrikaans-speaking former civil servants)	Smaller/short-term/unsecured loans
3	Informal microlending sector (neighborhood moneylenders—*mashonisas* in black townships and villages)	Smaller/short-term/unsecured loans

Figure 1: Credit supply

salaries and grants from the state came to serve as collateral: the term *unsecured* for such loans is thus misleading. Lenders, having direct access to the bank accounts into which the salaries of this new swath of civil servants (or the grants of welfare recipients) were paid, were easily able to recoup their debts. Whereas the informal neighborhood lenders or *mashonisas* in sector 3 used the system— only outlawed at the end of the 1990s—of confiscating a debtor's ATM card and identity document in order to ensure repayment (for a similar practice in India, see Parry 2012), many lenders in sector 2 used garnishee or emoluments attachment orders (EAOs) to get installments deducted directly from debtors' bank accounts. Such an order is issued by a magistrate's court against the salary of a debtor, provided that the application for it is willingly signed by that debtor. If a creditor is owed money and then presents an employer with the order, the latter must allow the former automatically to deduct a portion of the debtor/employee's monthly pay before the employee receives it, with the creditor bearing a 5 percent charge (James and Rajak 2014: 455–56; James 2015: 61–64, 74). Retailers in the mainstream (sector 1), continuing but intensifying a long-standing practice, were similarly dependent on the use of EAOs, as seen in the deduction stories with which this article began. Some lenders originating in sectors 2 and 3 have formalized and effectively entered sector 1; these include African Bank and Capitec, both of which explicitly aim to cater to the low-income earning population.[9]

---

9.   The "unsustainable" business model of African Bank, which offered loans but took few deposits, were exposed when, in 2014, it sought reprieve and the Reserve Bank

What is crucial to note in this picture of credit supply and demand is the role of state salaries and grants. The situation in South Africa, with its developed capitalist sector and high levels of economic formality, both converges with and differs from that of the countries where informal/underground or "second" economies (MacGaffey 1991) are prevalent. State employment in the Congo, as in Ghana and Uganda, was important mainly for the fact that jobs brought "access to the profitable opportunities of a parallel commercial system developing in the heart of the state" (MacGaffey 1991: 15) rather than for actual salaries, which often remained unpaid. In South Africa's posttransitional civil service, by contrast, salaries *are* regularly paid. In this newly financialized setting, they not only fund recipients' livelihoods, they also underpin an informal or second economy of credit: through their use either as a kind of "start-up capital" in an informal *mashonisa* business or, conversely, as a means of repaying one of these (alongside other creditors). Dependence on moneylenders in the less-developed African countries of MacGaffey's book is often unavoidable, given the absence of alternatives "to those exploitative relations and the crude 'social security' provided by patron-client relations" (Beckman 1988, cited in MacGaffey 1991: 32). In South Africa, in contrast, alternatives *do* exist. These are used *alongside* illegal/informal moneylending by those newly liberated from the restrictive (or nonexistent) credit offerings of apartheid. MacGaffey claims that civil service employment provides "access to resources" and "opportunities to . . . extort from those lower down the social scale" (1991: 36). In South Africa, salaries can function equally as means to repay the extorters. In the case of the *mashonisas* (illegal moneylenders or loan sharks), this is achieved by the use of the confiscated ATM card; in that of buying a washing machine on instalments or borrowing from a registered microlender, deductions are made—with endorsement by the clerk of a magistrate's court—directly from the salary or grant. (Those without such incomes—or who are not receiving regular welfare payments—often find it difficult if not impossible to get a loan.) The interpenetrating first and second economies of MacGaffey's book (1991: 154) are thus equally present, but with a different modality, in South Africa.

---

forced the "big four" mainstream banks to bail it out. Moody's then downgraded the credit ratings of all these banks. For details on this process, see Tim Cohen, "Editor's note: UnAbil to unwind," *Financial Mail*, August 14, 2014; Agency Staff, "Moody's downgrades Standard Bank, Absa, FNB and Nedbank," *Business Day*, August 19, 2014; *Times Live*, August 17, 2014.

DEDUCTIONS AND COUNTER-DEDUCTIONS

I have a problem. People are debiting the money from my account. That is why I am not getting that much money. I have been working in security. And I have to pay some of the accounts, like Jet, and those accounts that I have to pay by hand.[10]

This statement by a low-wage, hourly paid worker, who I met when he was attending debt counseling, conveys something of what it feels like to be caught in the web of automatic repayments whose origins have been sketched above. Besides those he was compelled to pay "by hand," his monthly repayments included those for store cards to the clothing retailer, Jet, alongside numerous others that were deducted. His statement represents, in microcosm, what a judge later described as the iniquity of a system in which "millions of people across the country" were having their wages docked to an unsustainable degree.[11]

Figure 2: Jet store branch with advertisement for store card (Photo by Deborah James)

---

10.   Richard Madihlaba, Pretoria University Law Clinic, September 3, 2008.

11.   http://www.sun.ac.za/english/Downloadable%20Documents/News%20 Attachments/ Judgment%20Universityof%20Stellenbosch%20Law%20Clinic%20 080715%20(2).pdf.

We turn, then, to the stories of deductions and counter-deductions with which this article began. The first, about the overpriced washing machine, is not atypical but it attracted unusual levels of public attention because it was disseminated through social media. In early 2016, an employer in the Western Cape town of George posted on Facebook an account of his gardener's battle with furniture retail giant Lewis, which included a photograph of a contract that the gardener had signed (fig. 3).[12] What ensued was a kind of moral panic. Commentators were shocked that a low-wage employee could end up paying R18,000 for a washing machine that retailed for R6,000. The markup did not consist of interest alone. The appliance store, said a newspaper report, had "managed to convince [the] 60-plus gardener" to sign a contract for

> a 14kg twin tub that, apart from the R5999 price tag, included: a R975 contract fee, R750 for delivery, a R1311 maintenance agreement, interest at 23% per annum, customer protection insurance of R2052 and, again, protection insurance for clients of R3785. The total is R17955 and [the] employee asked him to have a look at the contract as Lewis Stores only asked him for R600 deposit and the gardener did not understand what the extra costs were for.

Lewis agreed to cancel the contract, but a bitter fight nonetheless ensued. The furniture retailer threatened legal action for defamation[13] and the gardener's employer unapologetically reaffirmed that its "lending practices are not fair to the poor and amount to exploitation." He also maintained that while a court would have to rule whether this was reckless lending or not, and he could not speculate about that, the gardener's "lack of ability to afford such a contract and lack of understanding of the full costs involved" made it quite likely that Lewis would "be found guilty of reckless lending."[14]

---

12. The story was reported in the local newspaper, the *George Herald*: https://www.george- herald.com/News/Article/General/r18-000-for-r5-999-washing-machine-20170711. It was later reported online at Fin24.com and the *Daily Maverick*: http://www.dailymaverick.co.za/opinionista/2016-01-25-the-exploitation-of-poor- debtors-is-routine/#.V7L_J_krLIU.

13. http://www.fin24.com/Companies/Retail/lewis-hits-back-in-r18k-washing-machine- row-20160122.

14. Shortly before this, Lewis's practices had been exposed—using "mystery shoppers"—by a consumer watchdog and self-styled auditor of the credit industry,

The term *reckless lending* was particularly emotive. In a manner somewhat reminiscent of the paternalism of the colonial authorities a century earlier, a regulatory framework had already been put in place—the National Credit Act—precisely in order to stop retailers and lenders from making offers to those manifestly unable to afford them. Its passing, informed by the kinds of scenarios that transpired between Lewis and the gardener, had been designed by the Department of Trade and Industry to counteract the egregious forms of "credit apartheid" that had earlier prevailed (DTI 2002), as well as tackling the effects of the new credit bonanza. But its umbrella organization, the National Credit Register, severely understaffed and hence little more than a "consumer advocate that is charged with registering lenders,"[15] was seemingly ineffectual.

Buying household goods in installments by those who cannot afford them outright is not in itself a uniquely South African phenomenon: in the United Kingdom, for example, a much-reviled company called Brighthouse has specialized in selling white goods in the same way.[16] What did mark off the South African case, and what led to the social media furor, was a set of associated practices (Schreiner et al. 1997). Retailers levied excessively high interest rates (despite having been able to ascertain—as with the washing machine purchase in George—that the purchaser has a secure line of income and hence did not pose a "risk"). They also charged for life insurance to cover the term of the loan, and added a fee for delivery. Retailers rationalize this as part of their "risk assessment" since it enables them to ascertain where—in a township, shanty town, or squatter camp—the customer lives and thus makes repossession easier should it come to that.[17] What outstripped all of these in notoriety, however, was the way such retailers—and others—were able to make "deductions" if payments were not kept up. It had become habituated practice for retailers and microlenders alike to do this by using emoluments attachment or garnishee orders (EAOs). Law Clinic attorney Stephan van der Merwe aptly summarized the situation:

Summit Financial Partners: http://www.summitfin.co.za/; https://www.youtube.com/watch?v=uZN2lw- LMYQ&feature=youtu.be.

15. Patrick McGroarty, "In South Africa, a consumer debt bubble forms," *Wall Street Journal*, December 26, 2012. https://www.wsj.com/articles/SB10001424127887324296604578177884108022670.

16. http://www.brighthouse.co.uk/.

17. Interview with Marlene Heymans, Pretoria, April 15, 2009.

"The rules . . . fail to cater for those matters where the judgment . . . [is] being abused to squeeze every last drop of blood from debtors" (2007).

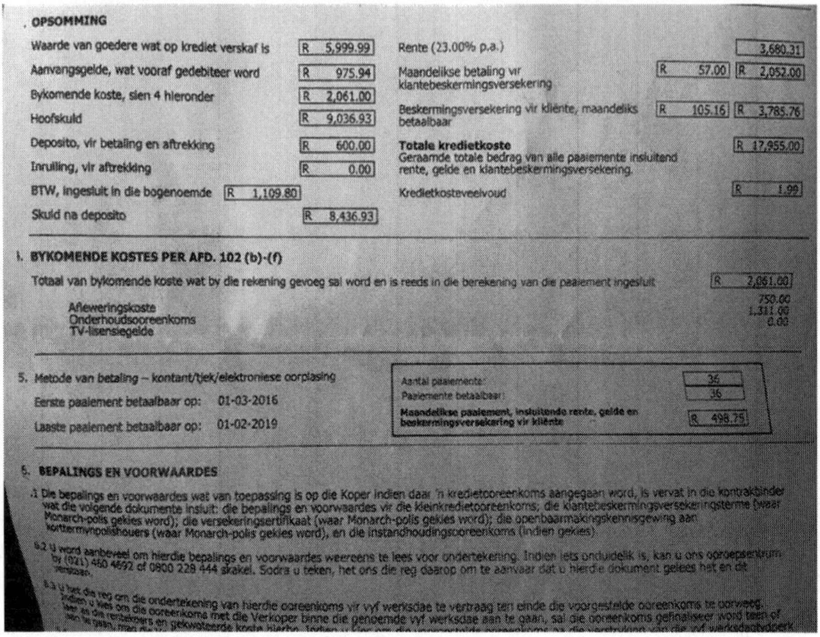

Figure 3: The gardener's contract posted on Facebook. (Photo by Onne Vegter, used with permission.)

This brings us to the second story. As in the washing machine case, things were once again instigated by a white employer from the left-liberal establishment: and this time court action was initiated not by a creditor hitting back at accusations but by an employer. What the cases had in common was the presence of one kind of (paternalistic) external control as a means to combat another (exploitative) variety, and the importance of the formal, legal domain as terrain on which these battles would be fought.

In the absence of meaningful action taken against reckless lenders by the government (which is what the drafters of the National Credit Act had intended), businesswoman and wine farm owner Wendy Appelbaum approached the Legal Aid Clinic at Stellenbosch University, which in turn instructed the pro bono practice of law firm Webber Wentzel. Several of the workers on Appelbaum's wine farm, De Morgenzon, she complained, were having "large portions" of their monthly pay deducted by the use of such orders.[18] In the judgment of the Western Cape High Court that heard the case, it was not this practice itself that was condemned. (It noted with concern, however, the epidemic levels at which such orders were being granted: in the case of one of the applicants the clerk of the court had "issued three EAOs on the same day attaching almost her entire salary.") Rather, it singled out the "predatory lending practices" and "large scale abuse" including "fraud" in the process of issuing such orders.[19] The fraud—eventually ruled against by the court—included debt collectors' use of counterfeit signatures. It also included the issuing of orders by incompetent or corrupt clerks rather than by magistrates themselves, and the practice of "forum shopping," in which retailers and lenders sought to have orders enacted in areas of jurisdiction, far from the debtor's place of residence, where clerks were known to be compliant. Those who had been readily using these fraudulent procedures, and were listed as respondents in the case, were not only the thirteen "credit providers" but also a firm of attorneys that specialized in debt collection on their behalf, and which had on its books debt to the "total value . . . of R1,597,585,832.00 (that is, over one and a half billion rands)."[20] With a rich income source thus threatened, the association representing the debt-collecting law firm—despite the judgment being widely hailed as a "great victory for the poor"—lodged an appeal. Even before the appeal was heard, however, there were signs that the numbers of "fraudulently" enacted EAOs had fallen. The Constitutional Court eventually ruled in September 2016 that no such order may be issued without authorization by the court "after satisfying itself that it is just and equitable and that the amount is appropriate."[21] The efforts made to bring the case to court, unusually, involved not just pro bono lawyers and legal practitioners with an interest in human rights. They also involved "those with

18. Desmond Thompson, "Emoluments ruling 'a great victory for poor in general,'" *Sunday Times*, July 15, 2015. For more information on how the system operates, see van der Merwe (2007).

19. These and the following citations are from the judgment: http://www.sun.ac.za/eng- lish/Downloadable%20Documents/News%20 Attachments/Judgment%20Universi- tyof%20Stellenbosch%20Law%20 Clinic%20080715%20(2).pdf. For the later judgment by the Constitutional Court, see http://www.saflii.org/za/cases/ZACC/2016/32.html.

20. At the time, this equated to £77,930,236.

21. http://www.moneyweb.co.za/news/south-africa/ombuds-complaints-salary-attachment-orders-fall/; http://www.saflii.org/za/cases/ZACC/2016/32.html.

resources and influence," such as the farm owner mentioned earlier, as well as a business in the private sector, Summit Financial Services, which had charged itself with auditing the unethical practices of creditors.[22] Effectively, the Court was here intervening at the highest level in a realm previously thought of as everyday, even banal. The collection of debts, once made through routine administrative measures, had been ruled as involving abusive practices, and as having negative implications for the rights and freedoms of South Africa's lowliest citizens.

In the third deduction story, reported in 2015, it was—as in the previous case—an employer who was made aware of the effect of the whittling away of salaries on employee morale that initiated proceedings to curb this practice. The huge multinational mining company Amplats "launched a legal battle" against salary deductions for outstanding debts.[23] The company was opposed, in particular, to the "12.5% fee charged by administrators, stipulated in the Magistrate's Court Act," and to the practice whereby attorneys undertaking debt administration were charging "what they wish" or were circumventing "the 12.5% cap by subcontracting their duties and adding that cost to the debt." The CEO's argument "that this could turn some heavily indebted people into 'indentured labour, working to pay off administrators as well as creditors—often for indefinite periods'" contained eerie echoes of the practices of nineteenth-century trader/labor recruitment agents enticing workers into the labor force by indebting them. In this type of deduction, practiced through "debt administration," rewards were again arising from inadequate policing of the Magistrates' Court Act of 1944 that governed such matters. Debt administrators, appointed to officiate over the accounts of debtors who were in default, received funds through the execution—yet again—of a deduction order from those debtors' accounts. Their official role was to divert these funds into a trust account in order to distribute them to the unpaid creditors. But they were often unqualified and unregistered, overcharged their clients, or failed to pay creditors as they had undertaken to do, with outstanding interest from the unpaid debts then accumulating to the detriment of the debtor. In one case, administrators extended a loan to one of their clients, added themselves as a creditor, and "distributed the better part of the client's installment to themselves and the remainder to the client's other

22. http://blog.6cents.co.za/garnishee-laws-updated-by-the-constitutional-court/.

23. http://www.bdlive.co.za/business/mining/2015/01/09/amplats-takes-debt-collectors- to-court.

creditors." In other cases, "administrators were attorneys who were struck off the roll or were themselves under administration" (Smit 2008: 14).[24] The blurred boundaries between debtor and creditor are here evident.

The final story in my quartet tells of similar deductions, likewise made with impunity until a challenge was launched—in this case, by public interest law NGO the Legal Resources Centre. In this case, however, the automatic deductions were being made from state welfare payments rather than from state pay packets, or salaries or wages paid in the private sector. What also made this case stand out was the way it combined the outsourcing of the state's redistributive function with sophisticated new technologies of registration that were bringing potential (poor) borrowers more easily within the ambit of businesses aiming to profit from them (see Breckenridge 2005, 2014; Vally 2016). "Pensioners," said the report "are signing over their social grants to a private lender in order to get loans." The report went on to document how Easypay, a service "launched by Net1/Cash Paymaster Services," had access to "the details of 21 million grant beneficiaries." It was using these to allow microlenders and funeral insurance salesmen—many of them subsidiaries of the grant-paying company—to target those beneficiaries by offering them loans and selling them products, then deducting payments from their grants on payday (Torkelson, forthcoming).[25] Ethnographer Natasha Vally, who documented these processes in the rural setting of Bushbuckridge over two years, noted that officials spent more time involved in the business of these subsidiary loan and insurance arrangements than in the work of actually paying grants.

> Ultimately, Net1 had acquired the machinery and other hardware, the knowledge of how to put them into practice in South Africa, the employ of people with the required skills and local knowledge to implement their infrastructure,

---

24. "Struck off" means removed from the register and prohibited from practicing as a lawyer.

25. https://www.pressreader.com/south-africa/sunday-times/20160221/28219653501 9414. Deductions from social grants: how it all works. https://www.groundup.org. za/article/deductions-social-grants-how-it-works/; https://www.groundup.org.za/ article/deductions-social-grants-how-it-works/
    Sophia's Choice: Farm worker has to decide which of her children to feed https:// www.groundup.org.za/article/sophias-choice-farm-worker-has-decide-which-her-children-feed/

and the information and databases that it needed in order to maintain a thriving business without direct connections to the state. (Vally 2016: 982)

The legal NGO involved in the case achieved some success: by the time of publication, a case in the Constitutional Court, in which human/consumer rights organisation The Black Sash had played a significant role, had led to the cancellation of the Net1 contract, and its awarding instead to the South African Post Office. "It is a shameful travesty of justice," said a spokesperson for the opposition Democratic Alliance, that such deductions had "been allowed to take place at all, from grants which are already way too small to survive on."[26] Significant numbers of welfare beneficiaries, however, had opted to retain their "Easypay" cards and to continue borrowing from Moneyline, one of Net1's subsidiaries. The story demonstrates, overall, how "the expansion of indebtedness and financial devices . . . [and] the impossibility of paying" feature prominently in accounts of settings where there is a "massive incorporation of people into the current market economy" (Neiburg and Guyer, Introduction).

MORE COUNTER-DEDUCTIONS

The burgeoning supply of and demand for credit, the indeterminacy about the exact figures involved, and the socioeconomic segments most affected, have been outlined above. So have the belated attempts to regulate and curb the practice of ensuring repayment through deductions. It remains to be asked whether any means have been found to counter that practice, apart from expensive legal action undertaken by wealthy and paternalistic employers.

One answer suggests a protectionist, and perhaps equally paternalistic, remedy. Drawing attention to the risky and unsustainable character of the unsecured credit market, those espousing this approach offer advice to unwary consumers. Finance Minister Pravin Gordhan warned in 2012 against using unsecured lending to feed consumption rather than for investment purposes: "Take it easy on the consumption side. Lower your levels of indebtedness. Distinguish

---

26. "Funeral policy deductions settlement a 'step towards protecting society's most vulnerable,'" *Dispatch Live*, May 27, 2016. https://www.africanewshub.com/news/5072284-funeral-policy-deductions-settlement-a-step-towards-protecting-societys-most-vulnerable.

between what you want and what you need" (cited in Schraten 2012). As the situation seemingly worsened and as it became clearer that waged employees were among the worst hit, financial corporations like Alexander Forbes, concerned with employee well-being, presented a series of talks to audiences comprising the trustees of pension funds (among others) that were aimed at raising awareness of the need for worker education and protection.[27] These analyses, again reflecting a high modernist stance, stemmed from the idea that a population unused to—because previously excluded from—the possibilities of formal borrowing, was not attuned to the conventional wisdom that "all loans and repayments should cancel each other out" (Shipton 2011: 217; see also Graeber 2011: 3–4). Far from overtly challenging or questioning that premise, consumers had been duped into borrowing beyond their means and would require "financial education" to stop them doing so in future. They should also be introduced to the benefits of "being banked," which would lessen their reliance on higher-priced loans from informal moneylenders (Ardington et al. 2004).

A second line of argument—one I have pursued in earlier publications—was that consumers knew more than they were credited with, and that neither education nor banking could remedy a deep-seated bias in favor of lenders. Those in need of financial services have long made use of them (James 2015: 107), and *have* been accustomed to make regular repayments. They have used their obligations to honor installment plan repayments as a savings mechanism or a way of selectively avoiding relatives' requests for money (or both). As elsewhere, they have been able to "negotiate and challenge" such demands by choosing to repay some debts rather than others or by juggling various creditors' claims against each other (see Guerin 2014). But these strategies cannot mitigate the fact that the cards are stacked in favor of lender/creditors. The ability of the latter to make automatic deductions from pay packets means they have little need of collateral, since wages serve as a collateral substitute in such cases (Roth 2004: 78), and their techniques for making deductions have, until recently, gone unchallenged. Borrowers therefore have little muscle. Unsecured lending enhances the principle of "advantage to creditors" that underpins existing insolvency law and that remains intact despite inconclusive attempts to provide debtor relief (Boraine and Roestoff 2002: 4; Schraten 2014; 2020). What marked the break with earlier arrangements, according to this line of argument, was post-1990s

---

27. The 2015 issue of their *Benefits Barometer*, to which I contributed, can be found here: https://issuu.com/alexanderforbescomms/docs/benefitsbarometer2015.

financialization, plus the extensive use of bank accounts by the populace at large. It was this that definitively enhanced creditors' advantage by facilitating the unimpeded flow of money, from salary or social grant, into the bank account at month's end and out of it again (James 2015: 110).

There is truth in both sets of claims, however. Some creditors do indeed exploit lenders with impunity, and have been able to shape-shift in parallel with changing legislation, avoiding all attempts to regulate their behavior. But many informal moneylenders (*mashonisas*), initially spotting the opportunities offered by lending money at high rates of interest but later prohibited from securing or otherwise unable to secure repayment through the financialized "deduction" system, have reverted (as an alternative, usually unsuccessfully) to the "formal" means of seeking repayment at the small claims courts.[28] For other *mashonisas*, the extent of their lending, the interest they can charge, and their ability to call in loans, is limited by community norms about moral and appropriate behavior (Krige 2011: 154–58; for Argentina see Wilkis 2015). *Spaza* (informal) shops are likewise often able to stay in business only by selling on credit and often have difficulties in recouping moneys owed to them.[29] As this suggests, creditors—including illegal ones—are not all-powerful, since borrowers (albeit not always distinguishable from lenders) have some means—and not only illegal ones—of protection against them.

Equally, borrowers have devised schemes to protect themselves from lenders. Many are ambivalent about using banks, feeling on the one hand that they seem trustworthy (Hull 2012), but on the other hand that they are being exploited or discriminated against on racial grounds by these institutions (Kibuuka 2006). Some resolve to steer clear of them. Even middle- to high-income earners have decoupled themselves from the world of financial formality. Some are keen to escape from the clutches of stores that sell furniture on installment plan. "I wanted to prevent members from buying goods on credit," said the founder of one savings club who had suffered the iniquities of "deductions" from his salary. "At the end of the year, you can buy what you want with cash" (James 2015: 144). Others explicitly state their preference for clubs over banks because of the higher interest rates they offer on savings and the lower rate charged for taking out loans. Showing particular astuteness, they prefer to transact savings and loans through clubs in order to avoid South Africa's notorious bank charges, the

---

28. Nickle Felgate and Pippa Reyburn, pers. comm., April 2015.
29. Interview with Marlene Heymans, Pretoria, April 15, 2009; see also Hart (1973).

highest in the world (Kibuuka 2006: 51). Those of more modest means, having tried the simple option of fleeing from one bank account to the next as creditors pursue them, have subsequently requested that employers pay their wages directly in cash or by using prepaid money cards delinked from bank accounts.[30] Formal and informal borrowing arrangements are judiciously combined, but people are sometimes forced by circumstances to convert from one to the other, and back again—or to combine all simultaneously.

Claims that excessive borrowing owes itself to a lack of education, then, are as well-rehearsed in South Africa as they are in many other settings where financialization is far advanced (see Lazarus 2016). The examples given here, however, paint a more complex picture of people's navigation through the financial landscape, suggesting that their decisions are founded less on ignorance than on a shrewd ability to evade obligations that are unduly onerous.

CONCLUSION

How, then, can we make sense of South Africa's post-1994 economy, in which repayment, deduction, and counter-deduction have played such a large role? Given the fierce battles fought out in the courts to rule against practices that often exist beyond the law, are tricky debt collection practices to be reckoned as entirely distinct from formal legal processes, perhaps in a new version of the formal/informal binary? Or do they form an intrinsic part of the totality of the country's (now financialized) version of capitalism? Do the high interest rates, paid by those formerly excluded, serve as a new version of the subsidy to capitalist production—a role formerly attributed by Marxist theorists to householders' rural cultivation (Wolpe 1972)? Or does refusal to repay amount to a repudiation of financial inclusion?

The boom in both micro- and not-so-micro-lending of the post-1994 period intensified the existing systems of extraction facilitated by technologies of deduction. These certainly fueled accumulation; new financial players like African Bank were founded on the back of that boom. When African Bank required a bailout this revealed the unsustainability of a scenario in which lenders had clambered over each other in their determination to offer loans to all and sundry, without reckoning borrowers' ability to repay. On the one hand,

---

30. Tony Beamish, pers. comm., April 16, 2015.

borrowers' efforts to counter deductions, through evasive action and court hearings alike, seem to suggest that borrowers were getting the upper hand. It might also be claimed, however, that the state was ultimately the loser in this system, with its salaries and grants being made the basis of illicit moneylending and the collection of high rates of interest. A regime that has been called *distributional* on account of its continued state spending (Seekings and Nattrass 2005: 314), and a setting where "neoliberal means interweave with and facilitate redistributive ends" (Hull and James 2012: 16) is what makes this possible. In the end, it is unclear who is exploiting, or subsidizing, whom.

As in the case of the Congo, it is true that "vested interests stand in the way of any reform" of the informal, illegal, second economy, and that the state and its agents are similarly reluctant to "clamp down" on it (MacGaffey 1991). But in South Africa, it is not only the "wealthy and powerful" that "consolidate their own position" through participation in these activities (MacGaffey 1991). Rather, a multitude of small, informal lenders exist alongside the larger loan sharks and the rapacious retailers whose activities have been outlined above. Profits—and losses—have been difficult to trace, making it tricky to add the debts deemed "uncollected" to any statistical reckoning of the size or shape of South Africa's economy seen as an integrated whole, or to identify a specific set of wealth flows or accumulations that it involves. An account of the *real economy* in MacGaffey's sense—one that includes both recorded and unrecorded economic activities, both deductions and counter-deductions—might become easier to track as ethnographic researchers continue to explore and monitor these multiple activities.

Ultimately, this economy is one in which high finance and the state's resources are inextricably entangled with the wages earned, consumption undertaken within, and debts paid (and unpaid) by householders. To typecast it as yet another case of neoliberalism, with the state enabling extraction to privilege big business /capitalism, would be to tell too simple a story. Neither does this case square up entirely with MacGaffey's analysis of the Congo. Where she wrote of jobs bringing access to profitable opportunities of a "parallel commercial system developing in the heart of the state" (1991: 16), that "system" in South Africa has taken on an unusual and unexpected form. Somewhere between the two characterizations, we may be witnessing a new formation of the state, with private sector actors like Easypay and Net1 taking over, duplicating, or hijacking its functions. Yet we also need to recognize the less readily acknowledged aspects of the economy, whether these be tacitly sanctioned illegalities or informal economic practices. This article has shown how other factors, too, need to be stirred into the analytical mix. The varying modes of control range from the paternalism of white employers and the state, which echoes that of the colonial authorities that clamped down on nineteenth-century "advances," to more direct forms of exploitation. The constitutionalism of the courts is also important: one presaged by the human rights focus of certain key lawyers, even when the depredations of apartheid were at their worst. Finally, we must acknowledge the redistributive tendencies of a newly installed democratic dispensation, such that elite profits and state resources are channeled and find their way into the pockets of the rank and file.

ACKNOWLEDGMENTS

Some of the material for this article was collected under a grant from the Economic and Social Research Council of the United Kingdom (award RES-062-23-1290), which I gratefully acknowledge. Opinions expressed are my own. Thanks to research participants (some names have been changed to protect identities), to Keith Hart, Agustin Diz, and Jonah Lipton for reading the essay, to the editors of this volume and to the anonymous readers of an earlier draft for their valuable suggestions.

REFERENCES

Anders, Gerhard. 2009. *In the shadow of good governance: An ethnography of civil service reform in Africa*. Leiden: Brill.

Ardington, Cally, David Lam, Murray Leibbrandt, and James Levinsohn. 2004. "Savings, insurance and debt over the post-apartheid period: A review of recent research." *South African Journal of Economics* 72(3): 604–40.

Barchiesi, Franco. 2011. *Precarious liberation: Workers, the state, and contested social citizenship in postapartheid South Africa*. Albany: State University of New York Press.

Beinart, William. 1979. "European traders and the Mpondo paramountcy, 1878–1886." *Journal of African History* 20 (4): 471–86.

———. 2012. "Beyond 'homelands': Some ideas about the history of African rural areas in South Africa." *South African Historical Journal* 64 (1): 5–21.

Boraine, André, and Melanie Roestoff. 2002. "Fresh start procedures for con-
    sumer debtors in South African bankruptcy law." *International Insolvency
    Review* 11 (1): 1–11.
Breckenridge, Keith. 2005. "The biometric state: The promise and peril of digital
    government in the New South Africa." *Journal of Southern African Studies* 31
    (2): 267–82.
———. 2014. *Biometric state: The global politics of identification and surveillance
    in South Africa, 1850 to the present.* Cambridge: Cambridge University Press.
Chanock, Martin. 2001. *The making of South African legal culture, 1902–1936:
    Fear, favour and prejudice.* Cambridge: Cambridge University Press.
Cichello, P., G. S. Fields, and M. Leibbrandt. 2005. "Earnings and employment
    dynamics for Africans in post-apartheid South Africa: A panel study of
    KwaZulu-Natal." *Journal of African Economies* 14 (2): 143–90.
Cooper, Frederick. 2002. *Africa since 1940: The past of the present.* Cambridge:
    Cambridge University Press.
Daniels, Reza. 2004. "Financial intermediation, regulation and the formal
    microcredit sector in South Africa." *Development Southern Africa* 21 (5):
    831–49.
DTI (Department of Trade and Industry)/Reality Research Africa. 2002. *Credit
    contract disclosure and associated factors.* Pretoria.
DTI (Department of Trade and Industry). 2004. *Consumer credit law reform:
    Policy frame- work for consumer credit.* Pretoria.
Feinstein, Charles H. 2005. *An economic history of South Africa: Conquest, dis-
    crimination, and development.* Cambridge: Cambridge University Press.
First, Ruth. 1983. *The Mozambican miner: Proletarian and peasant.* New York:
    Palgrave Macmillan.
Graeber, David. 2011. *Debt: The first 5,000 years.* New York: Melville House.
Guerin, Isabelle. 2014. "Juggling with debt, social ties, and values: The everyday
    use of microcredit in rural South India." *Current Anthropology* 55, Supple-
    ment 9: S40–S50.
Guyer, Jane. 2004. *Marginal gains: Monetary transactions in Atlantic Africa.* Chi-
    cago: University of Chicago Press.
Han, Clara. 2012. *Life in debt: Times of care and violence in neoliberal Chile.*
    Berkeley: University of California Press.
Hart, Keith. 1973. "Informal income opportunities and urban employment in
    Ghana." *Journal of Modern African Studies* 11 (1): 61–89.

———. 2009. "Money in the making of world society." In *Market and society: The great transformation today*, edited by Chris Hann and Keith Hart. Cambridge: Cambridge University Press.

———. 2015. "How the informal economy took over the world." In *Informal market worlds reader: The architecture of economic pressure*, edited by Peter Moertenboeck, Helge Mooshammer, Teddy Cruz, and Fonna Forman, 33–44. Rotterdam: nai010 Publishers.

Haupt, Frans, Hermie Coetzee, Dawid de Villiers, and Jeanne-Mari Fouché. 2008. *The incidence of and the undesirable practices relating to garnishee orders in South Africa*. Pretoria: GTZ (Deutsche Gesellschaft für Technische Zusammenarbeit).

Hull, Elizabeth. 2012. "Banking in the bush: Waiting for credit in South Africa's rural economy." *Africa* 82 (1): 165–83.

Hull, Elizabeth, and Deborah James. 2012. "Introduction: Local economies and citizen expectations in South Africa." *Africa* 82 (1): 1–19.

———. 2015. *Money from nothing: Indebtedness and aspiration in South Africa*. Palo Alto, CA: Stanford University Press.

James, Deborah, and Dinah Rajak. 2014. "Credit apartheid, migrants, mines and money." *African Studies* 73 (3): 455–76.

Kear, M. 2013. "Governing Homo subprimicus: Beyond financial citizenship, exclusion, and rights." *Antipode* 45 (4): 926–46.

Kibuuka, L. E. 2006. "Informal finance for the middle and high income individuals in South Africa: A case study of high budget 'stokvels' in Pretoria." MSc diss., University of Pretoria.

Krige, Detlev. 2011. "Power, identity and agency at work in the popular economies of Soweto and Black Johannesburg." DPhil diss., University of the Witwatersrand, Johannesburg. http://wiredspace.wits.ac.za/handle/10539/10143.

Lazarus, Jeanne. 2016. "Educating poor people to 'real economy.'" Paper presented at Real Economy: Ethnographic Inquiries into the Reality and the Realization of Economic Life workshop, Rio de Janeiro, June 16–18.

Lund, Francie, and Caroline Skinner. 2003. "Integrating the informal economy in urban planning and governance: A case study of the process of policy development in Durban, South Africa." *International Development Planning Review* 26 (4): 431–56.

MacGaffey, Janet. 1991. *The real economy of Zaire: The contribution of smuggling and other unofficial activities to national wealth*. London: James Currey.

Marais, Hein. 2011. *South Africa pushed to the limit: The political economy of change*. London: Zed Books.

Martin, R. 2002. *The financialization of daily life*. Philadelphia: Temple University Press.

Maurer, Bill. 2012. "Mobile money: Communication, consumption and change in the payments space." *Journal of Development Studies* 48 (5): 589–604.

Neiburg, Federico. 2016. "A true coin of their dreams: Imaginary monies in Haiti." *HAU: Journal of Ethnographic Theory* 6 (1): 75–93.

Neiburg, Federico, and Jane I. Guyer. 2017. "The real in the real economy." *HAU: Journal of Ethnographic Theory* 7 (3): 261–79.

Neves, David. 2018. "The financialisation of the poor and the reproduction of inequality." *The new South African review: The crisis of inequality*, edited by Gilbert M Khadiagala, Sarah Mosoetsa, Devan Pillay, Roger Southall, 84–100. Pretoria: Human Sciences Research Council.

Neves, David, and Andries Du Toit. 2012. "Money and sociality in South Africa's informal economy." *Africa* 82 (1): 129–46.

Parry, Jonathan. 2012. "Suicide in a central Indian steel town." *Contributions to Indian Sociology* 46 (1&2): 145–80.

Roth, James. 2004. "Spoilt for choice: Financial services in an African township." PhD diss., University of Cambridge.

Schapera, Isaac. 1947. *Migrant labour and tribal life*. London: Oxford University Press.

Schraten, Jürgen. 2012. "Managing a consumer debt crisis." Paper presented at Towards Carnegie III, University of Cape Town. http://carnegie3.org.za/docs/papers/238_Sch-raten_Managing%20a%20consumer%20debt%20crisis.pdf.

———. 2014. "The transformation of the South African credit market." *Transformation* 85: 1–20.

———. 2020. *Credit and Debt in an Unequal Society: Establishing a Consumer Credit Market In South Africa:* New York, Berghahn.

Schreiner, Mark, Douglas H. Graham, Manuel Cortes Font-Cuberta, Gerhard Coetzee, and Nick Vink. 1997. "Racial discrimination in hire/purchase lending in apartheid South Africa." Paper presented at meeting of the American Agricultural Economics Association, July 27–30, Toronto.

Seekings, Jeremy, and Nicoli Nattrass. 2005. *Class, race, and inequality in South Africa*. New Haven, CT: Yale University Press.

Shipton, Parker. 2007. *The nature of entrustment: Intimacy, exchange and the sacred in Africa*. New Haven, CT: Yale University Press.

———. 2011. *Credit between cultures: Farmers, financiers, and misunderstanding in Africa*. New Haven, CT: Yale University Press.

Smit, Anneke. 2008. "Administration orders versus debt counselling." LLM diss., University of South Africa.

Soederberg, Susanne. 2015. *Debtfare states and the poverty industry: Money, discipline and the surplus population*. Abingdon, VA: Routledge.

Torkelson, Erin. forthcoming. "Taken for granted": cash transfer as debt transfer. *World Development*.

Trapido, Stanley. 1978. "Landlord and tenant in a colonial economy: The Transvaal 1880–1910." *Journal of Southern African Studies* 5 (1).

Vally, Natasha. 2016. "Insecurity in South African social security: An examination of social grant deductions, cancellations, and waiting." *Journal of Southern African Studies* 42 (5): 965–82.

Van der Merwe, Stefan. 2007. "Failure to discharge: A discussion of the insufficient legal recourse afforded to judgment debtors in the South African context." *AGORA International Journal of Juridical Sciences*. http://scholar.sun.ac.za/handle/10019.1/79636.

Verhoef, Grietjie. 2009. "Concentration and competition: The changing landscape of the banking sector in South Africa, 1970–2007." *South African Journal of Economic History* 24 (2): 157–97.

Wilkis, Ariel. 2015. "The moral performativity of credit and debt in the slums of Buenos Aires." *Cultural Studies* 29 (5–6): 760–80.

Wolpe, Harold. 1972. "Capitalism and cheap labour power in South Africa: From segregation to apartheid." *Economy and Society* 1 (4): 425–56.

CHAPTER THREE

Resisting numbers
The favela as an (un)quantifiable reality

Eugênia Motta

INTRODUCTION

Numbers, like words, are forms of expressing and creating the existence of things (Desrosières and Kott 2005); they provide a way to conceive the world through which we move, and transform it. The subjects of this text are "large numbers" (Desrosières 1993) or "public numbers" (Porter 1995) and operations involved in their production and use. As well as being one of the main modern modes of building social knowledge, large numbers are a key element of state reality, providing the reference point through which various agencies are mobilized in the effort to govern (Neiburg 2011; Mitchell 2002; Cohn 1996). Indeed, they occupy a fundamental place in the construction of the units, objects, and domains of state action, yet they are not purely state forms.[1]

As Theodore Porter argues, "statistics, preeminent among the quantitative tools for investigating society, is powerless unless it can make new entities" (1994: 398). In this chapter I discuss the production of a specific entity, the

---

1. A version of this text was published as an article in Portuguese (Motta 2019).

favela, based on operations involved in its creation and use as a statistical reality and, therefore, as an object of a certain kind of agency. My aim is to highlight the relationship between the difficulties and obstacles involved in the quantification and conception of favelas as abnormal (or subnormal), problematic and dangerous. Ian Hacking calls attention to the proximity between two ways normality has been understood in the development of statistics, and affirms it is one of the most important ideas of the twentieth century. For the author: "The normal stands indifferently for what is typical, the unenthusiastic objective average, but it also stands for what has been, good health, and for what shall be, our chosen destiny" (1990: 169).

Statistics are produced through an extensive chain of transformations (Thévenot 1995) that involve agreements, conventions, negotiations, translations, and codifications (Desrosières and Kott 2005). The processes of producing and using public numbers involve various kinds of negotiations and conflicts in which, in the effort to quantify the world, difficulties arise in collecting and classifying data, and contestations flare up over their accuracy. These are the critical dimensions in the production of statistical reality that interest me. I shall examine three types of oppositions to quantification, which I call *resistances*. They neither impede nor rule out the possibility of producing numbers, but on the contrary, form part of this always incomplete and conflictual process.

Quantification is understood here as a way of creating realities, categories, and objects of a particular kind. Reality (or realities) is understood to be the arrangements of elements and relations that people conceive as existent, relatively autonomous and external to subjectivities, observable, tangible, and intelligible—that is, it is a *common* reference point in both senses of the term: shared and ordinary. In adopting this approach, it not only makes sense to approach *realities* in the plural rather than *reality* in the singular, it is essential that we do so.

The object of the statistics discussed here are favelas, places deemed problematic ever since they first emerged (Valladares 2000, 2005). The origin of these spaces dates to the occupation of hillsides in the center of Rio de Janeiro at the end of the nineteenth century. Since this chapter explores the definitions of what favelas are, it would be somewhat hazardous to offer any kind of objective description, given that the analysis that I propose questions precisely that kind of endeavor. Nonetheless, the reader must be at least minimally situated. Provisionally, we can affirm that favelas are identified by distinctive landscape characteristics, such as high-density occupation by constructions, most of which are considered incomplete (lacking paint or other coverings), along winding, unplanned streets and passageways, and very often located on slopes and hills, although not always. They are taken to be equivalent or similar to what are referred to in the English literature as slums, informal settlements, or shantytowns.

Figure 1: View of Complexo do Alemão, Rio de Janeiro, 2014. Photo by the author.

The analytic proposal presented here originates in ethnographic fieldwork I have conducted since 2012 in a favela in the large region known as the Complexo do Alemão in the North Zone of Rio de Janeiro, which combines various neighborhoods considered to be favelas, though they constitute a fairly uniform urban continuum.[2] My initial interest was to investigate people's ordinary economic practices through long-term and in-depth insertion in the life of one

---

2. For reasons explained above, it is somewhat problematic to present statistical data with any descriptive objective in this text. Recognizing the importance of statistical reality in the social sciences, however, I suspend the analysis for a moment to provide some information to the reader. According to the municipal government of Rio de Janeiro, some 60,500 people live in the Complexo do Alemão in approximately 18,000 households (Cavallieri and Vial 2012).

family. This work revealed an intrinsic relationship between economics, family practices, and houses. The centrality of houses in the social life of the people in this community[3] formed the basis for an approach that also considers houses to be analytically central. However, residents are not the only agents who act and think about their houses and the space in which they live or act in.

It was certainly relevant to the questions that interested me that the people with whom I conducted my research lived in a favela—for many reasons, such as the forms of economic and building regulations existing for these spaces, the stigma that they carry and even the fact that few researchers have been interested in understanding the economy of favelas. But what are favelas? Or more precisely, what makes these spaces what they are? Among the numerous meanings that this word contains and ideas to which it refers, many are associated with disorder and the need to act. These are central dimensions in which quantification plays a key role.

I use three different kinds of materials as empirical sources for studying the production of favelas as quantified realities. One of them is the previously cited ethnography of everyday life in a specific community. The second are the written documents produced by the Brazilian Institute of Geography and Statistics (IBGE)[4] in different periods, which I use to establish continuities between the first formulations concerning favelas and the categories employed today in the national census, which are conducted by IBGE. Finally, I analyze the public debates that occurred in the wake of a self-census conducted by local organizations in the Maré region of Rio de Janeiro. This case contains a deliberate and explicit articulation of the same kind of critiques of numbers that I had perceived in a more diffuse form in my fieldwork in the Complexo do Alemão.

I argue that by using these different empirical sources, it is possible to produce a new approach to the multiple dimensions of producing statistical realities. The ethnographic interpretation, therefore, is not limited to description, but refers to a proposal to depict the interconnections of diffuse practices and meanings related to social worlds that, in principle, are at some distance from each other, and where people conceive and experience favelas differently (public policy managers and residents of favelas, for example). This composition

---

3. The word *comunidade* (community) is the most common way residents in the favela where I conducted fieldwork (and many others) refer to the where they live.

4. The National Institute of Statistics was officially created in 1934 and began operating in 1936. In 1938 it became known as IBGE.

is justified by the nature of the object itself. My attempt is to investigate the production of statistical realities, a process that involves the diverse efforts, oppositions, and practical and symbolic operations involved in the creation of an unstable agreement.

The idea of resistance that I am proposing highlights the relationship between dynamics that are distinct but share their presentation of oppositions and difficulties and their demand for solutions. What resists is the very object of quantification while it is being created. It is the disorder of occupied hillsides, the movement of people and houses, the favela residents themselves. Each form of resistance explored here corresponds to dissonances, and to a contraposition to a crucial aspect of statistical realities: measurability, stabilization, and accordance.

The idea of resistance employed here is not directly, nor even necessarily, related to opposition pursued by marginalized persons or groups, as discussed by James Scott (1985), for instance. I do not intend to examine interpretative disputes (though they also form part of my analysis) but dissonances that echo the main and pervasive questions that favelas raise in the public domain: how to recognize the favelas and, mainly, how to measure them, and what should be measured. Resistance here is whatever opposes effort, and ordered and intentional action.

I examine three forms of "resistance" by favelas to quantification. After a first section in which I sketch a panorama of the favelas and their historical construction as problematic, I examine the category *aglomerado subnormal* (subnormal agglomerate)—which is used to describe favelas in official statistics—and discuss how a particular, spatialized conception of poverty has been produced through the construction of the claim that these spaces are difficult to count. Hence, the aim is to explore how quantification is employed to conceptualize poverty as a reality—that is, as something existent, comprehensible, and upon which it is possible and necessary to act. By comparing the place of favelas in three different censuses (1950, 1991, 2010), I intend to show the nexus between *normalization* of the favela as a socially broad category and the idea that these were places in which and for which it was—and still is—difficult to produce numbers.

Second, I contrast the *domicile*, a statistical category that fixes and stabilizes persons and residences with "houses" as lived by favela residents. The endeavor to construct the residence as a discrete unit, fundamental to the construction of demographic statistics, contrasts with the constant movement involved in the production of homes, as lived by favela residents. These spaces are difficult to count precisely because there is instability and movement within them.

Finally, I discuss the resistance that emerges through the explicit contestation of this census data by the arguments and justifications for a "self-counting" carried out by local organizations. The statistical realities produced by official agencies are described by ordinary people engaged in local organizations as false, the methodology used is considered inadequate and to be based on prejudices and stigmatization. Producing their own numbers, organizers of the local census argue, entails challenging the way that favelas are publicly perceived and treated by state agents.

FAVELAS AS A PROBLEM SINCE THEIR ORIGINS

The category *favela* is difficult to define. It is employed daily by all kinds of people, including public administrators, as a self-evident reality and can be used in a purely descriptive form. It would not be an exaggeration to say that practically all of Rio de Janeiro's residents and most Brazilians have an idea of what a favela is. The word is used routinely without any need for additional description or explanation. Despite the naturality of its usage, the word contains multiple meanings and many concrete places exist whose categorization as favelas is open to discussion and dispute, given that the category associates landscape with violence and insalubrious conditions. Derived words like *favelado*, which refers to "a favela resident," are commonly used with a negative moral connotation. *Favelado* may be used as a strong term of accusation, implying that the person is badly educated and violent.[5] To *favelizar* a location, for instance, generally implies allowing or inciting urban deterioration and impoverishment.

The end of the nineteenth century saw the first clusters of houses made from cheap and reusable materials, built on hill slopes close to the center of Rio de Janeiro. According to the narrative that became widespread and persists until today—an origin myth according to Lícia Valladares (2000)—the first such place to be occupied was called the Morro da Favella (Favella Hill). The existence of a space with houses made from precarious materials, built in a

---

5. *Favelado* does not always have a negative meaning. Activists from local organizations in favelas strive to affirm their identity in a positive way through its use. Some researchers use the term to describe residents.

disorganized form on lands that did not officially belong to the people who had built on them, soon became a public issue. Over time the word favela became more widely used and transformed into a generic term for a kind of urban form, associated with concerns about their alleged ugliness and insalubrity, and for supposedly harboring dangerous people.

More than a century later, rather than vanishing, as had long been the goal of public policies, Rio's favelas have grown in number and size, and today much of the city's population lives in this kind of space. They continue to be a major theme of public debate, and are omnipresent themes in election campaigns and activities, for instance. Favelas were and continue to be seen publicly and treated by governments as a "problem" that needs to be addressed (Machado da Silva 2002). Paradoxically, one of the main arguments repeatedly used in support of intervention is that these are spaces where the state has always been absent.

In the twentieth century, various solutions were discussed and executed in relation to what was called the city's "cancer," ranging from proposals in the 1960s and 1970s for their complete extinction through demolition of housing, to the 1980s and beyond through urbanization programs and the installation of infrastructure (Burgos 1998). The association with poverty began early on; studies almost always focused on poverty and the place to study urban poverty was the favela (Valladares 2000, 2005).

The most recent modality of problematizing favelas began in the 1980s and became more firmly established in the following decade. The emergence of armed groups that controlled drug trafficking and favela territories led to a new and unique configuration of crime in Rio de Janeiro (Misse 2002, 2007). These places became perceived as the loci responsible for producing "urban violence" (Machado da Silva 2010). The dismantling of entire favelas, the implementation of urbanization projects, and investment in welfare policies still remain part of government actions for favelas, but they are accompanied practically and symbolically by the alleged need for police action.

The most recent interventions in favelas have been projects developed as part of the federal Growth Acceleration Program (*Programa de Aceleração do Crescimento*: PAC)[6] and the installation of Police Pacification Units (*Unidades*

---

6.   The PAC was a federal government program essentially designed to fund large infrastructure projects. Created in 2007 during the first Workers Party (PT) and Lula administration, it was one of main vectors of economic growth during the 2000s and one of the chief banners of Dilma Rousseff's first presidential campaign.

de Polícia Pacificadora: UPP).[7] These programs represent the two main ways state governments perceive favelas, through the themes of poverty and violence. The first creates a focus on urban infrastructure and corresponding "social" policies. The second sparked a new security policy.

In discussing the construction of favelas as a statistical reality, I show one aspect of their production as localities where order must be established. Considering that the statistical reality is the main device used in the planning and implementation of state actions, examining its construction entails analyzing the technical and moral foundations of the government of spaces and persons. Nevertheless, this process is not pacific, but involves various kinds of oppositions.

FROM THE FAVELA TO THE SUBNORMAL AGGLOMERATE: POVERTY AS A SPATIALIZED REALITY

In this section I analyze the uses of the categories *favela* and *subnormal agglomerate* in IBGE documents relating to three censuses: the 1950 census, the first to "see" favelas; the 1991 census, the first to use the term "subnormal agglomerate"; and the most recent census, conducted in 2010.

The 1950 census was the first national survey to include the population of favelas. The IBGE prepared a specific document analyzing the information collected in these locations, in which it identifies the difficulties involved in collecting and classifying the data:

> In the favelas, the building-household survey generally proceeded in the same way as in other areas, but entailed different kinds of tasks that required additional efforts to be achieved. The terrain to be covered is not always easy to access, indeed it often demands hard work for the surveyor to gather data for the entire area. (IBGE 1953: 18)

---

7. The UPPs were a program of the Rio de Janeiro state government to which the Military Police are subordinated. The declared objective was to enable close-range community policing as a strategy to contain armed conflicts in the favelas. For some time, in most of the favelas where they were installed, the UPPs led to an effective reduction in gun battles, but gun battles have returned to being near daily occurrences. About the uses of the category of "pacification" in different historical moments in Brazil, see Oliveira (2014).

The document also highlights the difficulties in proposing an objective definition. The IBGE's approach was based, therefore, on places considered favelas by
"social consensus." Based on this research, the institute proposed the following
definition for these spaces:

Hence, included in the conceptualization of favela were human agglomerates that possess, totally or partially, the following characteristics:

> 1. *Minimal proportions*—Groups of buildings or residences formed by units gen-
> erally numbering higher than 50; 2. *Type of habitation*—Predominance in the
> grouping of small houses or shacks, rustic in type, constructed primarily from
> tin or zinc sheeting, planks or similar materials; 3. *Legal status of occupation*—
> Unlicensed and unsupervised constructions on lands belonging to third-parties
> or of unknown ownership; 4. *Public improvements*—Absence, either entirely or
> partially, of a sewerage system, electricity, telephones and piped water; 5. *Urbani-
> zation*—Non-urbanized area without street paving, numbers or signs. (IBGE
> 1953: 18)

This definition presumes the concrete existence of the favela as a real phenomenon, which can be technically and objectively characterized through data collection and field observations.

In 1991 IBGE included the category "subnormal agglomerate" in the census
as a type of "census sector."[8] Both categories are referred to as "operational." In
other words, they are used in the data collection phase rather than the logical
and analytic organization of the information. A census sector is an area defined
by the capacity of a single census worker to carry out all the activities related to
data collection within a certain time interval. The definition of the subnormal
agglomerate is as follows:

> The special sector defined as a subnormal agglomerate is a group composed of
> at least 51 (fifty-one) residential units (shacks, houses . . .) most of which lack
> basic public services, and occupy or had occupied, until recently land belonging

---

8.   "The census sector is the territorial unit established for the purposes of registration
     control, formed by a continuous area, situated in a single urban or rural block, with
     a size and number of domiciles that enables its survey by a census officer. Hence,
     each official will proceed to collect information with the aim of covering the census
     sector designated to him or her" (IBGE 2010 Census Guide: http://censo2010.
     ibge.gov.br/materiais/guia-do-censo/operacao-censitaria.html).

to a third party (public or private) and generally built in a disordered and dense layout. Subnormal Agglomerates should be identified on the basis of the following criteria: a) Illegal occupation of land, i.e. construction on land belonging to a third party (public or private) either currently or recently (acquisition of the land deed in the past ten years); and b) Possession of at least one of the following characteristics: urbanization not complying with existing standards—reflected by narrow roads built in an irregular layout, plots of unequal sizes and shapes, and constructions built without permission from public authorities; and precarious basic public services. (IBGE 2011: 27)

The definition of the subnormal agglomerate is clearly based on the definition of the favela from the 1950s. Both highlight the lack of urbanization and an illegal land ownership system.[9] The difference between them is that the older expression concerns the posterior description of a reality external to the statistics. In the second case the category refers to a kind of place whose characteristics generate difficulties for data collection.

Subnormal agglomerates, along with other spaces like indigenous villages and prisons, for example, were defined as units linked to a supposed difficulty of collecting information in the field.[10] They shape a kind of practical and quotidian resistance to the work of the researchers.

Since 2010, when the last national census was conducted, the category became considered a unit of analysis and not just an operational category. As part of the results of its survey, IBGE published a specific document on subnormal agglomerates, which contains maps and tables, aggregated by state and region. There was a change in reference to the spatial units to which the term refers: a

---

9.　The relation between the categories is revealed by more than a logical perspective. The internal code used for the subnormal agglomerate in the documents completed by the researchers is "FAV" (IBGE 2010 Census Guide: http://censo2010.ibge.gov. br/materiais/guia-do-censo/operacao-censitaria.html).

10.　The "subnormal agglomerate special sector" is one of the types of "special sector," defined as an area "that presents characteristics that make it necessary to adopt a different approach to collection compared to the common or non-special sectors." The other special sectors are: "Military Barracks and Bases Special Sector," "Lodging and Encampments Special Sector," "Vessels, Boats and Ships Special Sector," "Indigenous Village Special Sector," "Penitentiaries, Penal Colonies and Jails Special Sector," and "Asylums, Orphanages, Convents and Hospitals Special Sector" (IBGE 2003: 228–29).

subnormal agglomerate, named after the ordinary name of the region, can be composed of various census sectors.[11]

These statistical framings try to make the *mensuration* of favelas a routine practice—data collection—placing it within the overall set of census units and categories. Beginning with a shared definition of the favela, the first form of incorporation is the result of an exploratory field trip by IBGE experts, based on an attempt to define favelas in technical terms. As an operational category, the subnormal agglomerate represents an expansion of the notion of favela through a shift away from the specificity of Rio de Janeiro that points to the specific difficulty of carrying out such surveys.

In 2010, the category was transformed from a purely operational category into a particular type of unit of analysis that violates the standard rule and more common way to conceive territorial units, which usually involves a successive aggregation in increasingly broader units that correspond to the sum, and only the sum, of a defined quantity of elements of the immediately preceding type. For example: a number of domiciles compose a census sector, a number of census sectors compose a neighborhood, and so on up to the level of municipalities that compose states, and the twenty-seven states that compose the country. This means that the units are more commonly considered as continuous spaces. In contrast to this procedure, presenting the population data for subnormal agglomerates per state, for instance, implies considering these places as the same significant *type* of space—which is also understood as an aggregate of persons— whose identity allows (or forces) us to go beyond the logic of successive encompassment of contiguous spatial units.

These three forms of framing reveal the favela's persistent resistance to quantification, considering the changing attempts to deal with them over time. They also reveal a progressive normalization through an abnormalizing typification. The idea of the favela is expanded and objectified to apply beyond the reality of Rio de Janeiro and is presented as a recurrent—and in this sense normal—form at the same time as it becomes an increasingly abstract category of abnormality, capable of encompassing an ever-larger number of cases.

---

11. Among the various platforms created by IBGE for publication of the 2010 Census Data is a specific web application for subnormal agglomerates. Visitors can use this application to search by state, city, and "name of the agglomerate" and access the information collected for each of the census sectors included in the agglomerate: see http://www.censo2010.ibge.gov.br/agsn/.

The category of subnormal agglomerate generalizes the idea of favela, maintaining their association with poverty and occupation of urban landscapes. Two characteristics were transposed from the common category of favela that IBGE transformed into an object of systematic inquiry between the 1950 and 2010 censuses. The first is a disorganized layout of the houses, roads, and paths, while the second is illegitimate occupation of land, presuming the construction and occupation of spaces that belong to other people or entities without their consent.

This statistical generalization of the favela as the spatialization of poverty is present in an IBGE document from 1953 and in analyses derived from the census. The citation below comes from the introduction to the data. It presents the technical principles and possibilities for interpreting data in time and space, making special reference to the limits to its generalization.

> Thus, the results presented in the tables in annex cannot be taken to refer to the entire favela population of the Federal District. They concern only the population present—including the inhabitants present on July 1, 1950, residents or otherwise—in the favelas listed in Box 7 and who represent, according to estimates, 90% of the total inhabitants of Rio's favelas, commonly recognized as such. (IBGE 1953: 16)

Another passage found in the document's "Final Considerations" points to a different kind of logical operation:

> What these results reveal above all is a snapshot of the life of poor populations in general, disseminated across all regions of the country and whose essential aspects probably do not vary much. This snapshot is useful, therefore, as a sample that indicates fundamental aspects of a socially defined portion of Brazil's population, providing an opportunity for productive research on the behavior of specific economically homogenous social groups, assembled, under specific conditions, in densely populated agglomerates. (IBGE 1953: 23)

Spatialized and "favelaized" through the category of "subnormal agglomerate," poverty is only considered indirectly as a lack of money through the inference that people living in these spaces are poor. What stands out is a certain kind of usurpation involved in defining the predominant form of land occupation as illegitimate or illegal. This association is a sign of the overlapping of the two meanings of normality mentioned in the introduction to this chapter and examined by Hacking (1990). Favelas and their practical resistance to measurement, because of their physical and urbanistic characteristics, serve as an abnormalizing and (im)moralizing modelization of poverty.

THE "DOMICILE" AS STABILIZATION OF PEOPLE AND HOUSES

The statistical reality of the population is determined by the establishment of fixed contacts. Exclusive relations need to be established between spaces and between them and people. The first stabilization operated by this kind of quantification, both in terms of data collection and in the construction of the logical framework for interpreting the data, is the association between persons and spaces through the idea of a residence and the management of resources for maintaining collective life. The category "domicile" defines the unit of data production—questionnaires are completed for each domicile—and represents the first form of aggregation of information about individuals, who, combined, form a "population." The successive forms of data aggregation—based on increasingly broader spatial categories—set out from the definition of each person's exclusive belonging to one, and just one, specific spatial and economic unit.

The favela, with its mutable houses, its intense and apparently disorganized circulation along narrow streets and alleys, and its family practices uncontained by the normative boundaries of organization in nuclear families, resists the stabilization required by the categories of the population census. What Pedro Abramo calls "urbanistic freedom" (2003)—that is, the loose or nonexistent relationship to state regulations concerning buildings and urban organization— makes the associations between built units and persons difficult to establish. Movement in the favela resists the stabilization required by the standards used by demographic statistics.

IBGE's definition of the domicile is the following:

> A structurally *separate and independent* place of residence, constituted by one or more rooms. Separation is characterized when the place of residence is delimited by walls, fences, etc., covered by a roof, *allowing the residents to isolate themselves, assuming responsibility for part or all of the food or residential expenses.*

Independence is characterized when direct access to the place of residence exists, allowing residents to *enter and leave without passing through the place of residence of other persons.* Domiciles are classified as private or collective. (IBGE n.d.: 16; my emphasis)

The notion of domicile operates in the first phase in the creation of a population. It links several individuals with a territory, based on their "isolation" and the management of the resources needed for "food and residence." It also encompasses the concept of "family," the ideal configuration of this set of individuals. One of the classifications of domiciles refers precisely to the family status of their residents. The domicile, therefore, contains relations between individuals, the domestic economy, family, and built spaces.

The relation with the idea of family is important in the definition of a concept that has acquired a central role in the discussion of public policies in Brazil, which is the so-called housing shortage. The calculation of the size of this shortage includes the number of "families" who live in the street, though the largest contingent refers to those who live in "inadequate" places, or share a space with other families. The ideal that one family, and no more than one, should correspond to one domicile plays a strong role in the form in which large-scale policies are designed, executed, and evaluated.

Through my ethnography in a community in the group of favelas known as the Complexo do Alemão, I show how these elements appear as part of the houses as they are actually lived in. While in a domicile relations are exclusive and the units discrete and stable, in the houses I have observed these relations are typified by constant transformation, instability, disjuncture, and movement. This discussion is inserted within the broader agenda of a new anthropology of the house (Cortado 2016). I shall quickly highlight three approaches that have been inspirational to my analysis. The first concerns what is typically labeled material culture, which I incorporate through an emphasis on the participation of constructed spaces, objects, and substances as vital dimension of social relations (Miller 2001; Buchli 2013; Appadurai 1986). The second approach is that of the so-called new kinship studies, which have suggested exploring the house in its multiple dimensions as the privileged locus and institution for the construction of family ties (Marcelin 1996, 1999; Carsten 2004). Its basis in subversive readings of the idea of *maison* developed by Claude Lévi-Strauss (1982, 1984, 1987, 1991) challenge normativity and the search for explanatory models, by radicalizing his proposal to take the native concept of the house as a starting point for building a new analytic foundation for kinship (Carsten and Hugh-Jones 1995). The third essential reference point are studies by Brazilian anthropologists that introduced a new approach to sociological and political questions central to the tradition of social thought, and that focus on economic relations, labor relations, and domination in Brazil (Heredia 1979; Palmeira 1977; Garcia Jr. 1975; Woortmann 1980).

Based on these three approaches, I propose an anthropology of the house that contemplates specific variations of some of the issues examined by these authors. The first is the attention paid to the *everyday economy*—that is, people's ordinary economic practices, setting out from a radically ethnographic approach, which means taking them not just to be immersed, as they of course are, in relations of family, friendship, and politics, for example, but considering these relations as a fundamental and inseparable aspect of these economic practices and vice versa. The second focuses on *forms of government* (Neiburg 2014; De L'Estoile 2014), specifically in relation to the debate on the construction of favelas as a problem and poverty and violence as realities in response to which it is necessary to act, but also to understand the ways in which houses are formed through daily life in favelas.

An anthropology of the house thus allows the comprehension of houses as a quotidian process, without failing to consider the various other agencies that participate in their construction in addition to those of residents, including the agency of state governments. By analytically placing the two conceptualizations of the house side by side—the statistical reality as a domicile and the reality of the way favela residents live in houses—my aim is to show the crucial importance of reciprocal resistances, dissonance and disjuncture.

The houses that I observed in my fieldwork are indissociably physical and symbolic constructions around which much of social life takes place. They are a place of care, where bodies and gendered persons are formed. People invest large financial and emotional resources in houses, such that their trajectories, relations, and prospects for the future are intrinsically linked to them. Houses are also constantly transforming, both physically and in people's imagination. They are constituted by and through movements of everyday life, and I specifically focused on three that dialogue directly with the foundations of the conception of the domicile as a statistical reality (Motta 2014).

Figure 2: Houses in Complexo do Alemão, 2014. Photo by the author.

One of the things that circulates most frequently between and within houses is money. There is a native expression for a specific form of separating and marking types of money; "house money." In practice, this money is defined by its source and the subsequent use made of it. It is usually composed of regular income from work, such as wages, or some kind of business. This revenue is used to cover expenses for household maintenance, including cooking gas, electricity, cable TV, internet access, cleaning materials, and food. But these expenses do not refer to a discrete unit: they also maintain a house's relations with other houses. This becomes clear when we observe the purchase of food, which is commonly used to prepare meals for many other people in addition to those considered residents of the domicile.[12] Children tend to be the most mobile between houses. For instance, in one of the families that I observed the children ate meals in their grandparents' houses during the week.

---

12. In this specific ethnographic context, "living" in a house is defined as having a place to sleep every day and store clothes or other belongings deemed to be linked to specific persons.

Loans and presents in the form of money are also common between houses. In most situations, they are considered obligations between persons who perceive themselves to be connected by family ties. Various authors have demonstrated the importance of food, substances, and their circulations in the construction of these relations (Carsten 2004). In the social universe that I observed, money is also an important means of making and sustaining ties (Zelizer 2005). House money is money that makes family.

The parents of young women who become pregnant, for instance, feel obliged to build a house for their daughter. This relation of origin between houses resides at the base of a hierarchical organization composed of moralities that transforms over time, but always involves specific forms of monetary circulation. What is thus in play in the houses as they are actually lived are not *discrete reference units*, as the statistical reality of the domicile presumes. These houses are constituted not through isolation but through relations, forming a *configuration of houses*.

Louis Herns Marcelin (1996, 1999) uses this notion to describe arrangements composed of various houses and their importance in the relations expressed through the language of kinship among black families in the Recôncavo region of Bahia state. The physical proximity between the houses in this ethnographic universe suggests that they comprise sufficiently self-evident units for the author to be able to identify the precise number of houses belonging to a given configuration. However, in the favela where I conducted field research, houses related within a configuration are not necessarily located close to one another. This is primarily due to the intense movement of persons between houses during the course of their lives; people move frequently between houses within the same favela.

Physical distances are an important issue in the configurations of houses insofar as they are practical conditions that influence the forms of everyday circulation of persons, substances, and objects. But differently than what Marcelin observed in Bahia or Flavia Dalmaso in Haiti (2014), spatial contiguity is not a necessary characteristic of house configurations in the favela. These facts led me back to the concept of configuration developed by Norbert Elias (1980) as a means of reworking the concept formulated by Marcelin. These arrangements are not isolated units, they are visible through the circulations between the relatively autonomous elements that constitute them. The relations between them are not symmetric: in fact, there is a marked hierarchy between the houses, related to the ties of interdependence between them. These ties, for their part, are not completely stable, such that every configuration an arrangement in constant movement that involves tensions.

The physical houses are also in constant movement: they are mutable. In addition to the successive annexation of new rooms when resources permit, houses can be transformed, for example, into business spaces. A living room can be turned into a hairdressing salon, later into a clothes store, and then back into a living room, as I observed in one case. This specific kind of mutability is central to money-earning strategies among the people with whom I conducted field research. The convertibility of house spaces also increases the value of the property on the favela's real estate market. Not even in terms of what may at first appear to be its most static aspect—its physical dimension—are houses stable.

The plasticity of houses and the intense mobility of people and things are related to forms of regulation *of* and *in* these places, which allow a significant constructive freedom and create a highly dynamic housing market. These places thus contrapose the stability and immobility needed to define statistical realities in various stages of production of numbers: from data collection in the field to the possible interpretation of population statistics in general.

THE FAVELA THAT COUNTS ITSELF

In this section I examine another kind of resistance made explicit by particular subjects: the questioning of census numbers. The resistance to quantification is specifically directed toward official statistical data and is transformed into an initiative for constructing alternative numbers. As I shall show, this explicit resistance to agreement on the figures expresses the ambiguity commonly related to public numbers, which, rather than invalidating them, strengthens them as a legitimate and common language in the dispute for public representation and government resources.

I began to frequent the Complexo do Alemão in 2012. IBGE had just released the first data from the Census conducted in 2010. According to the institute, the population of the region was around 69,000 inhabitants.[13] I do not know precisely how people came to know about this figure, but it was a frequent

---

13. A difference exists between the number of inhabitants of the Complexo do Alemão recognized by different state agencies, even when based on the same census data. This is because the "Complexo do Alemão" is, formally speaking, an "administrative region," a territorial unit defined for the purposes of management of municipal public policies. In this unit, some areas are considered "subnormal agglomerates" by the IBGE and others are not.

topic in talks with my interlocutors for weeks. I overheard conversations in bars and various people approached me, presuming my interest in the data, to tell me that the information was untrue. Some people knew the exact figures published by the IBGE. All the contestations that I heard ran along the same lines. They affirmed that "in reality" the number of residents was much higher. The data released by IBGE, especially the number of residents attributed to the Complexo do Alemão, was an important issue for many residents, including activists from local organizations, and many others.

People cited as evidence of the false data the fact that they themselves, and many others who they knew, had not been "counted." They alleged that the census officers may have omitted or lied about data because they were afraid to venture far into the favela, or were incapable of identifying the many residences invisible from the street. Almost always, other estimates would follow, ranging from 100,000 to as many as 200,000 inhabitants.

Maré is another huge cluster of favelas, not far from the Complexo do Alemão, built on flat land across most of its territory. It was in this locality that the first "self-census" initiative took place. It began in 1999 and became consolidated through a project organized by the Maré Study and Solidary Action Centre (CEASM) (Silva 2002). A second Maré Census was undertaken in 2011, through the initiative of other organizations, namely Redes da Maré (Maré Networks) and the Observatório de Favelas (Favela Observatory). In addition to the population count, the base maps for the region were updated (Observatório de Favelas and Redes da Maré 2012) and an Enterprise Census conducted, to survey businesses and the jobs they generated.

The justifications for the need to mobilize residents and local organizations to collect the data focused on two types of arguments: the inability of the IBGE information to account for the specificities of the region, the real needs of the residents, and the form in which the stigmatization, prejudice, and ignorance of researchers foreign to the community impede well-conducted research. According to a more formal criticism:

> Innumerable methodological distortions still persist in the surveys carried out in favelas. Most derive from the imprecision of the base maps, but it is also impossible to ignore the existence of biases arising from judgments about the favela whose impacts range from planning for the research to how interviews are conducted, such as the construction of marginalizing premises that hinder or prevent approaching the public. The process of stigmatization is one of the

innumerable historical effects of how favelas have been conceived and represented, since their appearance, in different fields of the social imaginary.[14]

This resistance discursively mobilizes two others that I mentioned earlier in this chapter: the association between spatial disorder, poverty, and movement and the illegitimate appropriation of spaces. On this basis, the organizations in Maré construct political and moral arguments to justify the effort to create new statistics.

Although the critique of official statistics may have been severe at times, the production of the Maré Census involved the participation of various government agencies. The National School of Statistical Sciences (ENCE), which is part of IBGE, and the Pereira Passos Institute (IPP) run by the Rio de Janeiro City Council, are cited as "partners" in the project, which was funded through a grant from the Banco do Brasil Foundation.

The relation with these agencies is a sign of something that traverses the dynamics of criticism and the production of alternative data: namely, the ambiguity between recognition of the relevance and real existence of the realities of statistics, combined with a permanent distrust toward them. Above all, it is widely understood that statistics portray reality as perceived by state agents and that, therefore, it is necessary to dispute them. As one activist from the Complexo do Alemão, who considers the population of the locality much higher than the number obtained by the census, affirmed: "A lower population, less investment."[15]

While on one hand the objective of the self-censuses was to adapt the methodology to local specificities, there was also another movement. In 2010, the research team from the Maré Census covered the entire area and, in addition to correcting the official maps that were outdated, proposed that residents organize themselves to name streets that did not have one. The mapping, therefore, is a reciprocal process of transformation between statistical reality and everyday reality.

Quantification and the kind of order that it implies are not only state supported normative ideals that "abnormalize" resistances. The Maré Census shows

14. http://www.fbb.org.br/tecnologiasocial/banco-de-tecnologias-sociais/pesquisar-tecnologias/detalhar-tecnologia-356.htm.

15. Lucia Cabral, from the NGO Educap, cited at: http://vivafavela.com.br/449-censo-nas-favelas-e-controverso/.

that the elaboration of a statistical reality can be a form of moral and political valorization of the favela that occurs by combining the order and rigor of data collection with the practices of activism—as an object of political struggle[16]—and the way residents experience spaces. One example of this process is the naming of streets.

FINAL CONSIDERATIONS: REALITIES THAT COUNT

Before my fieldwork in favelas, for two years during my doctoral research I accompanied the everyday practices involved in constructing a statistical information system. Following the creation of the National Solidarity Economy Office in 2003, it was necessary to produce statistics that could serve as a basis for policies in the region. The concept of the "solidarity economy" was not part of the vocabulary of national public administration at the time. It was necessary to create the reality that would be the object of intervention. The process took years, hundreds of meetings, accusations and fights over how to produce this information. The argument of most those involved was that it would be impossible to quantify the solidarity economy and, worse still, such quantification would be a violent reductionism that would put at risk its most characteristic aspects. I was apprehensive at the launching of the publication produced to disseminate the first data from the statistical study that was eventually produced. Several of the staunchest opponents of the so-called mapping were at the ceremony. One of them was on the event round table and spoke to the audience in a packed auditorium. He began his speech with the document in hand, shaking it in the direction of the public, and said: "Here it is! Now we exist!" (Motta 2010).

An ethnographic approach to the production of statistics provides intelligibility to the apparent paradox that appears in the episode described above. Recognizing that different agents, practices, and concepts are involved in the production and use of large numbers makes their processual dimension and

16. "Many citizens do not recognize the favelas as an integrated part of the city. Nonetheless, to overcome the invisibility of a place, its residents also need to recognize and valorize their belonging to it. The Maré Census is above all a means for discussing the reasons why favelas are stigmatized and basic rights neglected there."
http://www.fbb.org.br/tecnologiasocial/banco-de-tecnologias-sociais/pesquisar-tecnologias/detalhar-tecnologia-356.htm.

complexity visible. Controversies, conflicts, difficulties—which I have treated here as "resistances"—emerge through this perspective and prove to be highly revealing.

The difficulties involved in collecting data, classifying a certain kind of space, and generating trust in numbers are all interrelated. This becomes clear when the urban morphological characteristics of the favelas justify classifying them as spaces where information collection is difficult, about which it is difficult to produce statistical data. In a space that is constantly mutating, the stabilizations needed for the production of populational statistics are more complicated. These issues are recognized to be problematic by technical staff and managers, who seek to produce better numbers, and also by residents, who seek recognition of local specificities and responses to their political demands.

This is another reason why the idea of resistance seems suited to analyzing different social dynamics. It allows us to discern the relations between practical and logical operations of the quantification process. The idea of a "chain of transformations" advanced by Laurent Thévenot (1995) is extremely useful because it emphasizes the different operations and types of investments needed to produce numbers. The perspective proposed here, however, questions the linearity presumed by the image of a "chain." The resistances make evident the reciprocal and continuous relations between the procedures involved in producing statistics.

Thinking about statistics implies thinking about the state government and its forms of agency. Through them and the studies of the tense relations involved in the production of statistical realities, the processual and distributed character of forms of government reveal themselves. These state categories are not ready-made instruments for imposing a centralized power, but the outcomes, always provisional, of negotiations between various agencies. The favela as a statistical reality participates reciprocally in the construction of these spaces as lived realities and urban realities, insofar as they serve as a basis for the production of diagnoses and solutions to problems that always need to be quantified.

In this chapter I have explored the possibility of bringing together different logics and scales of analysis. By identifying the transformation of the idea of the favela in Brazil's demographic censuses and the fundamental place of the concept of stabilization based on domiciles, I sought to show that the forms in which people construct and live in houses are interconnected, relevant, and subject to the action and concern not only of residents. Based on the analytic strategies presented here, I explore the relation between issues that are commonly examined separately: domestic and family life, public policies, political disputes for recognition, numbers, and elaboration of the statistical realities.

The processes for producing public numbers, resistances, negotiations, and incorporations unfold around the forms of classifying and framing people, spaces, and relations. Examining these quantifications, therefore, involves examining the dynamics involved in the definition of the realities that are relevant, and suitable for discussion and dispute, and thus what are the realities that count.

REFERENCES

Abramo, Pedro. 2003. "A teoria econômica da favela: quatro notas sobre a localização
residencial dos pobres e o mercado imobiliário informal." In *A cidade da informalidade: o desafio das cidades Latino-Americanas*, organized by Pedro Abramo, 189–224. Rio de Janeiro: Sette Letras.
Appadurai, Arjun. 1986. *The social life of things: Commodities in cultural perspective*. Cambridge: Cambridge University Press.
Buchli, Victor. 2013. *Anthropology of architecture*. New York: Bloomsbury.
Burgos, Marcelo. 1998. "Dos Parques Proletários ao Favela-Bairro." In *Um século de favela*, edited by Alba Zaluar and Marcos Alvito, 25–60. Rio de Janeiro: FGV Editora.
Carsten, Janet, and Stephen Hugh-Jones. 1995. "Introduction." In *About the house:* Lévi-Strauss and beyond, edited by Janet Carsten and Stephen Hugh-Jones, 1–46. Cambridge: Cambridge University Press.
———. 2004. *After kinship*. Cambridge: Cambridge University Press.
Cavallieri, Fernando, and Adriana Vial. 2012. Favelas na cidade do Rio de Janeiro: o quadro populacional com base no Censo 2010. Rio de Janeiro: Instituto Pereira Passos. http://portalgeo.rio.rj.gov.br/estudoscariocas/download%5C3190_FavelasnacidadedoRiodeJaneiro_Censo_2010.PDF.
Cohn, Bernard. 1996. *Colonialism and its forms of knowledge: The British in India*. Princeton, NJ: Princeton University Press.
Cortado, Thomas. 2016. "Houses made out of eyes: An ethnography of brick walls at the urban fringe of Rio de Janeiro." Paper presented in the European Anthropological Association Meeting, Milan.
Dalmaso, Flavia. 2014. "Kijan moun yo ye? As pessoas, as casas e as dinâmicas familiares em Jacmel/Haiti." PhD diss., PPGAS / Museu Nacional / UFRJ.

De L'Estoile, B. 2014. "'Money is good, but a friend is better': Uncertainty, orientation to the future, and 'the economy.'" *Current Anthropology* 55 (S9): S62–S73. https://doi.org/10.1086/676068.

Desrosières, Alain. 1993. *La politique des grandes nombres*. Paris: Éditions Découverte.

Desrosières, Alain, and Sandrine Kott. 2005. "Quantifier." *Genèses* 58 (1): 2–3.

Elias, Norbert. 1980. *Introdução à sociologia*. Braga: Edições 70.

Garcia, Afrânio Raul, Jr. 1975. "Terra de trabalho." MA thesis, PPGAS/ Museu Nacional/ UFRJ.

Hacking, Ian. 1990. *The taming of chance*. Cambridge: Cambridge University Press.

Heredia, Beatriz. 1979. *A morada da vida*. Rio de Janeiro: Paz e Terra.

IBGE. 1953. *As favelas do Distrito Federal e o Censo Demográfico de 1950*. Rio de Janeiro: Mimeo.

———. 2003. *Metodologia do Censo Demográfico 2000*. Rio de Janeiro: IBGE.

———. 2011. *Censo Demográfico 2010. Aglomerados Subnormais. Primeiros resultados*. Rio de Janeiro: IBGE.

———. n/d. *Glossário PNAD*. IBGE. http://www.ibge.gov.br/home/estatistica/populacao/trabalhoerendimento/glossario_PNAD.pdf.

Lévi-Strauss, Claude. 1982. *The way of the masks*. London: Jonathan Cape.

———. 1984. *Paroles données*. Paris: Plon.

———. 1987. *Anthropology and myth: Lectures 1951–1982*. Oxford: Blackwell.

———. 1991. "Maison." In *Dictionnaire de l'ethnologie et de l'anthropologie*, edited by Pierre Bonté and Michel Izard, 434–36. Paris: PUF.

Machado da Silva, Luiz Antonio. 2002. "A continuidade do 'problema da favela.'" In *Cidade: história e desafios*, edited by Oliveira, Lúcia Lippi, 220–37. Rio de Janeiro: Editora FGV/CNPq.

———. 2010. "'Violência urbana,' segurança pública e favelas: o caso do Rio de Janeiro atual." *Caderno CRH* 23 (59): 283–300.

Marcelin, Louis Herns. 1996. "A invenção da família afro-americana: família, parentesco e domesticidade entre os negros do Recôncavo da Bahia, Brasil." PhD diss., PPGAS / Museu Nacional / UFRJ.

———. 1999. "A linguagem da casa entre os negros no Recôncavo Baiano." *Mana* 5 (2): 31–60. https://dx.doi.org/10.1590/S0104-93131999000200002.

Miller, Daniel. 2001. "Behind closed doors." In *Home possessions: Material culture behind closed doors*, edited by Daniel Miller, Daniel, 1–9. Oxford: Berg.

Misse, Michel. 2002. "Rio como um bazar: a conversão da ilegalidade em mercadoria política." *Insight Inteligência* 3 (5): 12–16.

———. 2007. "Mercados ilegais, redes de proteção e organização local do crime no Rio de Janeiro." *Revista Estudos Avançados* 21 (61): 139–57.

Mitchell, Timothy. 2002. *Rule of experts: Egypt, techno-politics, modernity.* Berkley: University of California Press.

Motta, Eugênia. 2010. "Trajetórias e transformações no mundo da Economia Solidária." PhD diss., PPGAS / UFRJ, Rio de Janeiro.

———. 2014. "Houses and economy in the favela." In *Vibrant – Virtual Brazilian Anthropology* 11, no. 1 (January–June). http://dx.doi.org/10.1590/S1809-43412014000100005.

———. 2019. "Resistência aos números. A favela como realidade (in)quantificável." In *Mana* 25, no. 1 (January–April). http://dx.doi.org/10.1590/1678-49442019v25n1p072.

Neiburg, Federico. 2011. "La guerre des indices. L'inflation au Brésil (1964–1994)." *Gèneses* 84 (3): 25–46.

———. 2014. "Questionando o Social 'Foucault em chave etnográfica: o governo dos guèto de Porto Príncipe.'" *Análise Social* 212 (49): 742–47.

Observatório de Favelas, and Redes da Maré. 2012. *Guia de Ruas: Maré.* Rio de Janeiro: Observatório das Favelas e Redes de Desenvolvimento da Maré.

Oliveira, João Pacheco de. 2014. "Pacificação e tutela militar na gestão de populações e territórios." *Mana* 20 (1): 125–61. https://dx.doi.org/10.1590/S0104-93132014000100005.

Palmeira, Moacir. 1977. "Casa e trabalho: notas sobre as relações sociais na 'plantation' tradicional." *Contraponto* 2 (2): 103–14.

Porter, Theodore. 1994. "Making things quantitative." *Science in Context* 7: 389–407.

———. 1995. *Trust in numbers: The pursuit of objectivity in science and public life.* Princeton, NJ: Princeton University Press.

Scott, James C. 1985. Weapons of the weak: Everyday forms of resistance. New Haven, CT: Yale University Press.

Silva, Eliana Souza. 2002. "Censo Maré 2000: Uma experiência de coleta e geração de informações sócio-culturais e econômicas numa favela da cidade do Rio de Janeiro." *Rio de Janeiro: Trabalho e Sociedade* 2 (3): 15–20.

Thévenot, Laurent. 1995. "Cifras que falam: medida estatística e juízo comum." In *A ilusão das estatísticas*, edited by Jean Luc Besson, 149–61. São Paulo: UNESP.

Valladares, Lícia. 2000. "A gênese da favela carioca—A produção anterior às ciências sociais." *Revista Brasileira de Ciências Sociais* 15 (44): 5–34.

———. 2005. *A invenção da favela: Do mito de origem a favela.com.* Rio de Janeiro: FGV.

Woortmann, Klaas. 1980. "Casa e família operária." *Anuário Antropológico* 80: 119–50.

Zelizer, Viviana. 2005. *The purchase of intimacy.* Princeton, NJ: Princeton University Press.

CHAPTER FOUR

What is a 'real' transaction in high-frequency trading

Juan Pablo Pardo-Guerra

Past the turnstiles and security guards, walking into a stock exchange today is much like walking into the administrative offices of most other modern organizations: greeted by sleek concrete, polished steel, and heavy architectural glass, visitors encounter areas peppered with conference tables, personal workstations, and communal sites for refreshments. One space is conspicuous for its absence: the trading floors where markets were once made in quick glances, jostling bodies, calculated voices, and the cacophony of crowds. Bar a few exceptions, these spaces have mostly disappeared. To observe the sites of feverish market activity (Simmel 2004) where millions of financial instruments are traded every day you need to look further afield, to the data processing centers where stock exchanges host their digital marketplaces. Resembling minimalist warehouses occupied by neatly organized rows of computer servers, these are the places where markets come to life, not through conversations and the density of social interactions but through the varying electronic signals received and processed by the automated stock exchange.

The computer servers and sophisticated communications networks of stock exchanges are subjects of various arguments about the "realism" of financial capitalism. This is clear, for example, in recent debates about high frequency trading, a series of practices that hinge on the use of computers, network configurations, and speed to exploit minute arbitrage opportunities in the electronic trading platforms that structure stock and foreign exchange markets (Chordia et al. 2013). High frequency trading, wrote the leading broker Charles Schwab in a statement in 2014, is "an explosion of *head-fake* ephemeral orders—not to lock in *real* trades, but to skim pennies off the public markets by the billions" (Russolillo 2014). The firms participating in these activities, noted Peter Henning (2014) of the *New York Times*, have "no *real interest* in the underlying value of the companies whose shares they trade." These critiques are underpinned by a fundamentalist conception of stocks as contracts that represent a materially valuable stake in a public corporation. A stock's price is supposed to reflect the value of its associated firm or a future-oriented judgement of its strategic actions. Yet when stocks are traded thousands of times every minute, the connection between price and value becomes less tenable. What does it mean, ask fund managers and other institutional investors, that high frequency traders own financial instruments for only fractions of a second?

This chapter focuses on one aspect of the realism of electronic, automated stock markets: it probes controversies about whether specific forms of market transactions are "real" or "fictitious." Specifically, it looks into debates surrounding a set of contested trades known as "spoofing" that involve creating intentions to buy or sell stocks with the objective of manipulating prices and other market participants. An exploration of how spoofing is constructed as a false transaction implies uncovering some of the "performances of reality" (Mol 1999) that constitute legitimacy and a collective sense of taken-for-grantedness in the worlds of automated finance. As data packages traveling through computer networks, spoofs and "true" trades are physically and computationally indistinguishable. What matters, then, are the mechanisms through which actors come to see transactions not only as legal or illegal, legitimate or illegitimate, moral or immoral, personal or impersonal, but more fundamentally as being real against the possibility of being fictitious.

To make sense of these performances, I turn to one of the key infrastructures of modern stock exchanges: the electronic limit order book, a computational list that captures and matches the orders to trade received by anonymous investors from across the world. In this chapter I argue that the "performances of reality" of automated trading involve a combination of knowledge about the market (such as market microstructure theory) and infrastructures of trading (such as the electronic limit order book) constituting the distributions of knowledge that make the actions of traders intelligible (Barnes 1988). What matters in the marketplace, surely, is not whether a transaction is real "in actuality" but rather the conditions under which participants come to evaluate it as such. The "regimes of truth" (Foucault 2012) governing electronic transactions are performed as much by the power of regulators, lawyers, and economists, as by the affordances, constraints, and possibilities of the material mechanisms that enable trades in the marketplace.

This chapter is organized as follows. In the next section, I introduce the empirical context that makes spoofing possible by overviewing the operation of electronic limit order books and their connection to automated trading. This is followed by a brief theoretical discussion that highlights how infrastructures, market relations, and knowledge configure performances of reality in finance. I then explore an example of how spoofing in an automated market setting was contested in the courts to then compare this to similar instances of price manipulation in face-to-face exchanges. This is followed by some concluding thoughts.

INSIDE THE MACHINE

Electronic limit order books are a fundamental technology of contemporary financial markets. Introduced at the margins of stock trading in the early 1970s, they became dominant exemplars of exchanges and other regulated trading platforms by the late 1990s (Castelle et al. 2016; Pardo-Guerra 2019; Gorham and Singh 2009). Order books are simple devices: they act as centralized lists that record the intentions to trade of investors and allow either a human or a machine to "match" compatible trades (or what economist William Stanley Jevons once referred to as the "double coincidence of wants"; Jevons 1879). Consider, for example, the order book for Apple Inc. on the electronic exchange BATS Global Markets (see fig. 1; BATS is now operated by the Chicago Board of Options Exchange). At any given moment in time, multiple investors might have slightly different valuations of Apple's stock. Some might think that shares of Apple command a higher price than what others deem them to, and vice versa. In the book, these valuations are expressed as "limit orders" sent in the form of electronic messages to the exchange's systems (the structure of individual messages often follows the Financial Information eXchange protocol, or FIX, that identifies the instructions contained in each message; see fig. 2). Within the computer warehouses of stock exchanges, incoming orders are time-stamped and logged in the order book according the moment of their arrival, their volume (the number of shares an investor is prepared to trade), and the price at which an investor is willing to buy or sell (an "ask" is the price set by sellers for the shares; a "bid" is the price determined by buyers). In the left columns of figure 1, for example, at 14:14:23 EST on September 28, 2017, the lowest amount at which an investor could buy 210 shares of Apple Inc. was $153.44. Conversely, the best price an investor could get for 601 shares in Apple Inc. was $153.43. In this instance, the difference (also called the spread) between the best bid and the best offer (or, the "top of the book") is $0.01. This is common in the most actively traded instruments—and is partly so by regulatory design: in the United States, in particular, shares cannot be traded in fractions of a penny. When an investor submits an order to buy at the best ask (or sell at the best bid), the system automatically matches these intentions and executes the trade. The right side of figure 1 shows the result of this automated matching: second after second, small lots of orders in Apple are traded at $153.44.

Figure 1. Apple Inc.'s top of book on BATS's EDGX at 14:14:32 EST on September 28, 2017. http://www.bats.com/us/equities/market_statistics/book/AAPL/?mkt=edgx.

From this very simple design of what is essentially an ordered list of intentions to buy and sell shares, order books can produce complicated dynamics. For instance, because order books are transparent in the sense that they are visible to all the investors that are connected to them, they quickly reveal strategies that can be gamed by other market participants. Imagine I wanted to buy one million shares of Apple Inc. Submitting an order at whatever prices are available (also known as a "market" order) would be an economically inefficient strategy. The order book only has 210 shares at $153.44, so filling the order would require going deeper into book, paying increasingly more for each batch of shares of Apple. Conversely, submitting a single limit order for a million shares at the best price would leave 999,790 shares outstanding and would likely trigger other market participants to increase their asks, thus increasing my overall costs. Much automated trading emerged around this problem of reducing "market impact." To trade large volumes of shares, algorithms slice orders into smaller lots that limit the effects and they have on the market: they try to "hide" the transaction, like minute whispers spreading through the interstices of a crowd. This slicing is paired with geographic diversification (Pitluck 2011); the strategy is pursued not in one but many markets, transmitting orders to several exchanges and trading platforms to obfuscate even more the original order—at the time of writing, Apple Inc.'s shares were traded in twenty-three different venues across the world.

8=FIX.4.2 | 9=178 | 35=8 | 49=PHLX | 56=PERS | 52=20071123-05:30:00.000 | 11=ATOMNOCCC9990900 | 20=3 | 150=E | 39=E | 55=MSFT | 167=CS | 54=1 | 38=15 | 40=2 | 44=15 | 58=PHLX EQUITY TESTING | 59=0 | 47=C | 32=0 | 31=0 | 151=15 | 14=0 | 6=0 | 10=128 |

Figure 2. A "typical" FIX message. Each element in the string of characters represents a meaningful instructions (PHLX, for example, corresponds to the Philadelphia Stock Exchange, or field 49 in this example).

High frequency trading emerged in this context. Betting on the long-term movements of stocks is still a common practice, but the fragmented, multisited, and electronic character of order books offers the possibility of profiting from miniscule price differentials across multiple trading sites. If the price of Apple Inc. is lower in Hamburg than anywhere else, there is quick profit to be made by arbitraging across this and other exchanges—buying shares in the cheaper to sell in the dearer. Traders equipped with the fastest systems are at an advantage because they are the first to observe and react to such differentials, creating a relentless incentive for an arms race in speed and connectivity (MacKenzie 2018). This leads to some well-known features of high frequency trading, such as the practices of colocation (where firms rent space next to the order books of stock exchanges at premium prices), or vast investments in telecommunications systems that reduce the transmission speeds between participants by small fractions of a second (generally, a few milliseconds; see MacKenzie et al. 2012). And while these practices were peripheral and somewhat controversial to the world of equities a decade ago, they are now more or less standard. In a short article in *Traders Magazine* titled "We're all HFTs now," Tim Quast notes that "today's stock market structure in large part reflects the pursuit of speed and price. . . . The entire structure has become high speed" (Quast 2017), diminishing the returns for even being called a high frequency trader.

THEORIZING SOCIETY IN THE ORDER BOOK

A frequent assumption about electronic order books is that they are altogether removed from "sociality," that they are emblematic of some form of "post-social" world where algorithms and humans are ontologically equal (see Arnoldi 2016). This is a common trope of financial automation: that through electronic devices and the apparent removal of humans, the social relations that once reigned on the trading floor are now entirely gone. This is incorrect: behind every electronic order, there is a trader, an institution, an organization; and the order book itself is not just a practical albeit anonymous informational device: above all, it is designed as a depository of intentions and "truthful" valuations. Limit orders are meant to represent what investors consider the value of a stock to be, in the same way that bids in an auction reflect, at a first degree of approximation, the preferences and senses of worth of collectors (Smith 1990). As Donald MacKenzie argues, precisely because they are spaces of perceived intentions, electronic markets are dense interactional orders (Goffman 1978) in their own right, populated by codes, expectancies, dissimulations, and multiple performances acted through, not without, the order book (MacKenzie 2019).

Studying the order book as an infrastructure for the social has two immediate theoretical implications. First, it underscores transactions as forms of relation-making rather than as ephemeral arm's-length exchanges. When two agents transact, they are tied for the duration of their exchange; they are related, even if through their membership of a community of exchange (Weber 1978). The order book frames this community—through its affordances, it bounds the membership and its codes of conduct, it defines who can trade with whom and how. Here, I am evoking the work of Marilyn Strathern (1995) and her provocative querying of "the relation" as a central analytical object in contemporary anthropological thought. Social anthropologists, writes Strathern, "route connections through persons," attending to "the relations of logic, of cause and effect, of class and category, that people make between things [but also] to the relations of social life, to the roles and behavior, through which people connect themselves to one another" (1995: 11). Such routing is the "substance of anthropological empiricism," she continues, creating a "double emphasis" on relations "known to the observer as principles of social organization and relations observed as interactions between persons." Social structure is located in relations that are "relevant to people's acts and intentions" (1995: 12), encoded in shared knowledge about society (Barnes 1988). The consequence of this "double emphasis," she adds, is that persons are discerned "by their relations to one another"—by shared, authoritative forms of knowledge that, like legal, informational, and scientific infrastructures, *establish* meaningful connections. Take the Paiela, for whom relations are "subjected to the test of time fall by the wayside depending on the warmth of that relationship" (Biersack 1982). Biological relatives that fail to provide support are "false" kin, whereas those that offer are thought of as "true" kin. More proximally, think of discussions about relatedness at the intersections of law and biomedical knowledge: transformations in reproductive technologies and legislations around their use imply that biological familiarity no longer guarantees relatedness in Western societies but does so only under finite combinations of law and its technique. A surrogate mother can only lay claim on her child in specific legal circumstances, in the same way that the donator of a gamete is not guaranteed relatedness to his or her genetic offspring. Relations are always underdetermined, be it by law, shared social knowledge, or by technologies of property and reproduction (Shalev 1998). The varieties of relevant relations are plentiful. As Strathern notes referring to Gregory Bateson's work with the Iatmul, kinship takes unexpected forms: for the Iatmul, "human beings are simply one manifestation of clan persons also manifested as every conceivable entity in the environment. . . . Yams have personal names, give birth, respond to speech, walk about at night" (1995: 16). The boundaries and dynamics of relations are never entirely trivial: the task at hand is finding how relations and personhoods are co-constituted, rather than taking for granted the existence of a dense relational system that serves as the basis of order and signification.

Like Strathern's anthropological relations, infrastructures deal with the apparent opposition between categorical and transactional accounts of social life. The question is not whether all transactions in the order book are meaningful relations, or if there is an abstract set of knowledge that defines—as if a view from nowhere—what constitutes a true trade. What matters is the interplay of infrastructures and knowledge, transactions and categories. For Strathern, the anthropological relation is divided:

> On the one hand are those relations seen to make connections through a logic of
> power of articulation that acquires its own conceptual momentum; on the other
> hand are those relations that are conducted in interpersonal terms, connections
> between persons inflected with a precise and particular history. (Strathern 2005: 7)

These two elements, the abstract and the particular, are necessarily conjoined
in a tandem. Interpersonal relations create what is conceivable, whereas the
conceptual apparatus provides social life to—or infuses with meaning—the
interpersonal:

> It is through the interacting with persons that diverse interactions and further
> connections become intellectually conceivable [the interpersonal creates possi-
> bilities for the conceptual], while it is through creating concepts and categories
> that connections come to have a social life of their own [the conceptual as a ter-
> rain for the potential interpersonal]. (Strathern 2005: 8)

Kinship provides an example, where the eminently abstractive conceptual apparatus of law meets the apparently thicker everyday experience of interpersonal,
familial connections. It is, as Barry Barnes might argue, a particular distribution of
knowledge that constitutes what can be known about actions, behaviors, and intentions (Barnes 1988). The law is not independent of these, as it is through court
cases and battles over relativeness that novel categories get made. Conversely, law
shapes our everyday experience: who can marry whom, who is deemed a sibling,
and who has parental responsibilities, are subjects of legal technique that affect
our capacity to create kindred groups in our intimate lives. Through the tandem,
Strathern evinces a connection between the relational and the infrastructural:
between densely inhabited proxies of concepts—worlds of classifications, gate-
ways, standards, protocols, measurements, templates—that make relations possible—by connecting machines, encrypting signals, or locating cases in the same
classification situations (Fourcade and Healy 2013). Infrastructures (the order
book) are to relations (intentional trades) what the abstract (market microstructure theory) is to the particular (the identification of "real" trades).

A focus on the order book as an infrastructure for relations is relevant for a
second reason. The concept of infrastructure matters not only because it speaks
of relation-making in a Strathernian sense, but also because it is doubly and
essentially relational. It is relational analytically, as Susan Leigh Star and Karen
Ruhleder (1996) observed: something is infrastructural not in and of itself but

only with respect to a particular community and set of practices—there is no substantive quality of being infrastructural *without* reference to practices and knowledges. But infrastructures are also relational in an operational sense: they enact relations by re-creating categories of membership, equivalence, and interoperability. Think of paradigmatic forms of infrastructure such as platforms, standards, and classification systems (Edwards 2010; Bowker and Star 2000) that, like relations, "summon to the field," discriminating between "all those possibly connected and those whom one choses to recognize." Standards and classifications order entities by locating them within specific categorical systems, but in doing so they also enact associations and dissociations, relations of similarity and relations of difference. This is visible in the recent work by Marion Fourcade and Kieran Healy (2013), whose Weberian-inspired analysis of classification situations points at how infrastructures—from credit scoring systems to crowd-sourced mechanisms for wine rating—operate as distributed sieves that sort people, things, and evaluations along specific orders of worth. Infrastructures facilitate this type of classification situations by making them durable and naturalized. The construction of a stable "reality" for market actors is necessarily predicated on the infrastructural work carried out by others (on the creation of a taken-for-granted arena of action): what is second nature to those involved in a transaction, what is obviously and blatantly a "meaningful relation" for parties to an exchange, is some other actor's rebuttable convention (Boltanski and Thévenot 1999) of counting, ordering, and technical interoperability. Order books and the forms of knowledge that make them intelligible constitute something similar to an "intersubjective spacetime" defined by a "likeness of intention" (Munn 1992: 264–65). Like Strathern's tandem, the double condition of infrastructures makes possible alternative accounts of how stable worlds emerge: they do so not only in reference to the creation of collective, intersubjective, front-stage categories shared by actors in a particular field, but also in connection to how relations are reflected upon the infrastructures that support the field's operation; contested relations are "tested" by how well they fit with extant infrastructures.

Note the potential shift in explaining sources of stability and change in the "real economy." Existing institutional, relational, and processual accounts place great emphasis on how, during moments of conflict and uncertainty, actors create shared repertoires (Swidler 1986), dominant cultural conceptions (Fligstein 2002), and accepted frames of interaction, narrative, and interpretation (Bandelj 2003; Goffman 1978) that allow closing controversies and coordinating action.

In Ann Swidler's classical account, for instance, unsettled times are wrangled by recourse to ideologies that bring together actors from distinct cleavages fixing them on common expectations (Swidler 1986). For Neil Fligstein, the key problem of market actors is curtailing competition by creating shared, field-level conceptions of governance, exchange, and control that produce stable and predictable worlds within the market (Fligstein 2002). And for Viviana Zelizer and Charles Tilly's (2006) account, actors participate in the ongoing construction of boundaries through which they collectively stabilize exchanges and tie these to extant social categories. In these as in other approaches, the "real" field of the economy is conceptualized as a space of front-stage action: what matters to markets and institutions are the knowledge and practices of the actors engaged in exchange—producers observe producers, firms observe firms, "real" actors with "real" relations. The dual condition of infrastructures, however, allows considering how front-stage actors refer to other operational planes to settle disputed moments and coordinate action. Actors do not invent the world anew every time there is a controversy or critical moment, nor do they constantly engage in a reflexive production of boundaries and classifications (cf. Bourdieu 1977, 2005; Zelizer and Tilly 2006; Barnes 1988). Rather, actors refer to "unquestioned conceptualization[s]" (Frank 1979) of what works *in practice* in taken-for-granted action. Infrastructures bootstrap the sense of reality shared by actors, anchoring accounts of what is possible, desirable, and permissible in moments of uncertainty. To determine what is "real" is to perform an infrastructural inversion (Bowker et al. 2009) that exposes the devices, techniques, practices, and objects assumed to ground action in the field, to then cool their meanings into a stable form.

An example of this form of infrastructural inversion is offered by how financial market participants deal with the "reality" of so-called spoofing in high frequency trading. Spoofing involves manipulating market prices by submitting "false" orders to buy and sell securities. In the context of electronic financial markets, spoofing has become a particularly notable object of contention for regulators and market participants alike (Lewis 2015): at the core, the issue is determining the reality of trades and the legitimacy of what seems, from the outside, an esoteric marketplace. Is a trade "real," the product of clear intentions to exchange, or is it simply algorithmic smoke meant to hide an underlying reality?

SPOOF!

What is at stake in the reality of spoofs? In addition to its pecuniary implications, spoofing elicits ontological and moral uncertainty in market transactions. Questions of spoofing remit to more substantive discussions about the makeup of society: if exchange is, indeed, productive of social cohesion (Bearman 1997; Mauss 1997), if relations matter for creating the forms that give life to the social, then "false" or "fake" exchanges corrode the character of markets. Fake transactions, like the danger of fake relations, challenge idealized principles of market and community, respectively.

Spoofs are challenging because they are difficult to identify: the process for generating a legitimate order to buy and sell securities and a spoof is much the same; both start their lives as standardized messages produced by the trading systems of brokers and other investment intermediaries that travel as electronic signals to the computer servers of exchanges where they are processed. A false order will not sink in water, nor will it look differently on the trading screen. Rather, what differentiates the real from the fictitious is the intent of whoever originated the trade or its underlying automated trading system. A real trade, market participants say, only exists when it was made bona fide. This is precisely how law singularizes spoofing: as an activity that distorts *true* prices through calculated (intentional) deception and manipulation. For example, since the securities markets reforms of 2001, it became unlawful, under Section 10(b) of the Securities Exchange Act 1934, "for any person, directly or indirectly [to] use or employ, in connection with the purchase or sale of any security . . . any manipulative or deceptive device or contrivance." Similarly, under section 17(a) of the Securities Act 1933, it is unlawful to "employ any device, scheme, or artifice to defraud, or to obtain money or property by means of any untrue statement of a material fact . . . or to engage in any transaction, practice, or course of business which operates or would operate as a fraud or deceit upon the purchaser." Legal prohibitions against spoofing in particular (rather than market manipulation in general) are even more recent: in the United States, they were only coded into law with the Dodd-Frank reform of 2010, when spoofing was defined as "bidding or offering with the intent to cancel the bid or offer before execution." This definition was reaffirmed in the courts, where spoofing was interpreted as "nonbona fide orders, or orders that the trader does not intend to have executed, to induce others to buy or sell the security at a price not representative of actual supply and demand."[1]

The notion of intent as a placeholder for reality is at the core of definitions of spoofing and market manipulation. Establishing intent, however, is notoriously difficult (for example, in parenting, see Coleman 1995; Wald 2006), particularly in the context of a system (the market) where actors mediate and delegate their behaviors onto algorithms, remain mostly anonymous, and act in ways that are supposed to reflect personal, subjective valuations and the ever changing state of public information (Malkiel and Fama 1970). It is not unlawful to be a bad investor, mistakenly digit a wrong number, or change one's mind. It is also not illegal to consider investment strategies that are contingent on other events ("Buy XYZ while ABC goes up"). It is also perfectly legal to submit orders that are completely nonsensical (and thus that have no real likelihood of being executed). But determining the existence of spoofing requires discerning the actual motivations of an individual trader or the designer of an automated trading system. "Identification of an abuse," writes legal scholar Jerry Markham "is itself problematic, since not every advantage or stratagem is abusive even if it provides advantage to its user at the expense of others" (2015). The phrasing of law is also far from trivial: if a strategy is based on a probabilistic expectation of execution (say, that 1 of every 100 orders submitted to an exchange will be executed, expecting to cancel the rest), can one speak of intent, as defined in Dodd-Frank? How to distinguish lousy, erratic, jittery, or informed trades from active forms of deceit? In other words, when is a transaction real? When do market participants say that a market relation exists?

A partial answer is provided by the Commodities Futures Trading Commission's (CFTC) Interpretive Order on spoofing, a document that serves as guidance in cases where there is suspicion of market manipulation.[2] For the CFTC, distinguishing between legitimate trading and spoofing requires evaluating "the market context, the person's pattern of trading activity (including fill characteristics), and other relevant facts and circumstances." To aid comparisons, the CFTC provides "four nonexclusive examples of possible situations for when market participants are engaged in 'spoofing' behavior, including: (i) Submitting or cancelling bids or offers to overload the quotation system of a registered entity, (ii) submitting or cancelling bids or offers to delay another person's execution of

---

1.   https://www.osc.gov.on.ca/en/Proceedings_set_20151211_panzz-oasis.htm.

2.   https://www.govinfo.gov/content/pkg/FR-2013-05-28/html/2013-12556.htm.

trades, (iii) submitting or cancelling multiple bids or offers to create an appearance of false market depth, and (iv) submitting or canceling bids or offers with intent to create artificial price movements upwards or downwards."[3] Note that within the CFTC's Interpretive Order, intentionality is framed with respect to specific technical conditions: "overload of the quotation system," "delayed execution," "false market depth," and artificial price movements. Indeed, although the CFTC does not interpret spoofing as an activity restricted to "trading platforms and venues only having order book functionality," it nevertheless ties its recognition to a specific technical device, the electronic limit order book. (Note, also, that the CFTC ties intent to individuals, not distributed *agencements* of humans and nonhumans. Regulation behaves "as if" all market actions are tied to a discernible human actant, the "market participant.")

Order books are infrastructural to finance in at least two ways. First, across countries and asset types, the majority of trading today is either routed through or executed in an electronic limit order book. In the United States, for example, at least 59.2 percent of the trades in equities are automated through order books (with a remaining 22 percent tied to manual, yet electronic, trading), whereas 97.1 percent of the most common (G10) foreign exchange operations go through the book. Indeed, soon after their introduction, electronic limit order books became the undisputed standard for building a market.

Second, and perhaps more important, trading strategies are often designed in reference to the order book's dynamics. Order books matter not only because they are operationally necessary; their technical details determine, to an important extent, the space of strategies available to market participants. A cursory exploration of "practical" publications in algorithmic and high frequency trading exposes this well: unlike a previous generation of textbooks in financial economics—concerned mostly with determining risk adjusted equilibrium prices—contemporary manuals focus on so-called market microstructure that involves understanding order book dynamics and the effects of variations in market design on aggregate patterns of trade and the profitability of specific trading strategies. Algorithms are designed to fit the functionalities of specific order books, exploiting different ways of signaling information, modifying orders, and executing trades (Balarkas and Ewen 2007; interview with platform developer, 2013). In addition to the very simple limit order (an order to buy or

---

3. https://www.cftc.gov/LawRegulation/FederalRegister/FinalRules/2013-12365. html.

sell a certain volume of securities at a certain price), an order book may process Calendar Spread Orders (that instruct to buy one delivery month of a contract and sell another delivery month of the same contract, at the same time, and on the same exchange), Deferred Orders (that sit on the order book until triggered), hidden orders (that are not visible to other users), or any other of the 1,200 order types available in American financial markets across the sixteen national securities exchange recognized by the SEC (Mackintosh 2014).

What matters is that action is tied to infrastructure in concrete ways. Such a tie (or tandem) is apparent in how the question of spoofing is resolved in courts of law. While market manipulation is as old as organized finance, the first legal criminal for suspected spoofing under the Dodd-Frank Act occurred only recently, in 2011, when the Commodity Futures Trading Commission of the United States and the Financial Conduct Authority of Britain brought charges against Michael Coscia and his Panther Energy Trading for illegally manipulating markets on the Chicago Mercantile Exchange and the Intercontinental Exchange. Agreeing with the Department of Justice, a grand jury indicted Coscia in late 2014 on six counts of commodities fraud and six counts of spoofing. During the ensuing trial, the government argued that Coscia knowingly "entered large-volume orders that he intended to immediately cancel before they could be filled by other traders" (*US v. Coscia*, Indictment, 2015). This case presents a useful illustration of the performances of reality surrounding high frequency trading.

Coscia's defense relied on two arguments. First, that the trial was procedurally incorrect because existing statutes against spoofing were simply too vague, encompassing "much routine, innocuous conduct by commodities traders" (*US v. Coscia*, Motion for Acquittal, 2015). Second, Coscia argued that both intent and manipulation were not evident. Since he never made an explicitly false statement or material representation about when or how he would cancel the orders submitted to the market, he rejected the representation of his actions as frauds (*US v. Coscia*, Memorandum opinion order, 2015).

For the prosecution, however, Coscia's intentions were clear: his strategy manifested the intent to cancel orders systematically, differentiating his conduct from other, widely accepted legitimate practices such as fill-or-kill and partial-fill orders. (A fill-or-kill is an order to buy or sell that has to be executed immediately upon receipt. If it cannot be executed, it is cancelled. Partial-fill orders, on the other hand, allow for the execution of only some of the order if the market does have enough depth to fill.) According to the government's legal team, Coscia manipulated the market by conveying "a misleading impression to customers" through his activity (*US v. Coscia*, Memorandum opinion order, 2015). That he had not misrepresented his intentions beforehand was simply immaterial. Indeed, much of the proof offered by the prosecution consisted in highlighting the logic of Coscia's strategy, consisting of so-called layering orders—that is, placing large orders to buy and sell instruments slightly above and under the best bids and offers in the book, creating a "false sense of supply and demand." Through this, argued the government, Coscia affected the offers of other (principally algorithmic) market participants and profited from market movements artificially created by his fictitious orders.[4]

Layering is important because it references order books as depositaries of "truthful" intentions—it indexes a shared, moralized expectation of what order books ought to be. Recall the explanation of the order book given earlier in this chapter. One strategy for manipulating the market is submitting trades that do not have the aim of being executed but that are meant to elicit actions from other participants. In the case of Apple Inc., the top of the order book has a slight imbalance: I can sell up to 601 shares, whereas I can only buy 210 shares at the top of the book. This means that it is more likely that the next transaction will move prices down rather than up (more people are willing to buy shares at a lower price than sell at a higher). If I wanted to fool market participants, I could submit limit orders just below the top of the book. These would give the impression that markets are likely to move in a specific direction (this is, for example, how trading algorithms are often programmed; see Lange, Lenglet, and Seyfert 2016; Goldstein, Kumar, and Graves 2014; Seyfert 2016). If I am fast enough, though, I can cancel these limit orders before they are executed and after betting against the likely movement of the market. This is what layering consists of: it involves creating deceitful orders in the book, playing with the system as a mechanism that ought to reflect true intentions. This form of trading is widely repudiated, and not surprisingly so: as fictitious trades, these deceits "fracture connectivities" (Munn 1992) in the order book and stand as threats against the market community and its alleged clarity of intentionality.

Note, with this, the nature of the evidence presented by the prosecution: it involved opening up the CME and ICE's order books—performing an infrastructural inversion, of sorts—to discern the aggregate nature of Coscia's actions by tracing the fine-grained logics of transactions. The indictment, for

---

4.   http://www.ft.com/intl/cms/s/0/7b9ccde8-638c-11e5-9846-de406ccb37f2.html.

example, accused Coscia of knowingly transmitting "to a CME Group server Euro FX currency futures contract orders that he intended to cancel before execution, so he could purchase 14 contracts at a below-market price and then sell them immediately thereafter for a higher price, in order to obtain a profit of approximately $175 in less than a second" (*US v. Coscia*, Indictment, 2014). (Though Coscia's indictment included only six counts of spoofing, none of which resulted in more than $500 in profits, Coscia is thought to have engaged in multiple events, earning $1.4 million over little less than three months.) The intent of these orders was not established from confessions or other first-person accounts, but rather was inferred from the strategy followed by the defendant in the context of what was possible and expected within the order book. In addition to testimony by Coscia's programmer, the government relied on the expert testimony of Hendrick Bessembinder, a professor of finance at the University of Utah and specialist in market microstructure theory, who set much of the tone for the trial. As *Bloomberg* reported, Bessembinder "went through data for the jury that showed that even after orders were filled there were attempts to cancel them by Coscia's algorithms" (Louis, Massa, and Hanna 2015). The construction of intent relied heavily on Bessembinder's representation of how the book works. "The only way trading is generated in electronic markets," noted Bessembinder,

> is through order submission. So if one is seeking to generate trading, seeking to generate a reaction, the only way one could do that is by inducing people to change their order submissions. [The] high fill rates on the small orders [suggest manipulation]. They were not only very high relative to the fill rates on the large orders, they are actually remarkably high for fill rates for other high frequency traders, so the high fill rates on the small orders are certainly very much consistent with the idea that the reaction that was generated was to induce other traders to submit orders to trade against, interact with the small orders. (*US v. Coscia*, Trial Tr. 1390, 2015)

Bessembinder did not speak directly of Coscia's intentions; he did not "implicate intent as to any element of the crime charged" (*US v. Coscia*, Memorandum opinion order, 2015). Rather, Bessembinder's testimony suggested to the jury what is expected of *normal* order book dynamics, signaling that the only possible way of making sense of Coscia's orders was as fictitious dealings. The order book linked native conceptions of intent with the specific technical repertoires of market microstructure economics. And the coupling was effective: in early November 2015 and after but an hour of deliberation, the Chicago jury found Coscia guilty on all twelve counts.

The trial of Michael Coscia was historically momentous in at least one important dimension. In addition to testing the waters of Dodd-Frank, it introduced a new way of establishing intent—of testing reality—within the increasingly electronic marketplaces of the American financial system. As economist John Montgomery commented,

> the recent enforcement and criminal cases [against spoofing and market manipulation] generally involve allegations that orders submitted by the defendant induced changes in orders submitted by other traders. . . . *It would then fall to economic experts to analyze whether such a pattern exists, and whether the trading suggests an intention on the part of the defendant to induce the other limit orders to be submitted.* The pattern described could be consistent with benign activity as well. For example, the trader could have orders on both sides of the market to benefit from the spread. A more aggressive trader could enter and submit more aggressive orders that then interact with the other side of the defendant's orders. Seeing those more aggressive orders, the defendant concludes the market is moving, cancels his/her open orders, and submits orders on both sides of the new market price. If a trader is alleged to have pursued spoofing as a strategy, *an analysis of the risk and expected return of the strategy can provide evidence on whether this is a plausible claim.*[5] (my emphasis)

There is, then, a test of "real" relations: if economic experts find risk-adjusted returns abnormal within the context of a particular order book design, something must be amiss. The result of such logic, argues Steven McNamara, is that *US v. Coscia* "takes the natural step of inferring a second-order intent in the programming of algorithms to accomplish certain tasks" (McNamara 2016). In this, the material cultures of electronic financial markets may not only be cultures of second-order-transparency, as Fabian Muniesa (2014) pointedly observes. It is also possible that, following *Coscia*, intentionality within the market is now observable only from a distance, through the judgment of experts that discern the boundaries of actions by discriminating between true and false transactions,

---

5.   https://ankura.com/wp-content/uploads/2018/10/Spoofing-Market-Manipulation.pdf.

real and fictitious market relations, according to how they are positioned within the order book.

MANIPULATION, IN ANALOG

That infrastructures matter in configuring relations, that they create and shape the communities that exist above them, can be seen perhaps by looking at the past as much as at the present. Consider, in particular, the trading floor, an infrastructure that contrasts sharply with the logic of the order book. Whereas order books operate under strictly symmetrical rules of price-time priority, trading floors are spaces of slightly more asymmetric interactions. Order books are organized as queues of electronic messages; trading floors take the shape of crowds of traders. Order books are mostly anonymous; the dynamics of trading floors are characterized by interpersonal knowledge and communication (Zaloom 2006; Hertz 1998). Yet spoofing is native to both, receiving quite different treatments across each setting. In the digital domains of electronic limit order books, spoofing is, quite clearly, an illegitimate transaction, a false relation that threatens the moral standing of the anonymous market. In trading floors, however, spoofing was at times tolerated, sort of a joking relation (Mauss 2013) through which traders on the floor teased and tested their market-kin.

One example jumps to mind: a case of spoofing on the floor of the London Stock Exchange in the early 1980s. Then, prices were mostly verbal, sometimes represented through whiteboards propped on the pitches of market makers on the trading floor. Over interview, a once young trainee at one of the most reputable market makers in London recalled how representations were used to drive prices in particular ways. The individual in question was assigned to work on the Australian mining book, which consisted of a list of mining shares selected and managed by a senior partner. As part of his research, the senior partner traveled to Australia to inspect facilities, talk with managers and engineers, visit brokers in Sydney and Melbourne, and buy shares for the firm's inventory. On an occasion during which the trainee was on the pitch, the partner had returned from Australia, bringing shares of a newly found mining company. The market, as the trainee recalled, was "a bit frothy," yet the price of gold was "really going through the roof." Before the market opened at 9:30, the senior partner introduced his new finding to the firm's members and trainees in the pitch: "Alright. I've got this company called GEM Exploration, which I've bought 250,000 shares of . . .

and I've bought them for the equivalent price of 3p. [We'll] see what we can do with them." So he wrote "GEM" on the whiteboard and next to it he wrote "5" as the opening price for the share. Because it was written rather than printed on the board, it was clear for everyone in the market that this was a new share. And so, the first brokers were drawn to it. The first to enquire about this strange new entry said "I see. . . . What's this GEM you've got up there? They look interesting. Tell me about that." As the one responsible for managing Australian mining shares, the senior partner replied: "Well, I went to Australia. I saw this company," and after explaining their business he mentioned he thought they were "a real prospect in the current market conditions." Intrigued, the broker asked for a quote. "They're 4 6" replied the senior partner. "What size would you like that?" asked the broker. "25,000" answered the market maker. "OK, well, thanks very much. I'll go away and have a think about that one," said the broker as he walked away from the pitch. Regardless of the fact that there had not been a transaction, the senior partner changed the price on the whiteboard, writing in blue the number 6. The next broker approached the pitch, seeing GEM Exploration on the board.

> "What are they this morning?" "Ah, well they're 5 7." "What's the size?" "Ah, well they're at bid for 25, offered in 10." Which showed that I'm a buyer, obviously. And he said "Oh, OK, well, I'll buy ten." The next guy comes along and literally, within half an hour, the things are trading at 25p. By the end of the day, they're trading at 40p, and we've turned over 2.5 million and we are long 350,000 shares instead of 250,000 shares.[6]

The case was blatantly one of market manipulation: the representation of prices on whiteboards was meant to elicit, like Coscia's orders, reactions within the market community. But any similarities obscure an important difference: these types of manipulations on the floor, although certainly contested, had an altogether different moral valence. To manipulate one's relative is one thing; to manipulate a stranger in an anonymous environment is quite another. Those were the days of the floor. As Gregory Meyer of the *Financial Times* wrote, technology "changes the nature of violations" (2015). But if it does so, it is necessarily because different technologies imply and enact different "mutualities of being" (Carsten 2013). The risk of spoofing is a risk of false, rather than joking,

---

6.   Interview with former market maker, London, July 2012.

relations—a challenge to the legitimacy, morality, and sense of reality of modern markets (Arnuk and Saluzzi 2012).

SOME FINAL THOUGHTS

So what do we gain by looking at infrastructures? First, they suggest focusing on relations and the mechanisms that bound, format, and enact them and their social worlds. The market is, indeed, an arm's-length setting: agents in financial markets today, for instance, have an ease of exit that is quite unparalleled historically. Yet markets are also bound by connections, mutual dependencies, and reciprocal obligations—materialized through settlement systems, contractual linkages, and connectivity standards, but also through associations, professions, employment matching patterns, and others. (As Turco and Zuckerman [2014] show, exit is indeed quite limited, even in the putatively rational and calculative spheres of private equity.)

Second, if relations emerge in connection to infrastructures, then the politics of relations cannot be contained within the categorizations of social actors and their mobilization. Relational economic sociology, like broader relational approaches, stresses the unequal distribution of power and resources as shaping categorical (and thus relational) work. This is certainly part of the story—but what an infrastructural inversion would advise is looking further afield than front-stage struggles. Definitional battles over spoofing were surely shaped by overt institutional politics (see Arnoldi 2016); but practical instances of spoofing depended on an altogether different articulation of intent on the basis of overlapping (yet disparate) forms of knowledge and expertise. Spoofing was not the object of ideological intervention—rather, it was at best a boundary object (Star and Griesemer 1989), linking the different ecologies of trading platform designers, lawyers, market microstructure economists, regulators, and a mixed gamut of market participants.

Third, infrastructures compel us to think of the "invisible"—not as an inherent quality of infrastructures but as a positional achievement, as something that happens when a device or system becomes infrastructural to a community (but certainly, the site of action and activity for others; see Larkin 2013). The question of spoofing is unescapably linked to issues about the nature of order books, the implicit assumptions they make about how things can (and should) be meaningfully connected, and the politics of their dissemination in finance.

To understand how reality was "realized" in finance, how specific modes of action emerged as second nature to market participants and their performances of reality as seamless parts of everyday action, requires tracing the histories of these invisible platforms and their multiple makers. For contemporary financial markets, so it seems, reality is partly manufactured by the invisible hands of others.

REFERENCES

Arnoldi, Jakob. 2016. "Computer algorithms, market manipulation and the institutionalization of high frequency trading." *Theory, Culture & Society* 33 (1): 29–52.

Arnuk, Sal, and Joseph Saluzzi. 2012. *Broken markets: How high frequency trading and predatory practices on Wall Street are destroying investor confidence and your portfolio*. Upper Saddle River, NJ: FT Press.

Balarkas, R., and G. Ewen. 2007. "Algorithms to help you trade aggressively." In *Algorithmic trading*, 2nd ed., edited by B. Patel, 1–10. London: TRADE.

Bandelj, Nina. 2003. "How method actors create character roles." *Sociological Forum* 18 (3): 387–416.

Barnes, Barry. 1988. *The nature of power*. Cambridge: Polity.

Bearman, Peter. 1997. "Generalized exchange." *American Journal of Sociology* 102 (5): 1383–415.

Biersack, Aletta. 1982. "The logic of misplaced concreteness: Paiela body counting and the nature of the primitive mind." *American Anthropologist* 84 (4): 811–29.

Boltanski, Luc, and Laurent Thévenot. 1999. "The sociology of critical capacity." *European Journal of Social Theory* 2 (3): 359–77.

Bourdieu, Pierre. 1977. *Outline of a theory of practice*. Vol. 16. Cambridge: Cambridge University Press.

———. 2005. *The social structures of the economy*. Cambridge: Polity.

Bowker, Geoffrey C., Karen Baker, Florence Millerand, and David Ribes. 2009. "Toward information infrastructure studies: Ways of knowing in a networked environment." In *International handbook of internet research*, edited by Jeremy Hunsinger, Lisbeth Klastrup, and Matthew Allen, 97–117. Dordrecht: Springer Netherlands.

Bowker, Geoffrey C., and Susan Leigh Star. 2000. *Sorting things out: Classification and its consequences*. Cambridge, MA: MIT Press.

Carsten, Janet. 2013. "What kinship does—and how." *HAU: Journal of Ethnographic Theory* 3 (2): 245–51.

Castelle, Michael, Yuval Millo, Daniel Beunza, and David C. Lubin. 2016. "Where do electronic markets come from? Regulation and the transformation of financial exchanges." *Economy and Society* 45 (2): 166–200.

Chordia, Tarun, Gideon Saar, Amit Goyal, and Bruce N. Lehmann. 2013. "High-frequency trading." *Journal of Financial Markets* 16 (4): 637–45.

Coleman, Malina. 1995. "Gestation, intent, and the seed: Defining motherhood in the era of assisted human reproduction. *Cardozo Law Review* 17: 497.

Edwards, Paul N. 2010. *A vast machine: Computer models, climate data, and the politics of global warming*. Cambridge, MA: MIT Press.

Fligstein, Neil. 2002. *The architecture of markets: An economic sociology of twenty-first-century capitalist societies*. Princeton, NJ: Princeton University Press.

Foucault, Michel. 2012. *Discipline & punish: The birth of the prison*. New York: Vintage.

Fourcade, Marion, and Kieran Healy. 2013. "Classification situations: Life-chances in the neoliberal era." *Accounting, Organizations and Society* 38 (8): 559–72.

Frank, Arthur W., III. 1979. "Reality construction in interaction." *Annual Review of Sociology* 5(1): 167–91.

Goffman, Erving. 1978. *The presentation of self in everyday life*. Edinburgh: Social Science Research Centre.

Goldstein, Michael A., Pavitra Kumar, and Frank C. Graves. 2014. "Computerized and high-frequency trading. *Financial Review* 49 (2): 177–202.

Gorham, Michael, and Nidhi Singh. 2009. *Electronic exchanges: The global transformation from pits to bits*. Burlington, MA: Elsevier.

Henning, Peter. 2014. "High frequency trading falls in the cracks of criminal laws." *New York Times*, April 7, 2014. http://dealbook.nytimes.com /2014/04/07/high-frequency -trading-falls-in-the-cracks-of-criminal-laws/.

Hertz, Ellen. 1998. *The trading crowd: An ethnography of the Shanghai stock market*, vol. 108. Cambridge, MA: Cambridge University Press.

Jevons, William Stanley. 1879. *The theory of political economy*. London: Macmillan.

Lange, Ann-Christine, Marc Lenglet, and Robert Seyfert. 2016. "Cultures of high-frequency trading: Mapping the landscape of algorithmic developments in contemporary financial markets." *Economy and Society* 45 (2): 149–65.

Larkin, Brian. 2013. "The politics and poetics of infrastructure." *Annual Review of Anthropology* 42: 327–43.

Lewis, Michael. 2015. *Flash boys: Cracking the money code*. London: Penguin.

Louis, Brian, Annie Massa, and Janan Hanna. 2015. "From pits to algos, an old-school trader makes leap to spoofing." *Bloomberg*, November 12, 2015. https://www.bloomberg.com/news/articles/2015-11-12/from-pits-to-algos-an-old-school-trader-makes-leap-to-spoofing.

Mackintosh, Phil. 2014. "Demystifying order types." KCG Working Paper. New York: Kiel Centre for Globalization.

MacKenzie, Donald. 2018. "Material signals: A historical sociology of high-frequency trading." *American Journal of Sociology* 123 (6): 1635–83.

———. 2019. "How algorithms interact: Goffman's 'interaction order' in automated trading." *Theory, Culture & Society* 36 (2): 39–59.

MacKenzie, Donald, Daniel Beunza, Yuval Millo, and Juan Pablo Pardo-Guerra. 2012. "Drilling through the Allegheny Mountains: Liquidity, materiality and high-frequency trading." *Journal of Cultural Economy* 5 (3): 279–96.

Malkiel, Burton G., and Eugene F. Fama. 1970. "Efficient capital markets: A review of theory and empirical work." *The Journal of Finance* 25 (2): 383–417.

Markham, Jerry W. 2015. *A financial history of modern US corporate scandals: From Enron to reform*. New York: Routledge.

Meyer, Gregory. 2015. "Technology changes the nature of violations." *Financial Times*, October 12, 2015. https://www.ft.com/content/7b9ccde8-638c-11e5-9846-de406ccb37f2.

Munn, Nancy D. 1992. *The fame of Gawa: A symbolic study of value transformation in a Massim (Papua New Guinea) society*. Durham, NC: Duke University Press.

Mauss, Marcel. 1997. "Gift, gift." In *The logic of the gift: Toward an ethic of generosity*, edited by Alan D. Schrift, 28–32. New York: Routledge.

———. 2013. "Joking relations." Translated and introduced by Jane I. Guyer. *Hau: Journal of Ethnographic Theory* 3 (2): 317–34.

McNamara, Steven. 2016. "United States v. Coscia as a case of first impression." *The CLS Blue Sky Blog*, January 6, 2016. http://clsbluesky.law.columbia.edu/2016/01/06/united-states-v-coscia-as-a-case-of-first-impression/#_ftnref14.

Mol, Annemarie. 1999. "Ontological politics: A word and some questions." *Sociological Review* 47 (1): 74–89.

Muniesa, Fabian. 2014. *The provoked economy: Economic reality and the performative turn.* New York: Routledge.

Pardo-Guerra, Juan Pablo. 2019. *Automating finance: infrastructures, engineers, and the making of electronic markets.* Cambridge: Cambridge University Press.

Pitluck, Aaron Z. 2011. "Distributed execution in illiquid times: An alternative explanation of trading in stock markets." *Economy and Society* 40 (1): 26–55.

Quast, Tim. 2017. "We're all HFTs now." *Traders Magazine*, September 14, 2017.
http://e.tradersmagazine.com/news/viewpoints/were-all-hfts-now-116672-1.html.

Russolillo, Steven. 2014. "Schwab on HFT: 'Growing cancer' that must be addressed." *Wall Street Journal*, April 4, 2014.
https://blogs.wsj.com/moneybeat/2014/04/03/schwab-on-hft-growing-cancer-that-must-be-addressed/.

Seyfert, Robert. 2016. "Bugs, predations or manipulations? Incompatible epistemic regimes of high-frequency trading." *Economy and Society* 45(2): 251–77.

Shalev, Carmel. 1998. "Halakha and patriarchal motherhood: An anatomy of the new Israeli surrogacy law." *Israel Law Review* 32 (1): 51–80.

Simmel, Georg. 2004. *The philosophy of money.* London: Psychology Press.

Smith, Charles W. 1990. *Auctions: The social construction of value.* Berkeley: University of California Press.

Star, Susan Leigh, and James R. Griesemer. 1989. "Institutional ecology, translations and boundary objects: Amateurs and professionals in Berkeley's Museum of Vertebrate Zoology, 1907–39." *Social Studies of Science* 19 (3): 387–420.

Star, Susan Leigh, and Karen Ruhleder. 1996. "Steps toward an ecology of infrastructure: Design and access for large information spaces." *Information Systems Research* 7 (1): 111–34.

Strathern, Marilyn. 1995. *The relation: issues in complexity and scale.* Cambridge: Prickly Pear.

———. 2005. *Kinship, law and the unexpected: Relatives are always a surprise.* Cambridge: Cambridge University Press.

Swidler, Ann. 1986. "Culture in action: Symbols and strategies." *American Sociological Review* 51 (2): 273–86.

Turco, Catherine J., and Ezra W. Zuckerman. 2014. "So you think you can dance? Lessons from the US private equity bubble." *Sociological Science* 1: 81–101.

Wald, Deborah H. 2006. "Parentage puzzle: The interplay between genetics, procreative intent, and parental conduct in determining legal parentage." *American University Journal of Gender, Social Policy, & the Law* 15 (3): 379–411.

Weber, Max. 1978. *Economy and society: An outline of interpretive sociology.* Berkeley: University of California Press.

Zaloom, Caitlin. 2006. *Out of the pits: Traders and technology from Chicago to London.* Chicago: University of Chicago Press.

Zelizer, Viviana, and Charles Tilly. 2006. "Relations and categories." In *The psychology of learning and motivation.* Vol 47, Categories in use, edited by Arthur B. Markkam and Brian H. Ross, 1–31. San Diego: Elsevier.

CHAPTER FIVE

Soybean, bricks, dollars, and the reality of money in Argentina

Mariana Luzzi and Ariel Wilkis

A few months after Carmen passed away, her children—Vicente (73), Sara (70), Paco (66), and Tere (58)—decided to embark upon what would become a never-ending journey: divvying up their mother's inheritance. Camila had owned three properties: a 50 sq. m. apartment and a duplex, all located in a suburb north of Buenos Aires. Two of her children were already living in the duplex: Santa had rented the ground floor unit for almost ten years; Pepe and his wife had recently moved in upstairs. When it came time to see what the properties were worth, the Torre siblings each called a separate real estate agent to appraise the three properties. There were no major differences in the appraisals given by the different agents, and the prices they finally agreed upon were the following: US$70,000 for the apartment, US$118,000 for the ground floor unit, and US$135,000 for the top floor unit.[1]

Camila had also left her children US$17,000 in savings. From the point of view of how much each sibling would get, it was simply a question of dividing by four the

---

1. Since the 1980s, the real estate market in Argentina has operated in US dollars. This applies both to the price of properties and to sales, the majority of which are cash transactions, even today. One important factor in this market is that home loans are practically nonexistent.

total amount to be inherited. In other words, assuming the three properties sold for US$340,000 plus the US$17,000 in Camila's savings, each sibling should have gotten US$85,000. Yet things did not turn out to be as simple or straightforward as this mathematical equation. Except for Toni, the youngest sibling, who expected to receive her inheritance in cash, all the others expected to get a property out of the deal. Victor wanted the apartment; Santa wanted the ground floor unit where she was already living, and Pepe wanted the top floor.

The difference in value of the different properties would lead to disputes over the amount of money to be paid and received by each member of the family. In other words, Santa should have paid her siblings US$33,000 to purchase the ground floor unit; Pepe should have paid US$50,000 for the top floor unit; Victor would not only get the apartment worth US$70,000, but also US$15,000 in cash; and Toni would get her US$85,000 from what Santa and Pepe paid, plus $2,000 from Camila's savings (with the remaining $15,000 going to Victor).

The Torre siblings were squabbling over the inheritance between 2012 and 2014, a time in which the Argentine government progressively restricted access to foreign currency and finally put an end to the legal purchase of foreign currency for savings purposes. This made the calculations even more difficult, because no one could access the exchange market in order to buy the dollars they needed to settle their accounts.

So, when it came time to agree on the payments in dollars, a series of issues led to disagreements among the siblings. At this point, the siblings took sides: Toni and Victor versus Santa and Pepe. Toni and Victor expected to be paid in the same currency in which the properties were appraised. Pepe and Santa, however, argued that the houses "are not in Miami, they're in Olivos" and refused to pay the price of the properties in dollars. Given the exchange restrictions, the only way Pepe and Santa could have come up with that amount in dollars would be to buy them at a much higher rate on the black market.

In summary, the problem was not about how much the properties were worth in dollars (its price) but what the equivalent rate would be in pesos to reach the agreed on sum. And that's where the negotiations stalled.

***

In the final months of 2011, just as Argentine President Cristina Fernández de Kirchner started her second term, the Argentine banking system suffered a massive withdrawal of dollars. According to the different analysts, and just as had happened many times since the mid-twentieth century, the run on the national currency revealed how different business sectors were pressuring the national government to devaluate the Argentine peso and thus make Argentine goods and salaries more competitive. Starting at the end of October 2011, the state responded to this pressure by changing the rules for buying and selling foreign currency. The regulations and controls got progressively stricter until July 2012, when the purchase of dollars or other currencies for savings was banned altogether. The restriction was partially lifted in January 2014, when it became possible to purchase dollars for savings once again, though some restrictions continued to apply up until December 2015, when they were completely eliminated by the new government.

There is nothing extraordinary about the inheritance of the Torre siblings: their story is just one example of the type of controversies and negotiations common in a context where currencies multiply and currency exchange is altered or interrupted, as occurred when the exchange market regulations were amended in 2012. As occurs more broadly in economic life, personal ties are mixed here with assets, appraisals, and economic regulations. In this case, though, calculations are simultaneously done in different units of account. The story of the Torre siblings reveals the types of situations that arise from limited access to the exchange market, but it is also one chapter in a broader social and cultural history. The family controversies occur in the context of currency exchange controls but are based on money practices and beliefs that formed over a much longer period of time.

In Argentina, the popularization of a financial repertoire articulated around the peso and the dollar was a long and slow-maturing process. Since the end of the 1950s, and in a context of recurring balance of payments crises, the US dollar started to be progressively associated with speculation practices of "small" investors who looked to benefit from the sudden and repeated devaluations of the national peso. If until that moment the foreign exchange market had been dominated by elites linked to international trade and the financial system, starting in the early 1960s, the purchase and selling of the US dollar became an operation extended to broader segments of the population. The media reports of that period bring continued attention to these new segments of the population with few financial expertise credentials; the figure of the saver who "keeps" dollars in his home to protect his patrimony's value started to appear in the interpretation of the "lack of confidence" in the Argentine peso during this period (Luzzi and

Wilkis 2017, 2019). The following decades accentuated the diffusion of this financial repertoire, which found not only particular macroeconomic conditions to develop (high inflation, devaluations, balance of payments crises, and fiscal deficit) but also cultural devices (movies, literature, newspaper articles, graphic humor, and publicity), which helped to legitimate dollar accounts and payments. The subsequent adoption of the dollar by certain markets—such as the real estate market—as means of payment further contributed to sediment a set of financial practices based on multiple currencies (Gaggero and Nemiña 2016).

The configuration of this financial repertoire can be interpreted in light of the literature that in recent decades, and in clear discussion with orthodox economic thought, has insisted on the normal—not pathological—character of currency pluralism. This notion is part of the developments from which different disciplines have reassessed the question about the nature of money. In the classic narrative, the figure of modern money is viewed as a "general equivalent of value" (Marx 1976), "the value of values" (Simmel 1978), or as an "all-purpose currency" (Polanyi 1983). In contrast, in fields like history (Kuroda 2008), economics (Blanc 2000; Théret 2007; Servet, Théret, and Yildirim 2008), anthropology (Guyer 2016a, 2016b; Neiburg 2016), and sociology (Zelizer 1994; Dodd 2014), a new narrative focused on multiple meanings of money has been constructed over the last two decades. Nigel Dodd (2014) has recently summarized this shift by arguing that while classic sociology focused on how money shapes culture, contemporary scholars do the opposite, revealing how money is formatted by culture. Unlike the perspective of money as an instrument that can be replaced or exchanged independently of the form it takes (coin, bills, checks, etc.) and of its origins, this new narrative brings up the question of the conditions and limits of its fungibility.

Jane Guyer's work has made a remarkable contribution to an empirically informed understanding of the multiplicity of money. On the one hand, her research shows that the multiplicity of currencies in the African economies is anything but exceptional (Guyer 1995, 2004): in fact, it has been characteristic of these economies and well documented at least since the 1950s, when Paul Bohannan studied transactions and currencies in the colonial world (Bohannan 1955, 1959). Unlike Bohannan, whose work was solidly rooted in Karl Polanyi's differentiation between primitive or "special-purpose" money and modern or "all-purpose" money, Guyer questioned this categorical division between coexisting currencies. According to the author, it is possible to find more modern features in precolonial monetary economies than what was once supposed, along with fewer modern (or all-purpose) characteristics in the twentieth-century currencies than one would have imagined. By following this line of research, Guyer departs from traditional perspectives in which currency is described through its functions (unit of account, method of exchange, payment method, and store of value), perspectives that treat the absence of any of these functions as an anomaly. This serves as a reminder that territorially united currencies are only one of the many currencies that have existed historically; it would be a mistake to consider such currencies as universal (Helleiner 2003). Thus, Guyer's works on the currencies in Western Africa—with its rich ethnographic descriptions and thorough historic inquiries—allow us to observe that currency pluralism is in fact characteristic of modern currency systems, as noted in other works as well (Blanc 2000; Servet, Théret, and Yildirim 2008; Théret 2008).

Guyer's more recent works have gone deeper into the issue of the multiplicity of money. According to her, starting in the 1990s the capitalist world entered a new phase of multiple currencies, which coincided with a proliferation of the circuits in which the US dollar became the sole common currency (Guyer and Salami 2012: 4). This second phenomenon spoke of a new economic and monetary configuration that began to be observed in the world at the beginning of the 1970s: from the point of view of economic theory, the primordial monetary function was determined to be storing value (Guyer 2016b; Orléan 2009) and from the point of view of the configuration of monetary economies and economic practices at the local level, the US dollar was consolidated as the currency used not only in foreign commerce globally but also as a common account and exchange unit in different regional and national scenarios.

This desegregation of monetary functions, no longer embodied in a single national currency—whose reign has been, in fact, comparatively brief—but in different coexisting ones, is expressed in the common distinction between soft currencies and hard currencies, where only those that serve as a store of value are considered "strong." Yet the point that interests Guyer is not only how these multiple currencies are configured but also the way in which each of these "currency innovations" forges a space for new conversions, new regulations, floating exchange rates, and new and existing agents who are forced to deal with a changing context on an everyday basis.

In line with these considerations, and in light of the Argentine experience, it is pertinent to wonder what happens when monetary regulations impact access and use of a currency—the dollar—that is identified as "hard." What does a context of limited access to the foreign exchange market teach us about the (historic and contingent) hierarchical dynamic of currencies and monetary functions? The context of foreign exchange restrictions we alluded to above is perfectly fertile for exploring a perspective that expands the thesis of monetary pluralism. As we will see throughout this article, the exchange constraints imposed between 2011 and 2015 and the monetary practices they generated reveal the dynamics of currency pluralism in today's Argentina. In a monetary system where different currencies exist side by side (where, for example, real estate transactions are done in a foreign currency), this was a moment when money hierarchies were altered; when it became necessary for people to decide how to continue to do existing transactions or what new transactions would replace them.

The Torres siblings' disputes over inheritance allow us to observe that in Argentina the implementation of accounts and payments in different currencies isn't necessarily problematic. On the contrary; the acceptance of monetary pluralism as a condition for negotiations between siblings shows how embedded the use of "hard" currencies—dollars—and "soft" currencies—pesos—are in Argentines' monetary practices. Nevertheless, given the context of foreign exchange restrictions, at no moment did the family consider that the payments be made with dollars in cash, as is usual in this type of transactions when there are not exchange control mechanisms in place. The disagreement between the Torres siblings referred to the appropriate conversion rate to divide an inheritance among the members of a family. What is the nature of the dollar in these negotiations? A hard but "imaginary" and "immaterial" currency, like the Haitian dollar analyzed by Federico Neiburg (2016)? What is the nature of the peso? A soft but "real" and "available" currency?

The long conformation process of this financial repertoire, in which the peso and the US dollar articulate, had a turning point starting in the mid-1970s, when the inflationary process started to accentuate (Canitrot 1981). In the successive economic crises that followed since the 1980s, the consideration consolidated, of the Argentine peso as an "ill" currency, whose evolution was always measured relative to the dollar, as a strong and "healthy" currency (Neiburg 2010). A decade later, those imaginaries found a definitive expression in the *currency board* regime (1991–2001), which established a fixed parity between the peso and the dollar as a part of a stabilization plan based on the "healthy" properties of the dollar as a means to "cure" the peso. This opposition between the dollar as a healthy or even true currency and the peso as an ill or even false currency (Muir 2015) remained usual during the 2001–2 crisis (for example, in the demands of bank clients whose deposits had been devalued [Luzzi 2016]) and after that crisis, when the distinction served as argument to justify safe investment strategies, such as real estate developments (D'Avella 2014).

The perspective we assumed in this chapter to analyze the context of foreign exchange restrictions—where the limitations to access the foreign exchange market combined with successive devaluations of the peso—allows us to have another approximation to these properties attributed to the Argentine peso and the US dollar in Argentina. A pragmatic point of view on monetary pluralism (Maurer 2006) allows us to go beyond the consideration of currencies and monetary functions based on attributes and fixed oppositions such as hard/soft, real/fictional, material/immaterial—to name some properties that repeatedly bring the nature of money into question (Neiburg 2016). The perspective we chose here identifies within specific transaction universes the level of analysis where it is possible to observe an intense and rich dynamic of imaginaries and monetary practices that establish orders and hierarchies between currencies and monetary functions. This allows us to understand, for example, how transactions go beyond state regulations that try to discipline practices and monetary imaginaries through the display of a plurality of currencies whose properties are temporally and relationally contingent. In the following sections, we will analyze two transactional universes embedded in the currency pluralism configured by Argentina's recent exchange restrictions. Based on qualitative fieldwork conducted between 2014 and 2015 in the cities of Buenos Aires and Santa Fe, Argentina, we will describe uses of the US dollar in two specific markets (real estate and soybean production), which have been extremely dynamic after the major socioeconomic crisis of 2001 and in which the dollar has served as an accounting or payment currency (or both) for at least the past four decades (Luzzi and Wilkis 2019). We will see how real estate developers and soybean producers make profits by organizing and establishing hierarchies of multiple currencies, disaggregated monetary functions, and differentiated monies. In these two cases we will also observe the creation of new currencies, relying on the definition of what is considered "real" in each universe (for instance, soy producers who take soybeans as the unit of account and store of value, or real estate developers who use square meters as a unit of account). As we will show, this multiplicity of currencies does not constitute an anomaly or create new borders or barriers, but does provide a new and profitable means for transactions.

Our work allows pluralism to be understood not merely as a dichotomy between soft/ hard, real/fictional, and imaginary/concrete currencies but by differentiating and establishing a hierarchy between the currencies that each

of these figures assumes. These hierarchies are multiple, conflicting, and mutually coexisting. The fact that it is not—even within the same market or set of
actors—a fixed hierarchy (dollar over peso, or soybeans/bricks over dollars), but
precisely that this varies both temporally and relationally, is the reason why it is
fundamental to destabilize interpretations that affix a stable property, be it soft/
hard, real/fictional, or imaginary/concrete to a currency or monetary function.

TRANSACTIONS

Real Estate Developers

The real estate market has been one of the main focuses of our research due to
the fact that it is almost entirely dollar-based. As the recent work by Alejandro
Gaggero and Pablo Nemiña shows, since the end of the 1970s, purchase and sale
transactions have been carried out in US dollars (Gaggero and Nemiña 2016),
as also seen in the story of the Torre siblings at the beginning of this chapter.

The construction sector witnessed a boom after the 2001 crisis; a great number of new office and apartment buildings were constructed across the city of
Buenos Aires. During this period, part of the impulse to invest in the sector
could be attributed to the appeal of investing in "bricks" (*ladrillos*) over savings accounts or time deposits. The experience of the *corralito* (the freezing of
dollar deposits and their conversion to pesos at an exchange rate lower than
the going market rate during the 2001 crisis) made Argentines highly distrust-
ful of banks. Encouraged by new investment options (real estate trusts), small
investors frequently opted to purchase new apartments.[2] The time in which an
investor's money was tied up was relatively short, two years at most, and part of
the investment—which yielded a high return—could be made in pesos and in
installments.[3]

---

2.   Over the past decade, trusts became a common way to finance new buildings. A
     pool of small investors makes an investment in dollars to finance the purchase of
     a lot; this investment yields an apartment in the newly constructed building, an
     apartment that will be handed over within a period of time established by contract
     (usually less than two years). This initial investment in dollars is usually combined
     with monthly installments in pesos over the course of the project. The investors who
     opt in during the later stages can make payments in pesos, at least until the building
     is finished.

3.   Nicolas D'Avella has reconstructed this period in great detail (D'Avella 2014).

The exchange restrictions put new limits on these transactions, historically done in cash. Since the late seventies, not only have most real estate sales in Argentina been cash transactions, they are also priced and paid in US dollars. This means obtaining actual dollar bills, which buyers and sellers must take with them either to or from the location where the transaction is carried out. As we saw in the story of the Torre siblings, limited access to the purchase of foreign currencies represented a challenge for real estate transactions. At the same time, the parallel currency market led to multiple exchange rates, making negotiations on the prices of properties even more difficult.

Gerardo is an engineer in his late thirties who owns a construction company and sells apartments. We wanted to know how real estate developers were carrying out sales transactions given the restricted access to the "official dollar," so Gerardo invited us to see his latest building venture. It was a group of three eleven-floor buildings, each with studio, one bedroom, and two bedroom apartments. One of the buildings was already finished but construction continued on the other two. He showed us some of the apartments and pointed out their advantages—the number of square meters and the quality of the materials.

The conversation continued at a coffee shop near the construction site. "Nowadays, I always tell my clients, it's up to you. I've got a building that's nearly done and one I haven't started on yet." This explanation was a summary of how this builder puts together his real estate transactions. If the market is paralyzed, with transactions occurring "in slow motion," to use the phrase of another builder we interviewed, profit margins are buttressed by combining currencies. Two different formulas may be used for constructions right next door to each other if these are at different phases in the business cycle. A finished property and a property under construction represent two different transaction types. A finished property is appraised in dollars; Gerardo left no doubt about that. Once the construction has finished, the dollar is the currency for establishing what the property is worth and it also serves as a payment instrument. The completion of the building brings the business cycle to a close, although until that point, the Argentine peso is a valid unit of account and payment method. There is a clear method to how builders do the numbers to determine the construction costs.

Like many other real estate developers we met during fieldwork, Gerardo uses the lot where the building will be constructed as the base value. Since the purchase of the lot will be in dollars, its impact on the final price will also be in dollars. However, the other two fundamental components, the workforce and construction materials, are calculated and paid for in pesos. The total cost of the construction is thus the sum of outlays in both dollars (the lot) and pesos (the workforce and materials). This formula permits multiple currency transactions in which different monies are used depending on the building's phase of production. Since after construction, the building no longer requires workforce or materials, the peso is excluded as a unit of account and payment method at this stage: the sale price is in dollars. At the same time, these transactions are connected with the start of a new business cycle for the developers, who must now acquire a new lot for the next project and pay for it in dollars. In contrast, the unfinished property (which is also up for sale) generates constant expenses in materials and worker salaries, and here the peso plays a fundamental role in the construction cycle. This part of the transaction, then, can be paid for in the Argentine currency, with prices stated in pesos. Since the peso is circulating during this stage, it can be used as a payment method for transactions like the developer's purchase of materials and salary payments.

The formula for calculating this transaction involves one additional element: a price index determined by the Argentine Chamber of Construction. Installments in pesos are adjusted by this index, which takes into account increases in the prices of construction materials and construction worker salaries, both stated in pesos. In 2007, this formula began to be used when inflation began to creep upward and the credibility of the INDEC (National Institute of Statistics and Censuses)—which also publishes its own Construction Cost Index—was challenged.[4]

In 2008, when the inflation index exceeded the rise of the US dollar against the Argentine peso, Gerardo decided it was time to "reduce risks." He started talking to his father about using the Construction Cost Index when selling an apartment in installments and in Argentine pesos. His father objected because of the price-indexing ban, which dated back to the times of the currency board (pre-2001) but remained on the books. Gerardo, however, thought there was no other option if they wanted to keep earning profits in a time when the production costs in pesos were rising more quickly than the US dollar. Convincing his clients to accept this clause in the sales agreement was the only way to ensure that a building would get finished without "anyone losing."

---

4. In 2007, the INDEC was subject to government intervention: the highest ranking officials were fired and technical personnel were replaced. The reliability of the index and the worthiness of its data have been a source of controversy ever since. As a result, new (and equally questionable) inflation indexes were introduced by private consulting firms. The inflation rates presented in these new indexes vary by up to twenty percentage points. For more on this issue, see Neiburg's article in this issue.

Gerardo tells us something that is reiterated by many business executives in different sectors other than finance or the exchange market. In terms of the transactions that take place within each sector, the dollar's importance abates. "For me, the dollar is just another good. Bricks are my business." A businessman from the timber industry had something similar to say: "I know what the wood is worth and how to make money off it; I don't need to calculate that in dollars or get my hands on dollars." This perspective changes when the question is not about planning a transaction but evaluating an investment or an increase in equity. Here the dollar acquires a new hierarchical position and competes with other currencies.

The builders' real estate transactions are developed according to their profit margins. These margins are modified when the *bricks*, to use their term, are added to the equation as their own currency. Thus several transactions take place here. On the one hand, builders can postpone the sale of real estate if it looks like the dollar is going to rise. "Stockpiling" square meters is a way to protect the value of their investments. On the other hand, the dividends of an investment are assessed in dollars, in a practice common among Argentine entrepreneurs, who use the US currency to calculate their equity or earnings; however, the quantity of square meters is also a benchmark of the investment. How many apartments or constructed square meters the developers will be able to offer involves adding this currency to a transaction which also depends on dollars and pesos. The developer knows that this is a relatively steady business with low risks. Gerardo followed in the footsteps of his father, who shared the secrets of the business with his son: real estate never goes out of style; you can get out easily; the risk is limited; and if things go south, the worst case scenario is no profit, but never forfeiting your initial investment.

"I think about how many square meters I can buy when the building is finished. My profits are based on volume, and I find people who want to grow by the square meter." Through the acquisition of "bricks" his investments have a profit margin even when pesos are subject to inflation and dollar access is limited. Both pesos and dollars can function as payment methods, while "bricks" or "square meters" function as units of account.

This reconstruction reveals that the currency pluralism that characterizes these real estate developers is embedded in myriad forms of experiencing and maneuvering the temporalities in which transactions occur. In a context of inflation and exchange restrictions, the Argentine peso serves as a current transaction payment instrument; the US dollar is a payment method, store of value, or a unit of account for transactions that will take place in the near or distant future; and finally, bricks are a unit of account to compare transactions over a long period of time. In this relationship between bricks and the long term, Gerardo's family has repeated the same adage since the 1960s: "Growing by the square meter is the secret to this business." And Gerardo could verify this saying with his own experience. After the fall experienced during the 2001–2 crisis, prices in the real estate market have gradually improved in recent years. According to the local Ministry of Urban Development (2013), while in 2001 the average value of an apartment in Buenos Aires was $891 per square meter, this value reached $2,000 in 2011.

Soybean Producers

"The soybean is like the dollar," a farm owner from the province of Santa Fe told us. This was one of our first visits to this region, whose social, economic, and productive milieu had changed since the expansion of soybean planting at the end of the 1980s. The soybean boom was accompanied by a true technological revolution in the countryside, thanks to the incorporation of genetically modified organisms (GMOs) and the direct sowing method (Hernández and Gras 2014). In the years since, the crop had transformed into a global commodity that contributed billions of dollars to the Argentine economy. According to the National Institute of Statistics and Censuses (INDEC), almost $20 billion from the export of soybean entered Argentina in 2014, which represented 30 percent of the foreign sales made by the country. It is no wonder, then, that an attempt by the national government in 2008 to increase the taxes on exporting soy farmers ignited one of the most severe political conflicts of the past decade. Farmers responded with a strike that stretched on for months, which led the minister of economy to hand in his notice and divided the government coalition.

Three years later, soy farmers were back on the front pages due to the exchange restriction policies. The government accused soy farmers—in conjunction with major trade companies—of attempting to "destabilize" the Argentine peso. Farmers, claimed the government, were stockpiling soybeans instead of selling them on foreign markets, thus keeping much-needed dollars from entering the country and speculating with the peso's devaluation. Such practices had been common during the 1980s, a decade of strong currency instability and drastic fluctuations in exchange rates.

San Justo is a small town located north of Santa Fe, the capital city of the province of the same name in the middle of the country. An area of small- and medium-sized farms, Santa Fe has undergone a profound transformation in the past fifteen years that has marked the entire fertile region of Argentina known as *la Pampa húmeda* (humid Pampas). Soybeans have gradually replaced other grains—and livestock—making this region almost monocultural. At the same time, this change has reduced the number of small farmers, who have increasingly rented out their lands to the large crop pools (Gras 2009; Manildo 2013), which have become more profitable than farming on one's own. In this way, although the structure of property ownership has remained more or less the same, the dynamics of production have changed entirely, as has the life of the rural towns in the region, where farmers went to make a new living after abandoning their trade altogether.

During our fieldwork, we found out more about the production and sales of this crop, which had been Argentina's number one export for over a decade. In San Justo, we talked with men and women from the countryside: old farmers who inherited the family farm and other new farmers who joined the bonanza of the past decade, employees of the cooperatives that stockpile crops, retailers selling agricultural machinery, and agricultural technicians working for large farms.

In these conversations, our informants discussed diverse accounts and transactions with multiple units of account. We thus learned that the yields were measured in different ways, such as by weight (in quintals, equivalent to one hundred kilograms); by the surface area of the lands where crops were planted (in hectares); and by their volume, in "trucks" (truckloads). Each of these units revealed the moment of measurement and different accounts: when production was measured in quintals, it was to calculate the profit of a crop; hectares were used when discussing net earnings; and "truckloads" were used to estimate the sale of grains and the accounts associated with them.

Abel was born on the farm his grandfather had bought after arriving from Italy at the beginning of the twentieth century, and where he had begun farming as an adult, following in his father's footsteps. Although the family had initially bred livestock, they had begun cultivating soybean slowly, starting with just a few hectares at the beginning of the 1980s. Now his entire farm is dedicated to soybean production. Abel explained the different ways grains are sold: through a co-op, that guarantees storage of the grain and makes contacts with the exporters, or through "direct exports" via the Rosario port (the most important port for grain exports in Argentina). Although the second option is cheaper, because it eliminates the commissions and other co-op costs, it is only available for major producers: "you have to fill the truck," as Abel explains. Only farmers with a volume of production by the truckload can contact exporters directly, and grain export is a highly concentrated business in Argentina. The truck option is also used for other accounts associated with the sale of grain. When he takes inventory of his production costs, Abel mentions the question of the dispute between farmers and the government on grain export retentions, which are set at 35 percent of their sales abroad. "Thirty-five percent is madness! Think about a hundred trucks [of grain]: they take thirty-five of those trucks: it's insanity! The taxes are unbelievable. . . . The government steals your money."

However, the units not only serve to measure production but also to price the products or raw materials. The basic calculation for the transactions of exporting farmers is based on the price per 100 kg of soy, which generally reflects its Chicago market value (in June of 2015, US$345.85 per ton). The production costs are comprised of different currencies. The workforce salaries, fuel, agricultural machinery rentals, and transportation costs are calculated in pesos. The dollar is the currency used for the purchase of seeds and agrochemicals sold by large multinationals like Monsanto.

Thus, the accounting involved in production costs always involves different currencies. The US dollar is the currency used to calculate the price of the grain, the machinery, and the agrochemicals. The Argentine peso is the unit used to express the cost of field workers, fuel, and utilities (like electricity). The cost of other production components is defined directly in soybeans. When a farmer rents the land of those who have left farming, it is done in two ways: either by paying the owner a percentage of what the renter ultimately makes or in an agreed quantity of soy quintals, regardless of the total crop yield. In both cases, the cost of the rental is measured in soy quintals and the final price depends on the price of soybean when payment is made. When equipment (harvest machines) is not used but rented, the agreement with the contractor is the same: the rental value is based on soy quintals, as a percentage of the harvest (usually around 9 percent).

Numerous devices help farmers in their daily calculations: websites, cell phone apps, and cable TV channels keep farmers abreast of the international commodity markets and the weather, other numbers that farmers check on a daily basis. Industry journals provide useful information for farmers to estimate their costs and earnings, periodically offering data on the cost of the raw materials. Although we mentioned that certain sectors are paid in pesos, the total value is estimated in dollars in order to have a single value for reference purposes. This means also converting to dollars whatever has to be paid in taxes.

This multiplicity of currencies configures the accounts and the transactions of soy farmers. The dollar clearly takes precedence as a unit of account, although it is rarely used as a payment instrument. Producers generally reinvest the pesos they receive in their fields, and pesos are usually the currency of everyday transactions. The most important currency in these transactions, however, is the soybean itself. As the farmer we interviewed said, the soybean functions like the dollar; but soybeans are easier to access, and farmers are more accustomed to this currency. Once the value of their soybean has been calculated in dollars, it serves as a payment method and a store of value. The dollar that farmers use for their calculations is the official dollar, which is what they receive for their exports, and the dollar known as the *soybean dollar*, which is the official price minus a government withholding of approximately 35 percent.[5]

"Soybean is a common currency. I pick up the phone and I've made a sale," explained one farmer in reference to soybeans stored by a co-op that sells his crops for him. The way grains are sold facilitates the currency conversion of soy: the crop is never sold all at once, but gradually, based on the producer's own needs. The portion corresponding to land and machinery rental, in addition to other running costs of the producer, is sold right after the harvest. The rest of the "truck" (truckload) is sent out according to the need to buy fuel (diesel) or agrochemicals for the next harvest or if investments in machinery are necessary. The storage co-ops play a key role in this system, as they store the majority of what is produced and thus allow resources to be used in different ways.[6] For this reason, others talk about the soybean as a financial circuit unto itself: it can be saved; it can be used as means of payment; and it also serves for currency speculation—that is, an upcoming devaluation of the national currency. The last option is the one that became most common after the exchange rate restrictions

5. In addition to these two dollars, the other reference dollar for businesses (though not for soybean producers) is the so-called blue dollar, which is the US dollar exchanged at the black market rate.

6. In the last few decades, development of "silo bags" allowed producers to store grain on their own farms and thus forgo the co-ops, which represents a paradigmatic example of the way in which productive processes can combine with technological innovations to generate an economic phenomenon. In any case, the use of these silos requires having space available (the grain must be stored "horizontally") and care (to avoid leakage or insects) that can make such storage costly in the long term.

were implemented. In the eyes of government officials, producers were destabilizing the Argentine currency; according to farmers, they were simply waiting for an upswing before selling.

As we can see, far from limiting producers, plural currencies offer the potential for a range of transactions. On the one hand, in a context of exchange restrictions, the hierarchy of soybeans (convertible in dollars) places farmers in a privileged position, allowing them to dollarize their transactions without the need to lay hand on a single dollar, in a context characterized by limited access to the US currency. On the other hand, beyond the restrictions, plural currencies allow them to multiply their profit margins, eluding intermediaries or expanding the time available for transactions (or both). As in all cases of a pluralistic configuration of the monetary system, the conversion processes are essential. Knowing when and how "to convert" soybean quintals into pesos, dollars into pesos, or pesos into dollars (or when and how to avoid these conversions) will be the secret to conducting (and understanding) their transactions.

The possibility of making these conversions shows how the soybean allows agricultural producers to maneuver different temporalities, from same-day sales to transactions in the near or distant future. Soybeans can thus be exchanged as part of day-to-day production (for a machinery rental, for example), saved for transactions that will take place at different points during the agricultural cycle or stored in a co-op for long periods. This even allows farmers to plan their retirement, as they contribute to a "pension fund" in the soybean silos. By maneuvering these transaction cycles (from the present to the near or distant future), producers can treat the soybean as an actual currency. This is why farmers say, "The soybean is like the dollar."

FINAL THOUGHTS

"I have a trauma, which is the *cepo* (clamp)," affirmed the ex-president of the Central Bank of the Republic of Argentina (BCRA), who was in charge of the regulatory authority of the monetary system when foreign exchange controls known as the *cepo* were implemented in 2011. The public that heard this statement was composed of young social science students who were attending the presentation on a book about monetary policy, in which the ex-official was the main commentator. The year 2016 was in full swing and several months had passed since those measures had ended. The new government had previously held as one of its main campaign promises the lifting of exchange controls. At the time, the president of the Central Bank had carried out a very active public defense of the restrictions as an instrument in a "cultural battle" oriented toward "undollarizing the minds" of Argentines. No doubt, the so-called trauma she confessed in 2016 responded to a profound sentiment of having lost that battle, given that despite the nearly five years of restrictions to foreign exchange transactions, Argentines' tendency to use the US dollar had not decreased.

The regulations oriented toward limiting currency pluralism—like the restrictions implemented between 2011 and 2015 in Argentina, or the attempt to prohibit the Haitian dollar, as analyzed by Neiburg (2016)—are efforts made to domesticate practices and imaginaries sedimented over a long period of time. During public debates regarding foreign exchange restrictions, Argentines' preference for the dollar constituted an "anomaly" that had to be corrected (Luzzi 2013). The "trauma" of the Argentine Central Bank's ex-president was the expression, in a psychoanalytic language, of the failure of those attempts when they clash with financial repertoires that present more resistance and flexibility than the regulations that intend to domesticate them. We have shown throughout this chapter that this flexibility and resistance corresponded to a plurality of currencies and monetary functions, with contingent and relational properties.

Table 1 presents our descriptions of the transactions we analyzed in the universe of real estate developers and soybean producers, where we discovered multiple currencies at work (pesos, dollars, constructed square meters/bricks, and soybeans). In addition, we noted a disaggregation of the functions of these currencies and a differentiation based on these functions, as the result of exchange restrictions (the official dollar, the blue dollar, the soybean dollar).

Table 1: Multiple currencies at work in different transactions

Money Functions	Real Estate Developers	Soybean Producers
Unit of account	US dollar constructed square meters	Official dollar Soy dollar (official—35%) Soybean (crop volume)
Means of exchange/ payment	Argentine pesos US dollar ("blue" or negotiated dollar)	Argentine pesos Soybean (crop volume)
Store of value	US dollar constructed square meters/"bricks"	Soybean US dollar

We find that the agents do not simply replicate patterns from the past. Beyond common traits such as rising inflation and exchange control policies, the scenarios are never quite the same and people reveal a localized ability to deal with them. And precisely because there are margins of innovation, profits are also possible. Yet, we never saw agents making instrumental decisions that respond only to specific situations, as other hypothesis would have it. Their transactions are innovative, always anchored in historic processes of economic socialization; they are reactivations of individual and collective lessons learned in unique contexts (as we have seen, "bricks" and "soybean" were not created as units of account *during* the exchange restrictions, but before).

In his study of currencies in Haiti, Neiburg (2016) showed "how nonunification [of different currencies] is in line (in the Weberian sense) with the ways in which people live in an environment of extreme monetary scarcity" (Neiburg 2016: 87). On our part, we have showed here how some economic agents in Argentine society find a condition to display their business activities, in currency pluralism. Despite the differences, both cases allow us to further understand the close relationship that exists between the ways in which currency pluralism is configured and the definition of particular imaginaries about the state, its capacities for regulation, and the resistances it encounters.

In this chapter, we found that agents define, handle, and experience different objects as real currencies. Currency pluralism expands when real estate developers treat "bricks" as a real currency and farmers do the same with "soybeans." In fact, developers promote bricks as the only real currency, since bricks keep their value over time. Similarly, soybean producers prefer soybeans to other currencies, as they can save soybeans, invest them, or exchange them for other goods, as if they were running a bank. The brick is a currency parallel to the state currency; developers add and subtract in square meters and convince their customers to do so as well. This account unit is more "real" than the peso since it allows them to make estimates and protect themselves from the fluctuations of an unstable currency. Accounting in square meters provides greater power over one's assets because it is done in a currency parallel to that of the state. On the other hand, for farmers, the soybean is a real currency that creates resistance and at times antagonism with the state. When a producer complains about the quantity of truckloads the state withholds, the producer is monetizing political criticism. When producers define soy as a parallel banking system, they reveal the social and political power anchored in the multiple reality of money. In this way, how they imagine money affects how they imagine the state, based on a currency whose reality expands in parallel to their opposition to the state.

From a certain interpretation, Argentina's recent monetary history, but also Israel's (Dominguez 1990), Ecuador's (Nelms 2012), Nigeria's (Guyer 2004), Russia's (Lemon 1998), and El Salvador's (Pedersen 2002), can be narrated through a currency pluralism that confronts a "hard," "healthy," or "real" currency (the US dollar) against a "soft," "ill," or "false" currency (in our case, the peso). Undoubtedly, these narratives contribute to the thesis about the recent configuration of a monetary pluralism articulated by the hegemony of US currency as store of value in heterogeneous spaces. Starting from the analysis of a particular context (the foreign exchange restriction from 2011–15 in Argentina), in this chapter we dialogue with this thesis, examining the contingent and relational dynamics of the properties of multiple currencies that integrate the financial repertoires. The two cases we present here—experiments in bricks and soybeans as real currencies—provide insight on the connection between dynamic currency pluralism and the temporalities of transactions. The hierarchy of currencies and currency functions is embedded in cycles both long and short, but also in the day-to-day maneuverings of agents eager to increase their gains.

Plural currencies allow agents to manage the different times in which transactions occur. Agents define bricks and soybeans as real currencies because these objects enable them to plan and conduct transactions in the near or distant future, giving them some leeway, and neutralizing or exploiting (as necessary) the uncertainty of the economic context.

In our reconstruction, currencies and their functions are associated with both the here and now (the peso is used in both cases), the near future (soybeans and bricks), and the distant future (the US dollar). However, this hierarchy is subject to fluctuations; real estate developers can swap the dollar for bricks as their currency for the distant future, just as farmers can "save" their soybeans for lengthy periods or use them for immediate transactions.

In this context, bricks, soybeans, and dollars can be considered *hard currencies*, to return to the term used in the narrative of monetary configurations since the end of the Bretton Woods Agreement. Yet unlike the usual classification, in which this figure is generally associated with the US dollar, our work allows pluralism to be understood not merely as a dichotomy between soft and hard currencies but also by differentiating and establishing a hierarchy between the currencies that each of these figures assumes. From this perspective, currency pluralism assumes a fluctuating hierarchy that can only be understood through an ethnographic reconstruction of the transaction cycles and ways to maneuver the temporalities established by each of the currencies.

ACKNOWLEDGEMENTS

The authors want to thank the coeditors, Jane Guyer and Federico Neiburg, for their valuable comments and critiques on previous versions of this essay. They are also grateful to the editor and the three anonymous reviewers whose suggestions have contributed to the elaboration of a richer and more precise text. And, finally, to all the participants at the Wenner-Gren/Museu Nacional/Federal University of Rio de Janeiro workshop Real Economy: Ethnographic Inquiries into the Reality and the Realization of Economic Life, who were the first readers of this text. None of them, of course, are responsible for the final result presented here.

REFERENCES

Blanc, Jerôme. 2000. *Unité et diversité du fait monétaire*. Paris: L'Harmattan.
Bohannan, Paul. 1955. "Some principles of exchange and investment among the Tiv." *American Anthropologist* 57 (1): 60–70.
———. 1959. "The impact of money on an African subsistence economy." *Journal of Economic History* 19 (4): 491–503.
Canitrot, Adolfo. 1981. "Teoría y práctica del liberalismo: Política antiinflacionaria y apertura económica en la Argentina." *Desarrollo Económico* 21 (82): 1–73.
D'Avella, Nicholas. 2014. "Ecologies of investment: Crisis histories and brick futures in Argentina." *Cultural Anthropology* 29 (1): 173–99.
Dodd, Nigel. 2014. *The social life of money*. Princeton, NJ: Princeton University Press.
Dominguez, Virginia. 1990. "Representing value and the value of representation: A different look at money." *Cultural Anthropology* 5 (1): 16–44.
Gaggero, Alejandro, and Pablo Nemiña. 2016. "La vivienda como inversión: El origen de la dolarización del mercado inmobiliario durante la última dictadura cívico-militar." In *De militares y empresarios a políticos y CEOS:*

Reflexiones a 40 años del golpe, edited by Guillermo Levy, 175–93. Buenos Aires: Gorla.

Gras, Carla. 2009. "La agricultura familiar en el agro pampeano: Desplazamientos y mutaciones." In *Trabajo agrícola: Experiencias y resignificación de las identidades en el campo argentino*, edited by T. Gutiérrez and J. M. Cerdá, 17–41. Buenos Aires: Ediciones CICCUS.

Guyer, Jane, ed. 1995. *Money matters: Instability, values and social payments in the modern history of West African communities*. Portsmouth, NH: Heinemann.

———. 2004. *Marginal gains: Monetary transactions in Atlantic Africa*. Chicago: University of Chicago Press.

———. 2016a. "Intricacy and impasse: Dilemmas of value in soft currency economies." In *Legacies, logics, logistics: Essays in the anthropology of the platform economy*, 165–80. Chicago: University of Chicago Press.

———. 2016b. "Soft currencies, cash economies, new monies: Past and present." In *Legacies, logics, logistics: Essays in the anthropology of the platform economy*, 220–37. Chicago: Chicago University Press.

Guyer, Jane, and Kabiru Salami. 2012. "Gaps, innovations and casuistic reasoning in currency dynamics: Nigeria, Eastern Europe, North Korea and their connections." Panel at Norms in the Margins and Margins of the Norm: The Social Construction of Illegality conference, Tervuren and Brussels, October 2012.

Helleiner, Eric. 2003. *The making of national money: Territorial currencies in historical perspective*. Ithaca, NY: Cornell University Press.

Hérnandez, Valeria, and Carla Gras. 2014. *El agro como negocio: Producción, sociedad y territorios en la globalización*. Buenos Aires: Biblos.

Kuroda, Akinobu. 2008. "Concurrent but non-integrable currency circuits: Complementary relationships among monies in modern China and other regions." *Financial History Review* 15 (1): 17–36.

Lemon, Alaina. 1998. "'Your eyes are green like dollars': Counterfeit cash, national substance, and currency apartheid in 1990s Russia." *Cultural Anthropology* 13 (1): 22–55.

Luzzi, Mariana. 2013. "La moneda en cuestión: Del estallido de la convertibilidad a las discusiones sobre el 'cepo cambiario.'" In *La grieta: Política, economía y cultura después de 2001*, edited by Sebastián Pereyra, Gabriel Vommaro, and Germán Pérez, 195–209. Buenos Aires: Biblos.

———. 2015. "Socialisation économique et hiérarchies monétaires dans un contexte de crise: Argentine, 2001–2003." *Critique Internationale* 69 (4): 21–37.

———. 2016. "Quelle est la monnaie de l'épargne? Controverses autour de la valeur des dépôts bancaires en Argentine." *La Vie des idées*, January 21, 2016. http://www.laviedesidees.fr/Quelle-est-la-monnaie-de-l-epargne.html.

Luzzi, Mariana, and Ariel Wilkis. 2017. "El dólar habló en números: Crónica periodística y publicidad en la primera popularización del dólar en la Argentina (1958–1967)." In *Saberes desbordados: Historias de diálogos entre conocimientos científicos y sentido común (Argentina, siglos XIX y XX)*, edited by Jimena Caravaca, Claudia Daniel, and Mariano Plotkin. Buenos Aires: Libros del Ides.

Luzzi, Mariana, and Ariel Wilkis. 2019. *El dólar. Historia de una moneda argentina (1930-2019)*. Buenos Aires: Crítica.

Manildo, Luciana. 2013. *La identidad chacarera en las grietas del paisaje sojero: Desplazamientos, transmisiones y apropiaciones intergeneracionales en las transformaciones recientes de la producción familiar pampeana*. Buenos Aires: Imago Mundi.

Marx, Karl. 1976. *El capital: Crítica de la economía política*. México: Fondo de cultura económica.

Maurer, Bill. 2006. "The anthropology of money." *Annual Review of Anthropology* 35:15–36.

Ministry of Urban Development. 2013. "2001–2012: Relevamiento de mercado inmobiliario en la Ciudad de Buenos Aires." Gobierno de la Ciudad de Buenos Aires.

Muir, Sarah. 2015. "The currency of failure: Money and middle-class critique in post-crisis Buenos Aires." *Cultural Anthropology* 30 (2): 310–35.

Neiburg, Federico. 2010. "Sick currencies and public numbers." *Anthropological Theory* 10 (1–2): 96–102.

———. 2016. "A true coin of their dreams: Imaginary monies in Haiti (The 2010 Sidney Mintz Lecture)." *HAU: Journal of Ethnographic* Theory 6 (1): 75–93.

Nelms, Taylor. 2012. "Una moneda de confianza: Dollarization, debt, and everyday economic organization in Ecuador." Paper presented at the International Sociological Association Forum, Buenos Aires, Argentina.

Orléan, André. 2009. "La sociologie économique de la monnaie." In *Traité de sociologie économique*, edited by Philippe Steiner and François Vatin, 209–46. Paris: PUF.

Pedersen, David. 2002. "The storm we call dollars: Determining value and belief in El Salvador and the United States." *Cultural Anthropology* 17 (3): 431–59.

Polanyi, Karl. 1983. *La grande transformation: Aux origines politiques et économiques de notre temps*. Paris: Gallimard.

Servet, Jean-Michel, Bruno Théret, and Zeynep Yildirim. 2008. "Universalité du fait monétaire et pluralité des monnaies." In *L'Argent des anthropologues, la monnaie des économistes*, edited by d'Eveline Baumann, Laurent Bazin, Pepita Ould-Ahmed, Pascale Phélinas, Monique Selim, and Richard Sobel, 167–207. Paris: L'Harmattan.

Simmel, Georg. 1978. *The philosophy of money*. London: Routledge & Kegan Paul.

Théret, Bruno, ed. 2007. *La monnaie dévoilée par ses crises*, 2 vol. Paris: Éditions del'EHESS.

———. 2008. "Les trois états de la monnaie: Approche interdisciplinaire du fait monétaire." *Revue Economique* 59 (4): 813–41.

Zelizer, Viviana. 1994. *The social meaning of money*. Princeton, NJ: Princeton University Press.

CHAPTER SIX

A political anthropology of finance in cross-border investment in Shanghai

Horacio Ortiz

This essay proposes to analyze global financial flows based on fieldwork carried out in a consulting company working in the domain of cross-border mergers and acquisitions in Shanghai. Marcel Mauss highlighted the fact that exchanges within and among social groups have multiple co-constituted meanings, which are, among other possibilities, economic, moral, political, and religious. The hierarchies within and between groups, constituted with those meanings, are thus both determining for and transformed by the objects exchanged and the modalities of exchange. Mauss thus stressed that the idea that the "economy" should be distinguished from the "political" or "religious" domains is itself part of a particular moral, political, or religious imaginary (Mauss [1923–24] 2016; Hart and Ortiz 2014; Sahlins 2013). This insight was central in Karl Polanyi's analysis of the political process establishing the "market" as an institution that would be separated from other social institutions ([1944] 2001). Michel Foucault showed how the theoretical formalization of this process by ordo-liberalism attempted thus to separate the "economic" from the "political," constituting the "market" as an institution with a technical character that would guarantee a distribution of resources, the justice of which would be politically neutral, and therefore politically undisputable (2004). Within this theoretical orientation—central in neoclassic economics and in financial regulation worldwide—money is considered as a technical medium that allows for exchanges in a "real economy," of which it is not a part. Jane Guyer (2016) shows, on the contrary, how the term *real economy* is mobilized with different meanings, reactivating certain "legacies," which must be understood as part of a political configuration, where the term plays particular roles in relations of forces. *Economy* can therefore be a slippery analytic concept, especially when one is doing research on practices that actors and analysts readily define as "economic," with all the potential of de-politicization this implies. To explore one of the ways in which this can be avoided, this essay proposes to consider global finance as an object of political anthropology.

In line with the Maussian insights highlighted above, this text considers that the meaning and uses of money are multiple, and relate to the social relations in which they take place (Dodd 2014; Guyer 2016; Hart 2000; Hart and Ortiz 2014; Maurer 2006; Zelizer 2009). This implies that money is defined by these social relations, but also contributes to define them in turn: gifts, debts, and expenses partially define kinship and friendship (Zelizer 2005); monetary policy contributes to define and legitimize a polity, its citizens and social hierarchies among them (Hart 1986; Hertz 1998; Neiburg 2006); indemnities imposed by the state against polluters shape conceptions of nature (Fourcade 2011); money rituals define the attributes of gods (Chu 2010); and consumption practices (Stark 2011) and budgetary disciplines (Zaloom 2016) can establish the standards of religious morality. Approaching these practices through this understanding of money allows for seeing how, as Mauss highlighted, different meanings and uses of money—which correspond to mutually constituted religious, political, and moral hierarchies established through the distribution of resources—can be combined in multiple ways, with conflicts, conversions, and the production of hybrid or new meanings in the process (Guyer 2004). Guyer (2016) has proposed to consider these sets of practices and meanings as a multiplicity of "repertoires" conforming "ecologies" navigated differently by different actors, in what are often (but not only) power relations (on this point see also Maurer 2015). I will use here the term *imaginaries* to talk about these repertoires, only to hint slightly more at their creative and labile character, as they can be vague, wavering, and not even recognized as changing by the actors themselves (de Certeau [1980] 1990).

This pragmatist approach (Maurer 2006) eschews the idea that money would be the representative of one particular form of practice or social relation, be it relations of production, as in the Marxian tradition, of exchange, as in the liberal tradition, or some universal moral idea, as proposed, differently, by Georg Simmel ([1900] 1978) and Mauss himself ([1923–24] 2016). In very different ways, all these approaches tend to stress what money "really" is, in a way that relates then to some definition of the "real economy." In the anthropology of finance, this can lead to considering finance as "fiction" or to focus on the sole issues raised by these approaches, such as relations of production or matters of calculation, knowledge, and information. The danger in this move is that the distinction between the "real" and its "other" may obscure the social processes in the latter that are crucial for the former.

One of the seeming advantages of these approaches of money and finance from the point of view of a "real economy" is that they often imply a much broader conceptual frame, which also contains a series of concepts and narratives providing for a political critique of the social processes under study. Pragmatism does not grant a politics warranted on a single reality. Instead, the "political" aspect of finance proposed here is itself termed along some possible uses of money that may allow for addressing a limited series of concerns. As money is constitutive of imaginaries of gender, kinship, religion, citizenship, and entrepreneurial profits, among others, it is also fundamental in the production and transformation of the social hierarchies that make sense according to them. Analyzing the multiple meanings mobilized to make sense of transactions such as mergers and acquisitions allows for understanding how this distribution of resources does not belong uniquely to the constitution of financial social hierarchies, but also to the constitution of political and moral relations of forces that cannot be separated from the former. As a series of organizations that collect, produce, and distribute money on a global scale, the finance industry ranks activities according to multiple conditions, rights, and duties, allowing some of them to exist at the expense of others. Thus, it articulates relations of forces that contribute to the production and transformation of the multiple social hierarchies where money plays a constitutive role, on a global scale (Hart 2015; Ortiz 2015). This use of the category *political* connects, thus, with Georges Balandier's definition of political institutions as those that organize relations of forces (1967), and Foucault's analysis of power as the production of differences in the capacities to act (1975, 1976). The political anthropology of everyday financial practices proposed here consists in studying the multiple repertoires that contribute to the production of these social hierarchies.

The research presented in this article is based on ten months of participant observation with a team of consultants based in Shanghai, conducting mergers and acquisitions (M&A) between Western Europe and China, and about fifty interviews with financial professionals, mostly concerned with cross-border investment, in Beijing, Shanghai, and Hong Kong.[1] Analyzing the way in which they channel money from a large corporation based in China to a medium-sized enterprise in Europe, through the purchase of one of its subsidiaries, this chapter highlights how the imaginaries of profit mobilized in the negotiations, calculations, and establishment of rights and duties in the deal were actually multiple, and how they also combined with different imaginaries of the state and cultural identity. These imaginaries, often vague, co-constitute each other, but can also be in conflict and disconnected. Thereby, this chapter shows not only that it is important to analyze financial calculation practices within other social processes—in particular, personal professional and nonprofessional trajectories, organizational issues, legal issues, stately and macroeconomic concerns, and imaginaries of the global (Montagne and Ortiz 2013)—but also that the imaginaries about "profits" are co-constituted with those about "states" and "culture," in ways that cannot be disentangled in everyday practice. Doing so, the article shows the fruitfulness of the pragmatist approaches of money outlined above to understand the practices and meanings whereby money is distributed around the world through these particular operations. The social hierarchies established through these exchanges make sense in terms of "states," "culture," and "profits," the limited possibilities of which are combined and transformed through the everyday practices described here. The analysis of these practices thus allows for locating the politics of distribution within these multiple imaginaries, instead of limiting it to problematizations in terms of the "economy."

The article will first show the multiple imaginaries of "profit" that were mobilized by the people observed, as they conducted a transaction that lasted more than two years. I will then analyze the importance, in the process, of imaginaries of "states" and "cultures." In the conclusion, I will come back to the complex relations between these imaginaries, and the questions that they raise for a critical and reflexive pragmatist approach of finance as an object of political anthropology.

---

1. Previous research was conducted with stockbrokers and fund managers in New York and Paris between 2002 and 2005, and in business schools in Paris and Shanghai between 2008 and 2014. In agreement with the people I observed, and to respect their anonymity, all names have been changed.

IMAGINARIES OF PROFIT

The jobs and income of Merge Consulting employees and owners depended on their capacity to attract clients whose service fees comprised the company's yearly sales of about 3 million euros. These fees came from different companies for different activities, and were distributed within Merge Consulting according to professional standards that comprise relations of collaboration, conflict, and hierarchy between people and between organizations. In professional finance, monetary gains can have multiple moral and political meanings, linked to the presuppositions embedded in the formulas and procedures (Maurer 2002; Muniesa et al. 2017; Ouroussoff 2010; Ortiz 2014a; Zaloom 2006) to organizational rules (Arjaliès et al. 2017; Godechot 2016; Ho 2009; Ortiz 2014b; Zaloom 2006), and to the macroeconomic and political context in which they operate (Hart and Ortiz 2014; Ho 2009; LiPuma and Lee 2004; Montagne and Ortiz 2013). In the case of activities such as those of Merge Consulting, "profits" meant different things, within several imaginaries about personal trajectories, organizational power relations, notions of entrepreneurship, and circuits of debt and credit with multiple more or less defined rights and duties and the possibilities to circumvent them, as they were claimed in conflicting ways by various stakeholders. I will present a transaction whereby a large company based in China purchased a small company based in Western Europe,[2] because it will allow us to see how these multiple imaginaries could be combined, opposed, or unrelated, as they were produced in particular situations.

Merge Consulting was composed of ten people. Four associates (who owned the company) and four employees were based in a mid-sized town in Western Europe, Villagiund, while two employees were based in Shanghai. The main source of income of the company came from its services as consultant in mergers and acquisitions. The client, a potential purchaser or seller, would pay Merge Consulting to find a counterparty in the transaction, and to assist at all the stages of the negotiation until the closing of the deal. In accordance with professional standards, clients paid "operating fees" upon completion of intermediate tasks, such as finding and establishing relations with potential counterparties and negotiating the price and the conditions of the purchase—for instance, in terms of the rights and liabilities of former owners or of potentially remaining

2.   In what follows, when I use the terms China and Western Europe without brackets, I refer to the territories.

management. These tasks could take between several weeks and more than a year and, according to the opinion of many interviewees in the profession and of Merge Consulting's members, usually less than half of the transactions that were started did reach completion. Once the transaction was concluded, Merge Consulting would be paid a success fee, potentially much bigger than the operating fees, of between 3 percent and 5 percent of the amount of the transaction. While operating fees usually were around 100,000 euros, distributed over a long period of time, the sale or purchase of a company valued at 10 million euros would imply payment of a success fee between 300,000 and 500,000 euros in one installment. This impacted the bonus distributed hierarchically within Merge Consulting, where the yearly salaries of financial analysts and the representatives of the company in Shanghai were between 40,000 to 60,000 euros and those of associates around 100,000 euros.

The company was established in the late 2000s in Europe, where it conducted most of its activities. In 2012, in order to develop its operations in China, the company hired Peter, in his late thirties, who had arrived to Shanghai from Europe two years earlier. When Peter decided to leave the company in 2015, I replaced him partially—as an external consultant in Shanghai—for ten months. During that period, one of my tasks was to assist in the purchase of one of Merge Consulting's clients, Bolbus, a small company producing medical molecules and devices based in Western Europe, by Alpha, a large company based in China, producing chemical and medical products. The transaction was eventually completed at a price of 15 million euros, which were paid to Bolbus' mother company, Calcus. This transaction allows for seeing how the members of Merge Consulting and the owners and representatives of these companies mobilized different imaginaries of profit.

The interactions between the members of Merge Consulting based in Europe and those in Shanghai were made of a daily stream of emails and regular conference calls, which happened at least once a week, and sometimes more, in particular when transactions reached moments that were considered to be crucial. The members based in Europe also came to Shanghai at least once a year, and, at the time of my observations, a trip to Europe was being planned for Vicky, who was previously Peter's assistant and who replaced him as head of the Shanghai office after his departure. In these exchanges, there were moments of misunderstanding that allowed for margins of play and clarifications that shifted the terms of the relations. But concerning the transaction, there was a clear agreement among all the members that they wanted the deal to be completed as soon as possible. All operating fees had already been paid the previous year, and any action by Merge Consulting on this project would only be funded in the event of a success fee. This would also be the first deal concluded with a Chinese company, and it could be used in marketing material to expand business. Merge Consulting had explored several potential buyers, and reached the final stage of the exploration with two of them. This meant the signing of confidentiality agreements between the potential buyer and the seller, so that the latter would disclose information deemed sensitive and confidential about its operations. Before the final negotiations that could ensue in the agreement about the price and conditions of purchase, the professional norm was that the representatives of the companies would meet personally. Just before the summer of 2015, the owners of Calcus and Mr. Hecks, head of Bolbus, came to Shanghai to meet the representatives of two potential buyers. While the way fee payments are organized presupposes that they "align the interests" of the consultancy with those of its clients, once the last stage is reached this turns into an explicit tension. The owners of Calcus did not want to sell Bolbus at just any price and under any condition, and although they wanted the transaction to take place, they preferred to go slower. The two days spent in Shanghai by Merge Consulting's clients were thus marked by a tension not only between the representatives of the buying and selling companies but also between Merge Consulting and its client.

The morning of the meeting, Vicky, Peter, and I met two owners of Calcus and Mr. Hecks in their hotel, and took them to the headquarters of Alpha, one of the two potential buyers, situated in an industrial park on the outskirts of the city. The first three hours involved an exchange between the representatives of the companies, mediated by Merge Consulting, followed by a lunch and a visit to Alpha's premises. At the negotiation table with representatives of Alpha, the owner of Bolbus who conducted the talk insisted on the idea that theirs was a family business; for the owners it was important to ensure that the sale of Bolbus would not create a difficulty for its employees and management, for whom they cared personally. They explained that the head of Bolbus, Mr. Hecks, had worked in the company for decades, and was practically part of the family. The presentation then shifted from the insistence on the morality of family entrepreneurship to presenting a particular arrangement for the deal. Mr. Hecks had worked in China for the last thirty years, and had established other companies there, some that were unrelated to Bolbus and some that had direct dealings with it. Calcus's proposal was that after the sale to Alpha, Mr. Hecks would continue to be the head of Bolbus, and that his own companies would still benefit from the contracts with it. Mr. Hecks then explained at length that the sale would help him to "spend more time in China"—in particular, to continue developing his personal businesses there, with and without Bolbus. He conducted most of the discussions with the representatives of Alpha concerning the qualities of Bolbus, staging the figure of an independent businessman with whom it was profitable to deal, not the least because he would remain a partner in the long term (as he was relocating to China). Alpha was listed in a Chinese stock exchange, and the negotiations were conducted in the presence of its management, composed of engineers, and of representatives of its main shareholder, Monatu, an investment fund based in another Asian jurisdiction. While the engineers mobilized arguments concerning the need to verify how compatible the technologies of the two companies were, implying that if they weren't, more investment was needed, and therefore the price of Bolbus should be lowered, the representatives of Monatu were concerned about the timing of the operation in relation to evolutions in the stock market. The announcement to the financial analysts that Alpha was upgrading its technology by purchasing top-of-the-line technology from Europe would boost Alpha's stock price, as long as the purchase could be presented as cheap enough. After all parties acknowledged that they considered the proposal by Calcus to be potentially acceptable, the lunch was spent talking about life in Shanghai and generalities, and the afternoon centered on technicalities of the medical devices.

The different meanings of the deal, staged at the negotiation table, were further explored in conference calls and exchanges of emails and documents. These meanings were partly connected to the attempt by all parties either to sell at a high price or to buy at a low one. But some arguments carried more weight than others or served different purposes. Calcus's management insisted that the sale was due to "purely industrial reasons," meaning that they considered that Bolbus was a very promising company; they were not selling it because it had no financial value but because operations needed further investment to profit from their potential expansion in China, and this was too far from Calcus's "core business." The talk of a family company only enhanced their argument that they would have preferred not to get rid of a technologically advanced asset. The responses from Alpha's representatives were ambiguous on this point. Insisting on the need to assess the technology was aimed at opening the door for a lower price. At the same time, the price proposed by Merge Consulting, 15 million euros, was acceptable due to differences in the methods of valuation for the acquisition of a company.

As I heard many times in interviews with professionals of cross-border investment (Ortiz 2017), the mainstream methods of valuations are the same in China and in Europe and the United States, with the exception of one. In Europe and the United States[3] a company would be evaluated by assessing the price of each of its assets, by comparing it to similar companies, and by calculating the potential cash flows that could be obtained in the future, discounted at a required rate of return. According to most interviewees, this last method is much less prevalent in transactions in China. These methods have moral and political meanings. The method of "discounted cash flows" is usually termed a "fundamental valuation," concerned with long-term ownership of the company, and it is intimately related to the idea that if "investors" search for all available information, in "efficient markets," this information will be "reflected" in the price, which will then serve as a signal contributing to a socially optimal allocation of resources (Doganova 2014). Valuing the company by its assets, or by comparing it to other listed companies, implies something closer to a "speculative valuation," with its "bubbles" and "crashes," where the aim may not be to profit from the company in the long run, but to sell it whenever market prices go up (De Goede 2005; Hertz 2000; LiPuma and Lee 2004; MacKenzie 2006; Muniesa 2007; Ortiz 2014b).

According to several interviewees, one of the practical problems posed by this difference in the methods of valuation is that when the parties disagree on the price, they may also disagree on what the object of the transaction is. In the current case, this difference had the opposite result. Using the discounted cash flows method, Merge Consulting's analysts considered that Calcus could gain 15 million euros by keeping Bolbus in operation. This price was lower than the stock price of comparable companies listed in China, taken as a standard of valuation by financial analysts of Monatu, and potentially by brokerage companies who would report on the deal. The purchase would be considered a bargain, and push up the price of Alpha's stock, and therefore the monetary value of Monatu's portfolio. The associates of Merge Consulting, connecting the technical and political elements of financial valuation, commented that the deal was therefore benefiting from this mismatch in valuation methods and from the inefficiency of the "stock market bubble" in China.

---

3.   But not exclusively.

The meanings of the 15 million euros paid by Alpha for Bolbus were therefore multiple. Some referred to different techniques of financial valuation, themselves predicated on different definitions of what a company is as financial investment and its relation to the technical and political meanings of market efficiency. But the money, considered a profitable transfer for all parties, was also supposed to make sense as part of a personal entrepreneurial project, as the "best industrial solution" for the development of an activity irrespective of its owners, or on the contrary, as the painful disposal of a family jewel, marked by employers' paternalistic moral responsibility toward employees. From the point of view of Merge Consulting, these different imaginaries were rendered compatible, in the deal, with the strategies of the associates to obtain a success fee and to expand their prestige and business in China. For employees like Vicky, the company's representative in Shanghai, this meant the potential upgrade of her position in the company, with the prospect, evoked by the associates, that she could herself become an associate in the future. These multiple imaginaries became more or less compatible or even mingled into one, depending on the situation, and their similarities, disconnections, and contradictions were used to articulate and defuse conflicts around price, rights, and duties in the transaction. Mobilized to strengthen or explore positions during the negotiation, their potential contradictions did not need to be explored further by the people involved as the transaction approached completion and tensions diffused. With technical, moral, and political aspects, they composed a complex set of possibilities, which marked the paths through which the actors concluded the transaction and went on with their lives. These imaginaries were inextricably linked to imaginaries of the state.

IMAGINARIES OF THE STATE

Merge Consulting's practices implied mobilizing imaginaries of the state that usually related in multiples ways to a broad understanding of a relative position between a rising Chinese economic power, where the state had played a central role in economic policy and wealth accumulation for forty years, and a decline in the places most affected by the financial turmoil that started in 2007–8, in particular the United States and Western Europe (Ortiz 2017). Yet these imaginaries did not conflate into one but were, on the contrary, sometimes disconnected and sometimes in contradiction with each other. Merge Consulting was itself partly an actor of different states that paid for its services.

Its associates understood their commercial strategy as benefiting from—and supporting—certain macroeconomic policies in China, with their narratives of nation building, socialism, and sustainable development. And the legal frameworks that were crossed by the transactions implied detailed strategies to avoid or profit from their provisions. In all these cases, the state was mobilized, among others, as a potentially mighty force orienting macroeconomic policy, as a series of unrelated entities, and in China, as an organization with a complex link to the Communist Party. It is therefore important to understand how the state is itself produced from its margins by actors who imply its existence, and who are officially not part of state bureaucracy (Abélès [1990] 2005; Das and Poole 2004). These imaginaries, in turn, must be understood in the case presented here as they were co-constituted with the imaginaries of profit described above.

Merge Consulting did not provide regulated legal services for its clients. Nevertheless, its associates, with decades of experience in M&A, did scrutinize closely each clause of the contracts that were signed between the parties of the transaction at each step of the process and when the final sale occurred. Thereby, the company's activities were constantly gauged against the regulatory frameworks that were brought together by the transactions. These frameworks could be perceived in terms of benefits—for instance, when it was considered that the contract should explicitly be covered by European laws because judges were supposed to be more independent of other state actors in Europe than in mainland China, or in terms of constraints that should be avoided—for instance, when establishing companies in Hong Kong to avoid certain tax requirements in Europe and China. This understanding of state regulation, which could be assessed and calibrated in detail in certain moments of the transactions, cohabitated with the fact that Merge Consulting sold its services to the municipality of Villagiund, where it was located, and to the municipality of a mid-sized Chinese town, Zhongzhen, in order to help them enhance the commercial relations between the companies operating in the territory under their jurisdictions.[4] This meant interpreting the political tensions within each municipality and the career prospects of the municipal teams. While municipal officials in Villagiund would use increased activity with China as an argument in electoral contests, for municipal officials in Zhongzhen, these activities responded to the central government's injunction to increase GDP and internationalization,

---

4.   The names of these two cities have been changed to preserve the anonymity of the people observed.

and could therefore help their career advancement within the Communist Party, and hence, within the state administration. These municipalities were not just clients paying fees but also facilitators, as they opened their contacts to Merge Consulting—for instance, when the consultants were looking for potential clients in Europe and buyers in China. Thus, just as the sale of Bolbus was being negotiated, Merge Consulting was working on another project, aiming to create a joint venture between a small company based in Europe and a state-owned company in China. This deal, which ultimately did not reach completion, was being brokered by the municipality of Zhongzhen, in whose industrial park the joint venture would be located, benefiting from tax rebates.

The transaction around Bolbus also activated another important imaginary of the state. The company produced avowedly high-tech molecules and devices that could be used in medical treatment. All the participants evoked as an evidence that this purchase, and the potential growth of Bolbus in China, was predicated on the hopes of success of the Chinese government's official project to reorient the economy from exports toward internal consumption, where middle-class consumption would take a leading role, in particular that of an aging and wealthier urban population. Investment was therefore supposed to go to sectors such as health, education, and environmental protection and away from heavy manufacturing or luxury, the latter being under attack by central government discourse as oiling the gift-giving circuits of state officials' corruption. Benefiting from the sale of Bolbus, for the members of Merge Consulting, thus implied navigating and trying to leverage the multiple facets of legislation, understanding and taking part in local-level politics in case they could be helpful if the transaction stalled, and participating in the application of government policy, within the understanding that the Chinese state indeed had the capacity to transform what was thereby supposed to be a malleable economic structure. This latter point contrasted with the assessment Merge Consulting's associates made of states in Europe, against which they held an explicitly "conservative" view that demanded less state participation in economic life.

These imaginaries combined with others where the power of the Chinese state was seen as a danger due to corruption and the weakness of the rule of law. On the same trip in which Mr. Hecks and the owners of Calcus met with the representatives of Alpha and started exploring the concrete modalities of the transaction, Merge Consulting had arranged a meeting with a representative of one of the largest state-owned investment funds, which was introducing as potential buyer the owner of a company of which the fund was an important shareholder. Contrary to his attitude in front of the representatives of Monatu, Mr. Hecks was extremely evasive, and did not disclose the fact that he owned a company that sold high-tech components to Bolbus. After the meeting, once we were back at the hotel, he explained to us that he did not want to deal with companies owned by the Chinese state. According to him, in that case, not only would it be very hard to negotiate the price and especially his right to stay in the company, but there was even the risk that the counterparty would send spies to copy the technology that he himself was producing in China and selling to Bolbus. This would make him lose the chance to expand his own business after the sale and, he claimed—following a narrative line that I had heard with many other professionals working in mergers and acquisitions and joint ventures between state-owned and foreign-owned companies—there would be no legal protection against this theft of intellectual property, as Chinese judges would not enforce the law against a state-owned company.

These imaginaries became further complicated by the events in stock markets in 2015. After a steady rise since the beginning of 2014, the summer of 2015 saw the collapse of most stock prices. According to the technical and political imaginaries of market efficiency described above, "markets" were "correcting a bubble," where prices had veered too far away from fundamental valuation. Members of Merge Consulting understood it thus as a "necessary" correction but also one that put the transaction of Bolbus at risk. If prices fell too low, the company, priced at 15 million euros, would start to look too expensive in relation to comparable companies listed in the stock markets of China. Monatu would then be unable to justify the purchase as a "good deal," and would either have to propose a lower price or put the transaction on hold, waiting for a new hike in prices. These fears were calmed by the intervention of the Chinese central government. Considering that the collapse of prices was dangerously hitting middle-class savings, the government used the rhetoric of market efficiency to claim that the fall was excessive in relation to fundamentals, and detrimental to a smooth economic life. A dedicated fund of US$200 billion, dubbed the "national team," was used to purchase stocks across the board, from most of the companies whose prices were falling. Intervening with media discourses and actual purchases, this strategy had the result of stemming the collapse and giving the fund 6 percent ownership of the whole market.[5] Even if prices did not

---

5.   Many of the companies listed in the Shanghai Stock Exchange were already, in one way or another, state-owned or state-controlled.

recover their levels of the beginning of the summer of 2015, they remained well above prices of the beginning of 2014, which allowed for a narrative of slow growth spurred by the government's protection against excessive volatility that did not respect the fundamentals. In informal conversations, Merge Consulting's associates wavered between the relief that the transaction could go on, reproving state intervention, and justifying it as a way to sustain market efficiency against speculation.

This state presence in the deal's valuation issues only rendered more complex the team's imaginaries about the state's role in the transaction. In the last stage of the transaction, the approval of the Ministry of Commerce was needed before payment money could be transferred. This added a few weeks to the conclusion of the deal, which the owners of Bolbus and the members of Merge Consulting had not considered. Fearing that any delay could derail the deal, they pressed the counter-party to speed up the process. In a conference call with Vicky and me, where we told the associates of Merge Consulting that representatives of Alpha communicated that it was a bureaucratic procedure that they could do nothing about—even in the case the Ministry's officials would refuse the deal—one of the associates, Jack, started to shout that such an answer was "unacceptable." He went on to explain that now that the state had invested in Alpha, the latter was part of "the system," and should be able to mobilize its newly acquired connections within the Communist Party to make the administration go faster and in the right direction. State participation in stock market valuation was thus translated into the capacity to bypass bureaucratic processes in order to secure profits by guaranteeing the completion of the transaction.

Merge Consulting's activities were carried out by mobilizing different imaginaries of the state that were more or less compatible, conflictive, or independent from each other. These imaginaries were co-constitutive of the imaginaries of profit. Valuation techniques, or the rights to set up a company and to expand its business, made sense in relation to certain understanding of the state, the legal framework, and the local politics of where profits could be made. Further, an investment project that aligned with the macroeconomic project of Chinese central government mobilized images of a state trusted for its capacity to steer the economy, an imaginary with ambivalences as to where political legitimacy lied, and which contradicted other imaginaries about European states' impact on profits. The technical, moral, and political aspects of valuation, entrepreneurship, and investment were inextricably linked to also technical, moral, and political imaginaries about states' multiple facets. Thus, "states" and "profits" were constituted as practical categories and concerns that were both different and partly defined by each other. These imaginaries were also co-constituted with imaginaries of "cultures."

IMAGINARIES OF CULTURE

The relations between the professional and nonprofessional, often termed "personal" lives in finance, are marked by the fact that certain social identities play a strong role in both domains, notably age (Ortiz 2014b; Zaloom 2006), social class (Godechot 2001), race (Ho 2009), and gender (Fisher 2012; Ho 2009; Roth 2006; Zaloom 2006), while the imaginaries of professional practice may at the same time silence or even oppose this. The "cross-border" character of the transactions in which the members of Merge Consulting took part was partly problematized as the crossing of a divide between what were loosely designated as two "cultures" or "mentalities," among other expressions: China, on the one hand, and the West or Europe, on the other hand. The meanings of these entities were multiple, and they were mobilized in often labile and contradictory ways. Yet, these imaginaries of culture played crucial roles in certain situations, articulating and diffusing conflicts, establishing common narratives to continue the transactions, and providing meanings and practices that were developed, feared, enjoyed, or accepted, among other emotional possibilities, in everyday professional and nonprofessional lives (Ong 1999). It is important, therefore, not to consider "culture," "China," or "the West" as our own analytic categories but to see how they are produced in everyday practice (Anderson [1983] 2006; Gupta and Ferguson 1992; Pieke 2014; Trouillot 2003). This will allow for understanding how these imaginaries of "culture" are mutually constituted with those described above, concerning "profits" and "states."

In interviews with financial professionals working on cross-border investment, three main narratives tended to be mobilized when articulating a difference between China and the West, Europe and the United States, or "the rest of the world," which could also be found in media and state-backed official reports (Ortiz 2017). They mobilized concerns about financial techniques, political organization, and personal trajectories of the participants. One imaginary built these entities as bound to become undifferentiated, either because China would become like the West, or because the opposite would happen. Another narrative considered that these entities were bound to enter into a violent conflict, since their differences were irreducible. A third narrative used words such as *hybrid* or *mixture*, developing the idea that something new was being produced, which took elements from both entities and put them together in a way that neither of them presented before. Merge Consulting's members tended to mobilize the third narrative the most. They insisted both on some unavoidable character of the differences between China and the West, and on the idea that these differences could be bridged by specialists like them.

In one of the associates' visits to Shanghai, as they were celebrating the fact that the sale of Bolbus had been completed, John, one of the founding associates of Merge Consulting, told to me as a justification that it was after an experience where "misunderstandings" had jeopardized a deal in China that he "realized" that it was only by "being there" that business was viable: only by having Chinese employees who lived in China could the company create a common understanding between parties in China and Europe and achieve transactions. This was also the company's marketing line to its potential customers in Europe. Many interviewees in the profession problematized the valuation differences described above in terms of "cultural differences." Although Merge Consulting's members, during my observations, did look for clarification concerning valuation differences, just like the other professionals I observed, and echoing an important production of manuals in cross-cultural management, they put forward "communication," "understanding," and "learning" between "cultures" as a central component of the company's activities.

I joined the company in replacement of Peter, who had lived in China for five years and had developed the Shanghai section of Merge Consulting in the last three years. We had first met for an interview and had maintained regular contact until he informed me that he was going back to Europe and could propose to the company that I replace him temporarily, given my research interests. He explained that my presence would be needed because "in some meetings, they just want to see an older white guy," a role that Vicky—"Chinese" and in her early 30s—could not fulfill. He considered that this was also necessary because counterparties are "usually older Chinese men, and they tend to not respect Vicky, because she is a woman and she is too young." In his narrative, these elements came together with other ones composing a distinctive "Chinese culture": "Sometimes it is really surprising that they really don't understand the simplest things. Vicky is very smart, but sometimes she just does not get it. I had many times the same problems with counterparts here. You send them the draft of the contract, it is crystal clear, and yet they ask you the most stupid question about how to interpret it." He would then give examples of deadlines that would not be understood to be strict, or guarantee clauses that would be doubted and needed explanation or rewriting.

These imaginaries of culture allowed for articulating conflicts with clients, as in the case presented by Peter, when a discussion and eventual resolution of the interpretation of a clause was not termed as an opposition of interests but as a "cultural misunderstanding." It also articulated, as evoked by Peter, relations within Merge Consulting. When Peter left, Vicky came to occupy a stronger position in the company, as head of the China office. Feeling that the arrival of an external consultant like me could threaten this, she initially insisted that I did not need to come to the office and that there was no need that I have access to the contracts that had been signed by clients with whom the company was still conducting operations. Her refusal to allow me to access the basic information I needed to work as a consultant for the company, and the insistence of the associates in emails and telephone conversations with me that I take a more active role in the company's daily operations, led to clarifying each other's positions in a conference call a few weeks after my arrival. The tense conversation found a point of compromise, when the associates insisted on the fact that Vicky would manage the office but that I would assist her in financial matters, on which I had a formal education that she did not have, and which was sometimes demanded by clients in Europe as part of the resources present in Shanghai. After this conversation, she stated her position, as a summary of the exchanges, in a long email, where she explained that I would only bring my expertise in financial technical matters, and that her role was centered on "cultural communication." She explained that Chinese counterparts did not understand the "European way to do business," and that they did not trust "Europeans" but would only express "what they think" "in Chinese" and "to a Chinese person." At the same time, in her narrative, Western counterparts, and even the members of Merge Consulting, did not know the "political situation in China" well enough to understand the reactions, fears, and expectations of Chinese counterparts. Her role in the company was therefore crucial. This email received the approval of the associates and my own, as a sort of chart of principles that would allow to clarify any potential conflict in the future, which eventually never occurred.

What is interesting about these mobilization of different elements around the idea of Chinese and Western "cultures" that needed knowledge and understanding was that it was explicitly accepted and found legitimate by the other members of the company, and that it combined, in a way that was specific to the situation, imaginaries of culture that could be found in other interviews and media or official reports. The assertion of Jack, Merge Consulting's associate, concerning Alpha's capacity to mobilize supposedly newly acquired connections in the Ministry of Commerce because the "national team" investment fund had acquired a share of its stocks was one of these instances. After the talk, as she understood that I was aware that this interpretation did not correspond in any way to Alpha's situation, Vicky explained, echoing John's own comments quoted above, that this was just an example of Merge Consulting associates' ignorance concerning China, and their need of a Chinese person to deal with clients and operations in the country. The formulation of misunderstandings and hierarchical conflicts within the company and between the company and its commercial partners could therefore be formalized in terms of "cultural" differences, in ways that reshaped the meaning of these relations, establishing specific possibilities and limitations.

These "cultural" entities were part of both professional and nonprofessional lives. This could concern attempts to understand the moral or political tensions that Merge Consulting's transactions were supposed to bridge by crossing the border. John, Merge Consulting's associate quoted above, combined European nationalism with an admiration for Chinese governmental policies. He explained that he did not want to live in China because he was "too old" and it was not "a place to raise your children," given pollution and the cost of a "good, quality education." In our first meeting, he expanded on how much Europe was "suffering" from the influx of immigrants. Conveying an avowedly conservative political view, he considered that the continent needed to start closing its borders in order to retain its social stability. He asserted that terrorist attacks were due to this European "openness," and that China could provide an alternative perspective, in particular with the way in which it dealt with what John considered to be Islamic terrorists, echoing the official discourse of the Chinese central government about the bloody attacks attributed to Uighur separatism. Considering that China needed European technology, he said that Europe could learn from China's political system. In his visit to Shanghai, remarking that all bags were screened in the access to subways, he said: "Maybe Europe could learn from China, after the terrorist attacks, and stop refraining from taking some measures in the name of the respect of individual liberties."

But the mobilization of imaginaries about culture could also articulate life and career trajectories. After five years in China, Peter told me that he was tired of being an expatriate, that he could barely connect with "other expats," who were too focused on "business alone," and that he felt "totally shut off" from becoming friends with Chinese people, due to language barriers but also—more importantly—to "cultural differences." He had a new job as a consultant for a large Chinese company, for which he would work while living in Europe, to contribute to its expansion through mergers and acquisition and business development there. He explained that this was part of a longer-term project, in which he wanted to develop a consultancy on "intercultural relations in business," connecting Europe and China, based on the experience he had accumulated during the five years he lived in Shanghai and after that. Vicky, in turn, explained that she would want to continue working for Merge Consulting and become an associate in the company. She explained that she could earn more money in a Chinese company, but that she was not interested in doing this because it was an environment that was much more hierarchical and where there were not many career prospects for someone who, like her, lacked political connections and an elite education. While she expressed her strong desire to travel to Europe and to acquire European luxury items, she explained that she would never want to live outside China, where she liked her life, was planning to build a family, and could enjoy closeness to her parents and friends. This was exemplified by the way in which she could use her Chinese name with Chinese counterparts, and her English name with non-Chinese ones. This practice was widespread in the profession and elsewhere where Chinese nationals worked with foreign companies, and it was common with many employees of Chinese companies that dealt with Merge Consulting. "Europe" and "China" were thus defined in multiple, vague ways that could be combined to make sense of the everyday professional and nonprofessional life of the people conducting Merge Consulting's activities.

Merge Consulting's activities mobilized several imaginaries of culture, China, and the West that gave meaning to the commercial strategy of the company, to conflicts and agreements between employees and between companies, and to life trajectories inside and outside the realms of professional practice. They concerned feelings of belonging, of trust and mistrust, differentiations between groups of people that could be recognized, as business partners and employees, and of imagined communities that connected with national identities and geographical borders and locations. These imaginaries were partly constituted by imaginaries about profits, concerning methods of valuation, of organizing companies, of negotiating contracts as a well as imaginaries about states, concerning citizenship, legal frameworks, the Communist Party, and imaginaries about the global, defined partly in terms of financial methodologies that could converge, clash, or be combined, but also in terms of geopolitical tensions, of "migration" and "terrorism." Thus, the production of *culture* as an entity that was supposed to give meaning to everyday practice was partly determined by imaginaries about financial rules and about states, and provided in turn some of the elements to make sense of the latter. These imaginaries contain technical, moral, and political aspects, they are labile, sometimes contradictory, and can be transformed within limits that are explored in particular situations but that connect with shared understandings and practices that never coalesce into a single narrative. This co-constitutive character of imaginaries of profits, states, and cultures allow for a questioning of the "economy" in the narratives of "real economy."

CONCLUSION

This essay has shown how, in the everyday practice of people engaging in cross-border investment, the categories of *profit*, *states*, and *cultures* have multiple meanings, which are mobilized to make sense of practices in ways that can be contradictory, vague, and disconnected, but that also make them co-constitutive of each other. Profits are understood within multiple temporalities and moralities, such as those of a life-long entrepreneurial career, the fast-paced movement of stock market prices, or the years-long development of Merge Consulting's operations. The meanings of owning a company and exchanging it for money vary accordingly. These meanings are co-constituted with those of states, which can be imagined as mighty actors capable of shaping the content and use of the law as well as the economic structure and particular transaction, but are also considered as commercial partners or legal frames that allow for manipulation and negotiation and as entities that can be themselves objects of investment. The political legitimacies of the Communist Party and the European project— when impacting stock prices through purchases by a "national team" or issuing licenses for deals that correspond to macroeconomic policy objectives—are part of the notions of market efficiency central in calculations and in justifications of prices, and play a central role in the design of long-term projects of business development in China and Europe by Merge Consulting, and its clients and counterparts in the transactions. Finally, the spaces designated as China and Europe, and the practices and imaginaries related to them, are conflated into more or less homogenized "cultural" entities, used as causal explanations in everyday interactions, but also central for the stabilization of the meaning of professional rules, career perspectives, and identities. In everyday practices, these imaginaries are co-constitutive in ways that may not allow for disentangling them. They make sense in connection to each other, even when they contradict each other, in particular situations, such as in the discourse of a same person in a same interview, or in different moments and by different people participating in the same transaction over a period of time that can last years. Their analysis here shows how this co-constitution implies that the social hierarchies established through the distribution of monetary resources, like the one effected through the purchase of Bolbus, are not uniquely "economic" but they relate to multiples meanings of "profits" that must be understood as part of legitimations also problematized in terms of states and cultural identities.

The political character of the distribution of resources becomes therefore more complex than what an analytical distinction between *real value* and *fiction* or between the *real economy* and *money* can allow to observe. These dichotomies obscure the processes under observation more than they help clarifying them. The practices of professionals like those of Merge Consulting contribute to channel money to particular activities at the expense of others, participating in the constitution of global hierarchies in the access to money articulated by the financial industry. These hierarchies cannot be understood if we only try to see them as "economic"—for instance, by focusing the analysis solely on how they relate to coordination through the production of information and knowledge or to a distinction between fiction and production. The imaginaries of profits, states, and culture described here mark a series of paths that are navigated, mobilized, and produced by financial professionals, but also in many state-backed official reports and discourses and financial and nonfinancial media, in order to organize, describe, and legitimize this particular distribution of resources. According to these imaginaries, contributing to the distribution of 15 million euros from a major chemical corporation based in Chinese territory to acquire the rights to expand the operations of a small company based in Europe and specializing in medical devices could be seen as a way to speculate in the stock markets, to enhance one's career, to develop an industrial project, to contribute to the reordering of social relations by the central government under the control of the Chinese Communist Party, and to bring together the cultures of China and the West, among others.

Stressing social processes that would refer to a particular disciplinary niche that connected more or less loosely with the way the people observed made sense of the situation—for instance, saying it is mainly a "cultural," a "stately," or an "economic" process—would mean risking to miss important parts of the social process itself, and also risking to reproduce some of the legitimizing narratives that the actors themselves put forth to make sense of the distributive effects of their practices. Thus, the practices described above allow for seeing that the notions of profit, states, and cultures, and those connected to them, such as *investor*, *market*, *law*, *corruption*, *China*, and *the West*, must be considered in the way in which they are used and produced, instead of being used as readily available analytic categories. The pragmatist definition of the political anthropology proposed here, following the practices of money production, collection, and distribution, with all the imaginaries they involve, allows for broadening the critical gaze to all the imaginaries mobilized to legitimize and reproduce these global hierarchies. Interdisciplinary dialogue is necessary to understand the imaginaries and social organizations whereby money is produced and used elsewhere than in the settings observed in particular fieldworks, making global social hierarchies possible. In this way, without claiming a grounding on a "real economy," a pragmatist approach of money can also open doors to explore the multiple places where global monetary distribution could be imagined to be different.

ACKNOWLEDGEMENTS

I wish to thank the editor and the anonymous reviewers of *Hau Journal*, where this essay first appeared, as well as the coeditors of this volume, Jane Guyer and Federico Neiburg, for their extremely useful critiques, comments, and suggestions. This essay also benefited from exchanges with Maxim Bolt, Kimberly Chong, Lily Chumley, Liliana Doganova, Keith Hart, Deborah James, Shao Jing, Jeanne Lazarus, Benoît de L'Estoile, Mariana Luzzi, Sabine Montagne, Fabian Muniesa, Gustavo Onto, Alvaro Pina-Stranger, Fernando Rabossi, Alexandre Roig, Wang Mengqi, Ariel Wilkis, Caitlin Zaloom, and Zhu Yujing.

REFERENCES

Abélès, Marc. (1990) 2005. *Anthropologie de l'état*. Paris: Editions Payot & Rivages.

Anderson, Benedict. (1983) 2006. *Imagined communities: Reflections on the origin and spread of nationalism.* London: Verso.

Arjaliès, Diane-Laure, Philip Grant, Ian Hardie, Donald MacKenzie, and Ekaterina Svetlova. 2017. *Chains of finance: How investment management is shaped.* Oxford: Oxford University Press.

Balandier, Georges. 1967. *Anthropologie politique.* Paris: Presses Universitaires de France.

Chu, Julie Y. 2010. *Cosmologies of credit: Transnational mobility and the politics of destination in China.* Durham, NC: Duke University Press.

de Certeau, Michel. (1980) 1990. *L'invention du quotidien 1. Arts de faire.* Paris: Editions Gallimard.

De Goede, Marieke. 2005. *Virtue, fortune and faith: A genealogy of finance.* Minneapolis: University of Minnesota Press.

Das, Veena, and Deborah Poole. 2004. "State and its margins: Comparative ethnographies." In *Anthropology in the margins of the state*, edited by Veena Das and Deborah Poole, 3–33. Santa Fe, NM: School of American Research Press.

Dodd, Nigel. 2014. *The social life of money.* Princeton, NJ: Princeton University Press.

Doganova, Liliana. 2014. "Décompter le future: La formule des flux actualizés et le manager-investisseur." *Sociétés Contemporaires* 93: 67–87.

Fisher, Melissa. 2012. *Wall Street women.* Durham, NC: Duke University Press.

Foucault, Michel. 1975. *Surveiller et punir: Naissance de la prison.* Paris: Editions Gallimard.

———. 1976. *Histoire de la sexualité, 1: La volonté de savoir.* Paris: Editions Gallimard.

———. 2004. *Naissance de la biopolitique: Cours au Collège de France, 1978–1979.* Paris: Gallimard, Seuil.

Fourcade, Marion. 2011. "Cents and sensibility: Economic valuation and the nature of 'nature.'" *American Journal of Sociology* 116 (6): 1721–77.

Godechot, Olivier. 2001. *Les traders: Essai de sociologie des marchés financiers.* Paris: Editions La Découverte.

———. 2016. *The working rich: Wages, bonuses and appropriation of profit in the financial industry.* London: Routledge.

Gupta, Akhil, and James Ferguson. 1992. "Beyond 'culture': Space, identity, and the politics of difference." *Cultural Anthropology* 7 (1): 6–23.

Guyer, Jane I. 2004. *Marginal gains: Monetary transactions in Atlantic Africa.* Chicago: Chicago University Press.

———. 2016. *Legacies, logics, logistics: Essays in the anthropology of the platform economy.* Chicago: University of Chicago Press.

Hart, Keith. 1986. "Heads or tails? The two sides of the coin." *Man*, n.s., 21: 637–56.

———. 2000. *The memory bank: Money in an unequal world.* London: Profile Books.

———. 2015. "Introduction." In *Economy for and against democracy*, edited by Keith Hart, 1–15. New York: Berghahn.

Hart, Keith, and Horacio Ortiz. 2014. "The anthropology of money and finance: Between ethnography and world history." *Annual Review of Anthropology* 43:465–82.

Hertz, Ellen. 1998. *The trading crowd: An ethnography of the Shanghai stock market.* Cambridge: Cambridge University Press.

———. 2000. "Stock markets as 'simulacra': Observation that participates." *Tsantsa* 5:40–50.

Ho, Karen. 2009. *Liquidated: An ethnography of Wall Street.* Durham, NC: Duke University Press.

LiPuma, Edward, and Bernard Lee. 2004. *Financial derivatives and the globalization of risk.* Durham, NC: Duke University Press.

MacKenzie, Donald. 2006. *An engine not a camera: How financial models shape markets.* Cambridge, MA: MIT Press.

Maurer, Bill. 2002. "Repressed futures: Financial derivative's theological unconscious." *Economy and Society* 31 (1): 15–36.

———. 2006. "The anthropology of money." *Annual Review of Anthropology* 35 (2): 1–22.

———. 2015. *How would you like to pay? How technology is changing the future of money.* Durham, NC: Duke University Press.

Mauss, Marcel. (1923–24) 2016. *The gift: Expanded edition.* Translated by Jane Guyer. Chicago: Hau Books.

Montagne, Sabine, and Horacio Ortiz. 2013. "Sociologie de l'agence financière: Enjeux et perspectives." *Sociétés Contemporaines* 94:7–33.

Muniesa, Fabian. 2007. "Market technologies and the pragmatics of prices." *Economy and Society* 36 (3): 377–95.

Muniesa, Fabian, Liliana Doganova, Horacio Ortiz, Álvaro Pina-Stranger, Florence Paterson, Alaric Bourgoin, Véra Ehrenstein, Pierre-André Juven,

David Pontille, Başac Saraç-Lesavre, and Guillaume Yon. 2017. *Capitalization: A cultural guide*. Paris: Presses des Mines.

Neiburg, Federico. 2006. "Inflation: Economists and economic cultures in Brazil and Argentina." *Comparative Studies of Society and History* 48 (3): 604–33.

Ong, Aihwa. 1999. *Flexible citizenship: The cultural logics of transnationality*. Durham, NC: Duke University Press.

Ortiz, Horacio. 2013. "Financial value: Economic, moral, political, global." *HAU: Journal of Ethnographic Theory* 3 (1): 64–79.

———. 2014a. "The limits of financial imagination: Free investors, efficient markets and crisis." *American Anthropologist* 116 (1): 38–50.

———. 2014b. *Valeur financière et vérité: Enquête d'anthropologie politique sur l'évaluation des entreprises cotées en bourse*. Paris: Presses de Science Po.

———. 2015. "What financial crisis? The global politics of the financial industry: Distributional consequences and legitimizing narratives." In *Economy for and against democracy*, edited by Keith Hart and John Sharp, 39–57. New York: Berghahn.

———. 2017. "Cross-border investment in China." In *Money in a human economy*, edited by Keith Hart, 147–66. New York: Berghahn.

Ouroussoff, Alexandra. 2010. *Wall Street at war*. Cambridge: Polity.

Pieke, Frank N. 2014. "Anthropology, China and the Chinese century." *Annual Review of Anthropology* 43:123–38.

Polanyi, Karl. (1944) 2001. *The great transformation: The political and economic origins of our time*. Boston: Beacon.

Roth, Louise M. 2006. *Selling women short: Gender and inequality on Wall Street*. Princeton, NJ: Princeton University Press.

Sahlins, Marshall. 2013. "On the culture of material value and the cosmography of riches." *HAU: Journal of Ethnographic Theory* 3 (2): 161–95.

Simmel, Georg. (1900) 1978. *The philosophy of money*. Translated and edited by David Frisby. London: Routledge.

Stark, David. 2011. "What's valuable." In *The worth of goods: Valuation and pricing in the economy*, edited by Patrik Aspers and Jens Beckert, 319–38. Oxford: Oxford University Press.

Trouillot, Michel-Rolph. 2003. *Global transformations: Anthropology and the modern world*. New York: Palgrave MacMillan.

Zaloom, Caitlin. 2006. *Out of the pits: Traders and technology from Chicago to London*. Chicago: University of Chicago Press.

————. 2016. "The Evangelical financial ethic: Double forms and the search for God in the economic world." *American Ethnologist* 43 (2): 325–38.

Zelizer, Viviana. 2005. *The purchase of intimacy*. Princeton, NJ: Princeton University Press.

————. 2009. *Economic lives: How culture shapes the economy*. Princeton, NJ: Princeton University Press.

CHAPTER SEVEN

Corporate personhood and the competitive relation in antitrust

Gustavo Onto

On the face of it, North American railroads are no longer controlled by trusts, and are therefore subject to free-competition; on the face of it, the Steel Trust has now been split off into forty independent companies that rival each other in terms of goodwill and fair prices. And now that Standard Oil has disappeared, innumerable oil pipelines transport oil to ports and reservoirs, with the price being set by a free market. The trusts have fragmented; it might appear that it is no longer the Rockefellers, the Schwabs, the Armours that control the oil, the steel, the canned meat. But everyone knows that behind this apparent compliance with the law, North American capitalists have held on to the essential part of their organizations. Their chosen men administer all the new companies. Most of the shares are still held by the same capitalists. And North American industry is increasingly under the "control" of certain groups of magnates.[1]

—Marcel Mauss, *La Nation*

---

1. "En apparence, les chemins de fer américains ne sont donc plus trustés, ils sont soumis au régime de la libre concurrence, en apparence la Steel Trust est maintenant

In July 2014, the Brazilian antitrust agency *Conselho Administrativo de Defesa Econômica* (CADE; the Administrative Council for Economic Defense) approved a merger between two corporations, Kroton and Anhanguera, which led to the establishment of the world's largest private higher education company. The new company began its life with a market value of approximately 10 billion dollars and over 1.2 million students. What most struck the regulators, more so even than the scale of new enterprise, was the underlying phenomenon that was sweeping through the Brazilian educational market. The merger was, in fact, the latest in a series of deals that had transformed the Brazilian educational sector into an extension of the national financial sector. Almost all the major centers of higher education were being bought up by banks and investment funds. This mass financialization posed a significant challenge to the antitrust authority and was considered by commissioners to be "a sensitive competition issue." Given that the ownership of these companies and, therefore, their administration, was distributed among similar individuals and/or corporations, it became increasingly difficult to pinpoint the extent of their influence on the market and, therefore, to distinguish between competitors. The question that arose was this: If market entities are apparently related, how is it possible to ascertain whether or not a market is competitive? This problem, so succinctly described by Marcel Mauss, is as old as antitrust itself. It raises fundamental issues about the relationship between corporate personhood, economic agency, and competition, which this chapter explores through an ethnographic perspective on regulatory knowledge practices.

In seeking to encourage fair competition, antitrust (or competition) policy in Brazil and elsewhere has followed two main directions. The primary is the launching of investigations into current or past business practices that might be harmful to other companies or consumers in a given market, such as the formation of cartels that increase prices for consumers on the basis of agreements

---

brisée en 40 compagnies indépendantes, et rivalisant de bonne volonté et de bon marché. Et la Standard Oil disparue, de nombreux pipe-lines indépendants mènent aux ports et réservoirs un pétrole dont les prix sont débattus par un libre marché. Les trusts se sont morcelés; apparemment ce ne sont plus Rockefeller, Schwab, Armour, qui possèdent le pétrole, l'acier, la viande conservée. Mais tout le monde sait que, sous les apparences d'obéissance à la loi, les capitalistes américains ont maintenu l'essentiel de leurs organisations. Ce sont leurs hommes qui administrent la totalité des nouvelles compagnies. Les majorités d'actions appartiennent toujours aux mêmes capitalistes. Et l'industrie américaine est de plus en plus sous le 'contrôle' de quelques groupes de magnats" (Mauss [1920] 2013: 306).

between companies.[2] In Brazil, where the antitrust authority is responsible both for the investigation and for the judgment of antitrust issues, companies found to have broken the rules face stiff penalties.

A second is the activity of so-called merger review, which is the focus of this chapter. The antitrust authority is responsible for authorizing or prohibiting corporate concentrations—mergers, acquisitions, joint ventures, et cetera. The decision is based on a finding as to the probability of the proposed concentration altering market conditions to the detriment of other participants in the near future. Each merger review case referred to the antitrust authority is dealt with in administrative proceedings that always involve a comprehensive investigation into the characteristics of the markets in which the relevant companies operate, including an inquiry into the conduct of competitors and consumers.

In order to decide whether to approve or reject a merger, antitrust regulators first of all need to identify all the participants in the market under investigation—that is, all the competing players, including, of course, those who submitted the merger application. They then need to consider the respective market share of the competitors, which is estimated in terms of the volume/quantity of products each one sells on the market, or by means of analysis of each competitor's turnover. This procedure is in line with the established (structural approach) view that a reduced number of participating competitors in a market increases the likelihood of the proposed merger causing excessive concentration. This concentration is, in turn, considered likely to afford the new company disproportionate "market power"—a market share that is significantly larger than that of the other participants (Hovenkamp 2005). On the other hand, when a market has several competitors in addition to the merger applicants, there is less likelihood that the merger will be harmful to competition, as the newly merged company will not be capable of prejudicing the other participants or consumers in the market. Thus, the identification of the agents that compete on the markets and the estimation of their relative market share constitute a prerequisite to assessing the effects of a corporate merger on market competition.

---

2. Corporate practices commonly deemed anticompetitive include cartels, price-fixing, exclusionary dealing contracts, tying (bundling), nontransparent, noncompetitive, and/or corrupt bidding processes. Anticompetitive practices may involve the actions of one company alone or may be "horizontal" when two or more companies act together.

Drawing on the ethnographic material taken from investigative procedures conducted by Brazilian antitrust analysts, this chapter describes how regulators identify or singularize market competitors in circumstances in which it is not easy to precisely quantify or identify them. This particular difficulty has become more commonplace in markets such as the private educational sector, in which the applicants seeking permission to merge are owned and controlled by investment funds. If a fund holds shares in more than one company in the market, or otherwise exercises administrative control over such companies, it may be capable of influencing the companies so that they do not compete with each other, because competition would be prejudicial to the fund itself. The problem then faced by analysts is how to know whether the company submitting the application for merger is in fact competing with other businesses in the same market, when a private equity firm holds shares in both the applicant company and in other market participants. When the investments of a private equity firm are apportioned between various companies, does this lead to all these companies effectively being part of the same assemblage, acting in a concerted and unidirectional manner? If that is indeed the case, then the companies that receive such investment cannot be considered competitors, or distinct economic agents but rather should be classed as part of the same economic group.

According to regulators, these difficulties in singularization are due to the fact that the legal form of corporations, presented when companies file a petition to merge, might not reflect the economic reality of the extent and nature of their participation in a given market. Recent work in the anthropology of corporations has highlighted practices of reification that confer upon corporate entities a marked degree of coherence, unity, and intentionality (Welker, Partridge, and Hardin 2011). These studies describe the manner in which different conceptions of corporations are enacted through routine internal corporate practices (Welker 2014) or by legal developments, including case law from the courts and the teaching of legal scholars. They also describe the effects of these reifications.[3] The manner in which corporate personhood is perceived,

---

3.   For studies that refer to US legal history and case law reflecting the transformation of the legal rights of US corporations, illustrating how companies have increasingly acquired legal status and treatment equivalent to that afforded to human beings, see Barkan (2013) and Coleman (2014).

ascertained, and classified has highly significant consequences in terms of corporate responsibilities and liability, powers, and duties.[4]

In a similar vein, this article considers "what is neglected or obscured when corporations are construed as persons" (Kirsch 2014: 210) in the context of antitrust policy. What are the effects of mobilizing corporate personhoods in merger reviews? These effects become visible when we contrast the usual legal-economic reifications of companies applying for authorization to merge with the more recent regulatory analytical procedures for the identification of competitors in a market, which suggest a relational perspective of corporations and economic agency. The task of identifying the agents that compete in a given market is complex, as examining property relations alone is insufficient to adequately distinguish between them (Strathern 1996). As I describe below, the analytical difficulties that follow on from the recent financialization of markets has led to a need for regulators to expressly consider the ontological nature of the entities being investigated, and to identify and characterize various forms of relations between natural and legal persons.

In the next section, I describe the dual legal and economic nature of corporate entities that are subject to regulation in accordance with Competition Law and demonstrate how this duality is taken for granted in most antitrust rulings. In the following two sections I recount the procedures that regulators adopted in order to identify the market share of a competitor in a 2013 investigation of a proposed merger in the private higher education sector. In the case in question, the issue of how to identify an economic agent led the investigators to question the standard ways in which governed entities were conceptualized in antitrust analysis and to adopt a fresh approach. I conclude the chapter with some remarks on the pragmatic meanings attributed to competition in antitrust practice, as evidenced by CADE's approach to the merger application I describe.

---

4.   An example of this is the research of anthropologist Suzana Sawyer (2006) into the legal arguments employed in a dispute between a US oil company and Ecuadorian rural dwellers. The author cites various instances in which the accused company, ChevronTexaco, was ascribed human qualities that rendered its actions comprehensible. This was applied to all the subsidiaries of the company in several countries, which were dealt with as the offshoot of a larger entity. According to the researcher, the representatives acting in the lawsuit used the personal pronoun *tu* (second person singular) to refer to the company. This form of qualifying the company, rendering its actions coherent, was one of the means used to hold the company legally liable for damage caused by a petrol spill in a rural region of Ecuador (Sawyer 2006).

LEGAL ECONOMIC MESHES[5]

The "competition sheriff" (as CADE is frequently referred to in the Brazilian press) is best known for its role in analyzing major mergers and for its investigation of the formation of cartels by large corporations. The Brazilian legislation on competition does not, however, limit the agency's role to the investigation of companies that are large enough to be known among the general public. In fact, the law does not even define the type of legal entity over which CADE is to exercise its powers.[6]

The "subject of Antirust law" is, in the words of the Brazilian jurist Paula Forgioni "any [person or entity] that is capable of performing an act that restricts competition" (2013: 145). However, the legal definition given to these acts means that they are generally deemed to have been committed only by entities that have the legal form of corporations. In industrialized countries, most of the goods and services used by the population are produced, distributed, and sold by business organizations rather than individuals. The violations of the economic order referred to in the Brazilian Competition Law are, therefore, committed by such business organizations, which compete with other similar entities in various markets. In terms of CADE's role in authorizing mergers, the premerger notification procedures and requisites mean that in practice only large organizations are subject to antitrust/merger regulation.[7]

---

5. Part of the material included here and in the following section was previously published in Onto (2017).

6. Article 31 of the Law 12.529/2011 establishes the following: "This Law applies to individuals (natural persons) or legal entities from either the public or private law spheres, and to any legally constituted or de facto associations of entities or of persons, even those constituted on a temporary basis, with or without having formal legal personality and even if they carry out their activities under the regime of legal monopoly." http://en.cade.gov.br/topics/legislation/laws/law-no-12529-2011-english-version-from-18-05-2012.pdf/view.

7. In relation to "acts of economic concentration"—mergers, acquisitions and other forms of union—the law, in Article 88, states that "the parties involved are to submit to CADE acts of economic concentration in which, cumulatively: I—at least one of the groups involved in the operation has registered, in its last financial statement, gross annual billing or total volume of business in the country, in the year prior to the operation, equivalent to or higher than R$400,000,000 (US$110,000,000); and II—at least one other group involved in the operations registered, in its last financial statement, gross annual billing or total volume of business in the country, in the year prior to the operation, equivalent to or greater than R$30,000,000 (US$8,300,000)" (June 2016 exchange rates).

The fact that the legislation does not expressly specify the legal personality/ form of the entities that are subject of legal rules on competition should not be considered a legislative oversight. It is, rather, characteristic of contemporary antitrust policy, in which regulatory decisions are based on economic analyses of the functioning of markets and market players. In these analyses, the legal form/ personality of the parties involved in a merger—that is, whether they are listed or closely held corporations, partnerships, or individuals ("natural" persons)—is less relevant than the manner in which these parties act and relate to other market participants. In other words, the antitrust agency aims to identify specific "economic agents" in the market, whatever their legal personality may be.[8] This can be clearly seen from the criterion stipulated in the legislation for the characterization of the unlawful act of "dominating a relevant market of goods and services." Article 36 of Law 12.529 provides that "a company or group of companies is presumed to have a dominant position whenever"

§ 2 [. . .] it is capable of altering market conditions in a unilateral or coordinated manner, or when it controls 20% (twenty percent) or more of the relevant market. CADE may alter this percentage share for specific sectors of the economy.[9]

The legislation therefore sets out certain requisites or markers that guide the antitrust investigation into acts of corporate concentration. According to the wording of the law, acts aimed at "dominating the market" constitute "violations of the economic order." As such, the characterization of market domination and of possible abuse of market position by the applicants for authorization to merge draws on a criterion of participation in the affected markets, also known as "market share." This numerical criterion provides to analysts an indication of the potential existence of violation of the statutory rules—that is, of the possible abusive exercise of market power. In Brazil, if the future company arising

8. It is worth noting that while the law applies the notion of *person* ("natural" person or "juridical" person), conferring rights and obligations accordingly, economic theory relies on the concept of *agent* to describe any entity that acts in a given market, producing or consuming products or services either as an "individual" or as a "firm" (these being the categories normally used in microeconomics). The use of the notion of agent implies that economic theory focuses precisely on the economic conduct of the entities and particularly the manner in which they make decisions and exercise choices relating to consumption or to production. For an analysis of the notion of agent in economic theory, see Ross (2010).

9. http://en.cade.gov.br/topics/legislation/laws/law-no-12529-2011-english-version-from-18-05-2012.pdf/view.

out of a merger will hold a market share of over 20 percent, CADE antitrust analysts are likely to consider that the merger will be prejudicial to competition in the market; in other words, that it will be harmful to other competitors or to consumers. Therefore, in line with knowledge practices common to many governmental bodies, the first step CADE officials usually take when presented with a request for authorization to merge is to seek information as to who the competitors are in the relevant market and to ascertain their respective market shares.

Estimating market shares presupposes a prior definition of precisely who the competing agents are. Each of these agents must be construed as a separate or discrete economic unit, which acts independently and competes with the others for the sale of specific products or services. In many cases, this singularization of economic agents is not difficult. Indeed, in most merger cases the analysts consider the economic agents in the relevant market to be the legal entities filing for merger and other legal entities that compete with them. In other words, for many (and possibly most) markets, there is no need to look beyond the legal form of corporate entities in order to establish the identity of the competing agents. That is possible because the owners and controllers of the companies do not generally have significant holdings in other companies operating in the same market. Furthermore, the corporate entities involved are usually owned by the same individuals that control them administratively. Even nowadays, the vast majority of Brazilian companies are family owned and administered, so that it is relatively straightforward for analysts to group the companies, their owners, and their administrators into one independent economic unit, as one competitor.

The fact that in most cases, the corporate persons requesting authorization for the merger can be taken as representative of the market competitors means that CADE's task of identifying and distinguishing economic agents is generally relatively straightforward. In addition to possessing this juridical-economic quality, these entities are deemed, during the administrative proceedings, to have a "volition" of their own (Foster 2010), which allow regulators to assume that they take rational decisions, based on the furtherance of their own interests and, most importantly, that these decisions are taken autonomously (see Welker 2016). Until recently, there did not appear to be any need for the investigating officers in Brazil to question these corporate meshes. However, because of the financialization of the economy, the lines have been blurred, as the scope and reach of market competitors appear to have extended beyond the defined limits of the legal form or personhood adopted by the companies applying for permission to merge. The difficulties of singularization or identification of the competition agents in a given market has become an obstacle to estimating market shares and, therefore, of ascertaining the likelihood of a competition issue arising as a result of a corporate merger.

REALIZING MARKET AGENTS

The antitrust authority, based in the Brazilian capital, Brasilia, is staffed by approximately 300 professionals who hail from various professional backgrounds, predominantly economics and law. Six commissioners, including the Chair of the Council (and Head of the CADE agency), sit on the Administrative Council and are responsible for the final ruling on cases. Each commissioner has either four or five assistants that help them in the investigation procedures and economic analysis.

Toward the end of 2012, I spent some weeks observing the work of the assistants to one of the commissioners on a merger between two small companies in the higher education sector.[10] One of the assistants, Camila, a thirty-five-year-old lawyer, explained the case to me, and also explained why CADE professionals considered it so significant, particularly bearing in mind that it was unlikely that the investigation would lead to CADE rejecting the proposed merger.[11] In fact, Camila's colleagues joked that she was "borderline obsessed" with the case, to the extent that her computer screensaver was a photograph of the eighty-year-old businessman who "was behind the investigated companies." This was the "the guy who commands the market," according to Camila.

The case on which Camila was working involved the acquisition of two education companies: Instituto Grande ABC de Educação e Ensino S/C Ltda (IGABC) and Novatec Serviços Educacionais Ltda, both members of the Anchieta Group and located in the São Paulo metropolitan region. They were

---

10. The material used in this section resulted from observation of the parties during an investigation undertaken as part of case number 08012.003886/2011-87, and from conversations and interviews of the officers responsible for the investigative work. I have also drawn on the public version of the case records, accessed via the CADE website (www.cade.gov.br) on February 15, 2014.

11. The reason for the subsequent approval of the merger was that the two education companies had only minor shares of the market in the geographical region analyzed.

being taken over by Anhanguera Educacional Ltda, which develops and pro-vides a range of higher education services in Brazil. In 2013, Anhanguera was "the largest private profit based professional training organization in Brazil and the largest listed company, in the Education sector, in terms of market value" (CADE 2013: 1881). At the time, Anhanguera had 54 campuses, 450 distance-learning centers, and over 650 professional training locations.

Camila told me that her initial interest in the case arose from the fact that it was clearly indicative of the increasing degree of acquisition by private equity firms of shares in companies providing private higher education ser-vices in Brazil. This development was already a cause of considerable concern to the CADE commissioners. As was stated in the opinion of the rapporteur Commissioner for the case (the jurist Alessandro Octaviani), the formation of large-scale private education groups in Brazil is a process "for which there is no precedent in world history" (CADE 2013: 1859). Of the five main Brazilian educational groups, four are run by companies from the financial sector (2013: 1861).[12] In the case in hand, the advisor (Camila) discovered on the internet, both in media reports and on the website of the applicant, that two companies in the private higher education market—namely, Anhanguera (the proposed incorporating company) and Anhembi-Morumbi (a supposed competitor) had some form of mutual relationship via legal entities and natural persons.

The assistant discovered a newspaper report bearing the headline "Two com-petitors and a professor in common" (*Duas concorrentes e um professor em comum*), published in the *O Estado de São Paulo* newspaper on June 11, 2012. Accord-ing to the report "Professor Gabriel" (Gabriel Rodrigues, the man on Camila's computer screen) had sold the administrative control (51 percent shareholding) of Anhembi-Morumbi (of which he was the founder) to Laureate Education Inc, a multinational company operating in the field of education. Despite hav-ing sold control of the company, which had been transferred to the majority shareholders, he continued to "advise on administrative issues" (CADE 2013: 1883). The company entrusted with putting into effect this corporate restructure of the Anhembi-Morumbi University was a well-known financial consultancy

---

12. As is set out in the Opinion of the commissioner, the Grupo Estácio is controlled by the GP Investments fund, Grupo Anhanguera is controlled by the Pátria bank and fund, Kroton is controlled by the Advent Internationale fund, and Anhembi-Morumbi/Laureate Education is controlled by the North-American fund KKR (Kohlberg Kravis Roberts). Only the Unip university did not, at that time, have an investment fund as its owner or controller (CADE 2013: 1860–61).

and fund manager, Pátria Investimentos, run by close acquaintances of Professor Gabriel's daughter, Ângela Rodrigues, who, in turn, worked at the Anhembi-Morumbi financial department.

In Camila's opinion, things "began to get complicated" when, according to the newspaper report, two years after the partial sale of Anhembi-Morumbi, Pátria Investments (which had organized the corporate restructure) was then hired to handle the public offering of shares of Anhanguera Educacional Ltda. To this end, Pátria set up a specific fund, the *Fundo de Educação para o Brasil* (FEBR, or Education Fund for Brazil), which purchased 17 percent of the shares in Anhanguera. The "Rodrigues family," the former majority owner of Anhembi-Morumbi, secured for itself via negotiation a guaranteed 70 percent share in the fund. Even with just 17 percent of the shares, the FEBR, a legal entity, became the controlling shareholder of Anhanguera, according to the report. Camila had therefore discovered that the founder of the Anhembi-Morumbi University, Professor Gabriel Rodrigues, who continued to have an influence over the decisions taken by his (former) company, was also a shareholder in a fund that held shares in—and controlled—Anhanguera.

As the advisor explained, the "Gabriel issue" gave rise to practical difficulties in the analysis of the private higher education market in the São Paulo metropolitan region and indeed in the country as a whole, since the extent of the market share of the applicant was unclear. In her view, although the case involved the takeover of a third-party company, Anchieta, it was necessary to establish Anhanguera's share of the market and to ascertain what type of relationship it had with its supposedly major competitor, Anhembi-Morumbi. If the common influence of Professor Gabriel Rodrigues imposed coordinated conduct on the companies, which rendered competition impossible, the market share of both companies, Anhanguera and Anhembi-Morumbi, would need to be considered together, because the two companies "would be operating as one agent in the market." As such, according to Camila, the CADE decision as to whether or not to authorize the merger required investigation of the relations that Professor Gabriel Rodrigues and his family maintained with these other companies.

In addition to researching newspapers, journals, magazines, and websites, the advisor sought relevant information from the records of the company registries (*juntas comerciais*) of the Federal District, the States of São Paulo, Rio de Janeiro, and Minas Gerais, which are available online. The information obtained cast doubt on the declaration made by the applicant Anhanguera in its petition (Request for Merger) to the effect that no member of the Executive

Board or of the Board of Directors of the educational group acted as director or executive at other companies operating in the same sector. According
to information set out in the Minutes of Board of Directors of Anhanguera
on September 15, 2010, submitted to CADE by the Applicant, Ms. Ângela
Regina Rodrigues de Paula Freitas, the daughter of Professor Gabriel Rodrigues, had a seat on the Anhanguera Board. Camila then discovered an entry on
the records of the São Paulo Companies' Registry (*Junta Comercial do Estado de
São Paulo*) that indicated that Ângela Rodrigues was also a director of ISCP,
the Anhembi-Morumbi/Laureate University (CADE 2013: 1888). Ms. Rodrigues also had other commercial relationships that linked the two (supposed)
competitors. For example, in accordance with the Minutes of the Anhanguera
General Meeting of October 29, 2010, Ms. Rodrigues had a personal office at
the same location as one of the campuses of the Anhembi-Morumbi/Laureate
University (2013: 1889).

In order to illustrate and explain some of the multiple relations involved in
the issue, Camila used the website MarketVisual, which gathers publicly available information on listed companies in Brazil and abroad. The website collects
data on the corporate, financial, and administrative structure of the companies
and publishes it in the form of tables or images of organograms or networks.
These tables or images identify different types of relations between individuals
and legal entities, as can be seen from the chart Camila used (see fig. 1).[13]

In her investigation, the advisor carried out a search of the name of Ms.
Ângela Rodrigues as well as other board members of Anhanguera Group. Using
the colored lines that can be selected on the website, Camila sought to highlight
the relations of corporate control such as seats on boards of directors or on
executive boards, as well as share ownership or financial control, family ties, or
even educational background (that is, the institution at which the individual in
question completed their higher education). The variety, multiplicity, and density of these relations that the lines on the chart demonstrated and made explicit
constituted what the CADE advisors called an irrefutable "relevant influence"
between the individuals and legal entities highlighted by the rectangles.

---

13. This image is available in the public records of the proceedings contained on the
CADE website (www.cade.gov.br) in black and white. The original image, however,
used colors that were (and are) an important part of the investigation undertaken by
the advisor. The different colors represent different forms of relations as indicated in
the box on the upper right corner of the image.

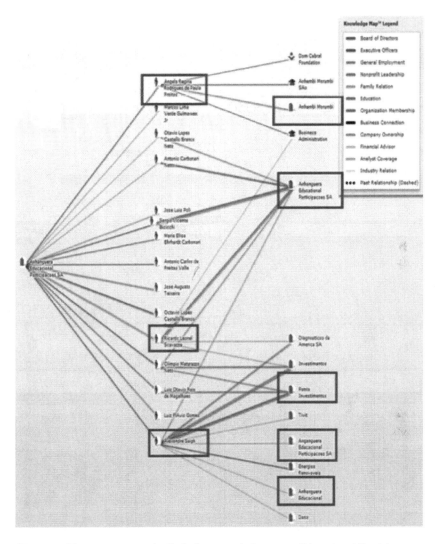

Figure 1: Chart setting out the "links between Anhanguera Educacional Participações S.A., Pátria Investimentos, Ms. Ângela Rodrigues and Anhembi Morumbi" (CADE 2013: 1898).

In his formal Opinion on the proposed merger, the rapporteur CADE commissioner, who drew on the findings of the advisor, held that it was possible to identify a "mesh of company relations (or holdings)"—in other words, a network of ownership links—and a "mesh of directors"—that is, a network of administrative control extending between Anhanguera and Anhembi-Morumbi and involving investment funds and individual members of the Rodrigues family. According to the rapporteur commissioner the evidence provided revealed the "true central organizer of the decisions, the *punctum saliens* of the business: the network commanded by Prof. Gabriel Rodrigues and his family, with the assistance of Pátria, which submitted two competitors, Anhanguera and Anhembi-Morumbi/Laureate, to its strategies" (CADE 2013: 1895). A diagram included in the Opinion of the commissioner-rapporteur enabled a clearer overview of this "mesh" (*novelo*), "central organizational nucleus" (*núcleo organizador central*), or "assemblage" (*arranjo*), as he variously termed it, based on the shareholdings of both of the supposed competitors:

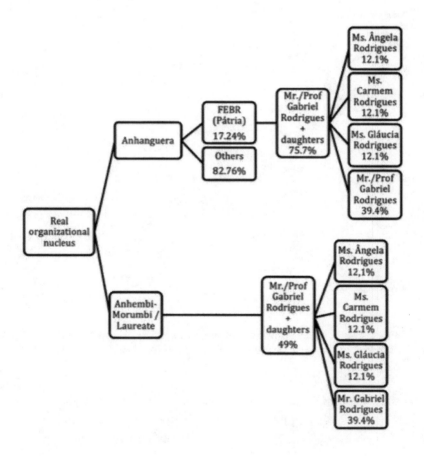

Figure 2: Chart labeled "Mesh of Shareholdings" (CADE 2013: 1900)

This "real organizational nucleus" (*núcleo organizacional real*) brought together the two companies: the investment funds that controlled them and the individual members of the Rodrigues family (who part owned and partially controlled/administered the funds). In the opinion of the rapporteur-commissioner, this nucleus could, in line with a previous CADE ruling, be classified as an "economic group." According to him, for the purposes of Economic Law, an "economic group" is deemed to exist when there is "central direction of competition, defined by the leadership of the group, whatever the form of its constitution, which the other members are expected to comply with" (CADE 2013: 1908). The relations between the legal entities and the individuals involved, in the case before him, meant that it was reasonable to infer that the two companies had mutual knowledge of their actions and strategies and did not act in any manner that was inconsistent or prejudicial to each other.

If all the entities present in this "assemblage" could be considered "to be, in effect, one competitor" for the purposes of enforcing Competition Law, then according to the commissioner it would be necessary to calculate "all the holdings and related resources of the Anhanguera/Anhembi-Morumbi-Laureate/Pátria groups" (CADE 2013: 1913), not only for the purposes of the proceedings at hand, but also whenever it was necessary to calculate the market share of participants in analyses involving any of these three companies. The investigation conducted in this case was able to demonstrate that the applicant Anhanguera had, given its ties with Anhembi-Morumbi (its purported competitor), a greater share of the market than it had formally declared.

A RELATIONAL REALITY

In handing down his decision on the merger of the companies, the antitrust agency's commissioner highlighted a key issue in the investigation undertaken by his staff. The question he posed in his written Opinion was this: "Do the legal (juridical) forms correspond to the economic fact" (CADE 2013: 1878)? He considered that the new context of dispersed share ownership and expanded administrative control of the companies required antitrust analysts to always inquire into the possibility of "convergence" between the legal personality of the corporations and their economic actions. As justification for CADE's extensive investigation into the corporate and administrative structure of the companies operating in the market (only briefly described above), the commissioner stated that he and his advisors had sought a "realistic interpretation of the facts," paying heed to "content, rather than just form, concrete effects rather than declarations and rhetorical statements of intent; to *de facto* articulation rather than the legal (juridical) forms that are merely the external appearance of the businesses; to the true centers of command rather than the corporate architecture that masks it" (CADE 2013: 1902). He stressed the fact that had his officers "merely analyzed Anhanguera in the precise terms set out in the case records by the applicants, [the analysis] **would simply not be in accord with reality**" (CADE 2013: 1882; emphasis in the original Opinion).

In the case in hand, the legal forms clearly did not correspond to the economic facts, in that one of the companies that had applied for authority to merge could not be considered an independent competitor of one of the other companies operating in the market. According to the commissioner, this had significant wider practical implications, in that the legal/corporate forms might have the effect of covering up the identity of the actual agent that the antitrust authority needed to identify. In fact, as Annelise Riles (2011) explains, legal personality produces an effect of opacity that companies may deliberately promote. These companies take advantage of their status as corporations to avoid the liability of the individuals that are "behind the company," in the event of said individuals engaging in unlawful conduct. The techniques and relations by means of which these market competitors are established and maintained, including the relationships of ownership and control, are concealed by the aesthetic effects of the legal form (Riles 2005).

Moreover, the fact that the applicant corporation Anhanguera insisted that it should be considered a single competitor in the relevant market was a very clear attempt at seeking to rely on its corporate personhood in order to be recognized as an independent unit for the purpose of antitrust analysis. Such treatment would be clearly beneficial to Anhanguera, in terms of reducing its estimated market share. The rapporteur-commissioner, alert to the consequences of relying on official form (legal or administrative) as an analytical criterion, stated the following:

As Mark Granovetter suggests, those that believe that the structure of a company resides in its official organogram or in the formal corporate structures are "like babies lost in the woods of sociology," because the "formal" organization of

a business organization (or indeed its informal organization, in many cases) are
not sufficient for the purposes of antitrust analysis. (CADE 2013: 1917)[14]

The commissioner was not, in his criticism, questioning or advancing some
theory of the legal personhood of corporations. He was merely stating that if
the aim was to ascertain economic reality, the legal forms in which companies
organize themselves should not be considered an accurate representation of
competitors. In his view, merely assessing competition in terms of the legal form
of the purported competitors would risk underestimating the degree of concentration in a market and could lead to the approval of mergers that prejudiced
consumers and other companies. In the case in hand, according to the commissioner, some characteristics of this reality, such as the shareholdings of the individuals involved (even if they were minority holdings), the coinciding business
strategies adopted by several participants in the market, and the interlocking
directorates, made it possible to identify economic agents that extrapolated or
were distinct from the legal forms presented by the applicants for merger and
other key players on the market.

In other terms, according to regulators, in cases such as this, economic agency can only be discerned from a particular internal perspective (Riles 2011),
one that foregrounds relational qualities. As anthropologists have previously affirmed, the nature of corporations is essentially ambiguous, being both personal
and impersonal at the same time—a company is simultaneously an abstract
socio-legal entity and a collective (grouping) of the individuals that work for
it or own it (Hart 2005; Riles 2011; Welker 2016). However, these particular perspectives on corporate personhood need to be qualified depending on
the context in which they are being employed. In antitrust cases, the epistemic
challenges faced extend beyond uncovering the internal ownership and administrative relations of companies. In considering a corporation solely in terms of
its legal/corporate structure, as well as an independent economic agent, antitrust analysts run the risk of overlooking relations between corporate entities
that are key to defining the competitive character of a market. Disregarding or
looking beyond corporate personhoods in merger reviews, entirely or in part,
can enable regulators to identify and highlight types and qualities of relations

---

14. The rapporteur cited in a footnote the well-known article by the North American
     sociologist Mark Granovetter (1985), referred to in the bibliography to this chapter.

between companies. This type of investigation requires the regulators to ponder and specify in greater detail their own definition of a competitive relation.

In the case examined in this chapter, the antitrust investigation, drawing inspiration from sociological studies of organizations and social-network analysis, demonstrated that one of the economic agents in the market (the Applicant), had a greater market share than it had formally declared, given that its supposed competitor, Anhembi-Morumbi, was part of the same organizational "assemblage." Despite that, following further examination of the facts, CADE approved the merger. The CADE commissioners took the view that competition in the affected markets in the greater São Paulo region would not be significantly reduced by the merger, even with Anhanguera and its supposed competitor, Anhembi-Morumbi, being considered part of the same group. However, the findings of the investigation highlighted the importance of detailed analysis of concentrations involving investment funds and led to CADE setting out clear new guidelines in its case law on the examination of merger reviews involving the higher education market in Brazil.

COMPETITION AS A FORM OF DETACHMENT

In *La Nation*, written in 1920, Marcel Mauss dedicated several pages to a phenomenon that, almost a century later, has emerged as a source of concern for Brazilian antitrust regulators. Mauss was somewhat more optimistic in his outlook than later regulators tend to be. In the chapter entitled "Economic facts," directed almost entirely to an analysis of the formation and effects of North American cartels and trusts, he set out the benefits of the new "capitalist collectives"—that is, corporations—characterized by a collective form of ownership, since they foreshadowed the future socialization of capital (Mauss [1920] 2013). For Mauss and for others, including Karl Marx (writing fifty years earlier), these new corporate forms might be considered an indication of a transition to a new economic mode of production (Barkan 2013). Others, such as the jurists Adolf Berle and Gardiner Means, were more skeptical about the benefits of these new corporate structures (Mizruchi and Hirschman 2010), and their concerns about the possible perverse effects of the separation between corporate ownership and control proved to be largely justified. They foresaw that the growth of these corporations would lead to excessive economic concentration in the market. Their predictions turned out to be accurate and this increased concentration gave rise to legislation such as the Celler-Kefauver Act in the United States (1950), which prohibited companies from buying shares in another if the acquisition was likely to lead to a reduction in competition between them (Sklar 1988).

The problems relating to the separation between owners and controllers of companies were examined in important North American researches into power structures in the 1960s and 1970s (see Domhoff 2005). This topic has also been the focus of considerable interest in the field of organizational sociology, with researchers seeking to identify the factors—such as personal relations (Burt 1983; Mintz and Schwartz 1985), position in the "organizational field" (DiMaggio 1985; Fligstein and Brantley 1992), "conceptions of control" (Fligstein 1990), among others—that influence the formulation of corporate decisions and goals. In sum, sociological research has sought to explain how companies or other organizations conduct themselves in an environment in which they are embedded in a set of relations with varying degrees of formality with other entities or with the state (Granovetter 1985).

The literature I refer to above focusses on the essentially relational nature of modern capitalism, which can be examined by considering the ties of ownership and administrative control of corporations. Recent antitrust practice in Brazil has also been influenced by sociological studies, and has sought to devise representations and definitions of economic agency by drawing on relational visualization techniques. Regulators have increasingly examined corporate entities in the light of the relations, positions, and professional trajectories of relevant individuals. In terms of the practical difficulties faced by Brazilian antitrust regulators to which I refer in this chapter, there is a complementary movement or perspective that is characteristic of antitrust policy and that merits attention. Their focus on the competitive relations in a market highlights the practices that separate, cut, or detach market entities. These entities are then defined in terms of the extent to which they are independent of each other. Inspired by recent attention in anthropology to detachment as a mode of relationality (Candea et al. 2015), I contend that the justifications put forward by companies seeking leave to merge and the considerations relied upon by antitrust analysts in defining the contours of economic agents (that is, where they "begin" and "end") clearly reflect this movement. That, in turn, calls for reflection on certain practical notions of competition in the light of detachment.

Competitive relations can provide an insight into the ways in which "detachment and engagement are interwoven; the ways in which they limit, complement and enable each other" (Candea et al. 2015: 2). Georg Simmel's (1955) definition of competition as a social form of interaction with a triadic structure in which two or more competitors struggle for the same scarce goods or audience (third party), *without directly* interacting with each other (see Werron 2015), already indicated that there are several possible forms in which it can be envisaged. An indirect interaction might be the result of a great variety of combinations of attachments and detachments.[15]

In the dynamics of corporate merger analyses presented above, we can see two possible practical meanings of competition, or the types of relationality that characterize it. As explained in the previous section, one of the main effects of the reification of corporations in antitrust practice—so that they are deemed to be, simultaneously, both legal entities and economic agents—is that any possible relationship between different corporate entities is denied or masked. In this context, corporate forms are means that are employed to enact detachment and segregate relations between economic agents, not simply hide internal relations within companies. Competition emerges here as a radical form of detachment that separates different persons/agents at the particular time companies file a petition to merge. Detachment in this sense is not an ethic (Cross 2011), but a corporate strategy that implies and provokes (Muniesa 2014) competitive relations to an external observer. The legal personalities and brand names employed by the companies are meant to convey to regulators (and also to consumers) that there is diversity in the market. For the legal and official representatives of companies seeking to merge, presenting the corporations and other entities in the market as being separate (or detached) from each other is a straightforward method employed to bypass potential antitrust investigations and merger prohibitions.

Regulators, however, are becoming wary of the formal means by which entities are defined in the market. For them, the indirect form of interaction that is competition can only be ascertained by defining certain degrees of detachment

---

15. The etymology of the term *competition* (and also *concurrence*) also indicates several possible modes of relationality. Up to the end of the fifteenth century the Latin verb *competo* had a relatively neutral meaning, denoting, in certain circumstances, simultaneity, reunion, parallelism, coincidence, or accord. Nowadays, in English, the verb *to concur* and the substantive concurrence embody this original meaning. From the sixteenth century onward, in Spain, the verb *concurro* began to be used in the sense of "running together" with overtones of "opposition" or "fighting." Competition was only associated with "rivalry" or "emulation" since the eighteenth century, with the work of Thomas Hobbes (Dennis 1977).

that are to be expected between market players. If the competing agents in a market are engaged in some form of relational assemblage, they can only be delimited in accordance with the intensities, temporalities, and the number and extent of the relations between them. The notion of "relevant influence" that is increasingly used by analysts, implies that even when there is a degree of influence and indirect relations between entities, only some of these relations and means of influence characterize a form of entanglement that signifies that the agents in question are in fact unified (and therefore not competitors for antitrust purposes). In general terms, a greater degree of intensity in relations arises from the physical presence of individuals in positions of ownership and administrative control. That may be the result or the manifestation of family/ friendship ties and may be indicated by the geographical locations at which the individuals involved live and work. A perceived excess or an absence or scarcity of relations between legal entities and individuals enables regulators to gauge the closeness/distance between agents in a market. Long-term presence of close relations indicates a heightened probability of coordinated conduct. Competition is deemed to exist or to be possible when an entity begins to acquire a certain minimum degree of autonomy.

Antitrust as a governmental policy designed to regulate conduct and market relations, frequently differs between nations; however, the overriding objective in all jurisdictions is to ensure fair competition remains a principle and, whenever practicable, a structural condition of markets. An ethnography of antitrust practices of evaluation/investigation of mergers and acquisitions reveals some of the difficulties that are inherent to a relational analysis in economic regulation. The means of ascertaining competition in a given market and of analyzing the entities found to be in competition is a source of conflict between antitrust analysts and the representatives and advisers of companies seeking to merge. The advisers of the companies tend to rely on formal legal aspects whereas regulators are increasingly drawn to a relational approach. In this chapter, I have sought to portray how the reliance on corporate personhoods and certain related reifications in antitrust analysis can be misleading for regulators.

Antitrust knowledge practices illuminate underlying ontological conflicts that are present in the formulation and implementation of economic policies or regulatory contexts. That is exemplified here in the recurring potential and actual divergences between legal and economic enactments of the real. The arguments pertaining to the conditions and extent to which a legal entity can be considered the economic agent for the purposes of antitrust are also a point of departure toward understanding of certain practical meanings that are given to competitive relations in regulatory knowledge practices. Competition is considered a form of detached agency in a variety of analytical procedures. This detachment may be in the form of a legal/formal separation of the entities, but it can also be envisaged in more subtle, relative distancing, ascertained from examination of the temporality and the intensity of relations between the agents.

ACKNOWLEDGEMENTS

This chapter is based on ethnographic research carried out between March 2012 and August 2013 into the Brazilian antitrust agency's analysis and judgment of administrative proceedings. The fieldwork was undertaken at the office (chambers) of one of the commissioners of the antitrust agency and at one of the antitrust coordinating offices. The research was funded by CNPq-Brasil. I would like to thank the participants in the Wenner-Gren Workshop, Real Economy: Ethnographic Inquiries into the Reality and the Realization of Economic Life, organized in Rio de Janeiro, June 2016, for their helpful comments on a previous version of this paper, as well as four anonymous HAU reviewers whose suggestions were essential to the development of this text.

REFERENCES

Barkan, Joshua. 2013. *Corporate sovereignty: Law and government under capitalism*. Minneapolis: University of Minnesota Press.

Burt, Ronald. 1983. *Corporate profits and cooptation: Networks of market constraints and directorate ties in the American economy*. New York: Academic Press.

Candea, Matei, Joanna Cook, Catherine Trundle, and Thomas Yarrow. 2015. "Introduction: reconsidering detachment." In *Detachment: Essays on the limits of relational thinking*, edited by Matei Candea, Joanna Cook, Catherine Trundle, and Thomas Yarrow, 1–31. Manchester: Manchester University Press.

CADE. 2013. Opinion of Council Member Alessandro Octaviani in Administrative Proceedings n° 08012.003886/2011-87. Brazil. 2013. Applicants: Anhanguera Educacional Ltda. and Grupo Anchieta. www.cade.gov.br.

Coleman, Leo. 2014. "Corporate identity in *Citizens United*: Legal fictions and anthropological theory." *PoLAR: Political and Legal Anthropology Review* 37 (2): 308–28.

Cross, Jamie. 2011. "Detachment as a corporate ethic: Materializing CSR in the diamond supply chain." *Focaal: Journal of Global and Historical Anthropology* 60: 34–46.

Dennis, Kenneth. 1977. *"Competition" in the history of economic thought.* New York: Arno Press.

DiMaggio, Paul. 1985. "Structural analysis of organizational fields: A block-model approach." *Research in Organizational Behavior* 8: 335–70.

Domhoff, G. William. 2005. "Power structure research and the hope for democracy." *WhoRulesAmerica*, April 2005. http://observatory-elites.org/wp-content/uploads/2012/06/Power-Structure-Research-.pdf.

Fligstein, Neil. 1990. *The transformation of corporate control.* Cambridge, MA: Harvard University Press.

Fligstein, Neil, and Peter Brantley. 1992. "Bank control, owner control, or organizational dynamics: Who controls the large corporation?" *American Journal of Sociology* 2 (98): 280–307.

Forgioni, Paula. 2013. *Os fundamentos do antitruste.* 6th edition. São Paulo: Editora Revista dos Tribunais.

Foster, Robert J. 2010. "Corporate oxymorons and the anthropology of corporations." *Dialectical Anthropology* 34 (1): 95–102.

Granovetter, Mark. 1985. "Economic action and social structure: The problem of embeddedness." *American Journal of Sociology* 91 (3): 481–510.

Hart, Keith. 2005. *The hit man's dilemma; or, Business, personal and impersonal.* Chicago: Prickly Paradigm Press.

Hovenkamp, Herbert. 2005. *The antitrust enterprise: Principle and execution.* Cambridge, MA: Harvard University Press.

Kirsch, Stuart. 2014. "Imagining corporate personhood." *PoLAR: Political and Legal Anthropology Review* 37 (2): 207–17.

Mauss, Marcel. [1920] 2013. *La Nation.* Edited by Marcel Fournier and Jean Terrier. Paris: Presses Universitaires de France.

Mintz, Beth, and Michael Schwartz. 1985. *The power structure of American business.* Chicago: University of Chicago Press.

Mizruchi, Mark S., and Daniel Hirschman. 2010. "The modern corporation as social construction." *Seattle University Law Review* 33 (4): 1065.

Muniesa, Fabian. 2014. *The provoked economy: Economic reality and the performative turn*. London: Routledge.

Onto, Gustavo. 2017. "O agente econômico e suas relações: identificando concorrentes na política antitruste." *Tempo Social, Revista de Sociologia da USP* 29 (1): 109–30.

Riles, Annelise. 2005. "A new agenda for the cultural study of law: Taking on the technicalities." *Buffalo Law Review* 53: 973–1033.

———. 2011. "Too big to fail." In *Recasting anthropological knowledge: Inspiration and social science*, edited by Jeanette Edwards and Maja Petrovic-Steger, 31–48. Cambridge: Cambridge University Press.

Ross, Don. 2010. "The economic agent: Not human, but important." In *Handbook of philosophy of science*. Vol. 13, *Economics*, edited by Uskali Mäki, 627–71. New York: Elsevier.

Sawyer, Suzana. 2006. "Disabling corporate sovereignty in a transnational lawsuit." *Political and Legal Anthropology Review* 29: 23–43.

Simmel, Georg. 1955. *Conflict and the web of group-affiliation*. Translated by Kurt H. Wolff and Reinhard Bendix. New York: The Free Press.

Sklar, Martin J. 1988. *The corporate reconstruction of American capitalism, 1890–1916: The market, the law, and politics*. Cambridge: Cambridge University Press.

Strathern, Marilyn. 1996. "Cutting the network." *Journal of the Royal Anthropological Institute* 2 (3): 517–35.

Welker, Marina. 2014. *Enacting the corporation: An American mining firm in post-authoritarian Indonesia*. Berkeley: University of California Press.

———. 2016. "Notes on the difficulty of studying the corporation." *Seattle University Law Review* 39 (2): 397.

Welker, Marina, Damani J. Partridge, and Rebecca Hardin. 2011. "Corporate lives: New perspectives on the social life of the corporate form: An introduction to supplement 3." *Current Anthropology* 52 (S3): S3–S16.

Werron, Tobias. 2015. "Why do we believe in competition? A historical-sociological view of competition as an institutionalized modern imaginary." *Distinktion: Scandinavian Journal of Social Theory* 16 (2): 186–210.

CHAPTER EIGHT

Making workers real on a South African border farm

MAXIM BOLT

On the Zimbabwean–South African border, migrant laborers toil in gangs of thirty to fill trailers full of fruit, or work their way, backs bent, along rows of cotton. Black overseers stand nearby, shouting to keep the pace up. A little farther away, black foremen and white managers look on from their pickup trucks. Occasionally a white farmer drives up, clad in khaki, an Alsatian alert in the pickup's passenger seat, to check on progress. As month-end nears, recent border crossers sit within reach, hoping that attrition will translate into opportunities for recruitment. After all, in the wake of Zimbabwe's political and economic troubles, the border's agricultural workforces—almost entirely Zimbabwean— are far from stable entities. Indeed, they are full of people who until recently never thought they would set foot on a commercial farm, who still have a hard time thinking of themselves as farm workers at all, and who in some cases keep going southward as soon as their first month's pay arrives. As night draws in, workers trudge down the access roads, past row upon row of crops, back to the barrack-like labor compounds where they are housed on their employers' land. In this landscape, characterized both by transience and plantation-style isolation, recent arrivals feel like they are barely in South Africa. Morning register is called in TshiVenda, the language of the border region, or ChiShona, the majority language of Zimbabwe. Only overzealous police, arriving with escorts from the border garrisons to load the undocumented into vans, remind workers that they are in a country with the best-resourced state institutions in the region.

Yet, if the farms are located on the geographical margins, they are also nodes in a globalized economic network. This is revealed by turning from the orchards and fields to the packsheds into which crops flow, and specifically to Grootplaas Estates, one of the border's citrus operations. Here, a huge double-conveyor system carries oranges and grapefruits from washing to waxing, to inspection and grading stations, and to packers' boxes via an optical machine that photographically organizes fruit by size. In the loading bay, pallets piled high with crates of oranges and grapefruits await trucks to the Indian Ocean port of Durban. From there, ships will take them to countries across Europe, the Middle East, and East Asia. Crate designs signal different agents, buyers, and brands: local, national, British, American. Michael, Grootplaas's personnel manager and packshed administrator, moves between the stacks, dressed in a white coat and armed with a clipboard as he prepares labels that detail each pallet's journey. The pallets evoke industrial-scale production, global connections, and the clinical formality of factories in the fields—far from the stereotypes of South African farms as quasi-feudal, anachronistic backwaters.

On display, at the very center of the packshed's network of conveyor belts and observation gantries, is Michael's harvest-time office, a statement about the importance of paperwork. Bureaucratic categories structure the whole packing process: fruit size; exportability versus rejection for local sale or juicing; export grade A or B, which affects price although it depends only on the superficial assessment of skin blemishes. By contrast, out on the lands, maintaining standards is restricted to the periodic admonishment of pickers who, in their haste, leave stalks attached (puncturing other fruit) or crowns ripped out (leading the fruit to rot faster). Nevertheless, paperwork extends into workers' lives. Alongside the export labels and documents lie Grootplaas's personnel records, for which Michael is also responsible. These follow him in a bank of filing cabinets, as he moves seasonally between the packshed and the farm's workshop. The contents tell a particular version of work and life on the border farms. Applications for employment, contracts, South African documents for "normalization" (regularization), and records of dismissal all speak in a corporate register—"thank you for your interest in our company." But, among these documents, Zimbabwean departure permits signed by thumbprint speak of other experiences—migrant workers fleeing the estate, even without their official identification.

For black workers, laboring on the border's white-owned commercial farms involves constantly relating to official and semiofficial documents and institutionalized arrangements. This is what we expect of formal employment. But how is formality realized? What does this tell us about the "reality" of this wage economy more generally?

On South Africa's border farms, formal employment absorbs migrants into social arrangements that organize space and time. Labor hierarchies bring around-the-clock authority that extends into the residential labor compounds. This reflects the enduring spatial significance of hubs of production in South Africa. Under apartheid, migrants' rights to residence and mobility in "white" areas came with formal employment. Resident workforces themselves represented sites of thoroughgoing incorporation, not merely income (Ferguson 2013). On today's border, being regarded as a "worker" rather than a "border jumper" legitimates migrants' presence in a strikingly similar manner, and attachment to officially acknowledged workplaces mitigates the extreme transience that characterizes the area.

Membership enables residents to use the labor compounds to anchor informal economic activities: trade such as running *shebeens* (illegal bars) and *spazas* (general stores); services such as running taxis, cutting hair, and repairing clothes; and smuggling, such as of cigarettes and marijuana. Considerable opportunities are created through proximity to the border, and the isolation on remote farms of hundreds of residents with monthly wages. Indeed, workers even acquire formal employment as a means to establish existing business activities. As I have argued elsewhere (Bolt 2012), what comes to matter is not remaining invisible to state officials. Rather, the necessary scope for diverse livelihood strategies is created by being visible and recognized in a particular way—as a farm worker.

This article traces how contracts, permits, and inspections shape and sustain the all-important notion of a formal "worker." This means going beyond a focus on labor dynamics themselves, and beyond examining divergences between management rules and employees' self-understandings and practices (e.g., Burawoy 1979). It means tracing fragmented "formalities" in the plural (see Guyer 2004), and appreciating how coherence emerges as an effect of different projects and interactions in and beyond a workforce. Different parties have a stake in upholding the reality of formalized labor relations, and the figure of the worker at their heart. For white farmers who are often considered apartheid throwbacks, a corporate style keeps regulatory authorities at bay, even though managerialism and personnel documentation have little reach beyond their offices. For state officials, recognizing workers as opposed to border jumpers is key to reading the landscape of the border, even if this is often arbitrary and relies on a murky negotiation of ambiguous documentation. For the employed themselves, recognition promises to stabilize the terms of everyday life, even if the ultimate goal is often to use institutional validation as a means to escape in search of better opportunities. In a turbulent border setting, formality remains fragile. But asserting it establishes the terms on which workers and the wage economy are experienced as real—and how that reality comes to appear self-evident (see Neiburg and Guyer, Introduction).[1]

FORMALITY, "THE ECONOMY," AND ECONOMIC LIVES

In what sense is the formal economy real? Substantial intellectual energy has been invested in understanding informality (see, for example, Hart 1973; MacGaffey 1991; Roitman 2004; Meagher 2010). This has produced the notion of a real economy as making a living *beyond* official measurement (see MacGaffey 1991), therefore exposing the restricted parameters of a state perspective. What happens under the radar is key on the Zimbabwean–South African border, where regulation has limited reach and livelihoods are patched together by multiple means. But how does formally measuring and recognizing workforce membership make a wage economy in such a setting?

If one version of the real economy is informal, recent analyses take a very different starting point. Here, "the economic" is produced as an object of expertise (Callon 2007), and through infrastructures of distributed human and nonhuman agency (see Çalışkan and Callon 2009, 2010). Indeed, it is through "socio-technical practice" and measurement, including from within the discipline of economics, that the economy itself is brought into being in this sense—by drawing together diverse practices into a single field of administration and

---

1.   This account draws on seventeen months of ethnographic fieldwork (2006–8), while in residence in Grootplaas' labor compound. During the citrus harvest, I worked unpaid in a picking team and grading fruit in the packshed. Much of border farm life has remained unchanged, and I write in the present tense to avoid an undue sense of distance, but I draw attention to relevant shifts.

engineering (Mitchell 1998, 2008). In this set of perspectives, economies are realized through networks of regulation and calculation, and their categories and effects. But they provoke questions about economic lives more broadly, and about a more expansive notion of the economy "as consisting of all the processes that are involved, in one fashion of another, in 'making a living'" (Narotzky and Besnier 2014: S5).

How might the realization of this narrower economy be brought into conversation with the other, under-the-radar "real economy"? How do people's attempts to make a living weave in and out of the infrastructures and the frames of reference that constitute "the economy" as object? As they do so, what other kinds of practical knowledge underpin the realization of formality's infrastructures and regulatory frameworks?

Timothy Mitchell (2002) helpfully notes that formalization is not simply a matter of representing economic activity, or a dichotomy between measurement and its object. The material economy comes to appear starkly opposed to immaterial and disembodied observation. Instead, however, the concrete practices of regulating and measuring create and sustain a distinct economic field. Measurement is part of the real economy, understood as the formal organization of diverse processes concerning wealth and livelihoods, as the latter come to be defined. Mitchell is interested in how national economies are realized, and his approach consequently restricts the use of the term *economic* in the manner discussed above. But his insights can usefully be applied to the intertwining of key economic categories and the pursuit of livelihoods at smaller scales—here, the figure of the worker in a single workforce. Workers are not simply catalogued and regulated through distant processes of formal documentation. Rather, processes of documentation are integral to life on the border farms, and the resulting paperwork creates workers—explicitly recognized by state and farm authorities as incorporated into settings that are both farmers' private worlds and globalized places of production. Where one body of scholarship presents the real economy as beyond measurement, and another defines it precisely as what is measured, this article explores the space in between. It examines the co-constitution of a regulatory regime and the broader livelihood projects that weave in and out of it.

If economies are at one level realized through regulatory regimes, the making of economic formality through documentary processes is far from straightforward. Documents are implicated in the diverse projects of workers, employers, and state officials. They thus enable performances of formality—including the coproduction of the figure of the worker—that are motivated by goals irreducible to formal logics. The corollary is that, even as documents produce shared understandings of formality, they fail to forge well-measured economic practices in the way recent scholars have emphasized.

Indeed, workers' visibility to and recognition by state officials and other actors may be fragmentary and multiple. That is why I take the metaphor of *spotlights* as a starting point here. State institutions "see" (Scott 1999) workplaces through spotlights such as inspections, permits, and employment contracts, and these do not simply comprise a coherent network. Connections emerge as the result of strategy and skill. They do so as different parties make use of the agreed authority of documents in a range of encounters, augmenting that authority in the process, to get things done in and beyond the labor setting itself. Hence, the second metaphor in this article: that of *stepping-stones*. Focusing on how projects are enacted by jumping from one document to the next reveals the goals and the techniques through which documentary networks are given a particular coherence. Crucially, in the kind of transient, migratory setting explored below, the status of worker may itself be a stepping-stone to something else.

Recent scholarship has explored the place of documents in governing people and space, and in the ways people "acquiesce to, contest, or use this governance" (M. Hull 2012b: 1). Documents are "graphic artifacts" whose "circulation . . . creates associations among people that often differ from formal organizational structures" (M. Hull 2012b: 18). Whether in large bureaucracies or on remote border estates, such associations have far-reaching consequences. As publicly acknowledged "traces"—"inscriptions" that attest to people's past acts and current status (Ferraris 2013: 253–54)—documents take on especial significance in a place where migrants strive for stability amid transience. In a range of settings, migrants are forced to navigate bureaucratic infrastructures and create their own coherence from the informal and improvised practices that characterize state institutions themselves (Coutin 2000; Vigneswaran et al. 2010; Tuckett 2015). This essay offers the view from within a workforce where the allure of formality lies at the heart of a migrant-labor regime. Formality is brokered through social relations, in which official and semiofficial paperwork—with its apparent fixity of meaning—becomes the focal point for negotiation and efforts to shape circumstances.

On South Africa's border with Zimbabwe, beyond the packshed with its labeled, bar-coded crates and its conveyor belts, formality is a diverse mosaic of connections to officialdom. Grootplaas's white farmers learn how to navigate these spotlights skillfully, presenting the farm appropriately while continuing to operate according to their own rules. In the process, state and farm institutions together shape black workers' lives while sustaining a field of delimited "personnel relations." Amid a range of patterns of movement and settlement on the farms, and a range of forms of trade and dependence in residents' livelihoods, official and semiofficial documents are key to recognizing workers—that is, to making *workers* real as a distinct category.

Grootplaas's workers also navigate the terrain of formality. Idioms of due process have little effect on personalized hierarchies, but a range of more or less official documents is key to employees' lives, strategies, and self-understandings. Migrants are extremely diverse in terms of their class backgrounds and places of origin. Many arrive with little other than their Zimbabwean identity cards and sheaves of qualification certificates, whose power comes from the presumed durability of their meaning and value through time. Once employed, different identity documents attaching workers to the farm enable new conditions for life. For workers, as much as for their employers, using documents takes adeptness: deciding when to reveal them; extending their uses to new circumstances; converting between them. Between the two extremes archived in Grootplaas's filing cabinets—corporate personnel records and abandoned identity cards and papers—is a world in which everyday lives and possibilities for the future are negotiated through the category of *worker*.

My emphasis on the production of formality offers an alternative way of approaching how workers are made. Given the context, a more obvious starting point would be migrants' subjection to the requirements of export agriculture in particular, and capitalism in general. Certainly, workers' lives on the border farms are powerfully shaped by the temporal regimes of capitalism. As I have explored previously (Bolt 2013), the relatively independent task orientation of permanent employees contrasts with their seasonal counterparts' tight labor discipline—the latter coordinated to harvest fruit for export within northern-hemisphere tariff windows. Yet, at a more general level, all workers are defined through the interchangeability of their different activities as abstract labor time, mediated by an equivalent standard of value created by the commodity form (see Postone 1993). Capitalism in Zimbabwe and South Africa was classically shaped by "delayed proletarianization": the persistence of rural agricultural bases that could supplement, although not ultimately reduce dependence on, commodities and waged employment (for Zimbabwe, see Arrighi 1970; Phimister

1988). Yet many Zimbabweans have seen even this eroded amid economic crisis, as rural homes come to rely overwhelmingly on remittances (Bolt 2015: 212).

This subjection to capitalism—life premised on the commodity and the wage—leaves migrants vulnerable. But it therefore becomes all the more important to understand how they work to stabilize the terms of their lives by gaining everyday recognition as workers, not simply by providing their labor. The view from one migrant workforce reveals attempts to control and stabilize the meanings of connections between workers, between workers and employers, and between the workplace and state officials. In turn, particular objects and processes enable the wage economy to be recognized as the real foundation of all of these interactions, by recognizing workers. Despite the imaginative power and apparent coherence of the formal sector and the figure of the worker in South Africa (Barchiesi 2011), workers and employers encounter formalities as a constellation of points through which to navigate. Yet the result is that formal registers of labor have a common-sense reality about them, as they become bound up with plans and projects for making a living. Formality—fragmentary, ambiguous, and emphasized and de-emphasized by different parties at different times—nevertheless anchors the everyday terms of life in a transient setting.

FORMALITY AND MARGINALITY IN SOUTH AFRICA

Grootplaas is one of a string of family-run crop estates on the southern bank of the Limpopo River, which marks the border. Large and high profile like some of its neighbors, Grootplaas employs 140 permanent workers, and 460 seasonal workers during the picking season. The farm reached one million crates of citrus in 2007, its oranges and grapefruits sold in British and other European Union supermarkets as well as in the Middle East and East Asia.

Tied into global supply chains, Grootplaas is regulated through both state and nonstate inspections. The Department of Labour, for example, visits the border farms for periodic evaluations of working conditions. GLOBALG.A.P. (formerly EUREPGAP), a standards agency that certifies produce for European markets, surveys hygiene conditions as well as "worker welfare." Some supermarkets have their own, even stricter investigation processes. It is during all of these that the filing cabinets of worker records become important, as they stand for proper procedure on the farm.

This appears indicative of a South Africa of far-reaching formality, in which the economy is dominated by regulated international linkages, oversight is the basis of a pervasive infrastructure, and workforces are governed by distinct and explicitly monitored codes. Formal logics of state and capital have a greater bureaucratic reach and imaginative hold than elsewhere in the region. Life on the ground is deeply enmeshed in interlocking public and corporate institutions (see, for example, James 2014; Ferguson 2015). Yet, analytical terms that constitute *the economy* as object can betray a bias to formal regulatory rhetoric (Guyer 2014). In debates about the fate of formal work (for example, Seekings and Nattrass 2005; Callebert 2014), what emerges is a world in which formality is a "sector," and in which workers' livelihoods might plausibly be addressed in the universalist, material/structural idiom of a "standard of living" (Guyer 2014: 149). South Africa can appear less messy, more structurally determined, more sharply categorized. But, like elsewhere on the continent, regulatory islands have stood in contrast to a conspicuous lack of information. The far-reaching ambitions of state and capital to register and categorize nonwhite people, beginning around the turn of the twentieth century, were always frustrated by incapacity and the profusion of blind spots (Breckenridge 2014). The South African state has been "defined by its control of the flow of resources, fiercely delimiting the transfer of benefits, constitutionally disinterested in and incapable of knowledge about the vast majority of its subjects" (Breckenridge 2014: 214).

Scholarship on wage labor in southern Africa has long explored the implications of inclusion in export-oriented enclaves (for example, Gluckman 1961; Moodie with Ndatshe 1994). Sites of formal employment—epitomized by South Africa's hyperpoliced, total institution-like mines—were built on migrancy but experienced as sharply distinct from hinterlands of subsistence. Yet inclusion did not mean conforming to anything resembling the official view of the workplace. The "institutionalisation of industrial relations" has remained fragile (von Holdt 2010: 128). Formal labor hierarchies, and official forms of recognition and regulation, are easily challenged by alternative—and often violent—"local moral orders" (von Holdt 2010).

Even centers of control, then, have been less planned that they appear. Nevertheless, places like Grootplaas are distinctly marginal in relation to centers of urban and industrial infrastructure. Official linkages are dim spotlights, exemplifying less order or regulation than is often assumed to typify South African labor arrangements. Hubs of production on South Africa's northern border have been shaped by cross-border migrants responding to periodic crises at home, and coercive but ad hoc regimes of policing and recruitment (see, for example, van Onselen 1976; Werbner 1991; Bradford 1993; Murray 1995; Bolt 2015). This, in turn, has meant that recruits have had little attachment to a thorough-going worker identity.

If industrial relations have been shallowly institutionalized elsewhere in South Africa, this is exacerbated on the border farms by the sheer diversity of employees, itself the result of spiraling hyperinflation, economic contraction, and the persecution of opposition supporters in Zimbabwe after 2000. Employ-ees hail from marginalized rural areas across the border and beyond, and from cities including the capital, Harare. They range from lifelong farm workers to erstwhile professionals. And they may have little education or be school gradu-ates, even occasionally university graduates. Indeed, recently displaced Zimba-bweans on the northern border actively deny being farm workers at all. Former teachers or nurses, or recent A-level graduates, speak of being "in exile," and of putting life on pause in the meantime. The police share this diffidence, for dif-ferent reasons—everyone is assumed to be a border jumper first. All of this, of course, renders documents still more important in making formal workers real; they do not simply confirm a widely accepted state of affairs.

One result is a highly vulnerable farm working population (Rutherford and Addison 2007; Rutherford 2008). Here, as elsewhere in the country, a floating reserve of migrant labor has proven useful for farmers responding to market liberalization (Johnston 2007). This setting resembles others where the vulner-ability of cross-border migrants is underpinned by gray legal regimes, which leave them perpetually "deportable" (De Genova 2005; see also Heyman 2001). Workers are often confined to their places of work, in a broader environment where they are potential fugitives, as elsewhere historically in South Africa. Such regimes support Ananya Roy's claim that informal lacunae are best understood as state effects: deliberate "suspensions" of legal order, defined as beyond the law but allowed to persist (2005: 149). Yet places like the Zimbabwean–South African border also reveal the complex configuration of employers' and workers' projects through which formality comes to be realized. This is especially visible on agricultural estates where state oversight has always been extremely limited.

Especially at its margins, South Africa has historically been characterized by limited state capacity and piecemeal accommodations. From the first half of the twentieth century, the northern border was the site of different schemes for achieving a measure of control, in turn the result of ever-shifting relations between state institutions and representatives (see MacDonald 2012). Further complicating the picture, a range of private individuals variously acted as informal intermediaries and operated as illegal "labour pirates" (Murray 1995).

Nevertheless, heated debates over regulation were the terrain for contesting the control of territory and human mobility. Messina Copper Mine, the border region's first major employer, attempted in the early twentieth century to gain formal jurisdiction over a large tract of land, ostensibly to prevent malaria but also to police the movement and enlistment of people. Farmers soon began cultivating the border in the same ecosystem of shadowy recruitment, and in periodic competition with ineffective state labor depots (see Bolt 2015). The result was a plurality of ambiguous forms of authority over land and labor.

On South Africa's farms, assumptions persist that white landowners enjoy paternalist sovereignty over their territory and "their people." Government bureaucrats anyway have little capacity to "see" the population they regulate (see Hoag 2010). But such assumptions further complicate what it means for estates like Grootplaas to come under state purview (see, for example, Rutherford 2008), and leave idioms of kinship competing with those of employment (du Toit 1993). If farmers' extralegal coercion on their "little republics" has largely receded, it has given way to vigilante justice presided over by senior black workers (Bolt 2016). What is more, labor compounds are unfenced, and gradually adapted over years (e.g., housing improvements, food gardens) by more or less embedded residents, all despite lacking security of tenure. Foremen and supervisors often cast themselves as headmen and elders, even holding court and judging disputes, rather than emphasizing formal working roles. Meanwhile, employment itself fluctuates. Even in a postapartheid era of minimum wages, required work conditions, and stipulated access to housing, determining what exactly is formal in farm employment—and delimiting recognizable categories of *worker* and *personnel* among farm dwellers—is no simple matter. And workers' rights are extremely difficult to defend as a result. Periodic inspections come and go, met with silence out of fear of repercussions. There is, anyway, little scrutiny of connections between workplace and residence—precisely those that complicate the category of "worker" in the first place, and that render much of the legal framework discretionary (Human Rights Watch 2006).

Farmers' experiences, meanwhile, are of making their own way. They provide their own infrastructure: graded roads; borehole and pump water; and school buildings for publicly employed teachers with sporadic attendance records. Nondigitized personnel records leave the farms further disconnected from state infrastructures. During my fieldwork, a Department of Health mobile clinic began coming to the farms, but its visits were infrequent. Different state institutions stand for particular kinds of regulation, with different interplays of attention and absence. But in this case, absence predominates.

The army and the police are notable exceptions. For workers and farmers, much everyday interaction with state employees means negotiating their presence. Displacement across the border because of the Zimbabwean crisis has produced a wider climate of popular and media hostility in South Africa, and a border regime of frequent, aggressive police deportation raids.[2] Fearing discovery, seasonal workers during the period of fieldwork would sleep in dry riverbeds in the bush. For farmers, the advantages of docile working populations (see Human Rights Watch 2006) were counterweighed by the bureaucratic nuisance of replacing workers. Deportees anyway generally returned to their jobs within days, after climbing back through the border fence. As for the police, their aggressive presence was only matched by their absence when it came to keeping the peace.

Yet even this coercive dimension of state attention is localized in important ways. Farmers regularly meet police and army chiefs to negotiate exemptions for their workers. As I discuss below, one result has been to recognize private farm ID cards. Farm workers have themselves localized the army presence. Soldiers, lonely in their garrisons, spend weekends at the farm compounds' *shebeens*, and even once assembled a football team to compete in the border's interfarm tournament. Workers draw on soldiers, with their apparently incontestable official positions and uniforms, to mediate disputes and underwrite everyday vigilante justice. By contrast, performance reports to superiors leave the lion's share of garrison life unmonitored.

While states are constituted through mobile presences (see Quirk and Vigneswaran 2015), spotlights of official attention are disconnected and ambiguous. Each is a point of partial regulation. Yet these spotlights become connected. In workforces, official and semiofficial documents are far from incidental. They have varying degrees of authority, which transcend the patchy reach of state institutions, and they become points around which a sense of formality is built through relationships in and beyond the workforce. And these locally authoritative documents become stepping-stones, as recruits try to get ahead as workers

---

2.   In 2009, deportations were suspended, and the Zimbabwe Documentation Project was instituted to register undocumented Zimbabweans en masse. This only reached a minority, and deportations recommenced in late 2011.

and subsequently make further plans. In a setting where the difference between a worker and a transient migrant is often just a matter of timing—as people make and revise plans about when to move and when to stop for a while—documents are the focal points for recognition. And this is especially so in South Africa and its wider regional political economy. Despite the stark deficiencies of grand attempts to register nonwhite working populations (see Breckenridge 2014), bureaucratic apparatuses and their lacunae have for a long time shaped people's experiences of capitalism. Nevertheless, even the legitimation that comes with established symbols of formality needs to be constantly negotiated.

THE CONTRACT

The farm's contracts make workers in a literal sense, by officially marking their recategorization. They make workers real, while also investing them in the reality of a chain of formal documentation. They therefore offer a useful starting point for examining how all this works. The contracts are especially limited spotlights, representing a juxtaposition of formal categorization and fixity, and half-hearted and flexible execution. They demand specifications of "position of employee," area of operation on the estate, working hours, and daily pay. Three lines for completion at the foot of the page—"on behalf of employer," "date," "employee"—suggest a parallel symmetry in the employment situation. But, within this rubric, matters are left as vague as possible. Most employees are simply "farm hands." The workplace of those not based in the packshed is usually "lands," the estate's vast hectares of orchards, and even this is flexible. And the employee may not actually sign the contract at all.

As for hours and pay, the form of the contract suggests that clock time predominates across the farm. The packshed, run around its conveyor belts, somewhat conforms to this model if one ignores unpaid "preparation time." But picking in the orchards is worlds away from the contract's abstract regularity. It is driven instead by the rhythms of gang labor, responding to the exigencies of piece rates and fluctuations in batch processing, and maintained by strings of insistent calls and insults. Teams, and especially their supervisors, compete aggressively and use chalk to mark tallies onto the backs of trailers—a form of inscription whose dynamics of incitement and rivalry are far more clearly connected to the labor process. Payday is a ritual affirming the formality of the contract. One at a time, workers "sign" for pay with a thumbprint, at a table outside the office, in return for a paper packet with an unverifiable amount typed onto the front.[3] In this interaction, employees who consider themselves simply in exile from happier lives confront the flip side of the corporate register of the contract itself. Being recognized as a farm worker by the farm offices means being assumed illiterate, and losing the capacity to sign with a pen.[4] Such treatment has especial historical resonance in South Africa, especially when seen alongside the farm's unsigned contracts. In the formative early years of apartheid, bureaucratic arguments for fingerprinting precisely undermined the autonomy of black people. Central was the contention that the latter's signing of labor contracts was an unnecessary inconvenience, in contrast to the efficiency promised by biometric identification. Meanwhile, workers needed written consent from white employers to leave agricultural and other jobs (Breckenridge 2014: 146, 157).

The contract, despite its selectivity and vagueness, draws life through its place in a chain of documentation—a self-referential assemblage in which an official story gradually accumulates (see Latour 2009). This chain is crucial to how workers live through and around paperwork. Their claims to formal identities are negotiated through documents, whose effectiveness comes from their material and aesthetic qualities (see Riles 2006; M. Hull 2012a, 2012b; E. Hull 2012), but which also require convincing performances when they are mobilized (Reeves 2013). Jane Guyer (2004) notes that formality often appears to people in African settings on the margins of bureaucracy through the apparent fixity of more or less official documents. In a workforce like Grootplaas, these work as fragmentary badges of formality—as putative connections to officialdom—because of people's investment in ensuring their authority and efficacy. Such investment renders the formal categories of the wage economy real, especially through the recognition of workers in interactions on and beyond the farm. The next section turns to how workers trace stepping-stone routes through their conversions between documents.

---

3. The amount always falls below the minimum wage. Piece rates are set so that workers cannot pick fast enough to make up their theoretical daily amount. There is no risk of added state scrutiny: reportedly, the state's loss of test farms since apartheid removed its capacity in this regard. Farmers must simply ensure that they coordinate their rates, in conversation with lawyers.

4. Literacy rates were strikingly high at the time of fieldwork, as many people experienced abrupt downward mobility. They may now be lower because of the decline since 2000 of Zimbabwe's famously strong education system.

DOCUMENTARY STEPPING-STONES

Workers are well aware that their stability relies on the skillful mobilization of documents. For new recruits, this awareness is doubly sharpened. Given their transience and vulnerability on the border, migrants' documents—as socially recognized inscriptions of their histories (Ferraris 2013)—represent a particular kind of stability. Zimbabwean national identity cards (*zvitupa*, singular *chitupa*)—durable metal plates—bear their owners' personal information, including area of origin. Sheaves of certificates bearing histories of qualifications—school and even university grades, and various courses and training sessions—are carefully protected in plastic, ready to be revealed and mobilized at the right moment. Yet the same transience presents a problem of everyday storage. I have shown elsewhere (Bolt 2014) that difficulties storing cash lead seasonal workers to entrust their pay to more established permanent workers, and this in turn underpins the farm hierarchy outside of work time. Similar challenges pertain with official and semiofficial documents as well as other possessions that promise to connect past lives to future prospects—from lists of contact numbers to photo albums that prove recruits not "really" to be farm workers. But documents that identify people and their potential value, especially, cannot be entrusted like money. Migrants hang onto the objects that make them who they are, at least until these are superseded by more effective ones. Once migrants are employed, they carry at all times the papers that make them workers in the eyes of police—stapled, tattered, their quarter-fold lines permanently marked with dust.

How does this conversion work? The self-evident way that Zimbabwean identity cards stand for their owners enables them to become points around which workers and jobseekers negotiate their positions. Officially, the recruitment of seasonal workers happens in the open: an official process in which a senior worker stands on a low wall and collects the cards from throngs of outstretched hands. But identity cards are also central to quieter recruitment offstage. The understanding is that if a senior figure agrees to take one's card, it means that one will be given work—an arrangement quickly learned by new arrivals.[5] There are risks in giving up cards. They are periodically misplaced, and

5.   This negotiation is highly gendered, as are dynamics in the workforce more generally. The predominately male senior workers are known to demand sexual favors from women in return for preferential access to employment. This may extend into

workers find themselves in the strange limbo of being on the farm's books but in danger of losing any officially recognized identity. This is all the more alarming because of the difficulty and expense of replacing them. Conversely, once migrants acquire alternative badges of officialdom, a few are willing to abandon their Zimbabwean cards altogether.

Those who do secure a job enter the world of farm paperwork. A corporate-style "application for employment"—which closes with the line, "Thank you for your interest shown in our company"—contrasts with the subsequent finger-printing and the queue for mug shots, in which exposure to objectification and humiliation by management introduces recruits to the farm's racialized hierarchy. As with the contract, the information requested is vague and its relevance appears confined to the filing cabinet. Linguistic ability is largely determined by self-assessment. The only two references from previous employers I found in the person-nel records simply stated that the workers moved on, "seeking greener pastures."

But the real importance of these documents is in laying the foundations for others that enable workers to be recognized in everyday terms. In other words, they are offstage parts of the documentary chain through which the formal wage economy is realized. The contract is a point where existing documents are converted into worker status. It asks for the recruit's ID document number, etched onto the metal card that has already circulated as part of recruitment. It also records any educational qualifications, which may affect getting a job, and some skill is involved in mobilizing them. If they need to be carefully guarded, they also need to be presented quietly and to the right people. One seasonal worker, a former teacher, had A-levels, a bachelor's degree, and a postgradu-ate diploma. Announcing his background to Michael, the highly educated per-sonnel manager, initially secured a clerical job. But a soured relationship with him—borne of a sense of competition—soon led to demotion back to picking. Michael himself had kept his certificates a secret, and then taken them straight to the farmer, not to a fellow worker.

The farm's own ID number, generated in completing the contract, gains its true significance after recruitment, because it enables a migrant to live as a worker. It is the basis of a farm ID card, made and issued by farms responding to huge delays in processing seasonal workers. Farm IDs are built on an enduring

---

demanding that women undertake domestic tasks, in relationships whose context is men's overwhelming control of accommodation. I describe the gendered character of farm life and workforce hierarchy in detail elsewhere (see Bolt 2013).

local understanding of what makes a farm worker. Dependence on proof of attachment to white landowners evokes apartheid-era pass laws, and underlines a legacy on both sides of the border of farmers' partial sovereignty over land and labor (see Rutherford 2001). Seasonal recruits have long been regularized after they start work, bearing the risks themselves, and then required to prove that they belong to particular estates—sometimes only tacitly and sometimes more explicitly, through ad hoc agreements between farmers, police, and army.

Farm IDs are recognized documents attesting to sponsorship by white farmers, which identify migrants as workers, protect them, but also confine them to their estates. Moving around on the border road, or elsewhere off the estates, is more dangerous. Yet the provisional security afforded by proof of connection to the farms is so valuable for diverse livelihood strategies that a market in forged employment cards developed in the Zimbabwean border town of Beitbridge. The cards' material form underlines the power relations they represent. As a "graphic genre" (M. Hull 2012b: 15), these documents stand for the private authority of farmers and their families, yet they are in effect semiofficial. Each is homemade, cut from a piece of paper prepared on a home computer. And on each, a cartoon-style, Clipart image of a fruit tree—the farm's logo—dominates. A monthly hole punch confirms that the bearer has been working on the estate since the card's date of issue.

Recruits with ID cards are generally considered workers, but this has to be negotiated and renegotiated. Given the market in forgeries, farm ID cards may not be enough to prevent arrest if workers flee when the police arrive—a response that itself renders them suspect. It does not help that farm IDs bear no photographs, unlike the pieces of paper that workers carry once they have been fully regularized. The cards are ambiguous: *semi*official (at least as they are treated by representatives of the state), *usually* accepted, *probably* issued by a farmer, but forged with relative ease.

The next stage in workers' recognition and realization is a work permit from Home Affairs. Michael, the personnel manager, decides who among the hundreds of recruits will be taken first to the border post to be processed. During the period of fieldwork, this meant receiving a Zimbabwean Emergency Travel Document (ETD, a photocopied sheet of paper[6]), with a photograph stapled to

---

6.   ETDs were developed to streamline the documentation of Zimbabwean farm workers, because of a shortage of passports. Access to Zimbabwean passports has since improved.

the front and a South African short-term visa subsequently affixed to the back. Some acquire official papers quickly. Others never receive legal documents, a situation worsened by the Home Affairs backlogs that became notorious during fieldwork. Key are connections to powerful senior workers whose threats Michael cannot afford to ignore, or Michael's own demands for favors or his attempts to build a retinue of dependents. Either way, gaining state-issued paperwork and realizing the unambiguous status of worker are inseparable from one's incorporation into around-the-clock farm hierarchies. Beginning in the orchards and the packshed, these extend to entrusting pay to superordinates, and even obtaining the protection required for informal trade and services in the compound. And it is not only that incorporation opens the way to formal documentation. As workers guard their paperwork in back pockets—as it disintegrates and becomes softer and darker, and perhaps accumulates more stamps and adhesive visas—it represents a record crucial for negotiating encounters with border patrols. Even so, police have been known to tear up workers' papers. The only way to be sure that one's worker status transcends particular encounters with police patrols—that it is really real—is to be attached to senior workers who can approach the white farmer, who in turn can chase up the case before deportation occurs.

Recourse to the farmer is most visible, of course, among permanent workers themselves. Fully documented, they are far less vulnerable, and there is no doubt that they are real workers, not border jumpers. Nevertheless, permanent workers' projects for still greater stability occasionally misfire, revealing the continuing importance of being recognized as part of a border workforce. Claiming questionable citizenship (reportedly by having dubious credentials confirmed by employers or purported kin) is risky.[7] One senior worker's ID featured a South African Venda name that he was unable to back up with sufficient local knowledge at a roadblock. The worker called the foreman, who in turn contacted the farmer, who intervened and had his employee released. Further bribes and appeals to the farmer would follow, in future encounters with police. The apparent fixity of meaning of documents gives them a powerful allure, but they remain

---

7. Others have legally acquired a South African ID (although not citizenship) following a letter proving long-term service on the farms. During the Zimbabwe Documentation Project (see footnote 2), some permanent workers were also able to acquire four-year South African visas. But this depended on being physically present at the farm when Home Affairs officials visited—and many workers were not—which emphasizes the contingent nature of access to documents.

subject to processes of everyday negotiation in which the ultimate fallback remains that farm residents are understood to be real workers.

A final twist is that as recruits build personal histories through documentation, being a worker enables a life beyond the border farms. Whereas papers attach a worker to a particular employer, for a fixed period, many see them as passports to more open-ended mobility. Police on the roads are assumed not to be able to check immediately whether the permits of absconded workers have been canceled. So many seasonal migrants head for Johannesburg, armed now not only with their certificates and contact numbers but also with pieces of paper—a permit and a visa-adorned travel document—that appear to render them workers in a less personalized and localized register than that of farm ID cards.

CONCLUSION

Regulation in practice is relational, and it produces formal people ("workers") in formal places ("workplaces"). While this may be especially marked in migrant labor regimes that perpetuate vulnerability and dependence on employers, formal regulation classifies people in other labor settings too (see, for example, Dunn 2005 on "standards"). Indeed, more generally still, "persons and relations" are "enacted and realized" through the categories asserted as basic to economic reality (Neiburg and Guyer, Introduction). This is often a piecemeal process. Workers and workplaces on the border are made through a multiplicity of regulatory lenses, with different purposes and different effects, mirroring the multiplicity of state institutions (see Abrams 1988). Especially noticeable in a setting like South Africa's margins, official spotlights are limited and bureaucratic infrastructures and documentary networks sparse—far from constituting a thick system of regularities.

Nevertheless, documents are more than just window dressing. Rather than simply standing as the opposite of a "real" informal economy, paperwork's relative fixity enables the realization of economic roles and places, and their stabilization through time. This fixity is inflected by South Africa's distinctive history of documentation. Capitalism has for over a century developed symbiotically with the bureaucratic registration of people and the regulation of their movement and settlement. Governmental fantasies of omniscience have always faced the reality of limited control, over people and over the very technologies used to identify them (Breckenridge 2014). Indeed, the awareness of these limits has been as formative as the ambition to achieve control: the particular South African penchant for fingerprinting, for example, began to develop at the turn of the twentieth century because of the "presumption of universal deceit" (Breckenridge 2014: 76). On the Zimbabwean border, fantasies of control have been especially challenged. Militarization jostles with state overstretch, and overlapping documentary regimes coexist with countless transient strangers. Resonating with South Africa's longer history of bureaucracy and its limits, attempts by officials and employers to identify and categorize, and by migrants to be recognized, become all the more important. Despite liberalization, the end of the apartheid order, and the lack of sufficient capacity to enforce new legal measures, paperwork continues to script a range of interactions. Paperwork's fixity, then, reflects its significance over a long period of time, in establishing the terms of life at the intersection of bureaucracy and capitalism.

Yet the result also produces and sustains everyday formality. Documents make workers, opening up possibilities through recognition in day-to-day encounters. As Ian Hacking (2004) notes, "making up people" requires understanding as much through Goffman-esque face-to-face interactions as through Foucauldian disciplining discourses. Workers learn to convert between different documents, using them like stepping-stones to realize an identity as a worker that carries weight with an increasing range of state officials. As people develop pragmatic logics for enacting official process from below (see Coutin 2000), they produce a real economy that is as much made of negotiated formal statuses as it is about their own contingent projects.

ACKNOWLEDGMENTS

For comments on drafts of this essay, I wish to thank Neville Bolt, Jane Guyer, Jessica Jacobson, Federico Neiburg, and participants of the Human Geography Seminar at King's College London, the DASA Staff Writing Seminar at the University of Birmingham, the WISER Internal Seminar at the University of the Witwatersrand, and the Wenner-Gren/Museu Nacional/Federal University of Rio de Janeiro workshop, Real Economy: Ethnographic Inquiries into the Reality and the Realization of Economic Life. Giovanni da Col and four anonymous reviewers at *Hau* offered extremely helpful suggestions. An early version of the essay was published in *The political economy of everyday life in Africa*, a

Festschrift for Jane Guyer, coeditor of this volume. Research for this essay was funded by the ESRC (PTA-031-2005-00006) during a PhD at the LSE.

REFERENCES

Abrams, Philip. 1988. "Notes on the difficulty of studying the state." *Journal of Historical Sociology* 1 (1): 58–89.

Arrighi, Giovanni. 1970. "Labour supplies in historical perspective: A study of the proletarianisation of the African peasantry in Rhodesia." *Journal of Development Studies* 6 (3): 197–234.

Barchiesi, Franco. 2011. *Precarious liberation: Workers, the state, and contested social citizenship in postapartheid South Africa.* Albany: State University of New York Press.

Bolt, Maxim. 2012. "Waged entrepreneurs, policed informality: Work, the regulation of space and the economy of the Zimbabwean–South African border." *Africa* 82 (1): 111–30.

———. 2013. "Producing permanence: Employment, domesticity and the flexible future on a South African border farm." *Economy and Society* 42 (2): 197–225.

———. 2014. "The sociality of the wage: Money rhythms, wealth circulation and the problem with cash on the Zimbabwean–South African border." *Journal of the Royal Anthropological Institute*, n.s., 20 (1): 113–30.

———. 2015. *Zimbabwe's migrants and South Africa's border farms: The roots of impermanence.* Cambridge: Cambridge University Press.

———. 2016. "Mediated paternalism and violent incorporation: Enforcing farm hierarchies on the Zimbabwean–South African border." *Journal of Southern African Studies* 42 (5): 911–27.

Bradford, Helen. 1993. "Getting away with murder: 'Mealie kings,' the state and foreigners in the Eastern Transvaal, c.1918–1950." In *Apartheid's genesis, 1935–1962*, edited by Philip Bonner, Peter Delius, and Deborah Posel, 96–125. Braamfontein: Ravan Press.

Breckenridge, Keith. 2014. *Biometric state: The global politics of identification and surveillance in South Africa, 1850 to the present.* Cambridge: Cambridge University Press.

Burawoy, Michael. 1979. *Manufacturing consent: Changes in the labor process under monopoly capitalism.* Chicago: University of Chicago Press.

Çalışkan, Koray, and Michel Callon. 2009. "Economization, part 1: Shifting attention from the economy towards processes of economization." *Economy and Society* 38 (3): 369–98.

———. 2010. "Economization, part 2: A research programme for the study of markets." *Economy and Society* 39 (1): 1–32.

Callebert, Ralph. 2014. "Transcending dual economies: Reflections on 'Popular economies in South Africa.'" *Africa* 84 (1): 119–34.

Callon, Michel. 2007. "What does it mean to say that economics is performative?" In *Do economists make markets? On the performativity of economics*, edited by Donald MacKenzie, Fabian Muniesa, and Lucia Siu, 311–58. Princeton, NJ: Princeton University Press.

Coutin, Susan B. 2000. *Legalizing moves: Salvadoran immigrants' struggle for U.S. residency*. Ann Arbor: University of Michigan Press.

De Genova, Nicholas. 2005. *Working the boundaries: Race, space, and "illegality" in Mexican Chicago*. Durham, NC: Duke University Press.

du Toit, A. 1993. "The micro-politics of paternalism: The discourses of management and resistance on South African fruit and wine farms." *Journal of Southern African Studies* 19 (2): 314–36.

Dunn, Elizabeth C. 2005. "Standards and person-making in East Central Europe." In *Global assemblages: Technology, politics, and ethics as anthropological problems*, edited by Aihwa Ong and Stephen J. Collier, 173–93. Oxford: Blackwell.

Ferguson, James. 2013. "Declarations of dependence: Labour, personhood, and welfare in southern Africa." *Journal of the Royal Anthropological Institute*, n.s., 19 (2): 223–42.

———. 2015. *Give a man a fish: Reflections on the new politics of distribution*. Durham, NC: Duke University Press.

Ferraris, Maurizio. 2013. *Documentality: Why it is necessary to leave traces*. Translated by Richard Davies. New York: Fordham University Press.

Gluckman, Max. 1961. "Anthropological problems arising from the African Industrial Revolution." In *Social change in modern Africa: Studies presented and discussed at the First International African Seminar*, edited by Aidan Southall, 67–82. Oxford: Oxford University Press.

Guyer, Jane I. 2004. *Marginal gains: Monetary transactions in Atlantic Africa*. Chicago: University of Chicago Press.

———. 2014. "Gain and losses in the margins of time: From West and Equatorial history to present-day South Africa, and back." *Africa* 84 (1): 146–50.

Hacking, Ian. 2004. "Between Michel Foucault and Erving Goffman: Between discourse in the abstract and face-to-face interaction." *Economy and Society* 33 (3): 277–302.

Hart, Keith. 1973. "Informal income opportunities and urban employment in Ghana." *Journal of Modern African Studies* 11 (1): 61–89.

Heyman, Josiah McC. 2001. "Class and classification at the US-Mexico border." *Human Organization* 60 (2): 128–40.

Hoag, Colin. 2010. "The magic of the populace: An ethnography of illegibility in the South African immigration bureaucracy." *PoLAR* 33 (1): 6–25.

Hull, Elizabeth. 2012. "Banking in the bush: Waiting for credit in South Africa's rural economy." *Africa* 82 (1): 168–86.

Hull, Matthew S. 2012a. "Documents and bureaucracy." *Annual Review of Anthropology* 41:251–67.

———. 2012b. *Government of paper: The materiality of bureaucracy in urban Pakistan.* Berkeley: University of California Press.

Human Rights Watch. 2006. "Unprotected migrants: Zimbabweans in South Africa's Limpopo Province." *Human Rights Watch* 18 (6) (A).

James, Deborah. 2014. *Money from nothing: Indebtedness and aspiration in South Africa.* Palo Alto, CA: Stanford University Press.

Johnston, Deborah. 2007. "Who needs immigrant farm workers? A South African case study." *Journal of Agrarian Change* 7 (4): 494–525.

Latour, Bruno. 2009. *The making of law: An ethnography of the Conseil d'Etat.* Cambridge: Polity.

MacDonald, Andrew. 2012. "Colonial trespassers in the making of South Africa's international borders 1900 to c.1950." PhD diss., University of Cambridge.

MacGaffey, Janet. 1991. *The real economy of Zaire: The contribution of smuggling and other unofficial activities to national wealth.* London: James Currey.

Meagher, Kate. 2010. *Identity economics: Social networks and the informal economy in Nigeria.* Woodbridge: James Currey.

Mitchell, Timothy. 1998. "Fixing the economy." *Cultural Studies* 12 (1): 82–101.

———. 2002. *Rule of experts: Egypt, techno-politics, modernity.* Berkeley: University of California Press.

———. 2008. "Rethinking economy." *Geoforum* 39: 1116–21.

Moodie, T. Dunbar, with Viviane Ndatshe. 1994. *Going for gold: Mines, men and migration.* Berkeley: University of California Press.

Murray, Martin. 1995. "Blackbirding at 'Crooks' Corner': Illicit labour recruitment in the Northeastern Transvaal 1910–1940." *Journal of Southern African Studies* 21 (3): 373–97.

Narotzky, Susana, and Niko Besnier. 2014. "Crisis, value, and hope: Rethinking the economy." *Current Anthropology* 55 (S9): S4–S16.

Phimister, Ian. 1988. *An economic and social history of Zimbabwe 1890–1948: Capital accumulation and class struggle.* London: Longman.

Postone, Moishe. 1993. *Time, labor, and social domination: A reinterpretation of Marx's critical theory.* Cambridge: Cambridge University Press.

Quirk, Joel, and Darshan Vigneswaran. 2015. "Mobility makes states." In *Mobility makes states: Migration and power in Africa*, edited by Darshan Vigneswaran and Joel Quirk, 1–34. Philadelphia: University of Pennsylvania Press.

Reeves, Madeleine. 2013. "Clean fake: Authenticating documents and persons in migrant Moscow." *American Ethnologist* 40 (3): 508–24.

Riles, Annelise. 2006. "Introduction: In response." In *Documents: Artifacts of modern knowledge*, edited by Annelise Riles, 1–38. Ann Arbor: University of Michigan Press.

Roitman, Janet. 2004. "Productivity in the margins: The reconstitution of state power in the Chad basin." In *Anthropology in the margins of the state*, edited by Veena Das and Deborah Poole, 191–224. Oxford: James Currey.

Roy, Ananya. 2005. "Urban informality: Toward an epistemology of planning." *Journal of the American Planning Association* 71 (2): 147–58.

Rutherford, Blair. 2001. *Working on the margins: Black workers, white farmers in postcolonial Zimbabwe.* London: Zed.

———. 2008. "An unsettled belonging: Zimbabwean farm workers in Limpopo Province, South Africa." *Journal of Contemporary African Studies* 26 (4): 401–15.

Rutherford, Blair, and Lincoln Addison. 2007. "Zimbabwean farm workers in northern South Africa." *Review of African Political Economy* 34 (114): 619–35.

Scott, James. C. 1999. *Seeing like a state: How certain schemes to improve the human condition have failed.* New Haven, CT: Yale University Press.

Seekings, Jeremy, and Nicoli Nattrass. 2005. *Class, race, and inequality in South Africa.* Scottsville: UKZN Press.

Tuckett, Anna. 2015. "Strategies of navigation: Migrants' everyday encounters with Italian immigration bureaucracy." *Cambridge Journal of Anthropology* 33 (1): 113–28.

van Onselen, Charles. 1976. *Chibaro: African mine labour in Southern Rhodesia 1900–1933*. London: Pluto Press.

Vigneswaran, Darshan, Tesfalem Araia, Colin Hoag, and Xolani Tshabalala. 2010. "Criminality or monopoly? Informal immigration enforcement in South Africa." *Journal of Southern African Studies* 36 (2): 465–81.

von Holdt, Karl. 2010. "Institutionalisation, strike violence and local moral orders." *Transformation* 72/73:127–51.

Werbner, Richard. 1991. *Tears of the dead: The social biography of an African family*. Edinburgh: Edinburgh University Press.

CHAPTER NINE

How will we pay?
Projective fictions and regimes of foresight in US college finance

CAITLIN ZALOOM

Attending college is an imperative of the middle class in the United States today. In the first fifteen years since 2000, however, as the median American household income slumped, the average cost of in-state tuition and fees for public colleges rose 80 percent (Fei 2016). The financial costs of higher education have been rising since the 1980s, though, with tuition at public and at private four-year colleges each roughly tripling from 1980 to 2010 (Draut et al. 2011: 26).

Federal and state governments, together with financial firms, have emphasized financial planning as a remedy for families facing this escalation. Government programs first define the achievement of higher education as a problem of household finance, offering options for saving and investing as a way to make paying for college possible. These programs require aspiring college students and their parents to ask the question "How will we pay?" and guide them to answers through policies that promote and support financial planning. Government programs and investment companies broadcast financial planning as the necessary activity of virtuous families.

Across my ethnographic work and more than 160 in-depth interviews conducted with middle-class American families throughout the country who faced
the daunting task of paying for college, I have seen the power of these government and financial programs to compose a calculative and moral field. Mothers
and fathers survey their tools and act on the promise that their children will reap
opportunities in the future. They then measure success and failure as mothers
and fathers by their children's results in the college years. In order to understand
such practices of middle class family life in the United States today, it is crucial,
first, to examine the policy frameworks within which they operate to be good
parents.

In this chapter, I compare two sets of household finance policy that promote
planning and analyze their distinct conceptions of economic and moral virtue.
Both hinge on paying for higher education and establish conditions for the
possibility of planning by configuring household trajectories and implicating
more extensive intergenerational relations of support. In doing so, they define
parents' responsibilities to their families' futures and call on them to organize
their current household economies around these obligations. I turn first to the
mid-twentieth century, examining the practices of planning established by the
GI Bill, especially its higher education provision, and Social Security programs.
Second, I examine the contemporary investment programs for higher education, which also promote particular procedures for establishing family futures.

Each of the institutional configurations examined here mobilizes what I
call a "regime of foresight," an institutionally sanctioned trajectory for family life that offers calculative devices for achieving these futures. The financial
tools do not act on families alone, however. Regimes of foresight gain traction
by endorsing future calculation as a moral project. From the postwar period
onward, US financial policies have shaped an ethics anchored in projecting
futures and ordering household economies around these forecasts. Through
policy and financial tools, the federal government and financial firms have established the conditions for planning and elaborated the project of household
calculation. Their sanction has rendered planning a critical moral project of
middle-class life.

Planning draws its compelling power from a notion of the "real" rooted in
the household. Federico Neiburg and Jane Guyer note that the concept of the
real has historically been tied to an idea of truth that both lies beyond human storytelling and that emerges from the laws of nature (Neiburg and Guyer
2017). Similarly, the category of the household constitutes economic reality by

contrasting the natural realm of reproduction with the public domain of finance, where the unnatural, impersonal multiplication of money takes place. Given the central role that financing college plays in today's middle-class households, establishing an ethnographic understanding of real economy, as Neiburg and Guyer propose, requires examining these links between household economies and the financial policies with which families must operate. Examining the institutional and moral ties between these historically opposed conceptual spheres also provides fodder for rethinking the real in an age of financial capitalism.

PROJECTIVE FICTIONS

The concept of reality employed by policymakers and financial institutions is shared, ironically, by those opposed to their programs and its broader ideology. Critics of neoliberalism, like political theorist Wendy Brown, argue that contemporary governmental regimes successfully deploy financial instruments and accounting logics as tools of social and political discipline, spreading economic calculation into even the most intimate spheres of life (Brown 2015; Martin 2002; Joseph 2014). Anthropologists too have consistently noted the success of neoliberal economic rhetoric and programs in harnessing and transforming the self-conceptions, agendas, and feelings of middle-class people, albeit sometimes with complex effects (see Cahn 2008; Dunk 2002; Freeman 2007; Shever 2008; Muehlebach 2011). Critics often share a central conviction with conservative policy-makers, as well as many liberal ones, in the sense that both give budgetary reckoning the power to define responsible action.[1] Calculation, according to each, reveals economic constraints that cannot be shaken off. Framed in this way, budgetary reckoning does not leave room for alternative evaluations or conflicting agendas. Both policymakers and their scholarly critics agree that contemporary governance appeals to economy as a central, irreducible reality.

---

1.   Here I have in mind policies like President Obama's college scorecard. The interactive online tool scores colleges based on the net price of attendance, graduation rate, loan default rate, average amount borrowed, and graduates' employment. Touting the program in his 2013 State of the Union address, the president affirmed both the possibility and the virtue of weighing the college decision in terms of household finance: "Parents and students can use [the scorecard] to compare schools based on a simple criteria: where you can get the most bang for your educational buck" (US Department of Education 2013).

The practices of planning, however, contradict this position. Planning requires imaginative acts that outstrip the confines of economic calculation. To understand the impact of the financial economy more fully we have to take a closer look at the processes and mechanisms of projection and the moral stories on which they confer governing authority. "Projective fictions" anchor a form of rationality essential to the regimes of foresight that have developed around college finance.[2]

Projective fictions are moral stories that organize visions of the future to direct economic activities in the present. Planning requires the anticipation of a range of conditions, potential college costs, income, future expenses, and how the broader economy will unfold. These projections are then layered into a model, which can be explicit but can also operate without full articulation. The model depends on defining a starting condition, designating a goal, establishing a timeline, and outlining the variety of conditions that can affect the outcome. The model generates an account of future success or failure, here related to whether or not the family will be able to pay their portion of a child's college expenses. These layered projections define a future course.

I employ the term *fictions* because projections sketch the outline of a world to come, one accessible only through imaginative acts. By fictions I do not mean loose fantasies, however, but rather structured narratives that proceed according to a set of conventions, or genres. In this, I extend Mary Poovey's analysis that generic conventions govern our understanding of economic facts. In *Genres of the credit economy* (2008), she argued that eighteenth- and nineteenth-century processes of generic differentiation divided the "hard" facts of the modern economy

---

2.   I distinguish between the practices of projection and those of prediction. Predictions calculate the likelihood of a particular event, based on probability. Risk assessments, like the likelihood of loan defaults, would come under the banner of prediction. Projections can encompass such probabilistic calculations, but include a much wider set of future-oriented forms of reasoning, like rule of thumb calculations, scenarios, and morally oriented trajectories, that come together both in policy domains and in households to give contours to the future and define a decision-making field. Recently, future orientations have become central to the study of capitalism. Political theorist Ivan Ascher posits that our financial economy has organized society through financial means of "prediction and protection" (Ascher 2016); in *Imagined futures*, sociologist Jens Beckert (2016) argues that temporality of capitalism is organized around future-oriented imaginaries. These works join anthropological work on the speculative and temporal dimensions of capitalism that foreground projects of future-making and control (Rajan 2006; C. Hayden 2003; Peterson 2014; Miyazaki 2013; Zaloom 2006, 2009).

from "fictional" literary accounts. This division continues to buttress contemporary notions of economic reality; it also obscures the imaginative foundations of economic knowledge and activities, like planning (see Poovey 2008).

At the same time, projective fictions mobilize generic, moral projects. In higher education, these center on the development of the nuclear family. In the process of assembling projective fictions, family members encounter themselves as a moral unit tied by bonds of obligation and devoted to a common future. The projection then becomes an object through which a family can work on itself, defining its trajectory in both moral and financial terms. The family's self-narration joins the narration of financial planning, guiding the family forward along a storyline sanctioned by government and financial experts alike.

The economic theories that subtend household financial policy also proceed according to their own generic conventions, including the fictions contained within their most basic concepts. Jane Guyer has drawn attention to the *life cycle* as such a fiction, one fundamental to ideas of economic rationality and household planning. The concept of the life cycle narrates a normative, moral story about approved economic behavior across time, such as investing in education. These behaviors are then associated with appropriate calculations. Departures from the life path described in economists' and policy-makers' projective fictions register as betrayal of reason itself.[3]

Government programs anticipate the sanctioned style of reasoning from citizens who stand to benefit from their largesse. They project macro-level outcomes based on expectations of disciplined behavior by citizens and allocate present resources accordingly. Expert projective fictions structure the resources available to families as they pursue their own visions of the future; they are embedded in the tools—like investment vehicles and loans—with which families must operate. These visions of the future shape action in the present. Like the government's scenario-based disaster planning strategies tracked by Andrew Lakoff and Stephen Collier, projective fictions govern households by shaping strategies and decisions in the present (Lakoff 2017; Collier and Lakoff 2014).

---

3. Jane Guyer's "The life cycle as a rational proposition; or, The arc of intermediate links" (2001) introduces the intellectual history of the idea of the life cycle and its imbrication with American federal policy through the theories of mid twentieth-century economics. Guyer's paper, and her work more broadly (2016), provide inspiration for this analysis, especially her observation that the life cycle concept forms "an economic plan, subject to rational quantitative calculation."

With government and industry-sponsored tools in place, planning becomes both a means of caring and a demonstration of citizen responsibility.[4] When families are unable to adhere to its steps, they expose themselves to both financial disadvantage and the disapprobation of the state, financial experts, and their fellow citizens. Once associated only with the poor (and, albeit less often, with the "irresponsible" affluent who blow vast fortunes), difficulty in planning has come to the middle class. The familiar moral accusations have followed: Those unable to plan are irrational, inept, or lackadaisical. Planning lies at the heart of the American moral economy today.

NEAR-TERM PRUDENCE AND DISTANT MODELING

Two US policies, each enacted at distinct historical moments and characterized by distinct qualities of planning, have shaped the projection of family futures into regimes of foresight. The first, which I call the mid-century regime of "near-term prudence," was organized around a bundle of federal policies that, together, ordered the projection of family futures: the education and housing provisions of the 1944 Servicemen's Readjustment Act, or GI Bill, and Social Security. These policies first had to summon the families that they would support, directing their interventions through the fiction of the nuclear family. They then mobilized resources to create a channel through which these citizen families could navigate. These government supports structured the life course, quietly guiding long-term visions, so that family decisions could focus on current conditions and present choices.

---

4.   Key professional groups—economists, policy analysts, and financial industry advisors—also endorse planning as both a financial solution and as a duty. In order to establish economic virtue in the eyes of government and financial experts, students and families must treat higher education as a problem of investment. Investment begins early with planning for future costs and investing savings, and results in a decision to attend a college that will yield profit—wage earnings—in the future (Akers and Chingos 2016). Laying bare their own moral economy, economists Beth Akers and Matthew Chingos, based at the think tanks Brookings and the Urban Institute, respectively, describe their prescriptions for funding US higher education as "predicated on the notion that borrowing for college *should* be treated as an investment decision" [Akers and Chingos 2016: 10; my emphasis]. The normative dimensions of these economic prescriptions are common in policy-oriented economics.

This contrasts with the second policy moment, which institutionalizes what I call a regime of "distant modeling." Within the distant modeling framework, families also engage financial policies for intergenerational support. To do so, however, they must marshal and deploy long-term projections across a much broader range of conditions. They inherit the middle-class definitions of family and its milestones defined in mid-century, but today's household finance policies enjoin citizen families to make models of the future, taking into account fluctuations in their incomes, in college pricing, and in the broader financial economy. They also must craft projections of their own behaviors under these conditions.[5] This regime of foresight operates through the genre of financial modeling. To examine this process, I turn to 529 plans. Named for a section of federal tax code, these investment vehicles, offered state-by-state, enable families to invest for college educations still decades in the future. Both in mid-century and today, government and financial programs gain purchase in households both by creating the conditions for financial success and failure and by distributing moral credit and blame for following or departing from these sanctioned paths.

Near-Term Prudence

Mid-century social policy was founded on a set of projective fictions that we would hardly recognize as realistic today, but which continue to structure American ideas about the trajectory of a good, middle-class life: the nuclear family led by a male wage earner and a predictable life course. The elements of this system were laid along the tracks of social policy and the economic theories it supported, in particular those of the New Deal, like the GI Bill. New Deal policies used federal power to promote the general social welfare through redistribution, and the GI Bill, historian Jennifer Frydl argues, may be the most comprehensive example of New Deal beneficence.

Of course, none of these policies covered all Americans as their more liberal designers would have liked and, in many ways, the policies reproduced existing hierarchies, especially those anchored in moral and racial ideas. The GI Bill's

---

5. Ethical management—employing calculative practices to balance conflicting moral agendas—appears in practices across the financial economy. Here, families engage in modeling to reconcile financial and parental responsibilities. See Zaloom (2016) for an analysis of American Evangelical practices in which ministries teach budgeting as a way to resolve tensions between God's kingdom and the ungodly demands of everyday economic life.

liberal architects themselves worried over the legislation's creation of a privileged group, although the veterans' moral "worthiness" proved critical in passing the bill through Congress. Conservative supporters ensured that important
provisions of the bill would work through private parties and through the states,
guaranteeing that white veterans would benefit more than their black partners
in war, and ensuring that the bill would provide not a general "hand out," but a
"hand up" to those they considered deserving (Frydl 2009).

Still, the GI Bill's benefits represented a broad New Deal goal related to
household futures. The GI Bill, like other mid-century social policies, was designed to blunt life's jagged edge. Such legislation could never *entirely* smooth
out the "hazards and vicissitudes" of life, as President Franklin Roosevelt noted
in his statement on signing the Social Security Act, another New Deal pillar.
The postwar order did, however, "smooth" the future for those it benefited. Institutional supports created conditions of predictability beyond the lives of individual families, and allowed for a style of reasoning that focused on decisions
about the near-term future. Moral evaluation was then focused on the activities
taken up, such as college education or parenting children; it did not hinge on
whether or not a family had planned and planned correctly.

I borrow the idea of a smoothed future from the field of economics. Starting in the 1950s with Milton Friedman's permanent income theory and Franco
Modigliani and Richard Brumberg's life cycle model, economists have described
the spending people engage in when they expect their fortunes to rise across
their lifetime as "consumption smoothing." The theory suggests that higher
spending—and taking on debt—in young adult life reflects the anticipation of
increased future income and the desire for relatively stable consumption across
the decades. In turn this spending raises near-term consumption toward the
higher levels of well-paid middle age, "smoothing" the graphed curve.

The projective fictions of consumption smoothing enable economists to
make macro-level predictions about the economy and guide policy toward government goals. Guyer (2001) has noted that these postwar economic theories
did far more than enable predictions and planning at the government level,
though. In the unacknowledged background of these theories lay the very government policies they purported to guide. Higher education subsidies, home
ownership incentives, and state pensions gave shape to the future for millions of
American adults in the period. Economists' ability to naturalize the fictions of a
generic life course and its operations depended on government institutions that
rendered privileged lives relatively predictable.

Economic theory promoted, rather than simply reflected, an imaginative vision of family futures and the operations that would bring them about: household budgeting and planning. In economists' expert modeling, citizens would be able to anticipate the broad outlines of their life's course and save and spend accordingly. Planning for a household future became the definition of consumer rationality at this intersection of theory and federal policy. But what kind of planning was shaped at this nexus? And what is its relation to the form of planning today?

Mid-century projective fictions established the conditions for what I call "near-term prudence," a style of future-oriented reasoning organized around preferences related to the imminent future rather than around long-term scenarios.[6] With projective fictions in the hands of the experts and policymakers, families could focus on future-oriented decisions over which they had significant control. A regime of near-term prudence meant that economic decisions could be based in experience and local information that would consistently yield the planned-for results. These policies set the expectation that individuals and the families *can* and *should* navigate their own course. Only those left out of or expelled from its framework needed to be engaged in the kind of planning taken for granted today.[7] For the designated beneficiaries of life-cycle institutions, as Guyer has argued, "active calculation becomes optional" (2016: 3). This alleviated both the institutional and the moral responsibility to plan.

The mid-century regime of near-term prudence departed from early twentieth-century history. With sufficient prosperity and longevity, defining a future

6. Jane Guyer has noted the shift in capitalism from a mid-century focus on the "near future" to the contemporary "evacuation" of that temporal zone. She argues that a bifurcated temporality has risen in its stead, one oriented to the present and to long-term futures without consideration to intermediate horizons. Although I demur from the idea of this evacuation, I am inspired by Guyer's incitement to gauge the conflicting temporalities within capitalist political economy (Guyer 2016: 89–109). Like Guyer, Bill Sewell argues that the conflicting temporalities within capitalism—which he characterizes as simultaneously "lumpy" and "eventful" and "smooth" and "predictable"—constitute a critical area of investigation for socially and historically minded analysts (Sewell 2008).

7. See Cybelle Fox, *Three worlds of relief* (2012) on the logic of "expulsion" from government programs directed at Latino immigrants, and Margot Canaday, *The straight state* (2009) on the expulsion of homosexual service members from the benefits of the GI Bill through dishonorable discharge. On the exclusions of African Americans from Social Security and other federal programs, see Ira Katznelson, *When affirmative action was white* (2005).

and fashioning a pathway toward its realization emerged as a distinctly modern problem in that period. For instance, the household budget as we know it came into being through the Home Economics movement of the Progressive Era. These educators, writers, and activists worked to organize middle-class households around the goals of "social advancement" or "higher life," propelling a family to higher moral standing through more efficient management of the home.[8] Home economists' columns and manuals for instruction promoted the budget as an essential tool for both projecting a future life and for realizing its operational assumptions.

According to the home economists, budgeting began with husbands and wives constructing a vision of their future lives. Together, preferably even with their children, the couple would define goals for education and training, spending and saving for the family. The household budget would guide the family toward social and economic advancement, the moral good as defined by the same set of reformers.

The budget book encoded these goals and set the terms for their achievement, directing spending and saving at weekly and yearly intervals along the way. These middle-class budgets placed responsibility in the hands of the nuclear family organized around the companionate marriage (itself a projective fiction of future-oriented conventions) and the goals of future family economic and moral growth. The responsibility for moral growth was mirrored in the responsibility to plan as a method of achieving the family's goals.

The period from the Depression through the aftermath of World War II developed the institutions of household planning as we know them today. In particular, Franklin Delano Roosevelt's landmarks, the 1935 Social Security Act and the GI Bill of 1944, established social policies that lay a path toward to the future for American citizens and took the responsibility for future projections into the hands of the federal government.[9]

---

8. My research into the history of the household budget has focused on the home economics movement and its promotion of future-oriented budgeting for middle-class families. I've found the writings of Christine Frederick, the home economics entrepreneur and columnist for *Ladies Home Journal* from 1912–19 to be particularly helpful in constructing this history.

9. As Jennifer Mittelstadt (2015) has documented, the US military has offered a comprehensive welfare plan for soldiers and veterans that has expanded in significance with the rise of a volunteer army and the parallel decline in other welfare supports outside the service. As with other welfare programs, I argue that

Together, the Social Security Act and the GI Bill created a powerful framework for envisioning family life over time and across generations. Based on projective fictions of family form and working lives, they established a defined life course and intergenerational pathway for millions. This is well known: education and training programs lifted GIs' incomes, while home values raised them up on the equity escalator, and Social Security alleviated the burden of caring for their parents and, eventually, themselves.

The details of these landmark policies and their subprovisions tell an important story and one that usually goes unnoticed. The GI Bill provided supports across a set of key life moments. These policies established an "arc of intermediate links," to use Guyer's term (Guyer 2001). For younger adults, the bill offered skills, workforce credentials, and an asset (their home) that would grow over the course of the husband's thirty-year working life. Arriving at the veteran's middle age, Social Security provided support for the GI's aging parents. Later, at old age, support was available for the GIs themselves. Examining these policies from the perspective of the state, we can call them the "safety net," providing security by taking on individual risks. Looking at these programs from the position of the household shows something different, and complementary: These policies created a decision field where GIs and their families could train their foresight on the near-term future and exercise prudence.

Let's start with the education and training provision of the GI Bill. The numbers of users were tremendous and so were the benefits: 7.8 million citizens—51 percent of returning vets—used this provision. The benefit offered up to 48 months of education or training. This included all tuition and fees, up to $500 per year (which covered all university costs at the time) and delivered a stipend to the GIs that increased in generosity with marriage and kids (Mettler 2007: 7). The Veterans Administration (VA) paid colleges and universities directly, and universities welcomed veterans by increasing seats and by building married student housing.

The GI Bill defined an avenue of household formation, upward mobility, and economic stability over the arc of a family life. This is particularly clear when looking at education and training in connection to the housing loan guarantees also offered to the returning GIs. From 1944 to 1952, the VA backed

---

it is important to think not only about the services and security offered through the military but also the provision of a predictable life course that makes military service appealing.

nearly 2.4 million home loans for World War II veterans. This provision, often credited for the growth of suburban America, also established a model for family responsibilities and working life tied to home ownership. The program provided a clear path for stability across decades and generations and offered a set of working assumptions from which GIs and their families could reap the benefit of full American citizenship.[10]

The provision didn't merely support GIs and their families, though; it also boosted the banks. The GI Bill guaranteed loans for up to half the purchase price of the home, securing the ability of banks and financial firms to recoup potential losses. At the time this was viewed as the creation of a virtuous cycle: By restructuring risk, banks could write loans to veterans with low interest rates; low capital costs allowed the GIs to purchase and build equity in their homes; security helped GIs shelter and provide for their new families. Within that arc, consumption took off.[11]

The home ownership provision created a direct and long-term relationship between veterans' and government's projective fictions, all organized through the financial system. The thirty-year loan operationalized a key government projective fiction: a population of homeowners bound by a three-decade loan and to a working life that would support it. At the same time, the loan enabled a young GI's family to wrap its individual projective future around the instrument that delivered the home, tying the stream of their wages to the future growth of their nascent family. The government-backed mortgage also normalized long-term debt relations with banks. They taught GI families that a large debt mobilized through a financial institution was the way to give institutional backing to their own imagined future.

The GI Bill in particular was an especially unusual policy in US history because it supported young adults during a critical period for establishing a household and for gaining the means of economic attainment later on (Sckopol 1997). One notable feature of the program was its regularity and ease of use (Mettler 2007). The direct institutional supports required little in the way of thought or advocacy on the part of the GIs and their families. The GIs reported

---

10. Historians and urban planners credit the growth of suburbia in large part to the home mortgage subsidies of the GI Bill and the patterns of family and residence it encouraged. See, for instance, Kenneth T. Jackson, *Crabgrass frontier: The suburbanization of the United States* (1987); and Dolores Hayden, *Building suburbia: Green fields and urban growth, 1820–2000* (2004).

11. See Louis Hyman, *Debtor nation: The history of America in red ink* (2011).

with gratitude that the VA was quick to enroll them and consistent in supporting them during their years in the program. The housing provision—except in conditions of default—worked without obvious government mediation between banks and households, rendering its intervention invisible in the GI's monthly payment checks, which they wrote to local banks.[12] Social Security raised the final strut in the infrastructure of near-term prudence for the GIs. The first regular, monthly Social Security checks started arriving in January 1940, relieving at least some of the financial pressure to care for parents in their old age as the GIs planned for their own future.

Instead of focusing on how to best access the necessary capital and project economic futures, these programs enabled participants to focus on questions whose answers they could reasonably judge from their own current experience. What kinds of work would they find satisfying and profitable? What neighborhood could they afford to live in? Thanks to government guarantees, GIs could answer these questions without having to worry about anticipating the fluctuations of the credit markets or its requirements of them. These institutions made it possible for members of a family to look toward the future and roughly approximate what was ahead. They generated enough stability to develop limited foresight, and kept beneficiaries' attentions trained on their local environments.

Mid-century policy did not cover all Americans, however, as has been well documented. Through exclusion of certain kinds of work and workers, Social Security distributed benefits in ways that gave weak or no support to large groups of American citizens, for instance, to women's domestic labor (both paid and unpaid), and to categories of work done at the time by African Americans (like farm work and, again, domestic labor). Gay and African American veterans also faced restrictions in using the benefits of the GI Bill. Until the 1990s, homosexual activity was grounds for dishonorable discharge from the armed forces, and disqualification from GI Bill eligibility. African Americans suffered a different kind of discrimination too. The federal Home Owner's Loan Corporation defined African American and mixed-race neighborhoods as financially risky, which led banks to deny mortgage loans to black vets, denying them the full benefit of their military service.[13]

---

12. Suzanne Mettler (2011) argues that such programs result in a "submerged state" whose benefits are invisible to those they benefit.

13. Even a single black family conferred a "mixed race" categorization on a neighborhood. See the "Mapping Inequality" project for a digital library of the HOLC maps across

By negatively defining the conditions for full participation, these exclusions lent force to the moral power of Social Security and the GI Bill. The programs established a powerful "ethical affordance" (Keane 2015), that planning constituted the grounds for household economic virtue. The excluded provided the critical negative case: they proved the virtue of those who could and did follow the projective fictions promoted by the programs from which they benefitted.

Exclusion from the policies left the excluded open to the moral invective that they did not or could not "plan"—that they were not future-oriented enough. From the 1970s on, anthropologists and sociologists alike have contradicted this charge with detailed descriptions, showing that planning under conditions of economic deprivation directs families' investments toward expanding and deepening relationships with kin and close friends rather than toward the formal mechanisms of saving and investment—like bank accounts—that undergird the planning apparatus (Stack 1974; Edin and Lein 1997; Venkatesh 2006). Without participation in the institutions that support the projective fictions of middle-class life, poor, often minority, citizens could not and did not plan in ways familiar to the white middle class. To reap the moral rewards of planning a citizen must be included in the projective fictions of policy and of the formal and lay economic theories they support.

The social supports of mid-century together created an infrastructure for foresight, delivered by top-down powers and taken up as central projects of family life by their beneficiaries. Today the regime of foresight has changed, but core projective fictions remain, like the middle-class family and its trajectory as well as, of course, the moral responsibility to plan.

Distant Modeling

Planning today operates within a different regime of foresight. Economic conditions have changed, as have the policies that enable planning. Instability in the job market, short-term and contract employment, financial market volatility, precarious housing values, and rising college costs have transformed the landscape in which middle-class families must craft projective fictions. Today's policies focus families on a long-term future, one often decades away. This future is made up of dissonant time frames established through a cacophony of

---

the United States. https://dsl.richmond.edu/panorama/redlining/#loc=4/36.71/-96.93&opacity=0.8&text=intro.

government programs and financial instruments, asking families to plan one, eighteen, thirty years out (and all of that at once) while carrying debts that tie future funds to past decisions. Planning relies on the possibility of crafting future visions, at the same time that the complexity of the scenarios today troubles the very idea of projection.

Comparison to the social policy of mid-century can be tricky since coherent policies like Social Security and the GI Bill have been replaced by investment choices, tax breaks, and loans of varied interest rates, which work through technical means and through the private household. Governments working through financial institutions is not new, however. An icon of New Deal liberalism, the GI Bill housing provision also operated through private banks and its education provision worked through payments to colleges and universities, both public and private, changing the terms of the school's broader finances. US policies have long delivered government direction through private financing. Today, however, the policies are layered and sometimes conflict. Contemporary planning requires families to assemble a set of projective fictions from these policy fragments.

Planning for a child's future education represents a hallmark of middle-class and aspiring US parenthood. Those who plan for college are the inheritors of the cultural goals of the returning GIs. For most American households today, college education—like the other major mainstream goals of home ownership and retirement—requires government supports. Few will have either the cash to pay out of pocket or have access to grant funds to cover the total cost. Government programs deliver a clear message to aspiring students and their parents, one very different from the college supports of mid-century: They should begin planning to pay for college early in a child's life. Children's college education requires families to plan decades in advance. Government programs define what financial paths families can and should consider, communicating to applicants that a solution lies in combining long-term investment strategies with debt across the college years.

As I have seen in my research, college-educated parents have learned this lesson. They hold themselves responsible for beginning to think about children's educations shortly after they are born. What will they have to pay? And how will they manage those costs? These questions assert themselves across their lives as they raise their children. With college expenses outstripping inflation and wages no longer able to cover it all, financial planning and its vehicles—investment programs and loans—extend the primary path for securing a college education.

Even the act of contemplating college launches families into a set of fictional projections vastly different from the conventions of mid-century foresight. The rising cost of higher education places a significant burden of payment on families, even those whose aid packages will diminish the often-shocking sticker price. And for those who have the possibility to save, anticipating college expenses requires elaborate projections. How much money should be socked away for college when enrollment might be eighteen years in the future? And how should they invest it? What will be the shortfall that might be financed with debt? When spring of the enrollment year arrives, how should families account for their income and assets to student aid agencies? When the "expected family contribution" decision arrives in the mail from the Department of Education, how should families plan to make up the balance? What loans should they take on and how much: subsidized, unsubsidized, Parent Plus, private loans, or home equity? Addressing these questions directs parents through a machinery of projective fictions, with a structure and plot far more complicated than anything the beneficiaries of the GI Bill could have imagined.

Consider state-based 529 plans. These tax-advantaged accounts encourage parents and other relatives to begin saving early in their child's life for their eventual college enrollment. Only the child's social security number and the contributor's own tax information is necessary to open an account. 529 plans allow family members to contribute up to $10,000 a year without paying current state taxes on the sum and the federal government sweetens the investment with its own incentives to be gleaned on withdrawal. Within the 529 plan, contributors select a mutual fund in which to invest. The program's design assumes that funds will grow as the child approaches college enrollment and throughout the college years. Funds can also be used for graduate school education, and if there are sums left over, can be transferred to siblings.

Uncertainty is a constitutive feature of these plans, however, as is the morality of planning. New York State 529 promotions intone, "One of the most important things you can do for your children is to save for their future. Many of us know we can't save all of the money we need for our child's college tuition. But every dollar you do save now is a dollar you and your child *may not* have to borrow later" [my emphasis].[14]

---

14. https://www.nysaves.org/home/college-savings-articles/content-secondary-col0/
     how-much-do-you-need-for-college.html.

Planners must then begin to craft their projective fictions, assessing future economic conditions, weighing the possibilities of gain and loss in securities investments, gauging the path of interest rates and inflation, anticipating the acceleration of college prices, and evaluating investment instruments for their effectiveness in this landscape. But how much should a parent save? What will college cost in 2035? These questions are answerable only with the projective fictions of financial models. 529 contributors must assume a growth rate for college costs and another for financial market rise (or decline). They also must model changes in their own nearer-term costs. If they invest too much and need the cash, they will have to pay not only the taxes owed, but also a penalty for early withdrawal. Assembling projective fictions requires students and families to act as specialists with regard to the complex expert system of finance.

Once the investment is made, the projective fictions shift to the experts behind the programs. The New York 529 assures potential investors: "You'll be able to take advantage of professional investment management from Vanguard, one of the world's largest and most respected investment management firms." Still, in order to construct their basket of mutual funds, these experts face similar uncertainties that require assessing the potential of individual companies' stock growth, of the future of industries, and of overall patterns of market volatility, or of assessing the future performance of other fund managers based on their past performance.

Even when outsourcing the modeling to professionals, parents need to have predictions about their own behavioral reactions. These will be completely opaque to their arms-length Fidelity investment managers. Will they be able to tolerate a downturn in the financial markets that may place their daughter's college fund in jeopardy? Will they adjust the portfolio, appropriately reacting to changing economic conditions? Or will they simply cross their fingers and hope?

Models of parents' own future behavior come into play as they choose in which among New York 529's sixteen funds to invest. Thirteen individual portfolios are adjustable according to "your own investment strategy and risk tolerance." For those who anticipate their own failures to monitor and appropriately adjust their investments, three age-based options automatically reinvest assets as children age, increasing conservative investments as college matriculation draws near. The "age-adjusted" options transfer the responsibility of adjusting investments from the contributor to the Vanguard manager. But either way, managing the account demands models of growth rates, risks, returns, and behavior that will guide decisions about how much to invest and how to invest and reinvest it. The family's financial reasoning relies on this layering of projective fictions.

As college matriculation comes closer and admissions decisions begin to roll in, families are thrust into another set of models, ones imposed by the federal government and colleges: the model of financial need. These models carry a different projective time frame. They assess the need over the coming next year by pressing the variables of last year's income and expenses through a hidden algorithm.

In the months before a child enrolls in college or begins a new school year, the families of rising freshman go through the spring ritual of filling out Free Application for Federal Student Aid (FAFSA). The FAFSA is a list of 108 fields, each of which asks for a detail of the student's household, earnings, savings, and national service status. Here are a few:

35. Student's Adjusted Gross Income   45c. Student's Child Support Received
73. Parents' number of family members   87. Parents' 2015 Exemptions Claimed

When the student or parent hits enter, the US Department of Education takes over, weighing eligibility for grants and loans and determining the Expected Family Contribution, the amount the government requires families to put toward their child's college expenses. Access to crucial financial assistance hang on this calculation, particularly subsidized government loans that are offered at a low interest rate. College-based student aid also depends on this calculation. Colleges take the FAFSA's information into account, sometimes supplementing it with their own model of family need. The amount of private loans—student, home equity, or credit card—also hangs on that number, since they are an alternative (and mostly higher cost) supplement to federal loans. Banks offer each of these private loans according to their own carefully calibrated models of risk and repayment. The federal models of need also interact with private risk assessments, as some federal loans hinge on private risk models. The Department of Education gives access to parent loans only after a review of family financial data.

The models of need and expected family contribution also interact with the projective fictions of earlier financial planning. For instance, monies that have grown inside a state 529 plan will not be held against the family in the federal government's calculation of their need. Savings account balances that have not been invested in the governmental projective fictions of college, however, must be reported.

As in the mid-twentieth-century programs, exclusions again structure the morality of planning. The results of privileged behaviors, like investing in education savings accounts and in home equity, receive a support that is at once financial and moral. 529 investments and house equity remain outside of the Department of Education's calculation of need. Those who have followed the government's model of a family organized around the projective fictions reap both greater assistance and the reward of their government's approval. Exclusion acts at another level here too. Those who have been unable to save, whose wages haven't offered more than life's basic needs, are taxed twice: first, by exclusion from the benefits from financial planning's vehicles, and second by the sense of failure that follows from the moral demand to plan.

Planning today stretches projective fictions across many years. For parents who want to send their children to college this can be almost two decades or more. Government and financial industry policies and instruments give families the narrative and the tools with which to engage this long-term future. They have created a situation in which families must model both their lives and coming financial conditions; they must engage the projective fictions they are given and, at the same time, create their own. Their virtue as parents and citizens depends on this act, while the outcome hangs on whether their modeling will approximate a future yet to come.

REGIMES OF FORESIGHT

Planning anchors both regimes of foresight examined above. In both, the governance of household policy produced conditions for calculation to guide "responsible" citizens toward their future lives. Tapping into an enduring moral imperative, policies from WWII onward have sought to establish prescience in American middle-class citizens. Citizens' responsibility to plan has remained constant but the tools and calculative practices of foresight have changed.

A temporal difference is central to these shifts. In mid-century, policies kept families focused on the near-term; today families must look decades into the future. This difference has reorganized the calculative nature of planning. While the rise of the household budgeting elaborated a moral requirement to plan, by mid-century, financial supports meant that planning itself carried few demands. Mid-century institutions elaborated a stable life course and organized household planning around a set of near-term problems. Families could rely on economic information from their local environments to develop judgments about the activities that would yield the future their family desired. I've called this form of reasoning *near-term prudence*. Families with access to these supports could advance their lives along a sanctioned path that included higher education. The moral economy of planning distributed virtue to those that acted with forethought defined by a near-future in which they could reasonably project their expectations and desires.

Today, foresight involves decades of anticipation. Planning requires families to engage in practices that resemble those of financial experts, and household finance policies present tools around which to craft models of layered projections. There has been also been shift in the subjects targeted for this work of financial fashioning. In the mid twentieth-century, household finance policies were addressed specifically to GIs and the white middle class; today parallel policies hail nominally universal subjects. In both, exclusions from the planning apparatus buttress its moral power.

Tracing this shift in regimes of foresight shows that the way capitalism organizes time both shapes rationality and defines notions of virtue for its citizens. The case of higher education allows us to see that as family futures have been stretched across longer time horizons, the rationality involved in planning family futures has been transformed. In this shift, assembling projective fictions and acts of modeling have become moral staples of middle-class family life. Still, current household finance policies and their promoters follow the mid-century moral assumptions of planning; failure to progress along a middle-class life arc indicates either self-inflicted errors of calculation or an abdication of responsibility.

Under financial capitalism, the future—often the distant future—has become a central category for citizens' household operations, one that recursively links household finance policies and family behaviors. The future has always been a central matter of family life, involving its central reproductive concerns. Today, however, the distant future is also a shaping force of the family, not only as an intimate personal unit but also as a constitutive unit of American political and economic life and the object of future-oriented policy.

Within the larger conversation of this special section, closely examining these evolving regimes of foresight also leads to new conclusions about the reality at the foundation of the economy. Historically, this reality was linked to nature and human reproduction, in contrast to the deviant reproduction of finance. Although this division continues today in economic concepts and vernacular understandings, families and their futures have become dependent on finance in essential ways. As I've shown, there is a tight feedback loop between the policies and governing institutions of finance and the modeling practices of families as they operate under the contemporary regime of foresight. In this system, the reality to which families are responsible is essentially financial. In the act of crafting projective fictions and modeling futures, they create family life. That which stood against finance is now founded in it.

ACKNOWLEDGEMENTS

This chapter benefitted from the reflections of the participants at the Wenner-Gren and Museu Nacional, Federal University of Rio de Janeiro Real Economy workshop, and the Calculating Capitalism conference at the Society for Fellows in the Humanities at Columbia University. Special thanks for inspiration and detailed readings to Jane Guyer, Federico Neiburg, Mary Poovey, Eric Klinenberg, Andrew Lakoff, and Natasha Schull. Thanks, too, to Max A. Cohen for manuscript assistance. I am grateful to the Russell Sage Foundation and to the Center for Advanced Study in the Behavioral Sciences at Stanford University for supporting the research.

REFERENCES

Akers, Beth, and Matthew M. Chingos. 2016. *Game of loans: The rhetoric and reality of student debt*. Princeton, NJ: Princeton University Press.

Ascher, Ivan. 2016. *Portfolio society: On the capitalist mode of prediction*. New York: Zone Books.

Beckert, Jens. 2016. *Imagined futures: Fictional expectations and capitalist dynamics*. Cambridge, MA: Harvard University Press.

Brown, Wendy. 2015. *Undoing the demos: Neoliberalism's stealth revolution*. New York: Zone Books.

Cahn, Peter. 2008. "Consuming class: Mulitlevel marketers in neoliberal Mexico." *Cultural Anthropology* 23 (3): 429–52.

Canaday, Margot. 2009. *The straight state: Sexuality and citizenship in twentieth-century America*. Princeton, NJ: Princeton University Press.

Collier, Stephen J, and Andrew Lakoff. 2014. "Vital systems security: Reflexive biopolitics and the government of emergency." *Theory, Culture and Society* 32 (2): 19–51.

Draut, Tamara, Robert Hiltonsmith, Catherine Ruetschlin, Aaron Smith, Rory O'Sullivan, and Jennifer Mishory. 2011. "The state of young America: The databook." New York: Demos, Young Invincibles. http://www.demos.org/ sites/default/files/publications/SOYA_TheDatabook_2.pdf.

Dunk, Thomas. 2002. "Remaking the working class: Experience, class, and the industrial adjustment process." *American Ethnologist* 29 (4): 878–900.

Edin, Kathryn, and Laura Lein. 1997. *Making ends meet: How single mothers survive welfare and low-wage work*. New York: Russell Sage Foundation.

Fei, Fan. 2016. "Median income is down, but public college tuition is way up." *ProPublica*, August 25, 2016. https://projects.propublica.org/graphics/ publictuition.

Fox, Cybelle. 2012. *Three worlds of relief: Race, immigration, and the American welfare state from the Progressive Era to the New Deal*. Princeton, NJ: Princeton University Press.

Freeman, Carla. 2007. "The 'reputation' of neoliberalism." *American Ethnologist* 34 (2): 253–67.

Frydl, Jennifer. 2009. *The GI Bill*. New York: Cambridge University Press.

Guyer, Jane. 2001. "The life cycle as a rational proposition; or, The arc of intermediate links." Paper presented at the American Anthropological Association meeting on Temporalities of Rationality, Washington, DC.

———. 2016. "Prophecy and the near future: Thoughts on macroeconomic, Evangelical, and punctuated time." In *Legacies, logics, logistics: Essays in the anthropology of the platform economy*, 89–108. Chicago: University of Chicago Press.

Hayden, Cori. 2003. *When nature goes public: The making and unmaking of bioprospecting in Mexico*. Princeton, NJ: Princeton University Press.

Hayden, Dolores. 2004. *Building suburbia: Green fields and urban growth, 1820–2000*. New York: Vintage.

Hyman, Louis. 2011. *Debtor nation: The history of America in red ink*. Princeton, NJ: Princeton University Press.

Jackson, Kenneth T. 1987. *Crabgrass frontier: The suburbanization of the United States*. New York: Oxford University Press.

Joseph, Miranda. 2014. *Debt to society: Accounting for life under capitalism*. Minneapolis: University of Minnesota Press.

Katznelson, Ira. 2005. *When affirmative action was white: An untold history of racial inequality in twentieth-century America*. New York: W.W. Norton.

Keane, Webb. 2015. *Ethical life: Its natural and social histories*. Princeton, NJ: Princeton University Press.

Lakoff, Andrew. 2017. *Unprepared: Global health in a time of emergency*. Berkeley: University of California Press.

Martin, Randy. 2002. *Financialization of daily life*. Philadelphia: Temple University Press.

Mettler, Suzanne. 2007. *Soldiers to citizens: The G.I. Bill and the making of the Greatest Generation*. Oxford: Oxford University Press.

———. 2011. *The submerged state: How invisible government policies undermine American democracy*. Chicago: University of Chicago Press.

Mittelstadt, Jennifer. 2015. *The rise of the military welfare state*. Cambridge, MA: Harvard University Press.

Miyazaki, Hirokazu. 2013. *Arbitraging Japan: Dreams of capitalism at the end of finance*. Berkeley: University of California Press.

Muehlebach, Andrea. 2011. "On affective labor in post-Fordist Italy." *Cultural Anthropology* 26 (1): 59–82.

Neiburg, Federico, and Jane Guyer. 2017. "The real economy: Ethnographic inquiries into the reality and realization of economic life." *HAU: Journal of Ethnographic Theory* 7 (3): 261–79.

Peterson, Kristin. 2014. *Speculative markets: Drug circuits and derivative life in Nigeria*. Durham, NC: Duke University Press.

Poovey, Mary. 2008. *Genres of the credit economy: Mediating value in eighteenth- and nineteenth-century Britain*. Chicago: University of Chicago Press.

Rajan, Kaushik Sunder. 2006. *Biocapital: The constitution of postgenomic life*. Durham, NC: Duke University Press.

Sckopol, Theda. 1997. "The G.I. Bill and U.S. social policy, past and future." *Social Philosophy & Policy* 14 (2): 95–115.

Sewell, William H., Jr. 2008. "The temporalities of capitalism." *Socio-Economic Review* 6 (3): 517–37.

Shever, Elana. 2008. "Neoliberal associations: Property, company, and the family in the argentine oil fields." *American Ethnologist* 35 (4): 701–16.

Stack, Carol B. 1974. *All our kin: Strategies for survival in a black community*. New York: Harper & Row.

US Department of Education. 2013. "Education Department releases college scorecard to help students choose best college for them." *US Department of Education*. February 13, 2013. http://www.ed.gov/news/press-releases/education-department-releases-college-scorecard-help-students-choose-best-college-them.

Venkatesh, Sudhir Alladi. 2006. *Off the books: The underground economy of the urban poor*. Cambridge, MA: Harvard University Press.

Zaloom, Caitlin. 2006. *Out of the pits: Traders and technology from Chicago to London*. Chicago: University of Chicago Press.

———. 2009. "How to read the future: The yield curve, affect, and financial prediction." *Public Culture* 21 (2): 243–66.

———. 2016. " The Evangelical financial ethic: Doubled forms and the search for God in the economic world." *American Ethnologist* 43 (2): 325–38.

CHAPTER TEN

Smuggling realities
On numbers, borders, and performances

Fernando Rabossi

If we follow the figures about smuggling that appear frequently in media reports in Brazil, we could conclude that there is grounded knowledge about the phenomenon. The same figures are used by and within different media and they are presented with regularity, accompanying the (reported) growing volume of smuggled products. Nonetheless, if we pay attention to the chronology of those numbers—their sudden emergence in the public discourse—to the actors enunciating them, and to the strategies used to publicize them, many questions arise. How are these figures produced? Who produces them? In which debates are these figures mobilized?

In this chapter, I will describe the efforts made to portray the so-called reality of smuggling by analyzing the instruments used, the actors involved, and the effects they produce. It is claimed that the Brazilian economy suffers great losses due to smuggling; provoked by the notion of this great figure, I discovered a transformation at the level of compositions, discourses, and practices that revealed the growing importance of smuggling as a productive trope for intervening in Brazilian political and economic dynamics.

Three fields of inquiry converge in my interest for these numbers: first, the economic practices that lie outside official accounts—what has been called informal or second economy (Hart 1973; MacGaffey et al. 1991); second, the government of ordinary economic practices, particularly through the Foucauldian notions of *illegalismes* and governmentality (Foucault 1975, [1977–78] 2004); and finally, the ethnography of public numbers—their production, circulation, and operation as instruments of government (Desrosières 1993; Porter 1995; Neiburg 2006, 2010; Hull 2012; Guyer 2016).

The estimates for smuggling have always surprised me, doing long-term ethnographic research on the dynamic border trade between Brazil and Paraguay. My research focused, precisely, on what doesn't count: the jobs and the wealth produced in those circuits. Is it possible to calculate the losses that smuggling produces without considering its gains? This is a naïve way of positing the question, of course. I raise it, precisely, to underline the perspectives that can inform our approaches to these issues and the limits that they have—here, I want to emphasize the selective character of the choices undertaken to depict the "reality of smuggling," which I will describe in this chapter.

Analyzing the estimates for smuggling led me to investigate definitions, measurement techniques, and models of analysis. In part, this text is about that, although it is much more than that. This is a text about the orchestrated production of definitions of reality constructed by certain actors, conveyed by the media, and expected to reach very specific goals—specifically, a reality that is productive, both in terms of political articulations and of legal transformations.

The chapter is structured as follows. First, I present the coverage by the main Brazilian television journal of the 2015 National Day to Combat Smuggling. Smuggling—suddenly—became such a huge problem in Brazil that even a National Day to Combat Smuggling was established. But when did that happen? Who was responsible for highlighting that "problem"? Next, I describe the legitimation of the discussion about smuggling in press conferences and through seminars organized by the print media (*Folha de São Paulo* and *Correio Braziliense*), which constitute crucial contexts for the presentation of "facts"— through the mobilization of research data—and proposals. Data from research became a crucial element to objectify a reality that—it is said—is considered to be known but "is not envisaged in its real dimension and consequences." The numbers produced by those researches are facts mobilized through the media and incorporated in official discourses. It is crucial to analyze these numbers in order to understand their performative character. Finally, I explore some of the effects they produce: the legitimization of corporate and industrial groups' claims, the spatialization of the problem of smuggling, and the criminalization of certain economic practices.

The issues analyzed in this essay are not unique to Brazil. As Peter Andreas and Kelly Greenhill pointed out in the introduction of *Sex, drugs, and body counts: The politics of numbers in global crime and conflict*,

> these difficult to observe phenomena are not perceived to be "real" until they are quantified and given a number. Consequently, death tolls, refugee flows, trafficking, and smuggling estimates are commonly inflated, deflated, or simply fabricated, all in the service of political goals. Identifying the sources of such numbers—as well as recognizing the agendas of their producers and proliferators—can be critically important in helping to mitigate some of their more pernicious effects. (Andreas and Greenhill 2010: 6)

I align myself with these interests, following a growing literature on control policies of border flows and markets in Brazil—particularly in its Paraguayan border[1]—and copyright enforcement and antipiracy strategies;[2] elements that are crucial in order to understand the growing importance of smuggling as a productive trope.

Both the contexts for the presentation of the problem of smuggling and the facts staged in those events *through* numbers need to be scrutinized in order to understand the interested nature of the interpretations presented in and through them. The contexts for the numbers were not the natural emanation of journalistic interest; neither were the numbers the descriptive expression of real dimensions. However, the interested claims presented through smuggling are gradually heeded—tax reduction, legal transformations—and the reality of smuggling constructed through these numbers and emplaced in certain borders and slums have concrete consequences for everyday life in those spaces. In summary, the chapter seeks to analyze the relationship between performances, numbers, and performativity in contemporary discourses on contraband in Brazil.[3]

---

1. See Rabossi (2004, 2013); Pinheiro-Machado (2010); Cardin (2011); Francisco (2014); Renoldi (2015). For the Brazilian border with Uruguay, see Dorfman (2015).

2. See Mizukami et al. (2011); Dent (2012, 2015); Castro and Mizukami (2013); Bandeira (2013).

3. As developed in performance studies, I use of the concept of performance as special events where participants "are thoroughly conscious of their action or practice as a

PERFORMING "PROTESTS" AND PRODUCING "NATIONAL DAYS"

On March 3, 2016, William Bonner, the anchorman of *Jornal Nacional*—the primetime news program of Brazilian television—announced that "This Thursday, the National Day to Combat Smuggling, there were several protests demanding more measures from the government." An off-screen voice described the protests while showing them: "In Brasilia, under rain, protesters walked before the Esplanade of the Ministries and stopped in front of the presidential building, the *Palacio do Planalto*. There was also a protest in São Paulo, in front of the government house, the *Palacio dos Bandeirantes*." The image switched to a man throwing cigarettes into a machine, while announcing that the Brazilian Association for Combating Counterfeiting (ABCF) destroyed smuggled cigarettes. After presenting several figures and places, another journalist appeared in front of a road saying, "Every time that a product enters in Brazil without paying taxes, Brazil is losing. Last year, smuggling rose 15% and produced a loss of R$115 billon," equivalent to US$30 billion at the time. On screen, the source was displayed: IDESF.[4] "Who produces according to the law and pays their taxes, complain of unfair competition" continued the off-screen voice, showing a seminar room with a table with eight speakers—seven men, one woman—and a canvas behind that read, National Day to Combat Smuggling. In a corridor outside the seminar room, Evandro Guimaraes, president of ETCO,[5] said that jobs, industrial activity, and all sectors were affected by smuggling, adding: "I would say that everything remains to be done at every government level." Less than two and a half minutes later,[6] William Bonner reappeared on screen to present the government version in ten seconds: the Ministry of Justice said that it

---

performance to be witnessed or participated in as such" (Kapferer and Hobart 2005: 11). The concept of performativity, although inspired in Michel Callon's proposal of studying the performative effects of economics on the economy (Callon 1998) and its subsequent developments (MacKenzie and Millo 2003; Neiburg 2006), it is taken in a broader sense to analyze the performative effects of discussions legitimated by numbers and staged in particular performances.

4.   IDESF stands for *Instituto de Desenvolvimento Econômico e Social de Fronteiras* (Institute for Economic and Social Development of Borders).

5.   ETCO stands for *Instituto Brasileiro de Ética Concorrencial* (Brazilian Institute for Ethics in Competition).

6.   2:16 minutes, to be exact.

had improved the structure of the Federal Police and the Federal Road Police at the border, and that it was carrying out special operations in the states of Mato Grosso do Sul and Paraná.[7]

The coverage by the *Jornal Nacional* can be summarized as the presentation of certain facts—the protests and the destruction of smuggled merchandise—and the interpretations given by several actors spurred by a national commemoration. However, when analyzed in detail, alongside the reports that were published in the newspapers, a different picture emerges. As I will try to demonstrate, what were presented as facts and interpretations were, in fact, performances and contexts for normative discourses. The same actors that orchestrated media coverage invented events such as the National Day to Combat Smuggling.

If we look at the images of the protest in Brasilia and São Paulo, we can see that the characters, the posters, and the aesthetic are all exactly the same. All the participants (almost sixty in each case) wore the same T-shirts—white with black stripes—that resembled prison uniforms. Many of them, especially men, used black knit caps and black gloves. They look like Lego characters of city burglars.[8]

The posters were the same in content, format, and material. They presented different slogans. "Brazil, smuggler country." "Welcome smugglers, our borders are open for you." "Paraguayan cigarettes, national preference." "More taxes, more cigarettes from Paraguay." "Government and smugglers, united to end your job." A photograph of Paraguayan president Horacio Cartes, with the motto: "Our hero, our president." Written on a huge packet of cigarettes, a question: "Economy going wrong? Join cigarette smuggling, the fastest growing industry in the country." In São Paulo, there were a lot of balloons saying: "Blah, blah, blah," mocking the governor who said that the fight against smuggling would be a priority.

Given the peculiar characteristic of the protests—people using the same costumes and carrying banners put together by the same hands (see fig. 1)—it is noteworthy that neither the news programs nor the newspapers mention anything about that aesthetic redundancy. I only found an explanation regarding

---

7. *Jornal Nacional*, "National Day to Combat Smuggling has protests," March 3, 2016, 22h20, *Rede Globo*, Channel 4 VHF (Jornal Nacional 2016).

8. See http://brickset.com/sets/853092-1/City-Burglars-Magnet-Set, corresponding to the 853092 City Burglars Magnet Set, released in 2011.

the nature of the protests in the website of the National Confederation of Industry (CNI 2016). At the protests, we can see the same numbers and details presented as we saw exhibited in *Jornal Nacional*. The activities displayed during the National Day to Combat Smuggling were organized by the *Movimento em Defesa do Mercado Legal Brasileiro* (Movement for the Defense of the Brazilian Licit Market), which gathers together entrepreneurs and representatives of different economic sectors. The protestors were described as groups of "smugglers" that, in a "playful protest," thanked the federal government for its inefficiency in combating smuggling, a practice that "only benefits organized crime."

Figure 1: Protest against smuggling, in front of the Planalto Palace (Brasilia). Credit: Antonio Cruz / Agência Brasil.[9]

The Movement for the Defense of the Brazilian Licit Market was created in September 2014, when the *Instituto Brasileiro de Ética Concorrencial* (ETCO) and the *Forum Nacional contra a Pirataria e a Ilegalidade* (FNCP), together with eighteen associations from several economic sectors, presented a manifesto in which they requested the support of candidates in the October presidential

---

9.   Empresa Brasil de Comunicação S/A—EBC. Licença Creative Commons Atribuição 3.0 Brasil.

election toward the protection of the licit market.[10] The subtitle of the manifesto expressed the scope of the point of view of enunciation: "A society united against smuggling, piracy, and counterfeiting."[11] The manifesto outlined twelve demands that revolve around the commitment to fighting piracy, smuggling, counterfeiting (tightening enforcement), the reduction of taxes, and the simplification of bureaucratic procedures (liberalizing the economy). At the end of 2014, the *Associação Brasileira de Combate à Falsificação* (Brazilian Association for Combating Counterfeiting—ABCF) and the *Instituto de Desenvolvimento Econômico e Social de Fronteiras* (Institute for Economic and Social Development of Borders—IDESF) also became organizers of the movement, which nowadays—they say—represents over seventy associations.

The Movement for the Defense of the Brazilian Licit Market represented a new articulation of several organizations financed by corporate actors and industrial sectors that work on intellectual property lobbying and advocacy, anticounterfeiting, and cross-industry coordination (Mizukami et al. 2011: 248ss). I will present the main institutional actors behind the constitution of the movement in order to identify the interests they represent. The proliferation of acronyms that makes the text difficult to follow can also be interpreted as part of the illegibility of this field.

The ETCO was founded in 2003 by the initiative of the several enterprises that constitute its current sectorial chambers: tobacco (Souza Cruz), beer (AmBev), soft drinks (Coca-Cola, Pepsi, AmBev), and fuel (SINDICOM—Fuel Distribution Association). It promotes actions for a better business environment through studies, legislative lobbying, and education. It focuses on the fight against illegal commerce, smuggling, informality, tax evasion, and corruption. Until October 2016, its president was publicist Evandro do Carmo Guimarães, who worked from 1979 to 2011 for the Gupo Globo—the main

---

10. The groups that signed the manifesto included several sectorial chambers (among others, tobacco, software, optic and sporting goods, and toys), interindustry coordinators, and intellectual property associations. The letter, with the complete list of institutions, can be found here: http://www.etco.org.br/11/wp-content/uploads/Carta_ETCO_v1_EMAIL_1.pdf.

11. Analyzing the meetings of the National Council on Combating Piracy and Intellectual Property Crimes (CNCP)—where the same groups analyzed here meet regularly with State officials—Pedro Francisco has already called attention to the use of the concept of civil society to nominate nonstate representatives, eclipsing the fact that they are private industrial representatives (Francisco 2014: 91).

media corporation of Brazil—and was responsible for its institutional relationships. The association's headquarters is in São Paulo.

The FNCP (National Forum against Piracy and Illegality) was established in 2003 during the Parliamentary Commission for Inquiry on Piracy and it was legally constituted in 2004. Its focus is the combat of piracy and counterfeiting, having among its associates several companies—like HP, Microsoft, Colgate-Palmolive, Xerox, Philip Morris, Souza Cruz—sectorial associations and other groups and organizations. Founded by the economist Alexandre Cruz, it has been headed from 2009 until 2016 by lawyer Edson Luiz Vismona, former Secretary of Justice of the state of São Paulo (2000–2002). In October 2016, Vismona assumed the direction of ETCO, showing the close connections between these institutions. The association's headquarters is also in São Paulo.

The IDESF (Institute for Economic and Social Development of Borders) was founded in 2013 in Foz do Iguaçu, in the border region with Paraguay and Argentina, the Tri-Border Area.[12] Its declared purpose is "to promote equality and integration in border regions," through diagnosis, research, education, and training with government and society, for the protection of the national market and the formal economy. Its president, economist Luis Stremel Barros, was previously (and for a long time) the representative of the Brazilian Association for Combating Counterfeiting (ABCF) in Foz do Iguaçu, before he came to run IDESF. He is also the Paraná Regional Director of the ABCF.

---

12. The Tri-Border Area—or TBA, as it is internationally known (the *Triplice Fronteira*, in Portuguese)—is the region where the borders of Brazil, Paraguay, and Argentina meet. Ciudad del Este, in Paraguay, and Foz do Iguaçu, in Brazil, are important commercial cities with the presence of significant commercial diaspora groups like Lebanese, Chinese, Koreans, and Indians, among others. During the 1980s, Ciudad del Este (then Ciudad Presidente Stroessner) became the main market for imported goods in Brazil, and Foz do Iguaçu was the main market for Brazilian goods in Paraguay. Since the 1990s, the region has been denounced as a regional security threat. For an analysis of the commercial circuits of the region, see Rabossi (2012). For a description of the Arab and Muslim presence in the region, see Rabossi (2014). For a deep ethnographic analysis of microcredit and financial technologies in Ciudad del Este, see Schuster (2015). Ieva Jusionyte (2015) undertook an ethnographic analysis of how security is perceived, constructed, and experienced through the lens of the media, particularly from the Argentinean side of the border. See Montenegro and Béliveau (2006) for an analysis of representations of the region. Carmen Ferradás (1998) also provides an anthropological analysis of the region.

The Brazilian Association for Combating Counterfeiting (ABCF) represents companies like Abbot, AmBev, Caloi, Coca-Cola, Globo, H.Stern, Johnson & Johnson, Kaiser, Levi, Motorola, Philips, Souza Cruz, Unilever, Votorantim, and others. It investigates and intervenes judicially in cases of counterfeiting of their brands, and gives support to the enforcement agencies of the state. Rodolpho Ramazzini is the association's main figure. Its headquarters is also in São Paulo.

As Pedro Francisco indicated in his research on Paraguayan cigarettes in Brazil while witnessing the emergence of IDESF,

> ABCF and IDESF can be classified as Operational Support organizations . . . with the provision of direct assistance to public authorities. . . . Assistance may be material—including direct funding through contributions—and logistical, with training and support for programs focused on repressive measures; and the advocating of interest in the form of public relations, lectures, research production and marketing anti-smuggling, focusing on messages about the damages to consumer health and to the national economy and the constant reference to organized crime. The ETCO and FNCP are crosscutting articulators, since they aggregate a number of stakeholders in the fight against illegal practices. Here, the modus operandi is also divided into two areas: lobby, with actions aimed directly to legislators, focused on specific legislative changes; and coordination of the activities above mentioned, between different sets of actors. Increasingly, it is this activity which is the main engine of the institutional system to combat cigarette smuggling. (Mizukami et al. 2013: 49, quoted in Francisco 2014: 94–95)

One of the first proposals of the Movement for the Defense of the Brazilian Licit Market was the creation of the National Day to Combat Smuggling, to be observed annually on March 3. The aim was to establish a day for drawing the attention both of the government and of society to the problems of smuggling. The media presented the first National Day to Combat Smuggling on March 3, 2015, without any reference to its unofficial character. The implicit officialization of the date in the media was possible thanks to the role played by some of its proponents: the president of ETCO was the lobbyist of the main conglomerate of Brazilian media for decades. On the other hand, the model of a national day to highlight a particular topic of the agenda of law enforcement was well known to ETCO, FNCP, and ABCF actors. It had already been implemented

with the National Day of Combating Piracy and Bio-piracy, which was established by federal law in 2005.[13]

CONTEXTS FOR NUMBERS

The first edition of the National Day to Combat Smuggling was in 2015. The
organizers prepared several main events, including the presentation of the results of research undertaken by the IDESF, in Foz do Iguaçu, and a meeting at
Brasília where the figures for smuggling and proposals for combating it were
presented. Each event was designed in accordance with a spatial inscription of
the logic of governance: the border as the scene for the facts of smuggling; the
capital city as the site for presenting demands to the government and influencing the legislative process.

In Foz do Iguaçu, which is one of the main points of entrance of merchandise from Paraguay, the scene was prepared for the presentation of data
on smuggling. In a press conference at the Brazilian federal revenue service
agency headquarters, the president of IDESF presented the results of *The cost of
smuggling*, research that would henceforth provide the numbers quoted in every
report on smuggling.[14]

At a modern convention center in Brasília, in the name of the Movement
for the Defense of the Brazilian Licit Market, the presidents of ETCO and
FNCP presented their demands: tightened controls at the border, a "positive
agenda" for Brazil-Paraguay relationships to find alternatives to smuggling, and
reduction of taxes for Brazilian products. Congressman Efraim Filho, from the
state of Paraíba and affiliated with the right-wing party DEM, presented the
proposals that he was putting forward to Congress: the official constitution of
the Parliamentary Front against Smuggling and Counterfeiting and a toughen-
ing of penalties against smuggling offenses.[15]

---

13. For an analysis of the Brazilian policies regarding piracy and the actors and
    coalitions that intervene in the field, see Mizukami et al. (2011). Their analysis was
    fundamental for my description and perspective.

14. The *Receita Federal do Brasil* (RFB) is a secretariat of the Ministry of Finance of
    Brazil. It administers the tax collection and the customs of Brazil.

15. The penalties for smuggling had already been modified in 2014 (Law 13.008/14),
    following a proposal by congressman Efraim Filho that created independent
    categories for crimes that had not been legally sanctioned as different infractions:

As the media treated the day as something given—particularly, the news programs of Rede Globo channels[16]—the intentions behind its creation were effaced and all that remained were the aims of its creators: to transform smuggling into a worrying problem that must worry everybody. The performance of two seminars organized by two of the main Brazilian journals, *Folha de São Paulo* and *Correio Braziliense*, was another step in constructing the context wherein smuggling would be raised to a national problem.[17]

The multimedia project "Everything about smuggling in Brazil" was organized by *Folha de São Paulo*, the newspaper of another key media group in Brazil, Grupo Folha. "Everything about smuggling in Brazil" was the result of two months of research undertaken by thirty professionals that sought to map and explain smuggling in Brazil. On March 18–19, *Folha de São Paulo* organized the seminar "Smuggling in Brazil" where it analyzed the impact of smuggling on the Brazilian economy, the relation between smuggling and urban violence, and the means to combat it. The speakers were federal and state officials—including the Minister of Justice—businessmen, politicians, journalists, and the spokesmen of the Movement for the Defense of the Brazilian Licit Market. In fact, the project and the seminar were sponsored by ETCO, FNCP, IDESF, and ABCF.

---

contrabando (introduction of prohibited or regulated products) and *descaminho* (introduction of merchandises without paying taxes). While descaminho remains a crime with one- to four-year prison sentences, the penalty for contrabando rose from two years to five years of prison time, which means that there is the possibility of preventive prison, no chance of parole, and the crime now only prescribed after twelve (rather than eight) years. A new proposal (PL 1530/2015) to penalize the drivers that transport contraband and the merchants that sell smuggled goods was sanctioned in January, 2019 (Law Nº 13.804). The Parliamentary Front Against Smuggling and Counterfeiting was established on May 14, 2015, including 230 members of the Congress and the Federal Senate and it is the parliamentary articulation for the modification of the law and for presenting demands to the government.

16. Besides *Jornal Nacional* presented above, see *Jornal da Globo* (Kirche 2015) and *Bom Dia Brasil* (2015).

17. Newspapers in Brazil are state-based, not national. In 2015, according to the *Associação Nacional de Jornais* (Newspaper National Association), based on data of the *Instituto Verificador de Circulação* (IVC), *Folha de São Paulo* was the third newspaper in circulation in printed version in the country—after *Super Noticia* (Minas Gerais) and *O Globo* (Rio de Janeiro). *Correio Braziliense* was the twentieth (ANJ 2016). If we include paid subscriptions with its digital version, *Folha de São Paulo* was the main journal in paid circulation in Brazil—with 335,895 daily readers in 2015—followed by *O Globo* and *Super Noticia*.

Some months later, on October 6, 2015, the *Correio Braziliense* newspaper and ETCO organized in Brasília the seminar "Smuggling in Brazil: Impacts and solutions."[18] The seminar was sponsored by ETCO, IDESF, FNCP, and ABCF, and was presented as an activity of the Movement for the Defense of the Brazilian Licit Market. Many of the speakers had already been present in the other media events produced by the movement, together with representatives of the industry, and auditor of the Federal Audit Court and the Minister of Justice, José Eduardo Cardozo.[19] The numbers mobilized in its announcement and coverage were also present in the other events. "A crime that cost R$100 billion to the country," was the headline in the newspaper the following day. A special issue on the seminar, entitled "Illegal market," was published in the *Correio Braziliense* print edition on October 15, 2015.

In little more than a year, the same actors, numbers, and arguments appeared repeatedly in the media, presenting smuggling as a huge problem for Brazil. Since the presentation of the Manifesto in Defense of the Brazilian Licit Market that addressed the presidential candidates in 2014 election, the movement managed to produce the contexts for its own presentations: press conferences, a "national day," and seminars in the newspapers. The centrality of the media coverage is crucial for us to understand the nature of these events: performances where certain facts and interpretations can be presented as news.[20]

The media attention that the movement gained was grounded in the trajectory of some of its members and in the power of the companies that they represent. When the manifesto was launched in 2014, the coverage of *Veja*— the leading weekly news magazine of Brazil, published by another media

18. As the main newspaper of the capital city (seat of the political power of the country), *Correio Braziliense* is important for the composition of its audience, not for the numbers that it sells.

19. The participants at the *Correio Braziliense* seminar were Evandro Guimaraes (ETCO), Efraim Filho (Federal Deputy), Rodolpho Ramazzini (ABCF), Luciano Barros (IDESF), Edson Vismona (FNCP), the president of Souza Cruz (British American Tobacco subsidiary), the president of Brazilian Association of Soft Drink and Non Alcoholic Beverages, Federal Audit Court auditor Mario Bertuol and the Minister of Justice, José Eduardo Cardozo.

20. The repercussion of these events was a permanent preoccupation for the organizers of the movement. See, for example, the 176-page report produced by FSB—the main communication agency of Brazil—to ETCO and FNCP, clipping all the media production about the presentation of the manifesto in September 2014 at the press conference in Brasilia (FSB 2014).

conglomerate, Grupo Abril—made no reference in the title to smuggling or to the movement. "The return of Evandro" was a small column, explaining that Evandro Guimarães had assumed the direction of ETCO, proposing to the presidential candidates several measures to combat smuggling and piracy. In an intimate tone, the text commented, "After a decade of services for Globo, Evandro left his position as the official lobbyist of the station in 2011."[21] In fact, he stopped being the lobbyist of one company to become the lobbyist of *several* companies. It is no surprise that all the Globo channels treated ETCO and the movement's interpretations as "givens." The main institutions of the movement sponsored "the interest" on smuggling of the *Folha de São Paulo* and *Correio Braziliense*; journals that produced seminars and special issues on the topic. The presence of the Ministry of Justice in the seminars organized by the newspapers shows the convening power that they managed to aggregate in very little time.

In short, the Manifesto in Defense of the Brazilian Licit Market turned smuggling into the reference trope that organized the discourse and the demands of the movement, and the IDESF's research as presented in the *Cost of smuggling* provided some of the numbers that were continually repeated since its release. Given the centrality of these numbers, it is fundamental to look into them.

SMUGGLING NUMBERS

The *Cost of smuggling* resulted from a study coordinated and applied by IDESF together with *Empresa Gaúcha de Opinião Publica e Estatística* (EGOPE), a company dedicated to market and public opinion research based in Lajeado, a small city of Rio Grande do Sul State. The study has three components: a description of the smuggling circuits that connect Ciudad del Este, Foz do Iguaçu, and São Paulo (general data); an analysis of the cost and profits of the ten most smuggled products at the time of their purchase in Paraguay and when they are sold in São Paulo (Top 10); and a description of the smuggled cigarette market.

General data—displayed as findings in the presentation of the research and amplified by the media—were derived from fifteen interviews with "smugglers" about topics such as income, number of persons that work for a boss, number

---

21. In fact, Guimarães's relationship with Globo dated from the end of the 1970s. For his trajectory, see MemóriaGlobo (2013).

of trips, and amount of goods transported. Indirect speech—such as "It is estimated" or "It was identified"—allowed the authors to present the data without the need to qualify it. Almost all the figures are presented without any explanation as to how they were calculated, including claims that "15,000 people are directly involved with smuggling in the Foz do Iguaçu region" (IDESF 2015a: 8), that the average income in the smuggling world is R$985, or that income is concentrated among the 2 percent that control the business. If the general data was obtained through qualitative methodologies, the text does not explain how it was transformed into quantitative data.

The *Cost of smuggling* report presents "The Top 10" most smuggled products, based on seizures by the Federal Revenue Service. The graph shows data that indicates the following products and figures smuggled through the Brazilian-Paraguayan border (in %): cigarettes (67.44), electronic devices (15.42), computers and accessories (5.04), clothes (3.03), perfumes (2.45), watches (2.03), toys (1.89), glasses (1.5), medicines (0.85), beverages and drinks (0.35).[22] When the report turns to the smuggled cigarette market, these percentages are projected nationally: "As we saw previously, cigarettes today represent 67.44% of all the smuggling that enters through the borders, the equivalent of R$6.4 billion considering losses for industry and taxation. Included among them, R$4.5 billion are taxes that the state fails to collect." (IDESF 2015: 11).

Before considering the procedure that generates these estimates, let's examine the numbers. The percentages were calculated from seizures at the Foz do Iguaçu Office of the Federal Revenue Service in 2014. Those percentages, however, were calculated without four items of the Federal Revenue Service list and the exclusion of these items was not justified in the report (see Table 1). In Table 1, we can see the percentages calculated by IDESF (the blank cells correspond to the items excluded). The second column (RF—Foz do Iguaçu) presents the percentages considering total seizures in Foz do Iguaçu (Lichacovski

---

22. After presenting the "Top 10" most smuggled products, the report presents a table with the gains that each item can produce; it compares the prices between in Ciudad del Este, Paraguay (provision market) and São Paulo (selling market). The prices were determined by consulting 180 stores in Ciudad del Este and 120 stores in São Paulo. The average price of the products—which is very interesting data—is accompanied by three other columns: the cost of smuggling for each product, the minimum gain, and the maximum gain. Although explained in the text, the reader does not have all the elements necessary to understand the percentage that appeared in each column for every product.

2015). The third column (RF—Brazil) presents the percentages of that merchandise in relation to all seizures done by the Federal Revenue Service in 2014 in Brazil (RFB 2014).

Table 1: Smuggling seizures in 2014, Brazil (% by products according to different sources: IDESF 2015; Lichacovski 2015; RFB 2014)

Products	IDESF		RF—Foz do Iguaçu		RF—Brazil	
	%	Position	%	Position	%	Position
Cigarettes	67.44	1º	51.86	1º	28.61	2º
Vehicles			16.57	2º	5.38	4º
Electronic devices	15.42	2º	11.86	3º	8.43	3º
Other products			5.92	4º	40.74	1º
Computers & accessories	5.04	3º	3.87	5º	2.29	7º
Clothes	3.03	4º	2.34	6º	5.24	5º
Perfumes	2.45	5º	1.88	7º	0.7	12º
Watches	2.03	6º	1.56	8º	2.18	8º
Toys	1.89	7º	1.45	9º	1.23	9º
Glasses	1.5	8º	1.15	10º	3.09	6º
Medicines	0.85	9º	0.65	11º	0.25	13º
Optical media (recorded)			0.46	12º	0.78	11º
Beverages and drinks	0.35	10º	0.28	13º	0.83	10º
Optical media (blank)			0.15	14º	0.25	14º
Total	100		100		100	

The distortion produced by the exclusion of certain items (that is, vehicles, other products, and both recorded and blank optical media) guaranteed the inclusion of other items (that is, beverages and drinks) among the Top 10 list of IDESF. The distortion was aggravated by the recalculation of the percentages without the amounts of the items excluded. To visualize that, we need to incorporate the total amounts reported by the Foz do Iguaçu Office of the Federal Revenue Service.

To recalculate the percentage of seizures with a smaller total amount ensures the inflation of the TOP 10 figures of IDESF (compare IDESF / RF—Foz do Iguaçu columns, in Table 1). Two other procedures transform these numbers in a superlative dimension. First, the report projects those numbers nationally ("cigarettes today represent 67.44% of all the smuggling that enters through the

Table 2: Comparison of seizures according to the Federal Revenue Service and the IDESF in 2014 (amounts, ranking, and resulting %) (IDESF 2015; Lichacovski 2015).

Products	RF—Foz do Iguaçu Seizures in $USD	RF—Foz do Iguaçu Ranking of Seizures	IDESF TOP 10 ranking	Amount used for calculating % by IDESF	IDESF TOP 10 %
Cigarettes	64,963,991.00	1º	1º	64,963,991.00	67.44
Vehicles	20,758,643.00	2º			
Electronic devices	14,855,021.00	3º	2º	14,855,021.00	15.42
Other products	7,405,453.00	4º			
Computers and accessories	4,852,927.00	5º	3º	4,852,927.00	5.04
Clothes	2,921,005.00	6º	4º	2,921,005.00	3.03
Perfumes	2,359,588.00	7º	5º	2,359,588.00	2.45
Watches	1,957,027.00	8º	6º	1,957,027.00	2.03
Toys	1,820,297.00	9º	7º	1,820,297.00	1.89
Glasses	1,440,367.00	10º	8º	1,440,367.00	1.5
Medicines	819,278.00	11º	9º	819,278.00	0.85
Optical media (recorded)	582,701.00	12º			
Beverages and drinks	338,152.00	13º	10º	338,152.00	0.35
Optical media (blank)	193,852.00	14º			
TOTAL	125,268,302.00			**96,327,653.00**	100

borders," IDESF 2015, 11). Second, it converts the percentage back again in a total amount of money ("the equivalent of R$6.4 billion considering losses for industry and taxation. Included among them, R$ 4.5 billion are taxes that the state fails to collect," IDESF 2015: 11).

The national projection of the arranged percentages produced by IDESF creates a gross misrepresentation in its portrayal of smuggling. The difference between the amount of cigarette smuggling according to IDESF and the seizures by the Federal Revenue Service in Brazil (third column in Table 1) is enormous: from almost 70 percent of all smuggling for IDESF to less than 30 percent according to *actual* seizures. That number not only captures the attention of the media—appearing in several headlines and TV spots[23]—but it is one of the main examples used by the spokesmen of ETCO, FNCP, IDESF, and ABCF to confirm the connection between the rise in taxes and the expansion of smuggling.

The conversion of the percentage back again into a total amount of money inflated the figure used to calculate losses of industry and taxation. The total seizures by the Federal Revenue Service in 2014 was R$1.8 billion and the seizure of cigarettes corresponded to R$515,319,232.73—equivalent to 28.61 percent (RFB 2014: 7). If we recalculate the total amount using the percentage produced by IDESF (67.44 percent of R$1.8 billion), we will have an amount of R$1.2 billion. That amount was multiplied by an apparently "official multiplying factor," which says that only between 5 percent and 10 percent of smuggled goods entering the country are seized.[24]

Next, the report calculates what the industries could have profited by producing and selling the same number of cigarettes that correspond to that amount of money, and how much the government could have earned with taxes. "Brazilian losses" are obtained from this kind of projection. However, at this point, we perceive that the aggregated numbers of losses are an assemblage of disparate sources, guesses, and manipulations. The limit between description and lobbying is blurred and the manipulation of numbers for imposing an agenda in the public debate becomes clear. As we have already seen, Souza Cruz (the British-American Tobacco subsidiary in Brazil) is a partner of IDESF; it is also associated with ABCF, ETCO, and FNCP. Philip-Morris is also associated with FNCP.

---

23. *Bom dia, Brasil,* for example, a television news program broadcast by Globo Channel, on the National Day to Combat Smuggling declared: "Cigarette is the most smuggled product in Brazil, points out research. The product represents almost 70% of all smuggling in the country. Brazil lost R$4,5 billons in taxes" (*Bom dia Brasil* 2015). The same claim appears in Jornal da Globo, the news program broadcast by Globo Channel at the end of the day (*Jornal da Globo* 2015) as well as in several reports and articles.

24. In the report, that estimation was credited to the Brazilian Prosecutor Service ("Foz do Iguaçu, 17/12/2014," p.4). In fact, the quotation corresponds to declarations of Federal Prosecutor Alexandre Collares Barbosa to the media. The prosecutor presented that estimation in a Civil Action against the Union asking for more federal agents to control the region. In the action, the estimate is also quoted in the indirect speech "It is estimated that. . ." without qualifying the agent of estimation (MPF 2014: 6).

Even if the figure for cigarette smuggling is a flagrant distortion, the "R$100 billion that Brazil lost with smuggling" that was reported in the first edition of the National Day to Combat Smuggling in Foz do Iguaçu and Brasilia did not even appear in the IDESF report.[25] It was a projection already taken for granted among the organizers of the Movement for the Defense of the Brazilian Licit Market,[26] a projection that was updated the following year—growing to R$115 billion—with no other specification than the worsening of the problem.

The figure of "R$100 billion lost with smuggling" corresponds to what Max Singer has called *mythical numbers*; numbers produced by guesstimating and made for exaggerating the scope and urgency of a portrayed problem. In the area of crime, he said, those numbers come to be "more mythical and have more vitality" (Singer 1971: 6).[27] Precisely, the difficulty of measuring unregistered markets and transactions opens the possibility for distortions and manipulations. As Peter Andreas affirmed, "illicitness makes possible a politics of numbers that is particularly susceptible to speculation, distortion, and sometimes even outright fabrication that is rarely questioned or challenged in policy debates and media reporting" (Andreas 2010: 23).

In Brazil, Pedro Mizukami and others called "magical numbers" those that were produced in the Brazilian enforcement context regarding the global value of the pirate market, the jobs lost to piracy, and the lost tax revenue (2011: 276–78). The "R$100 billion lost with smuggling" is a direct derivation of these magical numbers. In the case of smuggling, the "politics of numbers"—to use

---

25. The regional director of the Federal Revenue Services, Luiz Bernardi, started to use that figure in 2005 when he declared that the damages to Brazilian economy produced by smuggling corresponded to R$100 billion (Agência Brasil 2005). He repeated the same number in 2013 (Wurmeister 2013), but the media presented that data as an official number. Luiz Bernardi is the head the 9th Region of the Federal Revenue Service since 2001. The 9th Region includes the estates of Santa Catarina and Parana, where Foz do Iguaçu is located.

26. The accuracy and the magnitude of the number turn it into a doubtful figure. In his field guide to identifying dubious data, Joel Best warns about Big Round Numbers. In his description, "Big round numbers make big impressions. They seem shocking: 'I had no idea things were that bad!' They are easy to remember. They are also one of the surest signs that somebody is guessing" (Best 2013: 30).

27. Singer's classic text analyzed the exaggerated number of property theft by heroin addicts in New York, derived from the hyperinflated number of addicted people in the city. Thirteen years later, in "The (continued) vitality of mythical numbers," Peter Reuter resumed Singer's analysis of mythical numbers regarding the drug market (Reuter 1984).

Andreas's expression—was a particular development of antipiracy politics that has produced specific effects: the legitimization of corporate and industrial groups' claims, a singular spatialization of the "illicit market," and the criminalization of economic practices. I will explore these elements to conclude.

FROM PIRACY TO SMUGGLING: SPATIALIZING PROBLEMS, CRIMINALIZING PRACTICES

Since the constitution of the Movement for the Defense of the Brazilian Licit Market, smuggling has replaced piracy in the practice and rhetoric of institutions such as ETCO, FNCP, and ABCF. The strategy of a "national day to combat" was accompanied by the same practices of lobbying, training, and educational campaigns that characterized their work against piracy. As with piracy, the presumed connection with organized crime is a crucial aspect of the construction of the urgency of the campaign. According to their script, the conditions that encourage smuggling are high taxes and a difficult environment for business. Behind every intervention denouncing the increase of smuggling and its connection with organized crime, there is a demand for tax reductions.

The FNCP launched the most transparent campaign in this regard, *Imposto cresce, crime agradece* (loosely translated, "Taxes rise, crime obliges"). As the logo of the campaign states, "When taxes on cigarettes rise, smuggling carried out by organized crime—together with arms and drugs—also rises." The campaign included television spots in which actors from Globo Television introduced "an interview" with a cigarette smuggler in what seems to be a slum house.[28] A blurred out figure with a distorted voice says, "To us, when taxes on cigarettes

---

28. While the smuggler talks, the legend on the screen says, "Interview with a cigarette smuggler by Adriana Bittar (15/04/2016)." The "interview" is part of a "documentary" presented by Adriana Bittar in a slum—"like any slum of any Brazilian city"— where she interviewed a bartender that sells cigarettes from Paraguay and the smuggler already mentioned (FNCP 2016). The last minute of the film shows scenes of armed robberies, confrontations, kidnappings, and armed displays of force in slums. Bittar's voice narrates: "Cigarette smuggling is directly connected with organized crime and violence." Her final words are revealing: "Taxes, organized crime, smuggling. That is a heavy load. . . . It is not possible for Brazil to carry it anymore."

rise, it is very good. It is very profitable. We thank the government. It is easier and better working with Paraguayan cigarettes than with arms and drugs."[29]

The campaign of the FNCP is coarse, as we saw in the "playful protest" presented at the beginning of this chapter, or in report produced by the IDESF about the amount of cigarette smuggling. A similar conclusion was reached in the analysis of the antipiracy campaigns in Brazil.[30]

> Studying anti-piracy public awareness campaigns in Brazil is a dismal exercise. Demagoguery and scare tactics are the norm, often to a degree that reads as comedy rather than instruction. All are localizations of templates developed at the international level, and all hit the same simple messages: "you wouldn't steal a car"; "kidnapping, guns, drugs . . . the money that circulates in piracy is the same money that circulates in the world of crime"; "tomorrow I will sell drugs in my school because of that DVD"; and "thank you ma'am, for helping us to buy weapons!" are typical. (Three of the four quotes come from recent spots produced by the UBV, the organization of Brazilian film distributors, which has developed a particular specialization in the genre. The spots run on TV, in theatres, and in DVD preview materials.) (Mizukami et al. 2011: 288)

Comparison with antipiracy politics is grounded on the notion that we are talking of the same actors, and elaborating the same strategies and arguments that they previously deployed. The introductory words of Joe Karaganis in the Social Science Research Council research on *Media piracy in emerging economies* (where the Brazilian analysis was carried out) are relevant:

> What we know about media piracy usually begins, and often ends, with industry-sponsored research. There is good reason for this. US software, film, and music industry associations have funded extensive research efforts on global piracy over the past two decades and, for the most part, have had the topic to themselves. Despite its ubiquity, piracy has been fallow terrain for independent research. With the partial exception of file sharing studies in the last ten years, empirical work has been infrequent and narrow in scope. The community of interest has

---

29. See http://www.fncp.org.br/impostocrescecrimeagradece/.
30. For a detailed analysis of a campaign against piracy launched in 2009 by the FNCP, see Dent (2012).

been small—so much so that, when we began planning this project in 2006, a substantial part of it was enlisted in our work.

That community has grown, but there is still nothing on a scale comparable to the global, comparative, persistent attention of the industry groups. And perhaps more important, there is nothing comparable to the tight integration of industry research with lobbying and media campaigns, which amplify its presence in public and policy discussions. (Karaganis 2011: 1)

A judgment that dismissed the application for the prohibition of the "Taxes rise, crime obliges" campaign television spots provides the clearest demonstration of the interests represented by organizations like ETCO, FNCP, and ABCF. The campaign was denounced by antitobacco activists as a way of reintroducing cigarettes into publicity spots. An action against the campaign was presented at CONAR (National Council of Advertisement Self-Regulation) but the judgment—unanimously—considered that it was not an apology for tobacco but a campaign of a productive sector against taxation, something that it is not against the Brazilian Self-Regulating Advertising Code. The vote of the counselor André Luiz Costa is revealing:

> The film does not advertise cigarettes. Although increasingly combated but legally established, the tobacco industry produces a free drug whose trade is regulated. This industry, to avoid losing even more ground with tax increases, uses advertising time and free expression to avoid changes in the tax burden of its sector, something that is legal. That's what is portrayed in the movies. While not doing cigarette advertising, the tobacco industry is free to manifest itself as productive sector. (CONAR 2016)

As the counselor explicitly states, it is the tobacco industry that is talking through the FNCP campaign, defending its interests: to reduce the tax pressure of the state.

After more than a decade crusading against piracy, smuggling has become the new privileged problem in the battles over taxes and property claims implemented by corporations and industrial groups in Brazil. Piracy, counterfeiting, and informality are still important, but at present they orbit smuggling. Perhaps this new emphasis on smuggling is related to particular conjunctures: the government transition of 2014, the economic crisis in Brazil, and the destitution of the elected president in 2016.[31] However, this emphasis allows us to follow the heightened commitment to the "licit market" that legitimates a moralizing discourse and a criminalizing strategy by corporate actors; that is, discourse and strategy that help consolidate the proliferation of new markets for law enforcement. The border becomes a privileged scenario for the emplacement of the markets for law enforcement through the proliferation of vehicles, radars, arms, drones, and all the technologies for control and surveillance.

Smuggling presupposes the border and the border is a perfect scenario in the battle for the "licit market." In a long-term perspective, seizures have been on the rise at the Brazilian borders. The tightening of controls was part of a general policy of integration of the economic space of Southern Common Market (Mercosur)—the regional trade agreement between Brazil, Argentina, Uruguay, and Paraguay—since the 1990s. During the first decade of the twenty-first century, São Paulo gradually replaced Ciudad del Este (Paraguay) as the port of entry of imported products for the Brazilian market (Silva 2014). This was further matched by a policy of repression at the borders and on the roads (Rabossi 2004; Pinheiro-Machado 2010).

The border had been already politicized in Brazil and abroad (Heyman 1995, 2004; Andreas 2009), long before it was highlighted by the antismuggling campaign. In the last decade, discussions on urban insecurity—especially during elections—started to single out Brazilian open borders as responsible for the arms and drugs that funnel into major Brazilian cities. Echoing the debates of the presidential campaign of 2010 that put the border as a threat to internal security, Dilma Rousseff's government inaugurated the Strategic Plan for Borders in 2011, which included the creation of the National Strategy of Public Security at the Border (Ministry of Justice) and the organization of operations mobilizing the Armed Forces (Agata Operations) and the Federal Police (Sentinela Operations). In 2014, the border returned to the fore with the pending elections. There seems to be a paradox between the growing control of the border

31. On July 28, the president of ETCO Evandro Guimares visited former Vice President Michel Temer, who occupied Dilma Roussef's position, to register the commitment and receptivity that the new government team has to their suggestions and the careful attention they are paying to problem. In his words, the Temer government team "has shown, in two and a half months, a willingness to listen to the affected companies and a determination that the competent body act to create barriers to smuggling" (Planalto 2016).

in the long run and the accusation of uncontrolled borders.[32] The creation of the IDESF signals a change for both the traditional antipiracy and counterfeiting agenda and for the border research and policy agenda. As a representative of the Brazilian Association for Combating Counterfeiting (ABCF), its president was part of the traditional strategies. However, IDESF started to further its own agenda, where knowledge of the border was becoming increasingly important. As he spoke about the elaboration of the data the *Cost of smuggling* presented, EGOPE[33] director and economist Adriano Strassburger said,

> In the first discussion we had with Luciano [Stremel Barros], president of IDESF, we tried to show him that there is no use in just showing a problem, presenting a difficult situation, often a bad one. . . . So, to the extent that one wants to know, it is necessary to look for data.

As we have already seen in the analysis of that research, looking for data does not mean that it will qualify as consistent or robust. At any rate, preoccupation with the production of data on the border could trace a different path. Three seminars where organized by IDESF in October 2014, 2015, and 2016—called Seminário Fonteiras do Brasil—and several publications followed The *Cost of smuggling* report: *Security operations in border areas* (2015b), *Characteristics of border societies* (2016a), and *Crime routes: The crossroads of smuggling* (2016b). The data used is different, and extensively employs secondary data. In 2016, together with the Association of Graduates of the Advanced School of War of Foz do Iguaçu and the ESIC-Business & Marketing School,[34] the IDESF initiated a postgraduate course in Management of Political Science, Strategy, and Planning, with an emphasis on borders. This new stance goes together with the traditional notion of advocating for the products of the companies that support the institute, like the main Brazilian tobacco company.

---

32. However, demands for control can go hand by hand with tightening controls. As Peter Andreas has shown in *Border games: Policing the U.S.-Mexico divide*, the growth of control and law enforcement at the border can further the escalation of risk and profits, of flows, and of demands for more law enforcement (Andreas 2009).

33. EGOPE was a partner of IDESF in that research.

34. ESIC was the first business school of Spain. It now has several international programs.

Once inscribed in the political agenda, borders have become a new governmental frontier that guarantee an infinite field of interventions and designs, where security and control businesses can flourish without restrictions. The militarization of the border is one of the outcomes of this transformation, which came together with the proliferation of products, technologies, and procedures (Andreas 2009; Heyman and Campbell 2012). Brazilian border policy is gradually moving in that direction.

The recent emphasis on smuggling undertaken by the actors portrayed in this chapter, managed to naturalize a view of the border that criminalizes certain actors and circuits but not others. Outside remains other points of entry that have an important place in the map of flows of products that came from abroad. For example, the luxury circuits of high and middle classes through which large quantities of merchandise are introduced by regular airports, and the markets of consumption for all these products, are completely absent from the portrait of smuggling that has become naturalize in the media.

The possibility of defining the reality of smuggling in so little time, efficiently naturalized, was related to a very particular conjuncture. The manipulation of data that captured the attention of the media worked because the scenario for its enunciation was already prepared to have the effect that it achieved. The gradual presentation of that reality and the repeated proposals for tackling it—reduction of taxes—underlines the lobbying strategy implemented by those actors. If the conditions were conjectural, the consequences are enduring: the tightening criminalization of certain practices, the circumscription of problems to certain spaces (borders and slums) and the naturalization of corporate claims as public interest.

"If men define situations as real, they are real in their consequences," wrote William Thomas and Dorothy Swaine Thomas (1928: 572). What became one of the most quoted sociological statements—at least among sociologists—condenses William Thomas's concept of definition of the situation as central to human action: the real is not something given outside a definition and, once defined in a certain way, it produces real effects in the world.[35] Thomas's classical formulation helps us to advance an agenda on the "real economy": Who defines what? With what means do they do so? For what reasons? Which consequences do these definitions produce? The power to define something as real and the

---

35. For a discussion of the "Thomas Theorem"—as it was named by Robert Merton—and the ways it was quoted and used in sociology, see Merton (1995).

knowledge and techniques used to do so are crucial to understand the world that we live in.

ACKNOWLEDGMENTS

I would like to thank (for their questions and suggestions) the participants of the Wenner-Gren Foundation workshop, Real Economy: Ethnographic Inquiries into the Reality and the Realization of Economic Life, organized by the Center for Research on Culture and Economy (NuCEC) of the Federal University of Rio de Janeiro. In particular, many thanks to Federico Neiburg and Jane Guyer for encouraging the discussion and organizing this collection, and to the invaluable editors for work on the essay. Thanks also to Luiz Costa for the comments on an early version of this essay. Finally, I wish to thank the Brazilian National Council for Scientific and Technological Development (CNPq) for the support to the workshop.

REFERENCES

Agência Brasil. 2005. "Receita apurou no primeiro semestre r\$ 109 milhões com apreensões de mercadorias." *A Tribuna de Paraná*, April 8, 2005. http://www.tribunapr.com.br/noticias/receita-apurou-no-primeiro-trismestre-r-109-mi-com-apreensao-de-mercadorias/.

Andreas, Peter. 2009. *Border games: Policing the U.S.-Mexico divide*. Ithaca, NY: Cornell University Press.

———. 2010. "The politics of measuring illicit flows and policy effectiveness." In *Sex, drugs, and body counts: The politics of numbers in global crime and conflict*, edited by Peter Andreas and Kelly M. Greenhill, 23–45. Ithaca, NY: Cornell University Press.

Andreas, Peter, and Kelly M. Greenhill. 2010. "Introduction: The politics of numbers." In *Sex, drugs, and body counts: The politics of numbers in global crime and conflict*, edited by Peter Andreas and Kelly M. Greenhill, 1–22. Ithaca, NY: Cornell University Press.

ANJ. 2016. "Maiores jornais do Brasil." *Site Associação Nacional de Jornais.* Brasilia. http://www.anj.org.br/maiores-jornais-do-brasil/.

Bandeira, Olivia. 2013. "A pirataria no discurso da mídia brasileira." In *Brasil pirata, Brasil original*, edited by Oona Castro and Pedro Mizukami, 147–70. Rio de Janeiro: Folio.

Best, Joel. 2013. *Stat-spotting: A field guide to identifying dubious data.* Berkeley: University of California Press.

Bom Dia Brasil. 2015. "Cigarro é item mais contrabandeado no Brasil, aponta pesquisa." March 3, 2015. https://globoplay.globo.com/v/4005808/.

Cardin, Eric G. 2011. "A expansão do capital e as dinâmicas da fronteira." PhD diss., Paulista State University, Araraquara.

Callon, Michel. 1998. "Introduction: The embeddedness of economic markets in economics." In *The laws of the markets*, edited by Michel Callon, 1–57. Oxford: Blackwell.

Castro, Oona, and Pedro Mizukami, eds. 2013. *Brasil pirata, Brasil original.* Rio de Janeiro: Folio.

CNI. 2016. "3 de março, dia nacional de combate ao contrabando." March 3, 2016. http://www.portaldaindustria.com.br/cni/canais/propriedade-intelectual/ noticias/3-de-marco-dia-nacional-de-combate-ao-contrabando/.

CONAR. 2016. "FNCP—Imposto cresce, crime agradece." *Representação nº 123/16* (Conselheiro André Luiz Costa; Segunda e Quarta Câmaras). Conselho Nacional de Autoregulamentação Publicitária. http://www.conar.org. br/processos/detcaso.php?id=4400.

Dent, Alexander S. 2012. "Piracy, circulatory legitimacy, and neoliberal subjectivity in Brazil." *Cultural Anthropology* 27 (1): 28–49.

———. 2015. "Intellectual property, piracy and counterfeiting." *Annual Review of Anthropology* 45:17–31.

Desrosières, Alain. 1993. *La politique des grands nombres: Histoire de la raison statistique.* Paris: Éditions La Découverte.

Dorfman, Adriana. 2015. "Contrabando: Pasar es la respuesta a la existencia de una frontera, Burlar es el acto simétrico al control." *Aldea Mundo* 20 (39): 33–44.

Ferradás, Carmen. 1998. "How a green wilderness became a trade wilderness: The story of a southern cone frontier." *PoLAR* 21 (2): 11–25.

FNCP. 2016. "Imposto cresce, crime agradece." Accessed October 14, 2016. http://www.fncp.org.br/impostocrescecrimeagradece/#documentario.

Foucault, Michel. 1975. *Surveiller et punir: Naissance de la prison.* Paris: Gallimard.

————. (1977–78) 2004. *Sécurité, territoire, population: Cours au Collège de France, 1977–1978*. Paris: EHSS, Gallimard, Seuil.

Francisco, Pedro Augusto Pereira. 2014. "Fronteiras estratégicas: O contrabando de cigarros paraguaios no Brasil." Master's thesis, Federal University of Rio de Janeiro.

FSB. 2014. *Clipping—Coletiva de Imprensa—Brasilia*. September 19, 2014. http://www.fncp.org.br/download/clipping_etco_fncp_coletiva_brasilia. pdf.

Guyer, Jane I. 2016. *Legacies, logics, logistics: Essays in the anthropology of the platform economy*. Chicago: University of Chicago Press.

Hart, Keith. 1973. "Informal income opportunities and urban employment in Ghana." *Journal of Modern African Studies* 11 (3): 61–89.

Heyman, Josiah. 1995. "Putting power into the anthropology of bureaucracy: The immigration and naturalization service at the Mexico–United States border." *Current Anthropology* 36 (2): 261–87.

————. 2004. "Ports of entry as nodes in the world system." *Identities: Global Studies in Culture and Power* 11 (3): 303–27.

Heyman, Josiah, and Howard Campbell. 2012. "The militarization of the United States–Mexico border region." In "Militarização nas Américas," special issue, *Revista de Estudos Universitários* [Universidade de Sorocaba, São Paulo, Brasil] 38 (1): 75–94.

Hull, Mathew S. 2012. *Government of paper: The materiality of bureaucracy in urban Pakistan*. Berkeley: University of California Press.

IDESF. 2015a. *O custo do contrabando*. Foz do Iguaçu: Instituto de Desenvolvimento Econômico e Social de Fronteiras.

————. 2015b. *Operações de segurança nas áreas de fronteira*. Foz do Iguaçu: Instituto de Desenvolvimento Econômico e Social de Fronteiras.

————. 2016a. *Características das sociedades de fronteiras*. Foz do Iguaçu: Instituto de Desenvolvimento Econômico e Social de Fronteiras.

————. 2016b. *Rotas do crime—As encruzilhadas do contrabando*. Foz do Iguaçu: Instituto de Desenvolvimento Econômico e Social de Fronteiras.

IfM—Institute of Media and Communication Policy. 2016. *Media data base*. Berlin: Institut für Medien- und Kommunikationspolitik gGmbH. Accessed October 15, 2016. http://www.mediadb.eu/en.html.

Jornal Nacional. 2015. "Contrabando provoca prejuízo de bilhões ao Brasil." March 3, 2015. https://globoplay.globo.com/v/4858301/.

————. 2016. "Dia nacional de combate ao contrabando tem atos de protesto." March 3, 2016. https://globoplay.globo.com/v/4858301/.

Jusionyte, Ieva. 2015. *Savage frontier: Making news and security on the Argentine border.* Oakland: University of California Press.

Kapferer, Bruce, and Angela Hobart. 2005. "The aesthetics of symbolic construction and experiences." In *Aesthetics in performance: Formations of symbolic construction and experience,* edited by Angela Hobart and Bruce Kapferer, 1–22. New York: Berghahn.

Karaganis, Joe, ed. 2011. *Media piracy in emerging economies.* New York: SSRC.

Kirche, Wilson. 2015. "Perdas com produtos ilegais chega a R$ 100 bilhões no Brasil, diz pesquisa." *Jornal da Globo,* March 3, 2015. https://globoplay.globo.com/v/4008307/.

Lichacovski, Leticia. 2015. "Receita federal superou R$330 milhões em apreensões em 2014." January 8, 2015. http://www.clickfozdoiguacu.com.br/receita-federal-superou-r330-milhoes-em-apreensoes-em-2014/.

MacGaffey Janet, with Vwakyanakazi Mukohya, Rukarangira wa Nkera, Brooke Grundfest Schoepf, Makwala ma Mavambu ye Beda, and Walu Engundu. 1991. *The real economy of Zaire: The Contribution of smuggling & other unofficial activities to national wealth.* Philadelphia: University of Pennsylvania Press.

Mackenzie, Donald, and Yuval Millo. 2003. "Negotiating a market, performing theory: The historical sociology of a financial derivatives exchange." *American Journal of Sociology* 109(1): 107–46.

MemóriaGlobo. 2013. "Evandro Guimarães." Globo Comunicações e Participações S.A. Accessed October 12, 2016. http://memoriaglobo.globo.com/perfis/talentos/evandro-guimaraes/trajetoria.htm#.

Merton, Robert K. 1995. "The Thomas Effect and The Matthew Effect." *Social Forces* 74 (2): 379–424.

Mizukami, Pedro N., Oona Castro, Luiz F. Moncau, and Ronaldo Lemos. 2011. "Brazil." In *Media piracy in emerging economies,* edited by Joe Karaganis, 217–304. New York: SSRC.

Montenegro, Silvia, and Verônica G Béliveau. 2006. *La triple frontera: Globalización y construcción del espacio.* Buenos Aires: Miño y Dávila Editores.

MPF. 2014. Ação Civil Pública Nº 5010354-05.2014.404.7002/PR (1ª Vara Federal de Foz do Iguaçu). Alexandre Collares Barbosa. August 1, 2014.

Neiburg, Federico, 2006. "Inflation and economic cultures in Brazil and Argentina." *Comparative Studies in Society and History* 48 (3): 604–33.

————. 2010. "Sick currencies and public numbers." *Anthropological Theory* 10 (1–2): 96–102.

Pinheiro-Machado, Rosana. 2010. "Caminos del contraband: La fiscalización en el Puente de la Amistad y sus efectos en la cotidianidad de la Triple Frontera." In *La triple frontera: Dinámicas culturales y procesos transnacionales*, edited by Verónica Giménez Béliveau and Silvia Montenegro, 99–118. Buenos Aires: Espacio Editorial.

Planalto. 2016. "Para Instituto Etco, governo está atento no combate ao contrabando." Planalto —Presidência da República, July 28, 2016. http://www2.planalto.gov.br/acompanhe-planalto/noticias/2016/07/para-instituto-etco-governo-esta-atento-no-combate-ao-contrabando.

Porter, Theodore M. 1995. *Trust in numbers: The pursuit of objectivity in science and public life*. Princeton, NJ: Princeton University Press.

Rabossi, Fernando. 2004. "Nas ruas de Ciudad del Este: Vidas e vendas num mercado de fronteira." PhD diss., Federal University of Rio de Janeiro.

————. 2012. "Ciudad del Este and the Brazilian circuits of commercial distribution." In *Globalization from below: The world's other economy*, edited by Gustavo Lins Ribeiro, Gordon C. Mathews, and Carlos José Alba Vega, 54–68. London: Routledge.

————. 2013. "Diámicas económicas en la triple frontera (Brasil, Paraguay y Argentina)." In *Seguridad, planificación y desarrollo en las regiones transfronterizas*, edited by Fernando Carrión, 167–93. Quito: FLACSO, IDRC-CRDI.

————. 2014. "Terrorist frontier cell or cosmopolitan commercial hub? The Arab and Muslim presence at the border of Paraguay, Brazil and Argentina." In *The Middle East and Brazil: Perspectives on the new Global South*, edited by Paul Amar, 92–115. Bloomington: Indiana University Press.

Receita Federal do Brasil (RFB). 2014. "Balanço aduaneiro—2014." http://idg.receita.fazenda.gov.br/dados/resultados/aduana/arquivos-e-imagens/balanco-aduaneiro-2014.pdf/.

Renoldi, Brígida. 2015. "Estados posibles: Travesías, ilegalismos y controles en la triple frontera." *Etnográfica* 19 (3): 417–40.

Reuter, Peter. 1984. "The (continued) vitality of mythical numbers." *The Public Interest* 75:135–47.

Romancini, Richard, and Cláudia Lago. 2007. *História do jornalismo no Brasil*. Florianópolis: Insular.

Schuster, Caroline E. 2015. *Social collateral: Women and microfinance in Paraguay's smuggling economy*. Oakland: University of California Press.

Silva, Carlos Freire da. 2014. "Das calçadas às galerias: Mercados populares do centro de São Paulo." PhD diss., São Paulo University.

Singer, Max. 1971. "The vitality of mythical numbers." *The Public Interest* 23:3–9.

Sodré, Nelson Werneck. (1966) 1999. *Historia da imprensa no Brasil*. Rio de Janeiro: Mauad.

Thomas, William I., and Dorothy Swaine Thomas. 1928. *The child in America: Behavior problems and programs*. New York: Alfred A. Knopf.

Veja. 2014. "O retorno de Evandro." *Revista Veja*, September 16, 2014. http://veja.abril.com.br/blog/radar-on-line/.

Wurmeister, Fabiula. 2013. "Contrabando cria prejuízo de R$100 bilhões por ano." *G1 Paraná*, June 7, 2013. http://g1.globo.com/pr/oeste-sudoeste/noticia/2013/06/contrabando-cria-prejuizo-de-r-100-bilhoes-por-ano-no-brasil-diz-rf.html.

The method of the real
What do we intend with ethnographic infrastructure?

BILL MAURER

Yes, words are useless! Gobble-gobble-gobble-gobble-gobble! Too much of it, darling, too much! That is why I show you my work! That is why you are here!

—Edna E. Mode, *The Incredibles*

The false use of passions, or of types, or the mere use of conventional gestures,—these are all frequent faults in our profession. But you must keep away from these unrealities. You must not copy passions or copy types. You must live in the passions and in the types. Your acting of them must grow out of your living in them.

—Constantin Stanislavski, *An actor prepares*

When I took my very first anthropology class in college, the professor, Walter Fairservis, assigned the bible of method acting, Constantin Stanislavski's *An actor prepares.* It was a class called Peoples and Cultures of the Soviet Union. It was the weirdest thing I'd ever experienced in a classroom setting at that point in my fledgling academic career. The book is written from the point of view of an acting student named Kostya who chronicles his lessons with "The Director," Tortsov, who is the fictional embodiment of Stanislavski himself. The reader is just thrown right into it. If you miss this at the outset, you will soon be lost. If you are not an actor, if you don't know anything about the theater, and especially if you have no experience with Russian theater or much else besides a little Shakespeare and Masterpiece Theater on television—my situation in 1986—it is rough going.

What kept my interest, however, and pushed me to slog through it, was Professor Fairservis's insistence on what he believed Stanislavski's mission really was. I just had to take his word for it, but I was game. That real mission, he told us, was to help teach Russians how to act on stage in order to convincingly portray Russians. He said, "He's trying to teach Russians how to act Russian." He said it over and over again, through the several class sessions where we read *An actor prepares* and then Chekhov's *Three sisters.* Somehow this was supposed to help us get at "the Russian national character." I still didn't quite get it, but I liked the problem posed and I liked that it was posed as an anthropological problem, a problem of the ethnographic method—even if I didn't really know what that was yet, either.

This experience came back to me while reading the papers from the Real Economy conference that generated this volume. What could be more "method" than the instructor's explanation in the workshop on the case method in business instruction quoted by Fabian Muniesa (Chapter 2 this book, p. 30): "The more the case is lived, . . . the more it is understood"? The business case is not a set of empirical facts from which to test hypotheses and draw conclusions but something to be "lived." In other words, the business case is not supposed to be incorporated in a student's preparation for the business world as a set of facts, but rather as a lived experience. This is the essence of method acting or of preparing the actor for the role on the stage. There is resonance with ethnography. As Keith Hart said at the conference in Rio de Janeiro where these papers were first presented, a difficulty for ethnography is that although it had "sold itself to the academy as a science," it cannot trace its truths to a "source."

This chapter uses the essays from the Real Economy conference to stage a series of questions about the sources of ethnographic truths. I am interested in the homology between what ethnography does or can do—as I will discuss below,

I am particularly interested in how anthropologists can discover new things in old ethnographies—and how anthropologists grapple with the relationship between plural economic formations and that thing we call "capitalism." The Real Economy project grapples with both the question of ethnographic representation and the sources of ethnographic truths, and the question of economic plurality. Even the designation of the "real" economy suggests there is something others are missing when they look at economic relations and forms. Anthropologists think we have specific insights to offer based on our attachment to certain kinds of methods. But I think we often miss possibilities for method in the impulse to be more revelatory than experiential, delighting in the reveal rather than in the doing. I will specify this "doing" in what follows.

How we understand economic plurality and how we do ethnography are intertwined, too, not just homologues. As ethnographers we live both problems: we live in plural economic worlds every day (and I do not mean "in the field" but "at home"); and we put ourselves in others' shoes during fieldwork and in the reading of others' ethnographic texts.

I am also interested in the family affinity between the Gens Manifesto (Bear et al. 2015) and the Real Economy project conveyed in this book. Both are concerned with multiplicity and plurality, and the need to "challenge the boundedness of the domain of 'the economic'" (Bear et al. 2015: §2). Both strain against, even as they try to analyze, the kinds of standardization and formalization particular to, or ideologically enforced by, totalizing dreams of the thing we call capitalism. Both want to grasp how diverse life forces get enrolled in value projects. Although I am interested in the relations and conversions that make this enrollment (sometimes) possible, if (always) conflicted, I am more concerned here in what these twinned efforts illuminate about the ethnographic project. If the Gens project draws attention to the bridges or infrastructures between noncapitalist and capitalist economic forms that facilitate the conversion and appropriation of value from the former to the latter, I use the Real Economy essays to put forward the notion of ethnography as a similar kind of bridge. It has other intentions, however.

METHOD ETHNOGRAPHY

Method acting tries not to represent or mimic the intention of the character one is portraying but to place the actor in a situation where he or she will embody it. At one point in *An actor prepares*, the Director asks a pupil named Maria to enact a simple scene of sitting on a chair. "Not knowing where to look, or what to do, she began to change, to sit first one way and then another" (1948: 32), awkwardly going through a variety of poses before the curtain fell. Others repeated the experiment; "their helplessness and desire to please were ridiculous" (33). Then, he asks Maria to come back up on stage, to the same chair she previously occupied, while he looks for something. She sits. "Her pose was life-like, natural" (33). Then the curtain fell. "'How do you feel?'" the Director asked. "I? Why? Did we act?" "Of course" was his reply. "Why, I didn't act anything," she protested. "That was the best part of it," he replied. "You sat and waited, and did not act anything" (34). Her intention was simply to sit. And she did. And it was marvelous.

In Juan Pablo Pardo-Guerra's account of fraudulent orders to buy or sell securities, what comes across is the centrality of "intent" to the determination of what is or is not a "real" trade. There is nothing that materially differentiates a true trade from a spoof. "Like a forgery," Pardo-Guerra writes, "a spoof is physically real" and is "materially identical to the other orders in the system" (2016: 13). This is why the discovery of intentionality matters so much to the identification of the spoof. Had Maria been intending to act as if sitting, and had done as well as she did when she did not realize she was "acting," then that would have been acting indeed.

Conceptions of the "real economy," as Jane Guyer (2016) outlines, wend their way through various Western political economic traditions. Yet "the potential for slippage, or for insistent precision, across the range of terms to which 'real' belongs is profound" (Guyer 2016: 245). Even in the field of economics, the *real economy* is a contested term. Prominent economists across the ideological and methodological spectrum appear to agree that the field has largely abandoned the real economy: "Economics has become an increasingly arcane branch of mathematics rather than dealing with real economic problems," wrote Nobel laureate Milton Friedman (1999: 137). Tony Lawson, the Cambridge critical realist economist, opened his *Economics and reality* with the headline from an edition of the *Times Higher Education Supplement*: "No reality, please. We're economists!" (1997: xii) before proceeding to launch a sustained case to "bring reality (or more of it) back into economics." Closer to anthropology, Michel Callon (2005) and Daniel Miller (2002) have debated whether economic theory constitutes economic realities or virtual fantasies of neoliberal ideology. Karen Ho (2009: 36) argues, based on her ethnography of shareholder value, that economic ideas are performative—but not in a total fashion—as well as being "virtual substitutions for real life complexity"—but again, not wholly so.

Not acting anything. The Director's statement implies a first-order reality in which resides the true nature of intention or purpose. Aristotle (2013) famously differentiated the primary and secondary uses of things, the former associated with their true, intended use, and the latter with second-order purposes to which they might be animated:

> Of everything which we possess there are two uses: both belong to the thing as such, but not in the same manner, for one is the proper, and the other the improper or secondary use of it. For example, a shoe is used for wear, and is used for exchange; both are uses of the shoe. He who gives a shoe in exchange for money or food to him who wants one, does indeed use the shoe as a shoe, but this is not its proper or primary purpose, for a shoe is not made to be an object of barter. (*Politics* IX)

Such secondary purposes are not necessarily immoral or unjust. It is only when the secondary use of a thing is employed in the service of unlimited acquisition that it veers from its intended use. Household management, for Aristotle, "has a limit," a natural one, determined by the size of the household and the provisioning of its members. Trade and money-making move beyond the confines of what is natural and good when they exceeds this natural limit and when wealth acquisition is undertaken as an end in itself. Such an end is unbound by any natural constraint or convention. The shoe, to stick with this example, starts acting in a whole new way when it is traded to make money beyond limit. When it is a shoe on my foot, however, it is not acting anything other than itself. It is simply being what it is, or what it was intended to be.

Anthropologists, for our part, have tended to assume that the real economy has those same natural limits that Aristotle postulated. This is perhaps borne of our longstanding interest in family, kinship, and household. It is also borne of our commitment to telling the reality of others' lifeways: what is "real" is generally understood to be what is "on the ground," as Jane Guyer has said to us in conversations about this workshop. What is on the ground tends to be the creation, maintenance, and sundering of familial and other interpersonal relations. So when we try to counter the "fictions" of finance, say, we seek out those "real" relations underneath or behind the fictions. Or when we try to sketch "real" economies, we find ourselves returning to the *oikos* or the "human scale".

This tendency is reflected in theoretical statements about the articulation of modes of production among the French structural Marxists (Meillassoux 1975), feminist anthropologists' criticisms of the French Marxists' naturalization of the biological generation of new humans, sidelining their social reproduction (Yanagisako and Collier 1987), and more recent work that understands capitalism and kinship as mutually implicated (Yanagisako 2002).

There is a tension, however, over whether those other social relations are sutured into a dominant mode of production, say, capitalism, or whether they exist outside, to one side, or sometimes out of phase with it, and when or whether it matters. For J. K. Gibson-Graham (2006), noncapitalist relations are all around us. Capitalism's apologists, promoters, and critics alike refuse actually existing economic plurality and diversity, and in so doing make out capitalism—and any critical response to it—to be singular or monolithic. Anna Tsing (2015a) is closer to the articulation of modes of production approach, in that she "look[s] for the noncapitalist elements on which capitalism depends" (2015a: 66). What she calls "pericapitalist" spaces are both inside and outside capitalism—say, Lao and Hmong mushroom foragers' trajectories of and relationships to war, displacement, and migration. In designating these as pericapitalist she foregrounds their articulation to or mobilization for "salvage capitalism" (Tsing 2015a: 106) in order to show how things "created in these non-capitalist processes are translated into capitalist value" (Tsing 2015b: ¶2). Indeed, "economic diversity makes capitalism possible" and at the same time provides the possibility for "instability and refusal of capitalist governance" (Tsing 2015a: 301).

Tsing's argument, and the analytical perspective on economic plurality presented by the Gens Manifesto (Bear et al. 2015), restages while challenging earlier Marxist accounts of the relationship between noncapitalist and capitalist modes and relations of production. Revisiting those debates gets us right into the thick of the "real"—and the association in anthropology between the real and the household, and how things "count" as real—literally and figuratively. There is an accounting problem here, and what Taylor Nelms (2015) has called a problem of delimitation: How do we understand kinship, gender, and the real economy and decide whether, when, and how these forms are alternatively opened up or closed off in people's practices, making bridges or articulations possible or not, sometimes or often, durable or periodic (as Nelms also argued in a paper that was circulated after the Rio conference).

Let's dig into anthropology's history for the often-overlooked antecedents of theories about economic plurality. Claude Meillassoux (1975) argued that there is a twofold dependency of capitalism on non- or precapitalist forms. First, capitalism depends on the reproduction of labor power in the household. Second, capitalism as a global phenomenon in colonial imperialism depends on reserves of cheap labor power and resources outside its core loci in the industrialized West. To paraphrase Bridget O'Laughlin's summary (1977: 4), capitalism preserves these pre- and noncapitalist forms in order to exploit them more fully; primitive accumulation from noncapitalist modes "is a functional requirement of the reproduction of capital" (1977: 8).

O'Laughlin criticized Meillassoux for naturalizing reproduction. Household, family, and biological generativity are simply assumed as coterminous and given. Take, for instance, Meillassoux's discussion of the supposed transition from land as a subject of production (among, say, migratory gathering and hunting bands) to land as an instrument of production (among quasi-settled horticulturalists). The ethnographic record on such quasi-settled communities contains examples of people developing systems of accounting between the full season and the fallow—they carry over surpluses and take stock of who has lent what to whom. Meillassoux describes them as resting on a system of "advances and returns"—credits and debts. This is because "production is delayed"—it takes time for those crops to grow—which requires ongoing "co-operation between members of the productive cell" (1975: 41). How is that cooperation organized and maintained? In addition to the social relations maintained between those who labor together, there are the relations over time between "the successive workers who, at each season, depend for their survival through the non-productive period and for the preparation of the next cycle on the subsistence food produced during the previous productive period" (1975: 41). Over time, he writes, the work team changes—but this establishes a relationship of debt to "those who came before" (Meillassoux 1972: 99–100). Thus elders gain authority over juniors, as being closer to as well as being an example of those who came before.

The problem O'Laughlin and others (see Collier 1988) identified, however, is that this account assumes what should be explained: the "contingency of the biological reproduction of workers" (O'Laughlin 1977: 7). In Meillassoux's account, elder men perpetuate their authority over junior men "by controlling both the distribution of women and access to the valuables young men must present to women's kin to validate marriages" (Collier 1988: 4)—the stuff of "primitive money," or the accounting or memory-devices that make up so much of the early ethnology of money (e.g., Quiggin 1949).

Jane Collier's account of marriage and inequality in classless societies further advanced O'Laughlin's critique by pointing out the obvious from the evidence of the ethnographic record: it's pretty clear that elder men don't control women at all, at least, Collier writes, "not in any ordinary sense of the word 'control'" (1988: 4). Rather, they are "constantly involved in litigation because unmarried girls have affairs and married women leave their husbands to run off with lovers or return home to mother" (1988: 4). Rather than controlling women, elder men face the accounting problem of "who owes what to whom" (1988: 4) and need to settle up with men jilted by their wives. Those primitive moneys, far from suggesting the price of a wife or compensation to the wife's family for her labor is better seen as a remedy to a conflict situation rather than a right to a woman's labor, reproductive or otherwise.

Read one way, Meillassoux's critique sounds like Friedrich Engels's account of the rise of private property—men gaining control over women's reproductive powers once the "discovery" of paternity inaugurates the institution of private property through inheritance from those (men) who came before. This, too, is the story from Louis Henry Morgan's (1877) reading of Numa Denis Fustel de Coulanges (1877), which was picked up by both Engels and Karl Marx. The defeat of the female line and common property by agnatic descent and private property represents the resolution for Marx and Engels of the first great world historic class struggle.

The classic Marxist version of the story depends on a "real" of biological re-production, lineage, and "blood." As Collier succinctly put it, however, "mating and marriage are not the same thing" (Collier 1988: 4). As O'Laughlin put it, "social reality can never be adequately analyzed in . . . empiricist terms because the surface world of appearances provides only a fleeting and necessarily incomplete glimpse of the contradictory social relations that underlie it" (O'Laughlin 1977: 23). And now we come to the heart of the thing. How do we get at what's on the ground—to return to Guyer—without falling into the empiricist trap? How do we "see," ethnographically speaking, what we see? And how do we analyze relations without being fooled by what we see?

When ethnographers witnessed the exchange of valuables at marriage, it appeared to them to be a payment for a wife, the exercise of control over social relations of reproduction that effected a transfer of rights of the biological capacities of the wife from her family to the husband. What they did not always see were the ways in which debts were socially organized, and in which the

delimitation and durability (à la Nelms) of relations among men were maintained or restored in the breach of such debts.

Consider, however, Collier's accomplishment in *Marriage and inequality*—
and the ethnographic accomplishment that actually preceded it. The book is
not based on fieldwork, but on rereading some old ethnographies. Collier "saw"
things in those old ethnographies that others had not. How so? By placing herself in the position of the women whose lives and conflicts could be imagined
through the pages of those ethnographies (and, admittedly, doing so by reading
across a host of such ethnographies). She admits, this was a just-so exercise, imagining one playing the game from her own point of view and perspective. But
nevertheless, it allowed her to open up the relations structuring social inequality
and the importance of marital instability (really, women's agency) in classless
societies. There was enough in those old ethnographies for Collier to imagine
herself in the position of the actors portrayed—even if only just off to the side,
just off stage—to ask herself, what would I have done?

EMPIRICALLY PLURAL

I rehearse the feminist debate over Meillassoux because I think it is restaged
in contemporary anthropological conversations about the real economy, and
provides a cautionary tale on the limits of empiricism. It also reminds us that
the translation of noncapitalist forms into capitalism has a prehistory in the
annals of anthropological thought. It is easy to see Meillassoux's first error—
naturalizing biological reproduction, which then prevented subsequent anthropologists from questioning the diverse forms of life-forces and their social
production and organization into other value projects (to borrow some language from the Gens Manifesto). It is more of a challenge to grapple with how
we might still be reproducing his second error—subsuming all noncapitalist
relations into capitalism. I think this is because revealing the subsumption of
the noncapitalist into the capitalist feels like the answer. Having found the
answer, we can then take our attention away from the "doing" on either side of
that operation of subsumption as well as from the operations or infrastructures
of conversion facilitating that subsumption. In effect, finding the answer is
like making those hyperexaggerated expressions of emotion Stanislavski made
fun of; attending to the doing requires just sitting in the chair, like Maria that

second time she was asked to do so, and acted convincingly by not playing at anything at all.

"Real" economic diversity, or "real" translation into capitalism: which one of these two constructs we as analysts or social actors take up, and when we do so, it seems to me, depends on the stakes of whichever game we are playing at whichever time or in whichever temporality. This, in turn, requires openness to these alternative times and games, or, to put it another way, openness to putting oneself in the shoes of those playing those games, much as Collier, but to the extent possible without caricature (about which, more below—I realize this is a perilous charge, and a place ethnography has been before . . . and not always a happy place!).

But we experience people doing this kind of operation themselves, out there in the "real" world. Take Nelms's argument (Nelms 2015, and in Nelms, n.d., which circulated among the Rio conference participants afterward): Variously positioned Ecuadorians either seek out those economic alternatives as a source of refusal of neoliberalism, or simply live them—not acting anything. Sometimes anthropologists (and some of Nelms's interlocutors) foreclose possibility in the name of ideological or analytical purity, or a desire to state what is "really" going on or what is "really" important, consequential, meaningful (such as incorporation into capitalist accumulation). I know that in refusing this foreclosure I am just putting forward another conception of the real; but I am going to do it anyway, to see what it might evoke, to muster whatever resources it may afford me and my own nature for the new contexts and configurations, indeterminate, yet to come.

And, nota bene, I am doing it *here*, in terms of ongoing conversations the Real Economy project has fostered. (In spite of statements about surfacing contingency and refusing totalizing purity in analyzing the things of the world, anthropologists remain pretty stingy in granting the same indulgences to each other!) I would very likely do otherwise in other venues, on another stage, so to speak, or in another time phase of this being that I call myself and my world. This, of course, implies a certain kind of being in a certain kind of world—one in which something called an individual in something called a society can occupy different roles, take on different perspectives. Marilyn Strathern (1991) has been a signal guide through the questions this sort of being/worlding evokes, and I will return to her in my conclusion.

Many of the actors described in the Real Economy chapters are themselves simply on a quest to sort out what's real from what's not. Whether they are trying to get an accurate count of something (the size of South Africa's economy, for James; smuggling into Brazil, for Rabossi; the numbers in the favela, for Motta) or trying to make themselves visible through formality and documents (as with migrant laborers at the Zimbabwe–South African border, for Bolt), or trying to determine whether a set of representations corresponds to a real economic fact (in securities trading, for Ortiz; in antitrust cases, for Onto; or in potentially fraudulent trades, for Pardo-Guerra), these actors' goals are often to establish an incontestable baseline to guide to their own and others' future action. To be successful as fact, that baseline has to be accepted by any parties that might consult it. It has to account for the real, and the activities that produce it have to be undertaken *for* real. Those *actions* cannot be an *act*.

Of course, this path to objectivity is littered with failure. It's hard to count certain things, and these chapters detail why, in particular cases, achieving a count that can stand as objective is often thwarted—by people's everyday practice, their negotiations and conversions of one form of value into another, their resistances, or the lack of fit between the counting tool and the reality "on the ground" being counted. Still, the belief persists that counting can give access to the "real" economy.

What is this real economy? For some of the actors described here, it stands in opposition to the fictions of the financialized economy. The real economy is the economy of stuff, labor, construction, or manufacturing or mining or whatnot, as opposed to paper or digital trading of representations of some supposedly more real assets backing them. These fictions can become so complex, however, that deducing the reality behind them is a puzzle for analysts and actors on the financial scene alike. There are contested claims, too, as we see in Horacio Ortiz's, Deborah James's, and Gustavo Onto's chapters: it is often difficult to differentiate what is economic from what is stately, or what is neoliberal from what is redistributive. Multiplicity, ambiguity, and the intertwining of relations and institutions that are supposed to be separate keep getting in the way. The real economy is also the economy of certain time horizons, which, as Caitlin Zaloom shows, involves a great many leaps of faith, not straightforward economic calculation.

Stanislavski warned that theater based on "conventions"—stylized gestures expressing inner states, like clutching one's head to convey anguished surprise—may entertain but will not truly move the audience. Hence, the quotation that I have chosen as one of the epigraphs for this essay. Stanislavski challenged such "unrealities" in favor of acting that grows out of living, or, what he elsewhere called "the direct co-operation of nature herself" as opposed to "representation" (Stanislavski 1948: 22). The direct cooperation of nature gives you true intent and thus real drama. Anything else is just play-acting.

If Muniesa's interlocutors are using cases to create subjective experiences that actors can draw on to guide future actions, some of Nelms's interlocutors crave cases, which they can turn into on-the-ground examples of alternative economic relationships or arrangements, not to experience but to implement, to make what they call a "real change." If Muniesa's worry that the real that business students seek can never be realized, at least some of Nelms's informants commit themselves, given this same condition, to keep on trying, to "hang in" and hang on. Their commitment is reminiscent of Slavoj Žižek's (1989) analysis of the ideological fantasy: ideology is not a veil masking the real, because we know full well that the real never lives up to its name. Yet we continue to persist in its fictions. This is analogous perhaps to drawing on one's real emotions, in cooperation with nature, while nevertheless on the stage. Or method ethnography, we might say: experiencing in cooperation with others their experiences, which are also yours.

It is a phase-shift in time. In method acting, I know I am not this guy (whomever it is I am portraying; and let's keep the masculine terms for now, for this is arguably a masculinist fantasy). But I have spent months, maybe years, turning myself into this guy—changing not just my physical appearance but my actual physical type, to the point possibly of causing health complications; not just reading about the lives of those like the one I will portray but partaking of their peccadillos or their perversions. So, *am* I that guy? Of course not. And yet . . . I have become him. And yet . . . I am not him. And so on. (An aside: I think ontology would have a tough time here).

The process is similar to what Nelms's informants describe, as they seek or embody economic alternatives. Or what James's interlocutors experience as they juggle debts and relationships, here becoming responsible and responsibilized borrowers or creditors, there falling into over-indebtedness and financial chaos—complexly intertwined, or again, at the "same" time yet out of phase, just as informal and formal or neoliberal and redistributive practices themselves intertwine. And it is in play in the multiplicity and plurality of both money and houses in Mariana Luzzi and Ariel Wilkis's chapter. In her chapter, Eugênia Motta tells an evocative story about a house in a favela whose owner styled hair. She reconfigured the main room of her autoconstructed house each time: what is today a living room would become tomorrow a hairdressing salon. So, which is it, *really*? How do we live it, have muscle memory of it as we move through it, inhabit it? As Luzzi and Wilkis relate, building materials—bricks—can be a store of value. But of course they are just bricks. And of course they are a store of value. But they're bricks. You get the idea.

INTENTIONAL ETHNOGRAPHY

In their exhortation to "live" the business case or to "live" the dramatic passions and types, Muniesa's business instructor and Stanislavski's Director might be describing the orientation in ethnography set out by Stephen Tyler in his contribution to the *Writing culture* project. Strathern's reworking of that orientation may give purchase on how ethnography can help us grapple with real economies. The real economy and ethnographic reality have something in common: they exceed representation. Tyler wrote that ethnography is "imperfect" (1986: 122)—one might say partial—because it does not produce a universal metalanguage nor truly describe in total another reality. Rather, it evokes "what cannot be known discursively or performed perfectly":

> [If] a discourse can be said to "evoke," then it need not represent what it evokes, though it may be a means to a representation. Since evocation is nonrepresentational, it is not to be understood as a sign function, for it is not a "symbol of," nor does it "symbolize" what it evokes. (Tyler 1986: 129)

In Tyler's view, "fragments of discourse" "evoke in the minds of both reader and writer" a "possible world of commonsense reality" that produces an integrative, even therapeutic effect (1986: 125). Such fragments create an object of joint attention that exceeds those fragments themselves (again, going back to Hart's insights, that is why for ethnography there are never clear or direct "sources" for truth claims). Taking the etymology of *intend*, they stretch or strain one's attention toward something. Why strain, I wonder? Perhaps because the thing is not really perceivable as such, not amenable to empirical observation. Like a "culture" or "society," much less an "individual." In any event: how like the method of *An actor prepares* or the case method of business instruction! The result is an "emergent holism" (Stanislavski 1948: 133), a "restorative harmony" (134). Tyler also invoked polyphony and temporality in his effort to craft a new realism (1986: 137).

The *limit* of evocation, however, is precisely this restorative harmony, this integrative therapy. As Strathern wrote of the situation of the ethnographer working "at home" in a generalized "Western" context or an English village, there is never any real integration. Rather, there is constant interruption. Whether from colleagues from other disciplines—sociology, economics—also working on the terrain of home, or our subjects, themselves theorists of their practices, there are constant "presences that impinge" (Strathern 1991: 23)—including the mundane knock on the door, new email, or administrative crisis that jolts us out of our research timespace and into our lives as bureaucrats (I speak for myself here). I would add: they impinge first in this time, then in another; here in one locus, there, elsewhere. There are different timespaces to these interruptions, and different spatiotemporal horizons. The situation is not limited to the ethnographer at home, of course. It is characteristic of any analytical or descriptive endeavor in which we hold onto the self in society, the concept of the person that denies its own partiality and multiplicity, its own distribution or dispersion across and within a social field, and its own interconnectedness with other such distributed entities. Strathern writes:

> Interruptions to the self do not guarantee a therapeutic return to the familiar. Rather, there is a sense of holding in one's grasp what cannot be held—of trying to make the body do more than it can do—of making a connection with others in a partial manner. (Strathern 1991: 27)

What Strathern and Tyler do for ethnography—as a site of connections and conversions—the Gens project (Bear et al. 2015) and Tsing do for capitalism. They "look beyond market exchanges and monetary forms to explore these conversions to take into account the full range of mediations: for example, between state debt and social debt, humanitarian projects and entrepreneurship, and non-human forms and commodities or resources" (Bear et al. 2015: §5), radically empirical without being irreducibly empiricist.

For those of us in Fairservis's class, to read Stanislavski and then (trying) to act Chekhov was a peculiarly effective way to stage the method of ethnography—and to stage it as "method" in the acting sense. To borrow one of Federico Neiburg and Jane Guyer's terms from their introduction to this volume, it "provoked," and it strained, pulled us toward a nonperceivable object. Despite our having been thrown into the *Writing culture* and deconstructive moment, words did not matter here so much. Showing was more important than saying, as

Ludwig Wittgenstein had it. We were put in the position of Maria in *An actor prepares*, on the stage without realizing that the acting had begun, by which fact we were able to act.

Can the ethnographer bridge scenarios, Neiburg and Guyer ask? Can ethnography itself be the bridge, the thing that facilitates that stretching-toward, that intention in the sense I've used above? That is to say, can ethnography of the real economy be the kind of conversion device, or infrastructure, that Bear et al. discuss in their reflections on capitalism? For the Gens project, conversion devices channel the values and possibilities of plurality and multiplicity into capital—at least sometimes, and contingently so. Toward what would ethnography channel the possibilities of the polychronic (Bear et al. 2015), the polyphonic (Tsing 2015a: 24), and the multiple timescapes in which human and nonhuman actors coordinate their activities (Bear et al. 2015: §8)? My own struggle has been to harness ethnography's infrastructures rather intentionally when setting off from the starting point of Gibson-Graham's world of economic plurality and possibility. I try then to come back again toward that world, but now dropping the "economic" frame altogether—in order to set our interests sometimes athwart capitalism as our primary object of concern and practice. This, anyway, is what I have intended to show.

ACKNOWLEDGMENTS:

I would like to thank Federico Neiburg and Jane Guyer for their invitation to write this Afterword, as well as Marilyn Strathern and Keith Hart for continuing inspiration, and Taylor Nelms and Tom Boellstorff for their comments on earlier drafts of this essay. Conversations with Jane Collier on Meillassoux and O'Laughlin significantly enriched this essay and clarified my argument. All errors, confusions, and inconsistencies are really mine alone.

REFERENCES

Aristotle. 2013. *Politics*. Translated and with an introduction, notes, and glossary by Carnes Lord. Chicago: University of Chicago Press.

Bear, Laura, Karen Ho, Anna Tsing, and Sylvia Yanagisako. 2015. "Gens: A feminist manifesto for the study of capitalism." Theorizing the Contemporary,

Cultural Anthropology website, March 30, 2015. https://culanth.org/fieldsights/652-gens-a-feminist-manifesto-for-the-study-of-capitalism.

Callon, Michel. 2005. "Why virtualism paves the way to political impotence: A reply to Daniel Miller's critique of *The laws of the markets.*" *Economic Sociology: European Economic Newsletter* 6 (2): 3–20.

Collier, Jane F. 1988. *Marriage and inequality in classless societies.* Stanford, CA: Stanford University Press.

Friedman, Milton. 1999. "Conversation with Milton Friedman." In *Conversations with leading economists: Interpreting modern macroeconomics,* edited by Brian Snowdon and Howard Vane, 124–44. Cheltenham: Edward Elgar.

Fustel de Coulanges, Numa Denis. 1877. *The ancient city: A study on the religion, law, and institutions of Greece and Rome.* Boston: Lee and Shepard.

Gibson-Graham, J. K. 2006. *A postcapitalist politics.* Minneapolis: University of Minnesota Press.

Guyer, Jane. 2016. *Legacies, logics, logistics: Essays in the anthropology of the platform economy.* Chicago: University of Chicago Press.

Ho, Karen. 2009. *Liquidated: An ethnography of Wall Street.* Durham, NC: Duke University Press.

Lawson, Tony. 1997. *Economics and reality.* London: Routledge.

Meillassoux, Claude. 1972. "From reproduction to production: A Marxist approach to economic anthropology." *Economy and Society* 1 (1): 83–105.

———. 1975. *Femmes, greniers et capitaux.* Paris: Francois Maspero.

Miller, Daniel. 2002. "Turning Callon the right way up." *Economy and Society* 31 (2): 218–33.

Morgan, Lewis Henry. 1877. *Ancient society; or, Researches in the lines of human progress from savagery through barbarism to civilization.* London: MacMillan and Company.

Nelms, Taylor. 2015. "'The problem of delimitation': Parataxis, bureaucracy, and Ecuador's popular and solidarity economy." *Journal of the Royal Anthropological Institute* 21 (1): 106–26.

———. n.d. "Realizing alternatives in post-neoliberal Ecuador: Performativity and durability." Unpublished manuscript, distributed June 2016.

O'Laughlin, Bridget. 1977. "Production and reproduction: Meillassoux's *Femmes, greniers et capitaux.*" *Critique of Anthropology* 2 (8): 3–32.

Quiggin, Alison Hingson. 1949. *A survey of primitive money: The beginnings of currency.* London: Methuen and Company.

Stanislavski, Constantin. 1948. *An actor prepares*. Translated by Elizabeth Reynolds Hapgood. New York: Theatre Arts Books.

Strathern, Marilyn. 1991. *Partial connections*. Savage, MD: Rowman and Littlefield.

Tsing, Anna L. 2015a. *The mushroom at the end of the world: On the possibility of life in capitalist ruins*. Princeton, NJ: Princeton University Press.

———. 2015b. "Salvage accumulation, or the structural effects of capitalist generativity." Theorizing the Contemporary, *Cultural Anthropology* website, March 30, 2015. https://culanth.org/fieldsights/656-salvage-accumulation-or-the-structural-effects-of-capitalist-generativity.

Tyler, Stephen. 1986. "Post-modern ethnography: From document of the occult to occult document." In *Writing culture: The poetics and politics of ethnography*, edited by George Marcus and Michael Fisher, 122–40. Berkeley: University of California Press.

Yanagisako, Sylvia J., and Jane F. Collier. 1987. "Toward a unified analysis of gender and kinship." In *Gender and kinship: Essays toward a unified analysis*, edited by Jane F. Collier and Sylvia J. Yanagisako, 14–52. Stanford, CA: Stanford University Press.

Yanagisako, Sylvia J. 2002. *Producing culture and capital: Family firms in Italy*. Princeton, NJ: Princeton University Press.

Žižek, Slavoj. 1989. *The sublime object of ideology*. London: Verso.